music of Yes

Feed///bACK

The Series in Contemporary Music

Volume 1

music of Yes
structure and vision
in progressive rock

Bill Martin

Open Court
Chicago and La Salle, Illinois

Open Court Publishing Company is a division of Carus Publishing Company

Copyright © 1996 by Carus Publishing Company

First printing 1996

Printed and bound in the United States of America.

Library of Congress Cataloging-in-Publication Data

Martin, Bill, 1956-
  Music of Yes : structure and vision in progressive rock/Bill
  Martin.
    p.   cm.—(Feedback ; v. 1)
  Includes discography (p.   ), bibliographical references (p.   ),
and Index.
    ISBN 0–8126–9333–7 (pbk. : alk. paper)
    1. Yes (Musical group)—Criticism and interpretation.
  2. Progressive rock music—History and criticism.   I. Title.
  II. Series: Feedback (Chicago, Ill.) ; v. 1.
  ML421.Y48M37   1996
  782.42′166′0922—DC20

                                                        96-42932
                                                           CIP
                                                           MN

For my friends in listening and life
Tim Crete
Kevin Condatore
Zane Edge
Lydia Eloff
Claudia Ericson
Nina Frankel
Tony Kirven
Gary James
Joanie Jurysta James
Chelsea Snelgrove
Garry Rindfuss
Mark Stone
Chet Williamson

The question is thus not the last word in language. First, because it is not the first word. At any rate, before the word, there is this sometimes wordless word which we name the "yes." A sort of pre-originary pledge *[gage]* which precedes any other engagement in language or action. But the fact that it precedes language does not mean that it is foreign to it. The *gage* engages in language—and so always in *a* language. The question itself is thus pledged—which does not mean linked or constrained, reduced to silence, on the contrary—by the pledge of *Zusage* [acceptance]. It answers in advance, and whatever it does, to this pledge and of this pledge. It is engaged by it in a responsibility it has not chosen and which assigns it even its liberty. The pledge will have been given before any other event. It is nonetheless, in its very coming before, an *event,* but an event of which the memory comes before any particular recollection and to which we are linked by a faith which defeats any narrative. No erasure is possible for such a pledge. No going back.

—Jacques Derrida, *of Spirit*

And the *yes* keeps restarting itself, an infinite number of times . . .

—Jacques Derrida, "Ulysses Gramophone"

Contents

Acknowledgments

This book was written as a true labor of love over the course of about four years. When I began writing *music of Yes,* I actually had little idea of whether or not there would be an audience for such a book. Not being plugged into the "scene" around Yes (or any other group), I was unaware that there remains a solid base of support for a group whose music and vision has been and should continue to be a force for redemption and against cynicism in the world. I first became aware of the extent of this support when I published an article on Chris Squire in *Bass Player* magazine in November 1994. I want to thank the editor and publisher of that magazine, Jim Roberts, both for publishing the article and for opening me up to many in the "Yes family" who have been supportive and helpful in this writing effort. Among these is especially Glen DiCrocco, who has been unsparing with advice and information. Among those who contacted me while I was writing the book, I would also like to thank David Orsini and Nick Kokoshis (the "Sunlight Caller") for their encouragement.

As always, my colleagues in philosophy have been generous with their time and ideas; I would especially like to thank Andrew Cutrofello, David Detmer, Alison Brown, George Trey, Al Cinelli, and Leslie Jones, six good friends who have also thought a good deal about music. In addition, Stephen Houlgate deserves special mention for sharing not only musical and philosophical insights, but also very useful information concerning things English.

I am most appreciative to Kerri Mommer for her hard and meticulous work as editor of this project. But I am even more appreciative to her for believing in the project and going to bat for it. Thanks very much, as well, to all of the folks at Open Court; I hope that this is the beginning of a long and fruitful exploration of the critical issues in and around music.

I had already known Kate Murphy for some time, as a graduate student in the department in which I am a professor, when we found that we had a mutual interest in the music of Yes. As it turned out, Kate had had other associations with the group as well. Kate supplied me with a very useful "Yes file," a rather large collection of articles, reviews, and interviews from over the years, and this was very helpful. Kate, thanks.

I am also fortunate to have Deena Weinstein as a colleague at DePaul University. In formal terms she is a sociologist, but I know her as our resident "professor of rock and roll." Thanks, Deena, for many valuable conversations and insights.

This book is dedicated to thirteen people who were my close friends in high school and college. Some of them remain close to me now. In two cases, I don't even know where these people are. Regardless, high vibrations go on, and they will continue to go on. These folks were there when I formed some of my initial views about Yes, and they played a large role in the formation of my views about music more generally. Wherever you are, I love you and wish you well.

Within this group, I would especially like to thank Claudia Ericson, Garry Rindfuss, Chelsea Snelgrove, Zane Edge, and Tony Kirven for teaching me much about music and life. (It occurs to me only now that each one of these friends and former bandmates is or was a drummer—hmm . . .) So, when are we getting the band back together?

For whatever reason, I seem to have a fair amount of vinegar in my constitution. As always, therefore, I must conclude by thanking my wonderful companion in life and thought, Kathleen League, for putting the sweetness in, and stirring it with a spoon.

Introduction: The ideologies of form

The music of Yes has been a force in my life for close to twenty-five years now. "Force," I believe, is the proper term, for I have always felt this music as a force, especially in the sense of something to be reckoned with. Words such as "force" and "movement" abound in Yes lyrics (which is to say, primarily, Jon Anderson's lyrics), and Jon Anderson said recently that the reformation of Yes in the early eighties had to do with the fact that he wanted Yes to be a force, once more, in music. Rick Wakeman said recently that the band Yes is simply defined as those musicians who have the honor of playing "the Yes music" (as he put it) at any given time. I think that is very perceptive, and the idea of a musical force, and perhaps something beyond simply a musical force, is felt here too, in the idea that the musicians themselves are the instruments of the music. Such a conception of music then invites the participation of others, and listening becomes, paradoxically, active. Paradoxically not because all real listening is not active, for it surely is, and a quality missing in many who would want to be musicians is precisely the ability to listen. Instead, the paradox is in the fact that the guiding conceptions of the band must have been larger than the members of the band itself, and so we, we listeners in the larger world, must have participated in some sense in making this music. For the creation of such a context, however, the musicians of Yes deserve all the credit, and it is the central purpose of this book, over and above the attempt to say something insightful and elucidating about the music of Yes, to give back to that music, albeit in a small way, some of the inviting force (what Jacques Derrida calls "absolute hospitality") that I and many others have felt for more than these twenty-five years.

Having said these things, it should be clear that this book will be very personal. For that very reason, however, I hope that a little of the force of Yes music will make itself felt here, in a way inviting of participation.

There are many paradoxes of Yes that I will discuss further in these pages. But I suppose that, by way of a beginning, something more needs to be said about two central questions: Why Yes? And, Why a book about Yes? To take up the latter question first, and then to leave it, and then to show why these two questions are really one, it would be very easy to say that, truthfully, no great music really needs a book. Steve Martin or Laurie Anderson or some clever person said that talking about music makes about as much sense as dancing about architecture. Perhaps John Coltrane and Beethoven, to take two of my personal favorites, need books to be written about their music as much as a fish needs a bicycle. There are interesting books on both, however, books that open up dimensions of their music that the listener has perhaps not heard before. There is a very interesting aesthetic question here. Can a verbal explanation cause one's aesthetic judgment to change? Can I "explain" to someone why he or she should appreciate the music of Coltrane—or, not just "appreciate" it, but *love* it, *embrace* it, *care* about it? This is a very old question (really going back to Plato and Aristotle in the Western tradition). I do think that explanations can alter our aesthetic judgments, and yet I don't think that anyone has proposed an aesthetic "science" that shows how these alterations take place. Immanuel Kant, in his *Critique of Judgment,* takes his theory of aesthetic judgment to just the point where categories break down, where the appreciation of a particular work of art is conditioned by categorical thought but is not the product of a formal calculus. This remains for me a central question, for it would be too easy to say that I've simply written this book for those who already love "the Yes music," and that I only want to deepen the appreciation of such people for this music. Admittedly, that will probably be the effect of this book, given that people who do not care about the music of Yes already are perhaps unlikely to be reading this. Perhaps there is only one thing to be said about music, only one thing that can be communicated in another medium (that is, through explanations): music has a structure. Some music has a structure that is "interesting," and yet, what it is that makes structure interesting is notoriously difficult to define. The music of Yes is music that is often structurally complex, and yet complexity is itself not always to be valued, and sometimes simplicity is the hardest thing to achieve. Sometimes Yes achieves a very beautiful simplicity, often one that emerges from complexity, as with the final part of "Gates of Delirium" (the part called "Soon"). How music achieves such effects is something that can be explained structurally, but which also cannot be explained structurally. This, of course, is the paradox of not only Yes music but all music. The "effect" does not seem to be something that is simply "there," to be isolated and studied. But, of course, it *is* "there," there is something in the structure that has caused the effect. To take away this mystery, and to try to replace it with a verbal explanation, would be to rip the heart out of music. The sort of explanations I aim at in this book, therefore, are geared toward deepening both understanding of the music, structurally, and to deepening the sense of mystery. In this sense we might recall the remark of the philosopher Emanuel Levinas, who said "the great thing about philosophy is that it fails." What I have attempted to do in this book is to explain the music of Yes in such a way that, in the end, it is clear that the explanation must fail.

These quasi-philosophical ruminations may show something about what books about art (including music) are generally up against, but have seemingly not brought us any closer to answering the question of why a book about Yes music is needed. The answer moves us from the question of the book to the question of "Why Yes?" Beethoven and Coltrane do not *need* books, and yet it is good that we have some of them. In other words, their music does not need a book in order to be what it is and to have great power. The same thing could be said of Yes, if we were only talking about "music" in some pure sense. The force of Yes music, and the structures that embody that force without fully defining it, would be what it is regardless of what, if anything, was written about it. In fact, given that much writing about rock music isn't very good, Yes music might be better off without writers fooling around with it. But that is just the reason for writing a book such as this. There is a canon in which Beethoven is firmly ensconced. This is pretty much the case with Coltrane as well, although, with the attacks on Black people and African-American culture that have never really let up in the United States, there is plenty need to listen to Coltrane and to write about him and to popularize his music. I wish that I could say that this music will never die, for, if anything seems eternal, it is the music of John Coltrane. Black culture in the United States, however, has never not been a constant struggle. Coltrane's music is a triumph of the Black struggle in particular and of the human endeavor in general. For that very reason the same social system that has never cared one wit for the human dignity of Black people seeks to deprive humanity of that victory, seeks to undermine it with a cultural amnesia that undermines and destroys people's culture in general.

Sometime later in my life, when I am more worthy of the subject, I hope to take up this complex of questions with regard to Black music, from Coltrane to Cecil Taylor. It would be wrong to simply use these reflections on musical canons and their cultural-material underpinnings to then raise questions of musical canons in general, for there is a particularity to the complex of questions around Coltrane and others (others who, more and more, must be named and discussed and written about if the force of their music is to be felt) that is politically charged and that demands justice. May justice be done and may we all work to see that it is done.

There is, however, a question of the "canon" concerning Yes music, and it also has its material-cultural dimension and its political dimension. Chris Squire points out (in the *Yesyears* retrospective set) that Yes is not really a "rock 'n' roll" band, and I think that most people who are attached to that label would agree. That sounds snooty, and I don't mean it to, except for the fact that, in the final decade of the twentieth century, rock 'n' roll is dead. It did not die slowly, rather it was killed in the space of a few short years by record companies, media conglomerates, and beer companies, all of whom continue to tell us that rock 'n' roll will never die. (So buy, buy, buy!) This is, of course, a story in its own right which will not concern us in detail until part 3 of this book. While it is true that Yes, at least in the period from *The Yes Album* to *Going for the One* is/was not a rock 'n' roll band, their music and the music of everyone else in (as Steve Howe charmingly puts it) "the rock field," will go the way of all rock music because of forces that are simply beyond music and beyond the control of most musicians. It is against such forces that I offer, in another medium, a discussion of the music of Yes.

There is much in rock music that is worthy of similar treatment, and in some ways the fact that I want to try to help preserve what it is about Yes that resists the corporate capitalization of everything, the colonization of every sphere of life, is really tied to certain personal facts about people such as myself who listened to music and were affected by it in a particular time frame, namely the late sixties and the seventies.

Who are "people such as myself"? One hates to say it, but in a certain sense the right label would be "seventies people." There's no other meaning to that term than "not sixties people," and here I think there needs to be some explanation. There are many different kinds of seventies people. Some, like myself, missed the revolution but wished we hadn't. At the same time, being seventies people, as opposed to eighties people (i.e., the young people who are my students now), and feeling sharply the sense that the sixties were over, we didn't see simple and pure nostalgia as an option. Some seventies people, for whom the revolution didn't mean anything, became yuppies. Others of us experienced a kind of inner migration of our alienation. "When there's a revolution going on, everyone's a revolutionary." During times of less turmoil and more boredom (known in this society as "stability") it's harder to be a radical critic of society and to work toward fundamental change. By the end of the seventies, and especially in the early eighties, I was moving more and more in this radical direction, and that is where my head and heart are today. Whether I am a typical Yes fan or not I cannot say, but I know that, in the doldrums of the seventies, there was a certain spirit that was preserved for me in their music. At the same time, I was challenged, both as a musician myself and as an attentive listener who *cared* about music, by the formal aspects of their music.

This was a time of many rock musicians and groups who had tremendous technical facility. When I said above that there has been much in rock music that deserves critical treatment similar to that which I will apply to Yes, I mainly meant groups such as Gentle Giant, Emerson, Lake, and Palmer, PFM, and Genesis. In a whole other category would be King Crimson because Robert Fripp had a very different approach to musical structure. In one sense King Crimson is very much like Yes, and both are very much unlike the other groups mentioned. That is, even though their sounds are very different, they are similar in being *projects*. In either case, the Yes music or the King Crimson music is simply the music that is made by the particular musicians who happen to be in the group at that time. Interestingly enough, Jon Anderson was the singer on a track by King Crimson ("Prince Rupert Awakes," on the third album, *Lizard*), and his voice became, for that moment, part of the King Crimson project. This is interesting, because, in my opinion, Anderson does not fit in well with musical contexts other than Yes. (More will be said on this point later.) What allowed Anderson to fit in with King Crimson was precisely the fact that King Crimson might be called a "musical project" as much as a "band," and this is true of Yes as well. So, even though the music of the two groups is quite different (although it should be mentioned that "Prince Rupert Awakes" is in song form, unlike much King Crimson music, and Fripp certainly knew what he was doing when he asked Anderson to sing the song), there was a deeper similarity in attitude. One might say that, all the same, it is clear that King Crimson was (is? will be? will there be a once-and-future King?) *Robert Fripp's* project, whereas it is not so clear *who* is the spiritual center of Yes. Surely this center is somewhere in the vicinity of Jon Anderson, and yet it is perhaps a crucial difference between the projects of Yes and King Crimson that the center of the latter was undoubtedly a particular "who" named Robert Fripp, while the center of the former was some-thing more like a force, a guiding spirit.[1]

Much more will be said on this subject in due course, and it will be useful to have further recourse to the comparison of King Crimson and Yes. Let it be said for now that, during the seventies, both seemed magical bands to me. Despite being informed by prodigious technique that was not simply technique, it was this characteristic of having a project that distinguished these two groups from the others mentioned above. This is an important point, because in one respect it seems more true of King Crimson than of Yes. That is, King Crimson is clearly more influenced by jazz (Bill Bruford set out originally to be a jazz drummer, but then he did eventually join King Crimson), while, stylistically, Yes has more in common with the other groups.

Another way of putting this is that Yes is more easily lopped into the category that some rock critics developed in the middle seventies, "techno-pop." Another term that was used was "classical rock," meaning rock that had been influenced by Western classical music. I certainly think that there were some magical moments in the efforts of the other bands I mentioned, but in many cases the technique and the gimmicks overshadowed the music. While it is very clear that Yes put a great deal of effort into making use of musical technology (sometimes taking part in the invention of new tech-nologies), and that Yes drew some inspiration from classical music, the overall musical project remained in the foreground. Two ways of seeing this come to mind. First, the sense of a musical project is sustained in Yes music over, relatively speaking, a long period. Perhaps this quality makes Yes more akin to classical music composers, perhaps more than any structural similarities between Yes and some classical composers. When I say "relatively speaking," it is legitimate to ask, relative to what? The answer is, relative to the work of other rock groups and musicians. The very fact that this point has to be raised means that there is a question of the validity of rock music as a form of music. Of course, the question was also raised by another label sometimes applied to groups such as Yes, ELP, and King Crimson, namely, "art rock." We will take up this question in due course.

The second way of developing this point about a musical project that is not overcome by technology, gadgetry, and technique-for-the-sake-of-technique takes the form of a little test. Sometimes when I listen to rock music, I think about how a piece would sound in a different medium. This question mainly applies to rock music that is not heavily influenced by jazz or the blues. Basically there are two possibilities. With pieces that are in song form, I ask how they would sound if arranged as *Lieder*—that is, as art songs in classical music, with just voice and piano. Incidentally, I find this a useful thing to think about when confronting silly comparisons, such as between the Beatles and Beethoven, that sort of thing. Usually the person who raises this comparison is comparing "Dear Prudence" to the Ninth Symphony or one of the late Quartets, which doesn't make any sense, really. Beethoven wrote songs too, and, to the extent that comparisons in music are guided by the desire to be constructive (perhaps a rare quality), the point would be to compare the Beatles' songs to them. I think that many Beatles songs come out fine on this comparison. Of course, the whole problem with comparison in music is the idea that one has to choose. I suppose there are plenty of cases where it makes sense to say one song is better than another, but there are also plenty of cases where we want to have both, and where the world is a much poorer place when the idea of competition wins out (perhaps because the idea itself is more competitive?) in every sphere of life. The point in this "comparison" is instead to strip a song down to its bare structure, and to see what power it has in this form.

Similarly, the second possibility concerns more extended pieces. I have in mind works such as "Close to the Edge" or Jethro Tull's *Thick as a Brick*. In listening to this music, I sometimes like to imagine it being played by a standard orchestra, perhaps augmented by a piano and drum set. I imagine the lyrics being sung by classically trained singers. If such extended pieces were arranged for orchestra in such a way as to maintain the same ranges of rhythm, harmony, and timbre, would they still be interesting? Would they still sound innovative? The timbres would be different, of course, but if the range was maintained, I think that these two pieces in particular, and the more extended works of Yes in general (along with Jethro Tull's *Passion Play*) would hold up. In fact, I hope that this is an experiment that will be attempted at some point, though it is hard to imagine with the present climate in the music business.[2]

Indeed, I think that we have reached the point where it will take a revolution in social relations for music to be what it could be once again. This is to connect with the earlier theme of bands in the seventies that combined vision and technique to extend the parameters of rock music. I will return to this point in a moment, but first I want to say a few more things about form.

There are many reasons to believe that structure is not separable from content in an artwork. Some of these reasons have more to do with "aesthetics" (inasmuch as this category is itself freestanding). In particular, there is the fact that content cannot remain disembodied (or that it never is, in fact, disembodied, so that the very idea of disembodiment is a nonstarter), and that, on the other hand, there is also no pure form that exists without content.[3] This point takes us beyond a supposedly pristine aesthetic realm (itself a construction of art-for-art's-sake formalism) and into the larger areas of politics and history. That is, form always has content in that its emergence is historically and socially determined—not in the sense of a mechanical determinism in which all events, including the emergence of new art forms and artworks, is predictable, but rather in the sense of a historical context which is the background from which human events, including artworks, emerge, and against which they appear as what they are. This background is always changing. Therefore, the meaning of any event cannot ever be completely determined. Still further, events themselves, including artworks, can and do have an effect upon the historical background, sometimes a crucial and epoch-making effect.

The foregoing assertions are parts of larger arguments in cultural and social theory. At the expense of having the mountain bring forward a mouse, I simply want to use this scheme of thinking, which has been employed by a great many theorists (Georg Lukacs, Susan Sontag, and Fredric Jameson, just to name a few) to look at the determinations of rock music, in particular the fact that it is music created by and for first an electric and later an electronic age. My experiment with rearrangement, with song form and extended form, has the limitation that it may be attempting an artificial leap beyond the historical determinations of rock music. By this I do not mean that it may be a way of making rock music more than it is, although that is a question in its own right. Would it be a valid thing, historically and aesthetically, to have "Close to the Edge" played by a symphony orchestra? On one level, the question does not seem any different than one about the validity of playing Bach or Debussy on synthesizers or bass guitars. But that is to restrict the question too much to a supposedly pristine aesthetic realm. Classical music purists are typically guilty of this restriction, or perhaps they are not aware—because they do tend to be aesthetes—of all of the dimensions of this question. I especially have in mind two concerns, one of which is "aesthetic," the other less so.

First, if there are new sounds that are possible with electric and electronic instruments, it is hard to see why, in principle, new artworks and new kinds of artworks could not be generated using these tools. This point has been explicitly recognized in Western classical music, both in the composition of works for new instruments, for instance the saxophone, and in the recognition, for instance, that Bach's keyboard music (excluding his organ music) was written for the harpsichord, not the piano, which did not exist in Bach's day. This is primarily a question of taking timbre to be an important element of music.[4]

Second, however, and not unrelated to this first point, there are all sorts of things presupposed by the existence of electronic instruments, and all sorts of things that seem to go with and follow from the use of such instruments, and it is entirely appropriate to raise questions about these things. For instance, one has to wonder if these instruments, and rock music especially, not only presuppose industrial society but, further, require it. If such a social form becomes problematic, because it is destroying the planet, then doesn't that seem to raise serious questions about aesthetic forms that are closely tied to this form of society? Some of Yes's music, for instance, is about the destruction of nature, by humans and social forms that are out of tune with nature. I am very much in sympathy with their concern. But doesn't the emergence of "arena-rock" depend on anti-ecological social forms and the destruction of nature? The dependence may not be absolute, but, historically and socially, things have certainly developed this way.

It is a good thing that Yes has taken up these themes, and I am not calling them hypocrites. Very rarely in classical music does one find the musicians or the audience taking stock of the historical conditions for the creation of the music. Even where there was originally a clear historical and political purpose involved in the creation of classical works, as in several of Beethoven's symphonies (most famously the Ninth), this purpose is mostly obscured or even cancelled in the aestheticized world of classical music training, performance, or listening. (In the latter case we might say "aestheticized at best," because most classical music concerts are simply occasions for wealthy people to show off their wealth and to feel superior about their supposedly superior tastes.) Furthermore, I find a real sincerity in Yes's taking up these themes, in that they also do not write songs with the misogynistic slant that one finds in much rock music. In fact, I suppose that one might say that Yes seems peculiarly "sexless" for a rock band, and in that sense once again not a "rock'n'roll" band, for better or worse. (I'll say more about this in a moment.) The way that these two themes, women and nature, have developed in Yes's music, demonstrate a certain sensibility that, while it may not be fully conscious (whatever that means; in other words, "while it may not exist in their minds as a fully worked-out philosophical perspective"—the point being that they are musicians primarily, not philosophers), is certainly demonstrative of a deep connection. I find this entirely laudable.

But there is another question. Namely, once the electronic-industrial age has developed (I won't say "progressed," because I'm more and more doubtful of this) to a certain point, one that was reached at least by the onset of the eighties, does it really matter what message or ideas rock musicians were/are trying to get across? In my little experiment with rearrangement, I imagine the music first of all existing as notes on paper, the idea being that the written music displays the form of the composition in a bare-bones way. (This is to leave aside the question of timbre or, perhaps, to beg the question in a way that foregrounds it.) Assuming that one can read music, there is a certain austere beauty to this form of a composition, and it can be fun to imagine the music being played by all sorts of instruments and combinations of instruments. Now, compare this extreme to the real situation of rock concerts, where the music plays a distant secondary role to the other activities generally going on: loud talking, hooting and hollering, smoking, drinking, groping, drug use, puking, and so forth. Whenever the music comes down a bit in volume, one immediately hears all this activity, and one realizes that most of the people aren't there for the music anyway. Recall the famous moment the Doors were performing "When the Music's Over," when the music got relatively quiet (a two-note bass pattern) and the main sound was all the yacking, and Jim Morrison shouted, *"Shut up!"* The next thing he said was, "Give the music some." It is now accepted that this is simply an unreasonable request at a rock concert. I suppose that it's very unhip to say this, and that the answer to these complaints is that a rock concert, like a classical music concert, is a social event, where music is just one of the things going on. And yet neither are these events to be compared to the medieval carnival, where social conventions are suspended for weeks, or even months, at a time. Or rather, rock concerts partake no more of this carnival spirit than do athletic events. The latter are at least what they are (and are sometimes the occasion of great feats which clearly have their aesthetic dimension). When the performance of music becomes an athletic event, at best, and simply a place to try to "score" (on various levels) at worst, then one can legitimately ask, without necessarily being a cultural elitist, What has happened to the music or the meaning that music can convey? To my mind, concerts become worse than pointless when this is the atmosphere in which they must take place.

But this is not to raise a question first of all about Yes as about the social-historical contexts in which all attempts to express meaning, especially meanings which go against the grain, are more and more flattened and killed. The more recent incarnations of Yes, from *90125* or perhaps *Tormato,* have been no more subject to these pressures than any other musician or group of musicians—no more, but no less. In part 3 these developments will be traced, in general and for Yes specifically, but I wanted to lay out the basic parameters of it at the outset. This is important not only for setting the background against which Yes, or any music, appears, but further, for allowing us to see what it was that Yes music was confronting at what I think was its high point, from *The Yes Album* to *Going for the One.* In other words, there was a period in which Yes was making the music that it wanted to make, and this was its better music, by far. I am not a music industry "insider," nor do I want to be one, but it is clear that record companies (which are, more and more, monopolistic media conglomerates) exercise more and more direct control over the creation of the musical "product."[5] One question that I will have to raise again in part 3 and the conclusion is whether there is something in the very form of the music that Yes plays that allows commodification to work its way into the music.

My suspicion is that this is the case, in two ways. First, as already mentioned, there is the fact that Yes music is very much connected, it would seem anyway, with the industrial age. When everything becomes geared toward platinum albums and arena concerts, then the same laws of capital, especially standardization and crass commercialism, that affect everything else will affect music, as "product," as well. There is, however, no ironclad law that says that music or musicians must become commodities—or, at least, that is my fervent hope, despite many signs to the contrary in recent years. Clearly, it was against these gathering forces of hyper-commodificataion that Robert Fripp came up with the idea of a "small, mobile unit." In order to pursue this idea, Fripp had to give up the quest for large concert audiences and album sales. One could say that what this means is that Fripp, or whoever pursues this sort of path, had to give up a certain amount of money. The idea that what is also being given up is the attempt to reach a larger audience can no longer be sustained, because the concert and record-promotion atmosphere is such that there is little of substance that a "larger audience" could be reached with. The attempt to resist complete commodification was also very much behind the emergence of punk music, with independent labels and shows performed in small clubs or even garages, with mostly cheap equipment and no laser light shows. Finally, the fact that, some years back, when offered a large sum for the use of his "Born in the USA" song in Chrysler advertisements, Bruce Springsteen could say no, says something both about a subject and about a structure. That is, this fact says something good about the integrity of Bruce Springsteen, bless his heart. But it also says something about art and artists, that there is a space there for resistance to the complete commodification of every aspect of human life. (One way to bring these two points together is to say that Springsteen, while quite wealthy, is not a capitalist; if he was a capitalist, he literally could not choose to not sell his song—unless he had a more lucrative offer or had a way of making more money with it himself—without at the same time deciding to not be a capitalist. I would like to think that such a decision is possible, but I do not know of a single example. Capitalism does not fundamentally have to do with intentions, but rather with the invisible hand of profit.) Now, as capitalism enters a period that I think can correctly be called "postmodern," in which the flattening logic of television (with MTV in the lead, where everything is jump-cut) makes meaning more and more a nonstarter, there is an attempt to destroy the space for all marginal production of meanings which go against the grain.

Again, I am getting ahead of the story. My point here is simply that the best Yes music was created in a social-historical period in which this space was more open than it had been for a long time. What was the reason for this openness? Basically that capitalism was in a period of retreat, even though it had not been defeated. The great upheavals of the sixties, coupled with the defeat of the U.S. military machine by the people of Vietnam and the exposure of that machine in the imperialist countries themselves, left capitalism, if not defeated, at least in a certain amount of disarray. In this space of about ten years (not that we can be so exact about it, but, roughly, from 1968 to 1978) a great deal of musical creativity flowered, including that of Yes. Around 1978 a new thing started to happen musically, the emergence of punk and reggae and other forms of explicitly oppositional music, generally of a far less utopian (and often quite dystopian) slant than the music of Yes. My argument is that we have to understand this social-historical frame in order to understand how a band like Yes could create their more innovative works and, further, that any formal analysis of these works must take into account the way that the historical frame marks the music that was created in this period.

This leads to the second reason we have to ask if there is something in the form of Yes's most creative music that necessarily led to its disillusion. I haven't really specified what I mean by this yet, but what I have in mind is that Yes, after *Going for the One,* was not able to update its sound in a way such that it remained on the cutting edge of musical experimentation. At the same time, they rightly recognized that there was no point in doing the same things over and over again. As I will discuss in part 3, Yes faced the same situation that confronted all of the progressive rock groups at the end of the seventies. The question I want to raise here has specifically to do with the fact that Yes's innovative music appeared at a time when the system of commodification was in retreat (even if it was regrouping and would later, as the seventies came to a close, begin to strike back with a vengeance, sometimes with open brutality, sometimes through a subtle incursion into every nook and cranny that is even more insidious for being subtle). Although it is clear that at least Jon Anderson and Steve Howe, in their lyrics, had a sense of going against the grain of the dominant culture, Yes has never been identified as an openly oppositional band.

At this point it will be helpful to briefly introduce some ideas from the philosopher and social theorist Theodor Adorno, which inform the analysis presented thus far. Adorno argued that the best way that art can be oppositional is for it to strive to be autonomous with regard to the culture that it opposes. Explicitly oppositional art tends to be too implicated in this very culture, often as no more than a crude mirror image, and it also tends to be too much like propaganda, and therefore to lose its power as art. Adorno made these arguments at a time when it made sense to talk about the avant-garde in art. Groups such as Yes were, for a while, considered to be the avant-garde of rock music. Now it is difficult to see how this category has any meaning anymore, for rock music or for music in general, or even for art in general. Furthermore, we have entered a period in which about the only way to get an oppositional message across is in a straight-up, harsh, uncompromising way. This is part of what makes some punk and rap musicians, from the Sex Pistols to Public Enemy to Consolidated to Nirvana not only powerful in their expressions, but even refreshing. It would be very difficult to imagine Jon Anderson singing either punk or rap—it's an amusing thought. (There is the case of "Almost Like Love," from *Big Generator,* of course.) Furthermore, whether more straightforwardly oppositional forms are really having an effect is itself open to question. My view is that art in itself can never bring about a revolution, though it may help galvanize a certain sensibility that could lead to subtantive radical change. Adorno's argument is that real oppositional art negates the dominant culture by already imagining, in an autonomous way, a different world, a world that is affirmed. I believe that this is what Yes's music does at its best.[6]

However, it is not clear that Adorno's strategies for art have been very effective. Or, at least, it is clear that these strategies need to be reconsidered in this period of emerging postmodern capitalism. Yes's music was created in a period in which some autonomous works in rock music became possible because of general disarray in capitalist ideology. Capitalism itself had not been defeated, but capitalist ideology was in disrepute. This created a space for creativity of a particular kind, and in that space emerged the music of Yes. On either side of that space one finds rock music of a more explicitly oppositional kind—Jimi Hendrix, Jefferson Airplane, Marvin Gaye, The Who, and so on, at the end of the sixties, and the explosion of punk, reggae, and rap at the end of the seventies and on into the eighties. There are two points, then, that are part of this second reason for wondering if there is something in Yes's music that necessarily meant that it would run into serious problems in trying to develop in an experimental direction beyond a certain timeframe. First, it really does seem, on this view, that Yes's period of greatest innovation was very much tied to its time. Second, it may be that, in getting farther away from "rock music," and certainly far away from "rock'n'roll," Yes got farther and farther away from those sources that have continually regenerated rock music. I'm referring especially to the Black roots of rock music and the fact that these roots partake of an ongoing, oppositional culture. The ironic fact is that, even though Yes in its more recent forms has been something more like a "rock'n'roll" band, it seems less associated with oppositional culture than ever. This may not be a fair assessment, however, and these questions will be explored in much greater detail.

I began this long set of ruminations on theoretical issues in order to try to understand what it was about Yes that allowed it to be such a force for the people who experience the music in that way. There was a period in which I did not listen to Yes at all, namely the decade from about 1978 to 1988 or so. It was very difficult to listen to "dreamer easy in the chair that really fits you" (a line from "Heart of the Sunrise") in a period in which it appeared that this capitalist social system, both in the U.S. (where it wore the face of Ronald Reagan) and in the predominant social relations worldwide might actually succeed in its deepest impulses, which are to obliterate our species (and many others along with it). Now, in the face of a New World Order which is no less insidious, just more clever but also already incredibly brutal, having announced itself with the murder of 200,000 Iraqis, I am in a true quandary about the role of music. If Yes music is somewhat tied to its moment, and if this moment seems to have passed, this seems no less true for the punk music that came next. Rap music is undoubtedly important, and one could certainly argue that its moment is upon us: it is where the radical messages (albeit often mixed with a large dose of misogyny— and a real revolution can't be made by dissin' the sisters) are coming from now, and it is a form of true popular culture, having been created on the streets and in the ghettoes by Black youths. But not all music can or should be rap. There is still a need to find a way to create autonomous forms that keep alive the idea of an alternative future. If my desire to recreate an appreciation of Yes has a bit of nostalgia mixed in, I hope that it is a kind of radical nostalgia. I think that it may be, because I am much more nostalgic for the music than I am for the period in my life, especially when I was in high school and college (which is roughly the period that I'm arguing was the time of a certain opening for creativity), when I was most engaged with the music of Yes. What I am nostalgic for is what that music did for me at the time, which was indeed to create an opening to a different world. This music, along with the music of King Crimson, John Coltrane, Cecil Taylor, and John Cage, also played a large role in my intellectual development. I find now, listening to the music on a daily basis for the first time in quite a few years, that this power is still there. I listen to "Heart of the Sunrise" or "Gates of Delirium" and I marvel even more at what the music can do, in terms of both structure and vision.

There is a thin line between utopianism and escapism. (One might also thematize the distinction between the utopian moment in art and a full-blown utopianism; the problem is that, in a cynical society, any argument for the former will almost always get you accused of the latter.) Art, when it is utopian, keeps alive in us the sense that the world could be different. This is what Adorno meant by autonomous art—the implication being that such art must necessarily resist the structures of commodification.[7] But if this sense of a different world becomes too distant from actual work to bring this different world into existence, then the line is crossed into mere escapism. Mere nostalgia would very clearly constitute such a crossing. However, I think that there may be a real role for a radical nostalgia in this time in which memory is more and more under attack (one of the key elements of postmodern capitalism) and in which the possibilities for creative thought and expression are progressively attacked and closed off.[8] This is a difficult question and even one that may prove to be, in a sense, empirical; that is, the question may be one of whether or not looking back to the particular frame of creativity in which Yes's music appeared really does fuel new creativity and autonomy and resistance in the present. I do not propose this as the "main strategy" for anyone, and I may even be grasping at straws, but I do think that we will need every conceivable resource to raise, once again, the possibility of a different future.

I do find it important, therefore, that the music of Yes is structurally innovative. This means that, as music, it may last in a way that, for example, the Sex Pistols' music may not. This is to take nothing away from the Sex Pistols or, for that matter, from other examples of good rock music that were intensely part of their time. Indeed, this seems to be the trade-off: I've tried to show that the Yes music of the seventies was very much a creation of its time, but it was never as intensely connected to this time frame as the Sex Pistols were to theirs. And yet, to listen to the Sex Pistols now, at the fin-de-millennium, would also be nostalgia (not that this shouldn't be indulged from time to time), and there isn't very much about the structure of the music that inspires critical reflection. But I do not sub-

scribe to the idea that music that "lasts" is somehow "timeless." What I wonder
about is the possibility of Yes's music not transcending history but rather participating in and pointing the way forward to what needs to come after this age.
This is where the intersection of structure and vision is crucial. The idea of this
book, finally, is to pursue this wonder, toward possibility itself.

That this will be a book primarily about music and the social circumstances
and effects of music should be clear by now. Although I said earlier that I didn't
know whether I could convince anyone who doesn't already appreciate the
music of Yes to start appreciating it, I hope that I will contribute to the appreciation of that music and the deepening of enjoyment on the part of those who
already care about the music. And perhaps those few brave souls who read the
book even though they do not like the music of Yes will find that some of these
arguments may be significant apart from the particular example.[9]

This, then, will not be a book about personalities, a "rock bio." Although I
am as curious as most people about what some of my favorite musicians may be
like as people, I do not believe that an analysis of the music of Yes is best served
by biographical investigations. Perhaps if I had some reason to believe that one
or more of the band members were horrible persons and complete hypocrites
there would be some reason to look into these sorts of things, but I have no reason to suspect that this is the case. In part 2, I do discuss briefly the class backgrounds of some of the core members of Yes. This is not primarily a matter of
biography, but instead an attempt to get at the social and historical context from
which Yes music emerges. And, while I find it interesting that the members of
the band were, in the period that will be my main focus and with the exception
of Rick Wakeman, vegetarians, I am mainly concerned with the values that are
embodied in the music. (Similarly, it's interesting that only some members of the
band are vegetarians now—with only Steve Howe keeping the strict discipline as
of this writing—but I don't want the analysis to depend on this sort of information.) I hope that the band members will see themselves in this book should any
of them ever read it.

Furthermore, I have not relied on interviews with group members, even
where these have been directly concerned with the music. This is despite the fact
that the band members are all quite articulate, as evidenced by the interviews in
the *Yesyears* retrospective video. Often, when I quote group members, it is from
the *Yesyears* retrospective. Otherwise, some of the better articles about and interviews with Yes are listed in the bibliography. In writing this book, I have also not
attempted to contact band members. Indeed, the idea is to step back a bit from
that sort of discussion of a rock group and its music. Instead, the idea is to, for
once, actually take up the music and to leave the other trappings of most books
on rock groups aside. The interesting thing is that, if you go to your local bookstore and look at the section on rock music, there are lots of books, but very few

of them have much, or anything, to do with the actual music. So, I'm trying to buck this trend.

Although this is not my main purpose, this book also provides a bit of an introduction to some key issues in philosophy, aesthetics, social theory, and other theoretical pursuits, for instance, around questions of meaning, intention, and representation in music. I try to not be too overbearing with this material. For some this will be new terrain while others will be very familiar with these ideas and may want to skip ahead. For those who want to explore these issues further, I have provided a basic set of sources in the bibliography.

Following this introduction, the book is divided into three parts and a "concluding note" (which I will also refer to as the "conclusion"). Part 1, "Before and beyond," introduces the original members of Yes and discusses the group's first two albums, *Yes* and *Time and a Word.* Part 2, "Perpetual change," deals with what I call Yes's "main sequence," from *The Yes Album* to *Going for the One.* In astronomy, a "main sequence" is the period in which a star is burning brightly, over a long period of time. I discuss in detail why I take *The Yes Album* to have been Yes's entrance into their main sequence, what I also call their "progressive rock" period. Part 2 is the centerpiece of the book. In Part 3, "In the beginning is the future," I discuss Yes's work beyond the main sequence, raising questions concerning the present and future viability of progressive rock music, and of Yes as a musical and cultural experiment. In the brief "Concluding note," I attempt to restate these questions in more broadly social and philosophical terms.

The analysis of the music of Yes, especially in the part covering the work from *The Yes Album* to *Going for the One,* will take this music in its totality. This means, especially, that I will treat the lyrics as an integral part of the composition. To this end I should say something about my approach to lyrics. I said earlier that it makes little sense to compare a song to a symphony. It may make more sense to compare the lyrics of a song or other piece of music to poetry, but there is still a problem with the comparison. Lyrics are meant, generally, to function as part of a larger whole. Some of Yes's lyrics, primarily Jon Anderson's, can stand on their own as poems, but this is not their main function. Sometimes Yes lyrics have been characterized as "bad Romantic poetry." I do not mean to say that Yes lyrics are always flawless, nor do I mean to say that it is wrong to see the influence of Romantic poetry in these lyrics. Indeed, I think that it is important to take stock of what this influence means. I just want to warn, once more, against comparing apples and oranges (or is it oranges and tangerines?). Other aspects of the totality (again, especially in the works treated in part 2) that I will discuss are album cover art (now pretty much destroyed by the advent of the compact disk) and production. These are very much integral to the music of Yes.

I would like to conclude this introduction by briefly introducing myself. I was born in 1956 in Columbia, South Carolina, and I grew up in Nashville,

Atlanta, and Miami. By training and passion I am a philosopher. I received my Ph.D. in 1991 from the University of Kansas. I teach philosophy at DePaul University of Chicago, and I write and publish a fair amount. Primarily I work in social theory (a term which designates the intersection of political philosophy and cultural studies). I also work in contemporary philosophy, both of the "analytic" and "continental" varieties (if these labels mean nothing to you, don't worry, they are not that important), philosophy of religion, and literary theory. Generally all of this work comes together for me under the heading of social theory and political engagement. My first couple of books deal with the work of the contemporary philosopher Jacques Derrida as it relates to social theory. My third book develops themes in radical social theory more generally, especially as they relate to the question of community. (*Music of Yes* is my fourth book.) As the reader will no doubt see, I have been influenced a great deal by the Marxist tradition as well, and I do not hesitate to call myself a Marxist and a radical communitarian.

I have played music for more than twenty-five years. My instruments are mainly bass guitar, but also guitar and cello. In the early and middle eighties I formed and played in an Ornette Coleman–influenced jazz group called "Chairman Mao," then in two punk bands, "Death Row" and "Evil Dad." All three were based in Columbia, S.C., where I lived from 1978 to 1985. I've never made any money playing music, although Death Row and Evil Dad were regionally popular in the punk scene (and Death Row's tape, "Burn This Town," was reviewed favorably in *Maximum Rock 'N' Roll*, where we were compared to Richard Hell and the Voidoids; others compared us to Gang of Four—I liked both comparisons). Whether and how these facts affect the analysis in this book I will leave for the reader to judge. Although I have taken part in countless hours of discussions concerning music, including a smaller but still near infinite set of hours discussing Yes, this is my first time writing an extended piece on music. I look forward, therefore, to readers' comments.

Now on to the hard part . . .

Part 1

Before and beyond

Introducing Yes

What if there had only ever been two Yes albums, the ones under discussion in this part? It's an interesting thing to think about. I must admit to almost complete ignorance of the records that were made by members of the first Yes before they formed the group. I did hear one of the Tomorrow albums on which Steve Howe plays, and of course Rick Wakeman was already known for his work with the Strawbs and as a session player on albums by David Bowie. When Alan White joined the group he was also well known as a session musician and for playing with the Plastic Ono Band, while Patrick Moraz had formed, with Lee Jackson and Brian Davison, a kind of updated Nice (The Nice was the group with which Keith Emerson had originally become famous), called "Refugee." But to this day I have not heard the groups that Chris Squire, Jon Anderson, Tony Kaye, Peter Banks, or Bill Bruford were with prior to their forming Yes.

Given what each member originally brought to the group, both in terms of styles and range of influences, the whole prospect seems a bit unlikely. The original nucleus, Anderson and Squire, were especially interested in vocal groups from the United States, for example, Simon and Garfunkel, The Association, the Beach Boys, and the Byrds, groups with a strong emphasis on harmony singing. Squire had a background in English church music, as a choirboy. His bass guitar style was clearly influenced by the greats of the day, Paul McCartney, Jack Bruce, and John Entwhistle, but even on *Yes* he was already exhibiting a unique, very trebly sound. Already the composed, contrapuntal bass lines that, in the later albums, could practically stand as complete musical works in themselves, were fully in evidence. The role of the bass guitar in Yes's music is something that we will return to at length.

Bill Bruford was something else again; his primary aim was to be a jazz drummer. In many ways it is an anomaly that he joined the group. There were many drummers in the "progressive" groups of the time, not least among them Ginger Baker, who were influenced by jazz, but few of them could really claim to be able to play jazz in the style of the important drummers from the U.S.— Max Roach, Elvin Jones, Tony Williams, and so on. Bruford, while at that stage of the game not yet a Jack DeJohnette, certainly had all the fundamentals. Since those early days he has developed his playing, especially through his work with King Crimson and with his own groups (most recently Earthworks), to become a very credible jazz-inflected percussionist and, of course, probably the most innovative percussionist in rock music. (This is not to take away anything from some of the very inventive rock drummers who have not become as well known as Bruford, for example, Christian Vander and Pierre Moerlin.) Bruford's style is deceptive. On the one hand, his playing is rhythmically very complex and, listened to for itself, abstracted from the particular Yes piece that it is a part of, funkier than one might at first expect. On the other hand, despite these attributes, there is a simplicity and clarity to all of Bruford's playing that resembles the drumming of one of rock music's most underrated drummers and musicians, Ringo Starr. It was Starr's contribution, one that very few rock drummers have successfully emulated, to be able to seemingly always play the right beat, in a completely uncluttered way. I almost said that Starr always played the right *note,* because his drumming is very melodic (perhaps the best example of this is the chorus to "Something," on *Abbey Road*). In addition, Starr's timing was truly immaculate. (George Martin's production should certainly also be credited with playing a major role in creating the crisp Ringo Starr sound.) Whether or not Bruford was consciously influenced by Starr's style, the remarkable thing is the way that he has combined a Starr-like simplicity, in terms of a clear, uncluttered approach, with a funky rhythmic complexity.

These elements, along with Jon Anderson's unique voice, were already in place and very much in evidence in the group's first efforts. The two factors that were not so settled were Tony Kaye and Peter Banks.

Peter Banks is a fine guitarist. I do not know what he has been up to in recent years. After leaving Yes he formed Flash, a group that sounded, I think, somewhat like a cross between Yes and The Who. The bass guitarist, Ray Bennett, and the drummer, Michael Hough, were very much in the Squire/Bruford vein, while singer Colin Carter's voice had some affinities with Roger Daltrey's. And, of course, Banks's contributions on guitar, which very much shaped the band's music as a whole, were expanded forms of what he had done on the first two Yes albums. Although I do not think that the Flash albums were nearly as strong as the Yes albums that were made after Banks left Yes, they are quite good and show Banks's development as a musician. This indicates to me that he was not able to develop in the framework of Yes, and perhaps this has to do with the presence of keyboards in Yes, while Flash employed only an occasional synthesizer quite sparingly (generally played by Banks or Bennett). It's a difficult thing to do, actually, to balance guitar and keyboards without the music becoming too cluttered. Banks is clearly a guitarist who deserves plenty of space, as evidenced even more on his solo record, *Two Sides of Peter Banks*. This is really an excellent album, all instrumental, featuring the rhythm section from Flash as well as Jan Akkerman and Steve Hackett also on guitar, Phil Collins (in the days when he was not only thought of mainly as a drummer, but also as one of the best drummers in rock music) on drums, and John Wetton on bass. There is one track,

"Knights (reprise)," on which all of the above, excluding Akkerman, play that it is amazing, especially the interplay of bassists and drummers. All of this is by way of not only recognizing Banks's musical accomplishments, but also recognizing that Yes was probably not the best vehicle for his skills.

Incidentally, Flash was not the only band that seemed to have a Yes-like rhythm section. Perhaps more interesting is the case of Genesis, where bass guitarist Mike Rutherford and drummer Phil Collins were also very much in the Squire/Bruford vein, while guitarist Steve Hackett's sound and style owes a great deal to Robert Fripp. It's a nice combination, along with Peter Gabriel's distinctive voice, and perhaps it shows us what Yes might have sounded like had Fripp accepted their offer to join after the departure of Peter Banks. But it also shows us that this combination was not as interesting as either tributary stream—Yes, King Crimson—was to become on its own.

Still more important, however, is the way that Squire and Bruford reinvented the rhythm section, such that the phrase "rhythm section" does not really do justice to the musical configuration that was emerging. This is a theme that will be developed at some length. Suffice it to say for now that neither Squire nor Bruford fit into the established mold for rhythm sections in rock and, while some movement in the direction that they were going had already been accomplished by Paul McCartney and Ringo Starr, the Yes musicians brought a qualitatively new sophistication to these roles. Further, in the band as a whole, there was a new kind of dissemination of these roles, such that it becomes difficult, even with the first two albums, to establish the rhythmic center of the group, inasmuch as this center generally falls with the bass and/or the drums in most rock music. Significantly, this is just as true with King Crimson, at least up until Bill Bruford joined the group. As much as Bruford deserves credit for this innovation, I think that Squire deserves even more, for he transformed not only the sound but the basic role of the bass guitar. In the final analysis, however, this transformation and dissemination of rhythm is the accomplishment of the group as a whole, and we will explore in greater detail how this came about.

Then there is Tony Kaye, who was with the band for the first three albums, rejoined with the *90125* configuration, and was also a part of the eight-person *Union* project. Although Kaye is not as accomplished an instrumentalist as the other members of Yes down through the years, he has the virtue, quite rare and worthy of considerable respect, of never overplaying. I'm not sure that that can be reported as an accomplishment of the other members of Yes either. In terms of style, Kaye was the least original musician in the first band. On the other hand, there are places in the later music where Rick Wakeman tends both to overplay and to clutter things up using too many different keyboards, where I sometimes think that Kaye's playing would have been more appropriate even if less interesting in itself. Clearly, Wakeman played the role of a catalyst of sorts, not so much in an immediately musical sense as in the direction that the band was then turning, especially with *Close to the Edge,* and I'm not sure that Kaye could have played this role. But for all that, Kaye sounds very much like the other keyboard—primarily Hammond B-3 organ—players of that period, there is a simplicity to his style that complemented what the band was doing at the time, sometimes better than Peter Banks's more complex guitar parts did.

As much as one can hear the elements of the later music in the first two albums, *Yes* and *Time and a Word* have an essentially poppish quality. (Interestingly, so does the album by the precursor to King Crimson, Giles, Giles, and Fripp.) But it is very much a pop sound that became possible *after* The Beatles' *Sergeant Pepper's Lonely Hearts Club Band* and the Rolling Stones' *Their Satanic Majesty's Request.* These albums opened a space for a kind of "experimental pop" music, and the musicians and bands and albums that came along to fill out this space, for example, Jimi Hendrix, Jethro Tull, The Who's *Tommy,* and many others, each aimed for maximum creativity and originality. Each aimed to have their own thing, to make a contribution both to the development of the music and to the spirit of the times.

As I discussed in the introduction, it was only in the spirit of a certain time, or rather, in certain historical and material circumstances, that something as seemingly oxymoronic-sounding as "experimental pop" could have emerged. Although there was little to Yes that could still be called "pop" by the time the band made *Fragile* (or certainly by *Close to the Edge*), it is important to mark the roots of the band in the period of experimental pop, and then, experimental rock. What characterizes this form? Three things, basically.

First, the music was rooted in existing popular forms. In the case of Yes, the music was rooted in several such forms, including rock (especially rock music that used harmony vocals, as with The Byrds), folk (both English and American), English church music, jazz, a little country music (in evidence in the opening and middle instrumental sections of "No Opportunity Necessary, No Experience Needed," the much-reworked Richie Havens tune that opens *Time and a Word*), and rhythm and blues. (Clearly there was also a "classical" influence even in the early Yes, including a certain amount of, shall we say, "borrowing" outright from works in the classical Western tradition.) After the Beatles, Yes was perhaps the most "multicultural" group of its time (and they became more so with the addition of Steve Howe; he is more than simply an imitator of diverse styles, he's a capable practitioner).

Second, experimental pop was characterized by the attempt to stretch those existing forms as far as they would go. In effect this was a new kind of avant-garde, whose only real precursor in the West was the experimental trends in jazz associated with John Coltrane in his last period, Ornette Coleman, Cecil Taylor, Albert Ayler, and others. Long before the time that Schoenberg set down the twelve-tone system as the next step beyond the hyper-chromaticism of Mahler, Western classical music had become dominated by an art-for-art's sake approach. There is something to be said for this form of art, to be sure, in the face of "popular" art that is so implicated in the culture industry that it can hardly work to spur critical consciousness—in most cases, quite the contrary. Art-for-art's-sake may seem necessary as a response to the pop song that serves double duty as a beer commercial theme. However, as a political strategy, it is not clear that Adorno's "autonomous art" has served any better to encourage critical sensibilities about (as Adorno put it) "totally administered society" than some of the more cutting songs of, for example, Jefferson Airplane. (My favorite is "Crown of Creation," a masterpiece of sarcasm.) By the early seventies, at any rate, the distinction between avant-garde and popular was beginning to break down. This breakdown in itself could be either good or bad. My point, however, is that, in the specific social and historical circumstances, a new kind of avant-garde was developing.

Third, and closely related to this last point, was the fact that the makers of experimental pop wanted both to push the material of popular music forms to their limits *and* to take much of the audience for those forms with them. This fact also marks experimental pop as a new kind of avant-garde. In general, I believe that it is a kind of avant-garde that can emerge, on the basis of all three elements enumerated, only within certain social and historical contexts. That is, it is not always possible for experimental pop to flourish—at least that is my hypothesis.

It is worth noting that, inasmuch as we are entitled to call the music of the later Coltrane, Coleman, Taylor, and so forth a kind of "experimental pop" (though clearly differing in important musical ways from what was emerging in the rock scene—but, then again, through the guitar work of Hendrix and Carlos Santana, Miles Davis's *Bitches Brew,* and other similar crossover efforts, there were some important musical and social connections as well), that is, an extension of a musical form that had a popular following, the context of the emergence of post-Coltrane jazz was different, even if experimental jazz and experimental pop were developing at roughly the same time. Even though some of the same social factors which created an opening for experimental pop, especially the multidimensional legitimation crisis that the social systems of many capitalist (including the so-called "Socialist" countries of eastern Europe) and neocolonial countries were facing, were also driving the development of experimental jazz, these factors created a far more intense context for the latter. The result was a music of great intensity; the music of Coltrane, Taylor, Archie Shepp, Albert Ayler, and many others cannot be understood apart from the development of a more militant civil rights movement and, further, the qualitative development from that movement of Black Power, personified in Malcolm X and the Black Panther Party. We can see now, with twenty-twenty hindsight, that it was in the later sixties that jazz began to lose touch with its longtime audience, especially among Black people in the U.S. (From this period forward jazz, although the chief innovators were and are still Black, came to find its primary audience among white intellectuals, such that many Black youths do not simply as a matter of course identify jazz as Black music.) But this increasing disconnection cannot simply be blamed on the musicians themselves, even if there was a bit of an attitude on the part of the musicians that the music had to head into the stratosphere whether the people followed it there or not. The fact is that the disconnection occurred as a result of harsh repression exercised against Black people in the U.S. The social system in the U.S. faces the necessity of breaking Black people, and it attempts to do this the way that any would-be master tries to subjugate the other, in part through the denial of the other's culture, and through shattering the memory of that culture. But Black people in the U.S. have not been broken yet, and the system, declarations of the New World Order notwithstanding, seems on the precipice of another downward spiral (hence the promotion of even more open racism and racist attacks in recent years).

For present purposes (that is, it is important to follow this line of reasoning further with regard to jazz and Black culture in general), my point is simply that the situation created for what then became experimental rock during the legitimation crisis was more "relaxed." The factors that allowed this new kind of avant-garde to appear among mainly white rock musicians also tended to ensure that, at least on the surface, the development of experimental pop had more of an "aesthetic" than a "political" orientation. Often, too, where the music did make comments about the direction of society, criticism was aimed at aspects of the society such as religion (I think especially of many Jethro Tull songs, also Emerson, Lake, and Palmer) that, while playing a real part in shoring up oppression and domination, are probably not the main target that social critique and activism need to aim at.

Incidentally, it may be that rap is the most recent expression of a kind of experimental pop. I believe that rap (and I mean the more interesting and militant forms, such as those created by Public Enemy, KRS ONE, and so on) meets the three criteria set out above, and it is definitely emerging in a historical conjuncture that encourages the merging of artistic and political innovation. The main difference in the conjuncture is that, while the late sixties and early midseventies saw the U.S. and other "great powers" of the West in both military and ideological retreat, the late eighties and early nineties have seen the system in military advance (although with serious contradictions and weaknesses—how strong can a system be if it has to get pumped up over invading tiny countries such as Granada, or massacring people in the desert?), while the ideological picture is much more complicated, with aspects of both advance and retreat, all wrapped around an essential cynicism. We will return to these points in the conclusion.

And, again, a comparison might be made between the reaction of the system to rap artists such as Public Enemy, and to experimental pop musicians of roughly the same period, such as the Talking Heads.

With these criteria in mind, I believe that it can be said that Yes was perhaps the best exemplar of musical crossings of experimental pop and experimental rock, especially when the first two albums are seen in light of their later trajectory. However, my reason for saying this is subject to scrutiny. That is, on the first criterion, that of working with established popular forms, the point is that Yes worked with a wider array of these forms than other bands did. King Crimson was clearly influenced by jazz and what used to be called "hard rock." (My friends and I used to call "21st Century Schizoid Man" an example of "heavy metal jazz.") Bands such as Jethro Tull and Genesis were very much influenced by the tradition of English folk music, while groups such as Emerson, Lake, and Palmer and Premiata Forneria Marconi (a.k.a. PFM) were influenced by both jazz and classical music. Although there were other influences as well with these bands, especially R&B (and few English bands were not influenced by R&B), I think that it is safe to say that Yes, more than the others, continually drew in more and more from the different streams of popular musics. This can be seen even more in what I'm calling the "main sequence" period, from *The Yes Album* to *Going for the One,* when African and Asian influences entered in as well. And, the country influence, which is apparent even on the first two albums, grew with the addition of Steve Howe, whose playing (consciously) bears the mark of Chet Atkins. Of the experimental rock bands of the period, I think it is safe to say that only Yes evidences this country influence in any deep-going way.

There are larger points at stake here, however. First, it seems to me that, long before the development in recent years of "world music" or "worldbeat," Yes and other experimental rock bands were bringing about a greater integration of diverse streams of popular musics than "world music" is doing today. Although there are some works in this "world music" vein that I personally enjoy, and although the creators of at least some of this music are truly motivated by a kind of internationalist spirit that is laudatory, I find that much of "world music" is *mere* eclecticism that, somewhat cynically, recognizes that all sorts of things can be played over a strong backbeat. Second, then, it seems to me that there is a level of integration in Yes's music, going back to the first two albums, that is quite beyond mere eclecticism. This integration represents an attempt to forge a broad musical language, and, at least until *Going for the One,* this integration was driven by a conjunction of aesthetic and social factors that were not primarily themselves driven by an all-encompassing desire for commercial success.

This conjunction, playing itself out in terms of the three criteria of experimental pop, was a fruitful one at least until *Close to the Edge.* After that, the music was, if anything, even more interesting, and certainly the band itself was still functioning within the criteria set out above. But more and more the third criterion could not be met: it became more and more difficult to take the audience for rock music in general along on these attempts to find the limits of the rock-driven and rock-based development of popular forms. This, however, contrary to what seems to be the popular and critical opinion, was not because of something the band was doing or not doing, but rather because the terms of the social and historical context were changing in the mid-seventies.

We will return to this discussion. For more immediate purposes, the point has been to understand better the context in which groups such as Yes emerged in the late sixties and early seventies. I have focused almost entirely on experimental rock groups from England, and then on only a certain range of these groups. It is clear that groups such as Yes, ELP, Genesis, Jethro Tull, and even King Crimson and Traffic have a certain affinity, and they have often been lopped together under the heading "progressive rock" or "art rock." But really the phenomenon was much broader, including not only other groups with clear avant-garde intentions (if not pretensions) such as Soft Machine, Henry Cow, Hatfield and the North, Egg, and so on but also groups based in the U.S. such as Weather Report, Santana, and The Mahavishnu Orchestra. These groups also meet the three criteria set out above. Yes was singular, however, even from the beginning, in the breadth of the musical language that the group was attempting to construct.

This breadth has its strength in a kind of aesthetic-political principle of building bridges among the different popular musical forms. But this breadth can work only if three criteria are met. First, there must be a backbone to the integration that is capable of also reaching out to the diverse forms for what they are. I think that Yes was able to construct this backbone from the language of rock music, in a way that much "world music," mainly relying on a backbone of heavy bass and drums, has not. Second, there must exist a certain level of musicianship to carry this off. With the exception of Tony Kaye (who all the same contributed some fine playing), there certainly isn't a more accomplished group of musicians in rock music than those in Yes. (Although there may be musicians as good as those in Yes, I cannot imagine what it would mean for there to be better musicians, in terms of technical facility.) Third, there has to be the authenticity to draw from different forms of music for more than purely "aesthetic" reasons, that is, to see different musical cultures as more than simply storehouses of interesting sounds that can then be exploited. It's a matter of respecting the peoples and the histories that give rise to these sounds. It's a hard thing to call, I suppose, but what emerges with Yes is a strong sense, discussed in the introduction, that structure must be infused with vision, with a guiding conception, and that that conception is not simply "musical," but indeed a kind of "responsibility to music," which is at the same time a more general social responsibility. These themes will be developed in greater detail below.

Let us return to the question that opened this chapter: What if there had only been two Yes albums, *Yes* and *Time and a Word?* As I've hinted already, it seems that the elements that have been laid out thus far in this chapter can be seen in the early Yes only with the benefit of twenty-twenty hindsight. For sure, the early Yes was a neat band, with their own style and sound. If the band had

ceased to exist after *Time and a Word,* the first two albums would still be interesting representations of what was a growing trend in rock music of the late sixties, much as the records of The Nice are. In the first two records Yes was developing both its experimental approach to structures and its guiding vision, but
neither of these two elements were at the point of consolidation or integration.
By "integration" here I mean a point of dialectical interaction where structure
and vision begin to drive each other to new levels of development. A real leap in
consolidation and integration was accomplished with *The Yes Album.* Of course,
there the obvious change was the replacement of Peter Banks with Steve Howe.
But other things were changing as well; the larger social and historical context
was in flux.

And yet most of the musical building blocks were in place with the first two
albums. First and foremost, on the instrumental front, Chris Squire's singular
approach to the bass guitar was already in formation. This in turn spurred Bill
Bruford to further develop his mix of jazz syncopation with a melodic touch, in
part so that the drums could be distinguished from Squire's use of high notes.

As we shall see in a moment, there were already elements of the Yes vision
in the first two albums, even if they were expressed at a somewhat primitive
level, and even if these elements were not yet fully integrated with the music and
with each other.

Before turning to this question, however, which will take us into a more
direct look at the particular songs that make up *Yes* and *Time and a Word,* I want
to take up, at least in a preliminary way, one more element of Yes's music that is
both unique and was there from the start.

I made reference, early in this chapter, to "Jon Anderson's unique voice,"
without developing the point. Perhaps the most interesting and provocative thing
about Anderson's voice is that it is, on the one hand, perfectly suited to the
music of Yes, and, on the other hand, hardly suited at all to any other music. This
latter category would include, to my mind, even a fair amount of Anderson's
own solo output, with the exception of *Olias of Sunhillow,* a very sweet piece of
music, and a few songs here and there. On the few occasions where Anderson
has sung on albums by other groups or artists, the results have been mixed,
mainly having to do with how much these other artists were going after a sound
somewhat similar to Yes's. Thus Anderson's voice is used to very good effect on
the song, "Prince Rupert Awakes," on the King Crimson album, *Lizard.* Clearly
Robert Fripp, who has a better sensibility about these things than most people,
appropriately chose Anderson for the song, which has lyrics by Peter Sinfield
that are not so different from some Yes lyrics. (It's unfortunate that this collaboration could not have been taken further.)[1] The larger point is that there is an intimate connection between Anderson the singer and musician and the music of
Yes. Although Yes, in their most creative period, was about as democratic in the
way that they went about putting music together as a group could be, it is not

wrong to say that the essence of Yes music, there from the start, is Jon Anderson's voice, Chris Squire's bass guitar, and, of course, their approach to music.

I emphasize the question of a particular approach to music in the case of Anderson because it is often assumed that singers are not musicians. This is perhaps often the case in rock music, that there is less deliberate effort on the part of singers to master a craft and make a musical contribution to the development of a group sound. (It's also hard to get most of them to carry equipment!) But this is clearly not the case with Anderson. For one thing, many of the parts that he sings are difficult in themselves, and, furthermore, they are part of compositions in which simply to get the part right takes a keen grasp of difficult structures. Of course, Anderson is responsible for the creation of many of these structures himself. Anderson's contribution as both singer and composer will be analyzed in greater detail, but my point here is that there is almost a one-to-one identification between the elemental energy and direction of Yes and his contribution.

From the start, Yes represented the intersection of a number of guiding conceptions, especially in the vicinity of Anderson and Squire, and the synthesis of these conceptions was and is the essence of the music of Yes.

Yes

Having said all that, it is still clear that *Yes* and *Time and a Word* are mainly pop albums, even if the form is stretched in various ways. The elements that would develop in the next few years were there, musically and lyrically, but by and large these were confined to the service of the shorter or slightly extended rock song. Then again, there are no songs on these albums that come in under three minutes; even though Yes produced quite a few "singles" over the years, they never really produced the standard radio single, which stereotypically comes in at around 2:30 to 2:59. And quite a few of the songs are more in the five- to seven-minute range. It's important to keep in mind that the first Yes singles (and the first Yes album) came out in 1969, a time when radio formats were being stretched, back when we used to speak of "underground radio." The situation has changed considerably, especially in the last ten or fifteen years, with media conglomerates fully consolidating their control of the radio airwaves and, in the U.S. anyway, government direction that has smoothed the drive toward homogenization. (There is a similar process going on worldwide.) Yes in 1969 was part of the wave of groups and musicians who were stretching out, essentially recreating the language of rock music.

Yes's first big break, in terms of public exposure, was as the opening band for Cream at their "Farewell Concert." Cream was part of the first wave of bands that really achieved a valid integration of other musical forms into rock, in their case blues. But rock came out of the blues and other Black forms, so Cream, Hendrix, John Mayall, and so on were basically dipping back into the well. At the same time, while the Beatles, the Stones, and others had experimented with orchestral sounds and sitars they didn't really go beyond using these sounds as novelties. However, the most important thing in 1969 was to be "happening." Creativity became popular because it became possible; and it became possible because it became popular; the breakdown of barriers was both aesthetic and political, and Yes, with its utopian, affirmative name and sensibility, was very much a part of that scene.

Yes and *Time and a Word* each featured eight songs, of which two were covers. To my knowledge, these four covers, along with "Something's Coming" by Leonard Bernstein and Stephen Sondheim, and "America" by Paul Simon, are the sum total of covers that Yes has ever recorded. On the whole the band did very well with covers, remaining both faithful to the spirit of the song and extending the musical material of each song. This, I think, is what makes a good cover version.

Probably the least successful of the covers was the version, on *Yes,* of the Beatles' "Every Little Thing." This may be in part because it is very difficult to improve on a Beatles song, if for no other reason than that these songs have such legendary status. I can think of very few successful Beatles covers; possible exceptions might be Joe Cocker's "I Get by with a Little Help from My Friends" and Earth, Wind, and Fire's "Got to Get You into My Life," but in these cases success is achieved because the original song borrowed on a form (blues and R&B, respectively) that the cover versions were able to achieve more directly. The "problem" with Beatles songs from the standpoint of cover versions is that these songs are generally quite melodic, but there is also a lot more going on with harmony, rhythm, timbre, dynamics, and so forth. The Beatles (and, again, George Martin played a key role) certainly used the full range of musical expression. However, most of the covers are made by singers who only express one dimension of the music, namely melody, and they often do even that in a schmaltzy way. So, in general, it is difficult to do a convincing Beatles cover. Although Yes do a number of interesting things with "Every Little Thing," beginning with a sort of loosely structured jam that contains a sweet guitar hook from "Day Tripper" and following through with some very fine vocal harmonies, they don't really add anything important to what the song already expressed in its original version. This, too, might be called a "general rule" of the cover.

Incidentally, it is difficult to think of Yes as very much of a "jam" group, in large part because of the way Chris Squire plays. Although there is one good example of a Yes jam, namely "Yours Is No Disgrace," especially the various live versions, this is mainly carried along by Steve Howe's incredible guitar improvisations. Although I think that it would be very interesting to hear Squire improvise in a small group setting, perhaps with drums and alto or tenor saxophone, he is not a "boogie" bass player. For that, listen to the Allman Brothers or the great Santana bands of the seventies (especially the *Lotus* live in Japan records). That's jamming where everyone is working at it, as opposed to the rhythm section just laying down a repetitive blur so that the guitar player can do his thing on top of it, which is more characteristic of the opening section of Yes's "Every Little Thing." In addition, Peter Banks's guitar is a bit of a mess in that opening section. And yet, having said all that, the song is fun to listen to, and, taken apart from the fact that it is a cover tune, it probably isn't the weakest song on the record.

The other cover on *Yes,* "I See You," is completely successful. The song was originally by The Byrds, and one key to its successful translation into a Yes song is the fact that Peter Banks has more affinity with the guitar work of Roger McGuinn than with that of George Harrison. In general the song is much more organized than the "Every Little Thing" cover. But the really nice thing about the song is its intimate sound, especially in Jon Anderson's vocals. Yes's version of Stephen Stills's "Everydays," which they perform on *Time and a Word,* is in a similar vein, both in terms of the original composition and what Yes does with it. (Of course, there were a number of affinities between The Byrds and Stephen Stills's group, Buffalo Springfield, which is what led to a nice blending of styles in the original Crosby, Stills, and Nash.) Both feature a form of singing that is half-talking, which Anderson does nicely in these somewhat jazzy contexts. Both have middle sections that are tightly controlled jams, if that isn't a contradiction. There is even a part in the middle section to "I See You" that sounds a little like the middle section of Led Zeppelin's "Whole Lotta Love," if you can imagine that! Also, the jazz flavor of each song allows Bill Bruford to get into the groove that he was looking for as a drummer in the first place, and here he shines in an area where few rock drummers do, in his cymbal work. These two songs make me wish there were more in this vein from Yes, or even simply from Jon Anderson. Although it is difficult to think of Anderson as a "jazz singer," he is able to convey an intimacy that we associate with jazz, especially when minimal instrumentation is used. On "Everydays" this minimalism is matched nicely by the keyboard work of Tony Kaye (which makes me think that an album with just Anderson and Kaye, just voice and piano, could be very nice.) Both "I See You" and "Everydays" are successful covers because they draw out the musical material of the original song in all of the important dimensions.

The cover of Richie Haven's "No Opportunity Necessary, No Experience Needed" will be discussed when we turn to *Time and a Word* in its entirety, while Yes's version of Paul Simon's "America" will be discussed in part 3, as it was recorded between the *Fragile* and *Close to the Edge* albums. However, one cover that should be discussed while we are on the subject is Yes's version of the Leonard Bernstein/Stephen Sondheim song, "Something's Coming." This is a song from the Broadway musical, *West Side Story*. Yes's version was released as a B-side for their very first single, "Sweetness" (from *Yes*). (The song is now available on the *Yesyears* retrospective album.) The Yes version also begins with a somewhat messy jam that does, however, have a few nice guitar hooks as well as a bass guitar quotation from Bernstein and Sondheim's "America"—the "only in America" part, which of course is meant ironically in *West Side Story*—which then appears again in the opening section of Yes's version of Paul Simon's "America." (This musical theme had also been popularized as a rock tune, in England at least, by Keith Emerson's version of the Bernstein/Sondheim "America" with The Nice—this was the tune in which, in concert, Emerson became famous for his histrionics with the organ.) I've always enjoyed a well-placed musical quotation, and this one works nicely.[2] As it turns out, Yes will employ quotations from their own earlier albums beginning with *Tales from Topographic Oceans,* which quotes from "Close to the Edge."

However, on the whole, Yes's "Something's Coming" is not that successful. Like "Every Little Thing" it is fun to listen to, and it has some good vocal harmonies, but it doesn't add anything important to the original. On the other hand, if we look at both of these covers as the work of a new band, which was trying to do things with musicianship, we see once again the elements of what was later to be achieved. This is perhaps what is most interesting about these songs, to see the seeds that were already there. Still, on the whole it was a good thing that Yes did not cover or try to write more songs like "Something's Coming." The "showy" sound of "Something's Coming" works well in *West Side Story* for, after all, Bernstein and Sondheim were masters of that genre, but it isn't the sort of thing that Yes is very good at—thankfully![3]

Now let us turn to the rest of the first album. "Beyond and Before," which opens *Yes,* begins by showcasing the propulsive sound of Squire's bass guitar. This is a good way to start, for it establishes that propulsive bass as a trademark of the band. Where most bass players fill their assigned role by laying down the bottom, Squire does it by setting up a rhythmic pulse that is at the same time melodic. Actually, it can be difficult to tell the difference between a high bass guitar note and a low guitar note on some of the songs on the first two albums. For sure, there are many points in which the bass is doing what one would ordinarily expect the guitar to do. Instrumentally the song is pretty good, lyrically less so (both music and lyrics are by Squire and a fellow named Clive Bailey). There is some good harmony singing without lyrics at the beginning of the song, followed by a lead guitar break that features what I've been calling, lo these many years, Banks's "vengeance" sound—it's got an edge to it. This sound is especially effective in the guitar solo for "Astral Traveller," from the second album. However, this gives way to what might be called Banks's "scrubbing" sound, chords played, usually with wah-wah pedal, that sound as if Banks is scrubbing the strings. To me it sounds like a mess, and it raises the aesthetic point that, in general, less is more: the parts of the song where Banks is making this messy sound would have been better if there hadn't been any guitar at all. The lyrics, on the whole, are pretty silly, kind of cosmic-psychedelic: "Sparkling trees of silver foam, cast shadows soft in winter home, swaying branches breaking sound, lonely forest trembling ground," and so forth. There is a nice march cadence employed in the final passage, and the ending, with acoustic guitar, is effective.

"Beyond and Before," then, demonstrates both the strengths and weaknesses of the band. The messy guitar intrudes often on the first album, not as much on the second. In terms of song structures, the two sides of the album somewhat mirror one another. Each side begins with Squire's pulsing bass; then there's a cover song; then there's a low-key, "romantic" song; then there's a final song that also begins with a strong bass line. The songs that work the best are "Harold Land," "I See You," "Looking Around," and "Survival." In other words, there's a great half-album here, which isn't so bad. None of the songs are terrible. The hard thing would be to try to listen to these songs "objectively," by which I mean in this case, without knowing what was to develop out of these musical seeds. I do not think that I am capable of listening to these songs in this "objective" sense, and I'm not even sure what the point of that would be except to be able to claim that, if Yes had not made the leaps they did with *The Yes Album* and subsequent albums, they would have simply been another neat band of the late sixties, like Strawberry Alarm Clock or Moby Grape or Egg (three really neat bands, to be sure), but nothing more. That's true enough, but fortunately we do have the pleasure of listening to Yes's early works with twenty-twenty hindsight (pardon the mixed sensory reference!). In this respect, even the weaker songs reveal a number of things about not only how the music of Yes got started, but also about the matrix out of which the later music came.

In considering even the weaker songs from *Yes* in this way I am violating the idea of the self-contained work of art, but deliberately so. This idea is perhaps best expressed in aesthetics by the "New Criticism," which was primarily concerned with literature and especially poetry. This form of criticism was predominant in literary studies in the U.S. from the thirties to the sixties. The New Critics applied the model of the "verbal icon." Under this model a poem, for example, is to be taken as an independent, self-sufficient *object,* which can be judged according to criteria that are completely formal. This severe formalism, which eschews all political, social, cultural, or historical contextualization of the work of art, was spoofed in the film *Dead Poets Society;* in one scene students are reading a textbook on literature that sets out, in order of importance, seven or eight criteria which can be applied as a kind of formal calculus for determining whether a particular poem has aesthetic value. Taken to extremes, as the New Critics were sometimes wont to do, formalism is sterile. But this does not mean that there are not important lessons to be learned from formalism, New Critical or otherwise. In considering some of Yes's weaker songs from a historical-contextual point of view, we cannot simply cast considerations of form aside. My whole point in this book is that, when structure and vision are both strong, a very powerful work of art can emerge. What I am primarily pointing to in the earlier songs, then, is the possibility of *enjoying* them from the standpoint of what was achieved later; this is something, and it is a good thing, but of course it does not make the weaker songs anything more than they ever were.

Incidentally, the very social trends and historical winds that brought the glory years of New Criticism to a close are also those factors which created, in the later sixties, an opening for experimental rock music.

Two of what I am calling the "weaker" songs, "Yesterday and Today" and "Sweetness" are just too "nice," too syrupy sweet, too schmaltzy. They do both have spare instrumentation, which is a pleasant change from some of the bombast that mars a couple of the other songs (especially "Beyond and Before" and "Every Little Thing"). "Sweetness" contains the line, "She puts the sweetness in, stirs it with a spoon." That's okay, I suppose. Although I admittedly use the adjective "nice" quite often, mainly to apply to parts of songs and not to songs or albums as a whole, on the whole I am not favorably disposed to "nice" songs, books, paintings, and so on in the sense that a work has to have an edge to it if it is going to play any sort of critical role. Not all works have to have that "edge" at every point or, perhaps it should be said that there is a dialectic of the edge just as there is of everything else because, without this dialectic, the edge itself cannot be maintained. (This is the reason why, for example, it makes sense to have *one* Sex Pistols album, i.e., *Never Mind the Bollocks,* which, in the social and musical context in which it appeared, certainly had more than an edge to it, but not three or five or ten albums. It isn't a question of whether that sort of energy could be sustained, but rather whether the repetition of what was accomplished on the first—and only real—album would turn that edge into its opposite. John Lydon seems to have understood this point well.) All the same, "Yesterday and Today" and "Sweetness" are just too syrupy, even if the latter is still fun to listen to. The song which is most like these two on *Time and a Word,* "Clear Days," which is performed with voice, piano, and strings, is still quite sentimental, but also a bit stronger. It would have been stronger still with just piano, no strings.

The four songs identified as the "stronger" ones are little gems. "I See You" is a cover, but Yes certainly made the song their own. (That this sort of thing can happen says something about artistic and intellectual property, and about property in general.) Before closing discussion of this song, it should be pointed out that the middle section features a long stretch that consists only in guitar and drums, basically a little jazz session. Such a combination is not typical in rock, and it represented an adventuresome experiment in 1969 and even, perhaps, in the nineties. Banks employs what was to become famous with him (and even more so with Jan Akkerman), the "violin effect." This is achieved by turning the volume down on the electric guitar, hitting the string, then easing the volume back up. Banks was to use this effect with even better results in Flash and on his *Two Sides of Peter Banks* solo album. Along with "Survival," "I See You" contains Banks's best guitar work on the album, showing what he is really capable of, which is considerable quality indeed.

I mention this partly because I believe that it is important to be able to listen for not only what is "there" in music, but also for what could be there, what is latent. This form of listening is not simply an idle aesthetic exercise, but rather is training in critical thinking, not only in music, but in general. The idea is to always look for the possibilities, to imagine them so that they can be developed further. As we shall see in the next part, this form of "practical optimism," rooted not only in an idealistic outlook but, even more, in the material structures that are just as much, if not more, "there," as the shortcomings and mistakes, has a great deal to do with the transformations that the music of Yes was to make from *The Yes Album* forward.

"Looking Around," by Anderson and Squire, is the strongest example of a pop song on *Yes.* The lyrics also have their silly side, but they work fine in the context of the song. It is important to remember that there is a difference between a song lyric and a poem that is meant to be read without music. Sometimes the former has or achieves the status of the latter, but it would be mixing apples and oranges to require the same standard of a lyric as of a poem. The important thing is that the lyric works in the context of the song as a whole. (Indeed, it is not out of the realm of possibility that there are great poems that would not work as song lyrics.)[4]

This brings us, finally, to the two songs in which just about everything works right, "Harold Land" and "Survival." Both are very strong lyrically and musically. Both exhibit, in their lyrics mainly, but reinforced instrumentally, the concern with struggle and war that would find its highest expression about six years later in "The Gates of Delirium" (from *Relayer*). To put it oversimplistically, "Harold Land" is about the ravages of war, while "Survival" is about the renewal of life through struggle. "Harold Land" has a gloomy tone that is uncharacteristic for Yes: "Harold Land with a wave of his hand said goodbye to all that." The song is about a young man going off to war, and its tone and theme are reminiscent of specifically English poetry about the First World War. The song closes with the lines, "In conversation it could be said, well after war your heart is dead. Well, it's not hard to understand, there is no heart in Harold Land."[5] Interestingly, there are no songs of this sort on *Time and a Word.* The next point at which this theme is taken up is "Yours Is No Disgrace" from *The Yes Album,* where there is a leap in understanding the character of certain wars. After a brief submergence, then, war and struggle emerge to become major themes in Yes's music. Still, the tone of "Harold Land" remains unique, for there we find a resignation that is not at all typical of Yes. This is not to say that everything is happiness and sunshine (though there is a lot of the latter, and of the sun itself, in Yes's music, through *Going for the One* and beyond) in Yes's subsequent music, but, unlike the whole of "Harold Land," including its ending, the wars and struggles in other songs or extended pieces all "work out" in the end. (Although the outcome is a bit ambiguous in "Yours Is No Disgrace.") These "happy endings" will be discussed in detail in subsequent parts; in particular, we will be interested in asking whether Yes's affirmation partakes too much of the affirmative culture, as Herbert Marcuse put it, of capitalist society.

"Survival" does, as a matter of fact, begin with "sunshine" (literally!). And yet the subject matter of "Survival" is a rather grim version of Darwin's natural selection: "The egg breaks, all is out; the crawling bird begins to scream and shout." The rhyme here threatens to trivialize the message, so perhaps it is useful to focus on three elements that make the song a success. First, the song opens with a powerful instrumental section, a two-part invention with a descending, heavy theme stated by wah-wah guitar and bass guitar, and a playful melody from organ. This emotional tension is restated lyrically, so that, second, the song evidences the sort of quasi-Buddhist or generally "Eastern" sensibility that Jon Anderson comes even a good deal closer to in subsequent albums. (The music and lyrics for "Survival" are by Anderson, so one sees a unified conception at work here—but fleshed out in a way that demonstrates a group effort on the part of highly original musicians, not the sort of thing that Anderson generally achieves on his solo albums.)

The interesting thing is that, as much as Anderson strives for a non-Western understanding, which he continues to aim for today, more than twenty-five years later, there is an underlying strife and tragic sense to his work that unfailingly shows that his is a striving from within Western frameworks. This question will be taken up at greater length in the next chapter, but we can set out some of the basic terms even now.

The tension is that between the grim realities of survival in the state of nature, and a sense that there is greater purpose at work in and beyond nature. On the one hand we have

> Sunshine is creeping in
> and somewhere in a field a life begins.
> An egg too proud to rape
> the beginning of the shape of things to come
> that start to run, life has begun, fly fast the gun.
> The mother flew too late
> and life within the egg was left to fate, ...

On the other,

> All that dies dies for a reason:
> to put its strength into the seasons. . . .
>
> And we're all going somewhere.

Keep in mind what I said about the difference between lyrics and poetry, for these excerpts do not do justice to the song. Really, what is going on here is quite complex, and possibly profound. The lyrics do not conclude on a note of resignation as with "Harold Land," and neither does the music, which ends with a crescendo derived from the playful organ theme—though stated, at the end, by guitar and bass. That the closing playfulness displaces the heaviness of the original guitar/bass theme is itself a testament to how Anderson resolves the tension in the lyrics.

The interesting thing here is that, whereas "Harold Land" was about human folly and catastrophe, "Survival" deals with both the forces of nature and the intervention of humanity. For, as it turns out, the "survival question" isn't one of the proverbial "law of the jungle" after all, but rather of the intervention of the "gun." "An egg too proud to rape" is a very strange line; perhaps it is the most concentrated and yet elusive attempt to capture the idea that there is greater wisdom in nature than in human schemes, again only represented here as violence and as the foolhardiness that thinks itself above the cycles of nature: "Could someone still remain who thinks he still could gain by escaping fate?" In order to understand fully what is going on here, let us consider a third element of the song, namely, the overwhelming feeling of *warmth* that accompanies the central part of the song, after the instrumental opening and a shorter, recapitulative instrumental conclusion. If there were no mention of the gun in this song, one could easily have a straightforward "primordial" reading of the piece: the opening section representative of the primordial and tumultuous forces that shaped the early Earth, before the appearance of life; the sweet sounds of the twelve-string guitar heralding new, vibrant, emergent lifeforms; the final lyrics, "we're all going somewhere," and the closing playful figure indicative of even greater things to come for our little green world.

But there is more; the song is more complicated. There is warmth and purpose and direction, not resignation, but, if anything, it is a warmth of the *reemergence* of nature after humanity has done much of its worst and is only capable of a few final acts of foolishness: following the question of "escaping fate," Anderson intones, "It's much too late." And yet even this is not meant as a dire warning, but an opening to the strength put into the seasons.

Does this opening fully connect with a non-Western sensibility? Of course, the musical setting is very much a work of Western harmonic structure, and this bears on what the lyrics communicate. Typically, music from the culture that gave rise to Hinduism and Buddhism aims at resolution, "peace," and "transcendence" of the world, but a transcendence that does not disdain the world (as with, say, the message of Jesus to "be in the world but not of it"). This is a "resignation" that is neither pessimistic nor optimistic, and indeed transcendence consists in not "going somewhere" but, we might say, "going nowhere," for there is no "where" there. Transcendence consists in recognizing the illusoriness of all attempts at "going somewhere," for any "where," any "there," *the world* in other words, is itself an illusion. The religious-philosophical culture of India is, of course, not the only group of non-Western traditions that might be drawn on (and the ideas of transcendence, illusion, and so forth just sketched may be common to various Hindu and Buddhist traditions, but they are not necessarily common to all Indian philosophical traditions), but the themes set out here are ones that have clearly influenced Jon Anderson. And yet it is also clear that he has, in "Survival," evinced a Western appropriation of these themes. In the years since 1969 Anderson has expanded his interest in non-Western traditions of thought, including in his efforts Native American thought (which is also diverse), and he has engaged in more systematic study. But one sees in "Survival" something that persists throughout Anderson's explorations of the others of the West, namely that he must continually set sail from Western shores and that he remains grounded in Western themes of struggle, of direction (or "teleology" and "eschatology"), of "going somewhere."

The important philosophical point here, and this is something that fans of Yes who see them as some sort of complete embodiment of non-Western religion need to think about, is that things could not be otherwise. Journeys from the West to exotic lands always take place with bags packed. There are two further questions here that are quite important. First, we might question the intention behind such exotic trips: is the aim a cultural raiding party on the cultures of non-Western peoples? Is the aim "orientalism," the gathering of exotic specimens for the entertainment of the Western Same by the other? In these cases nothing like a "heterology" is achieved—on the contrary, the exotic is simply appropriated by the logic of the Same, especially by the logic of commodification. But there is another possibility, namely that of reaching out, opening up, *listening* (for music is first of all about listening, and, as I argued in the introduction, the greatest musicians are the greatest listeners): to the other, for the other. Anything done "for" the other, however, is very dangerous—there is a thin line between a more active listening and opening and the forms of cultural colonialism and imperialism described just now (and always undergirded by the most violent colonialisms and imperialisms in the more standard sense).[6]

Indeed, the assimilation of the other in our century is what raises the second question here, namely, Where anymore is the not-West that one might explore? Eurocentric assimilation has proceeded to the point where there can be no simple exploration of non-Western cultures. In this situation, the danger is that an "opening to the other" will be no more than a facile orientalism.

When I attempt to visualize the landscape of "Survival," I see not a jungle and a tooth-and-claw struggle, but instead a great pastoral field ("somewhere in a field life begins"). All English music and poetry that has a utopian aspect to it will sooner or later find itself in such a field, and will also eventually allude to the "satanic mills" characteristic of the dirty, industrial city (the expression comes from William Blake, "Jerusalem"—Emerson, Lake, and Palmer, as is well-known, perform this hymn, while a much later incarnation of Yes, the band with Trevor Horn and Geoff Downes that made *Drama,* invokes the satanic mills in the song, "Machine Messiah," perhaps the first, but not the last, "cyberpunk" song by Yes). With this I have no quarrel, as long as it is not simply an invocation of better times for what became a far-flung scheme of enslavement and exploitation, the British Empire. Surely Jon Anderson makes his cultural-philosophical excursions to the not-West with different aims in mind than the British East India Company, but there are dangers regardless of one's aim. Let us leave this discussion for now, however, and take it up again in more detail when we deal with other works by Yes that raise the question. The interesting thing is that there is little more than an evocation of such questions of the not-West and their attendant philosophical-religious frameworks until we get to much later works of Yes, especially *Close to the Edge* and *Tales from Topographic Oceans.* To be sure, songs such as "The Prophet" (*Time and a Word*) and "A Venture" (*The Yes Album*) conjure images of wandering holy men, not unlike the Buddha, but they also remind us of those Jewish and Christian traditions that are foundational for the West and yet are not really so straightforwardly assimilated to "the West" as we have come to know it in the image of European modernity. (The same goes for Plato and the Pre-Socratic philosophers.) To bring this preliminary discussion of the encounter of Yes with the not-West to a close then, let us emphasize the idea that ultimately captures the meaning of "Survival" and that remains regulative for other such adventures (up to and including "Where Will You Be," from *Talk,* twenty-five years later): the advent of the beyond comes before, the going out comes from within. Within what? Not the self, not the singular subject, but rather from within the terms of a culture's self-understanding, and from within persons formed in light of such understanding.

Time and a Word

Bill Bruford has compared Yes's second album, *Time and a Word,* to King Crimson's *In the Wake of Poseidon* and found the former wanting. Although Bruford doesn't use these terms, you might say that King Crimson was an "avant-rock" group from the start, having worked through some of the possibilities of experimental pop in its previous version, Giles, Giles, and Fripp. To be sure, Robert Fripp in his experimental pop phase was not nearly as good at it as Yes in their first two albums; interestingly, one might argue that both groups returned to experimental rock in the eighties, after the heyday of progressive rock. In any case, whereas the Crimson King announced itself on the scene as already something that had little to do with popular music or rock'n'roll, and then became more and more experimental from that point onward, Yes's transition from experimental pop to avant-rock was much more gradual, not fully consolidated, one might argue, until *Close to the Edge,* the group's fifth album.

Further comparisons of these two trajectories will be useful in this study, but for now let us simply emphasize the fact that one very important member of the original Yes was becoming a bit impatient with the poppish direction of the group. What's interesting, however, is the fact that Bruford identifies Yes's poppishness with the group's use of vocal harmonies. (All of this is in a brief comment in the *Yesyears* video.) This is significant for two reasons. First, King Crimson never placed much emphasis on vocals. Indeed, apart from Greg Lake, the group never had a truly great singer—and, the singer almost always did double duty on some other instrument, most often bass guitar, that was really the primary task of the singer in the group. There are perhaps one or two pieces in the entire King Crimson corpus that use vocal harmonies (even there not "featuring" them), and long stretches on King Crimson albums with no voice at all. This contributes to the feeling that King Crimson was always already playing music more in the vicinity of Webern and Stravinsky and post–*Bitches Brew* Miles Davis. Yes, on the other hand, with their second album were still clearly working in the domain of stretching the material of the popular song, as refracted through some of the musical innovations of The Nice and Vanilla Fudge and the vocal harmonic innovations of the Fifth Dimension, Simon and Garfunkel, and The Association.

In back of it all, you might say, was The Beatles, and it is important to note that this was a common reference point for both Yes and King Crimson (or at least for Jon Anderson, Chris Squire, and Robert Fripp).

The second reason to take note of this difference is that, while King Crimson began by approximating what, after Arnold Schoenberg and John Cage, came to be called "contemporary music" (even a "song" such as "21st Century Schizoid Man" is no exception), Yes came closer to sounding like a "contemporary music ensemble" by working through and beyond song form. Again, more on this later, but the point is that song form, and the voice, remain central to Yes's music, and everything they have done has been launched from these shores (yes, even *Tales from Topographic Oceans,* which bears the same relationship to the shorter song form, or *Lieder,* as does most opera).

One might say, then, that Bruford's frustration couldn't have been from not doing something as well as he felt he might have, but rather from actually wanting to do something else. This desire for something else brought some very interesting elements to Yes's music, especially with *Fragile* and *Close to the Edge.* What we will look toward when we discuss the transition from Bill Bruford to Alan White is the fact that, while many listeners think of Bruford as both the best drummer in rock music and as *therefore* the better Yes drummer, it may be that White is a better drummer for Yes, a better fit with the core conceptions of Yes's music.

So, *Time and a Word* was not *In the Wake of Poseidon,* not in conception. What *was* Yes's second album, then? It was an important step in the maturation of the group's conception of what they could be. This was not yet a qualitative step, as with *The Yes Album* and the two albums after that, where each represented a qualitative leap into new domains. But certainly this was a quantitative development that showed great potential. Potential for what? This was the great uncertainty, but let us come back to this question after giving *Time and a Word* some focused attention.

I should mention that, at least until I discuss *Union* and *Talk,* I intend to address Yes's albums as they (and all other recordings at the time) were made to be listened to, as long-playing vinyl records, with two sides. Although this time of two-sidedness seems but a relic of a hoary and unretrievable past, of the now-forgotten pre–Compact Disk age, the fact is that musicians in the time of vinyl put together their albums in the full consciousness that each side was itself a semi-autonomous work. This is simply a roundabout way of saying that each side had to stand somewhat on its own, or else the likelihood that the listener would flip the record over was diminished; over time, the experience of an album might come to be exclusively identified with its stronger side, the weaker side mostly forgotten except as territory to avoid. (The upside of this equation is that people might be happy enough with one good side.) The practice of playing album sides on FM radio, the rise of which is concurrent with the time of progressive rock, reinforced this trend, as did the rise of the "concept album" in the post–*Sergeant Pepper's* period. But *Time and a Word* was not a concept album— even in the very loose sense that the term came to have (in the strict sense of a unifying theme, perhaps only *Tales from Topographic Oceans* is truly a concept album, though certainly, from *The Yes Album* forward, Yes made concept albums in the sense of taking the album itself as the level at which the music, production, cover art, and so on come together as a complete work of art). Despite what I have said previously about not wanting the musical experience to be overwhelmed by technological factors, the seemingly contingent fact that records were made with two sides does very much influence the listening experience, and there are good reasons to try to listen to these records in the terms in which they were made.

In that light, then, one easily sees the way that the two sides of *Time and a Word* mirror each other. Each side begins with a somewhat loud and bombastic anthem, each beginning with an organ from some other-than-orthodox church (shades of the organ solos to come in "Close to the Edge," and "Awaken"), each extolling the listener in prophetic tones to take up one's cross. Each side ends in a bit of sweetness, the first side with "sweet dreams can solve the future, sweet dreams provide the past" (to the accompaniment of "you're gonna smile again, you're gonna love again"), the second side with "There's a time and the time is now and it's right for me, it's right for me, and the time is now; there's a word and the word is love and it's right for me, it's right for me, and the word is love." Altogether very nice, and even the prophetic lyrics and tone of "No Opportunity Necessary, No Experience Needed" and "The Prophet" tend, in this context, to become merely anthems of self-improvement and blithe optimism, and not the stuff of true prophetic declaration, the calling down of God's wrath upon the people of Israel for they have forsaken the path of righteousness and the upbuilding of Zion.

The quantity-quality question looms large here, for indeed, something like a true prophetic voice does emerge in later efforts, from "Yours is No Disgrace" to "The Gates of Delirium" and beyond. How does this happen? And, is it only in retrospect that *Time and a Word* is a "good album," as part of a larger trajectory and narrative? I think this is for the most part the case, but that, on the other hand, there are some real gems on Yes's second album.

As Bill Bruford has noted, Yes's reworking of Richie Havens's "No Opportunity Necessary, No Experience Needed," makes the song into an anthem of "multiculturalism" before its time, as well as a bit of a postmodern pastiche of eclecticism. Yes's version runs the gamut from symphonic bombast to "Big Country," with an incredibly driving bass line throughout much of the song, the sort that would have introduced a nitroglycerin burst to the car music typical of the Beach Boys and other Southern California groups a few years before. Getting caught up in the sheer fun of the song, it is difficult to ask whether the version is any good or not. Let's just say that there is very little subtlety to it—as there is with Havens's original. Like many North American listeners, I only first heard Yes with "Roundabout" and then the rest of *Fragile;* it was some time later that I went back to the first two albums. So I cannot capture the sense of what it would have been like to hear "No Opportunity" as the opening of the next phase of development after *Yes.* What I was struck by from the perspective of going back to *Time and a Word* after already being quite familiar with *Fragile, The Yes Album,* and *Close to the Edge* (in that order), is that Jon Anderson sounded much more like a "rocker" in "No Opportunity" than I had been prepared for. This is a "belt it out" voice that one does not hear very often from Anderson, and it is easy to forget that he can do this (another good example is found in Yes's version of Paul Simon's "America"). All the same, as much as I *enjoy* listening to Yes's "No Opportunity," I cannot say that it is an "aesthetically significant" piece of music.

This of course presents us—or, I think, *should* present us—with a bit of a philosophical quandary. The problem has been with us since Plato and Aristotle, and is posed much more acutely when we consider it in relation to questions of ethical significance: How can I *know* the good and yet not *do* the right thing? Conversely, How can I think that something is not good, and yet want or appreciate that thing all the same? Despite the fact that both are areas in which the key term is value, aesthetic questions just do not seem to have the same weight here.

And yet it might be argued that our world is no less in need of aesthetic value than it is in need of ethical value—but I suppose that we would have to have an ethical argument for this claim. Furthermore, where there might be agreement that what we seek in ethics and politics is "what is right," "what is fair," and "what is good" (as in "the good person, the good life, and the good society," the terms that have come down to us from Aristotle), it is less clear what we might seek as the key value in works of art. "Beauty," of course, has been the prime candidate across the ages, but there is undoubtedly much that is great in art that is not beautiful. In our own age—however this may be defined—beauty in art can be seen as an insult to the disasters that humanity has had to endure. We will come back to this question when we discuss the specific aesthetic values that Yes music may be said to embody.

Assuming for the moment, however, that I have some sense of what it is that is "good" in art, how can I then have a liking for a work in which I do not find this good? And, is such a work "art," or does it fail to achieve that status? Is there no such thing as "bad art," but instead only "art," which is at least minimally "good," and that which, failing to meet this standard, is not art after all? These questions may seem at some distance from our main discussion here, which concerns *Time and a Word,* but there is always that larger question: What contribution has Yes made to the art of music?

Yes's version of "No Opportunity" is more a contribution to the more technical art of arrangement than it is to the art of music; the version is more artifice than art. And yet we can learn something from this. Even in their most extended works, with works such as *Tales from Topographic Oceans* and "Close to the Edge" obviously representing the far limit, Yes remains tied to song form. The proper analogy would be to Verdi or Puccini in opera, as opposed to Wagner. What Yes did with Richie Havens's song was to bury it in a sometimes ingenious arrangement, rather than to let the extension of the basic song remain more faithful to the sonic material that was there in the song itself. This could also be said of the version of The Beatles' "Every Little Thing" from *Yes.* As I argued before, it is very hard to do a version of a Beatles song because most of them are perfect to begin with and quite tamper-resistant. Yes was more successful with "I See You" (*Yes*), "Everydays" (*Time and a Word*), and "America" (the long version can be found on *Yesterdays*)—not because they necessarily stayed closer to the original versions of the song, but because the Yes versions have a logic throughout consistent with the material available in the original. Through pursuing this logic, Yes made these songs their own in a much less violent, less expropriative way. Perhaps this is to say that there is certainly an art to creating good arrangements, and while, just as with good interpretation in, say, literature, there is much more to it than simply trying to capture the intention of the author (which I think is in many ways not capturable, even by the author her- or himself), there is still the possibility of a kind of "co-composition" that works from the logic of the "original." (If this is done well enough, the logic of "originality" itself is displaced.)

A whole other line of reasoning might simply take "No Opportunity" as a good opener for the second album, and treat the song mainly in that context. Then we might ask, too, what tone Yes was trying to set for *Time and a Word* in doing this. It seems that Yes was trying to start off by showing that they could "rock," even if this was not in the form of a basic rock'n'roll song, but instead with an extended arrangement of a folkish hippy-trippy song that Yes ran through a multicultural blender. In this interpretation, Yes is already moving toward an "album-length" conception of its work, and then appreciating the song—and the question of how good it is—becomes a different matter. For now it isn't simply a question of the song by itself, but rather of one part of a larger whole. I think this is the better interpretation, or at least a perfectly valid interpretation, though I don't know that this fully gets us out of the woods with regard to the questions raised concerning aesthetic value. There is still the question of how much the part contributes to the value of the whole. But let us return to this question after discussing some other aspects of the album.

Although the third song, "Everydays," is also a cover version (of a song by Stephen Stills that had originally been performed by Buffalo Springfield), there is a good deal of affinity between the second and third songs. Both are a bit jazzy, especially the percussion parts, as might be expected, and Jon Anderson's lead vocals, as might be less expected. Bill Bruford is one of the very few drummers in rock music who can, in the style of the great be-bop jazz drummers such as Max Roach and Kenny Clarke, drive a band with cymbal work. Be-bop introduced into jazz a percussion style in which the cymbals carry the beat, with the drums themselves, including the bass drum, playing the role of punctuation, emphasis and ornamentation. This is just the opposite of most rock drumming (perhaps with the key exception of the great and inimitable Ringo Starr, especially his work on *Abbey Road*), where the drums pound out the beat and cymbals are used for punctuation. Bruford's cymbal work cannot be disconnected from Chris Squire's trebly Rickenbacker sound and use of many high notes, but it is remarkable all the same.

"Then" and "Everydays" are similar in having a basic three-part structure, an opening vocal part, a somewhat bombastic instrumental part, and a closing vocal part. "Then," like "No Opportunity" and "The Prophet," begins with Tony Kaye's overdriven Hammond B-3 organ, though this time with ten measures of two-note chords playing an elongated downward arpeggio. The B-3, it should be mentioned, is one of those brand-name instruments that became, as with the Rickenbacker 4001 bass guitar for Chris Squire, a sound in its own right, something other than simply "organ" (or electronic organ). Although Kaye has some nice piano (and electric piano) work in a number of songs (my favorite is "A Venture," from *The Yes Album*), clearly the B-3 is his instrument, and he has returned to it in recent years. (All of Kaye's contributions to *Talk* are on the B-3.) How did this instrument gain such popularity in rock music? Interestingly enough, there are again jazz roots to be pursued, for the person who really popularized the Hammond B-3 was jazz organist Jimmy Smith. The key aspects of his sound that came into rock music were his phrasing and his use of the percussion effect on the B-3, which gives a very nice "punch" to the organ's sound, especially on single notes. Keith Emerson got a good deal of his organ sound directly from Smith (not to take anything away from Emerson—he's been a brilliant practitioner of this sound within the context of rock music), and Emerson's work with The Nice then influenced a good many other rock keyboardists. (Another excellent Smith-influenced rock B-3 player is Brian Auger.) Whether or not Kaye was more directly influenced by this Jimmy Smith–Keith Emerson combination I do not know, but his organ work was certainly part of a general trend that emerged in the late sixties.

And yet, especially in the organ introductions to many of their songs (more significantly "The Prophet" than "Then"), one cannot help but make other associations with Yes's use of the organ, even if it is the Hammond B-3, basically religious sorts of associations. These associations are also there in the music of The Nice and Emerson, Lake, and Palmer, though often turned in a more irreverent and even antireligious (or anticlerical, at any rate) direction.[7] Significantly, such introductions, prevalent on *Time and a Word,* are entirely absent from *The Yes Album.* In any case, although Jimmy Smith was probably behind Kaye's B-3 in some way, Kaye's playing was far less blue-note inflected than most of the rock organists who were similarly inspired. (I mean the good ones, of course.)

Characteristically, after playing a major role at the beginning of "Then," the organ drops back significantly as the other instruments come in, especially Squire's commanding, pulsing bass line. The other neat thing about the opening part of the song is the very crisp, near-buzz roll that Bruford holds for the longest time, basically throughout the first verse. There's a sense of suspension, of anticipation, of the song perched and ready to take to the air and yet still having its feet on the ground even as the rest of the body stretches toward the sky. It is a wonderful tension, especially as it is resolved not in the obvious way that it might have been, with some sort of complete release, but instead with the new bass line and drum pattern that begins with the second verse. This is a really terrific transformation, almost one of quantity to quality, as there is the simultaneous sense of continuity and the recognition that something quite different is now happening in the bass and percussion. The vocal line is percussive as well, driving, but not in an overdone, histrionic way, but really quite subtle and jazzy. Perhaps this is the first place in the Yes music up to this point, including *Yes,* where we get the sense of just how good a singer Jon Anderson is. Sometimes in jazz criticism there is a funny sort of term that pops up from time to time, not "singer," but "song stylist." With "Then" we hear Anderson as song stylist.

In the middle, instrumental section, there is again a bit too much bombast (as with "No Opportunity"), but the second part of the instrumental section justifies this. Still, the bombastic part could have been presented with a bit more subtlety, if that makes sense, or perhaps what I'm trying to say is that the first part of the instrumental section is simply too busy. There are some nice changes there, however, from a series of fast, bass guitar propelled runs, to a bit with horns that sounds something like a Broadway show tune (they still had some of that in their system, apparently), ultimately transmogrifying into a kind of reel or Irish folk dance. (At the end of this part there is some especially fine cymbal playing.) An exhaustive eclecticism that is exhausting! Then, when this bombast comes to an end, it is as though the bottom has fallen out, and we're once again in the tension that we found ourselves in at the beginning of the song. Out of this black hole comes an intermittent bass line that plays around the beat without ever quite stating it, with some very nice, warm guitar chords and violin-effect single notes and more excellent cymbal work wrapped around this line. This is spacy, intimate music, music to listen to in the dark. And then, out of the dark, or rather in the intimacy of this warm, dark place, we hear the delicacy of Anderson's voice, a voice tentative and vulnerable.

This voice, both warm and almost frightened in texture, again leaves us with the tension that has now enveloped the entire song, but now emphasizing the role that the lyrics play in creating this tension. For the song, on the one hand, is once again an anthem of hopefulness, of "a new kind of day." The final lines, whispered in your ear, in the dark, very intimate and undeniably sensual:

And, in a time that's closer,
life will be even bolder, then;
Love is the only answer,
hate is the root of cancer, then;
Thoughts will be thought together,
soon in our minds forever . . . then . . .

I have punctuated this more in accord with the actual cadence of the vocal line rather than strictly as printed in the *Yes Complete* edition that I am working from. The final word, "then," is drawn out, but when the period comes, it comes with finality, even though, on top of this period there is a persistent afterglow of several tenor saxophones spreading in different directions like the opening of a flower that has petals the size and consistency of elephant's ears. (Okay, it's a trippy image, but I think it captures the moment.)

Despite the utopian content of these lines (this is the only verse, sung twice, and the chorus stays with this theme), there is on the other hand something very *existential* about the song, something that is jazzy, but in more of a Parisian than New York way. And this atmosphere continues into the third song on *Time and a Word*, Stephen Stills's "Everydays." This one is more jazzy to begin with.

"Everydays" opens with bright piano chords cut across with strings that have a touch of angst to them, but more in the mode of a cinematic melodrama than some bitter irony. Still, one thinks of "Georgie Girl," or perhaps even Petula Clark, the vibe of someone who has come to the big city for the great experiences that might be found there, to forge an exciting life, but feeling a bit ground under on this particular day. And a bit lonely. "Well, well, well, another day . . . well, well, well, a . . . nother day," sounds a bit trite out of its musical context. In context the lyrics, as handled by Jon Anderson at any rate (not that I've heard many Buffalo Springfield songs I haven't liked), are a perfect depiction of the vague wandering/wondering that one finds oneself lost in at times in the city. We know that, only a couple years later, Anderson will expressly say, "I feel lost in the city" ("Heart of the Sunrise," *Fragile*). The town and the countryside will emerge as a theme in Yes music, as it perhaps must for any utopian minded artists, and certainly if they are from the land of Blake, Shelley, and Wordsworth.

(I meant Percy Shelley, but, by and by we'll see a bit of Mary Shelley as well, for example in "Machine Messiah" [*Drama*].)

The bass line, too, starts out jazzier from the start, with a warm, burnished figure (not everything Squire does is completely metallic!) that employs some comfortable fifths. (This line, incidentally, anticipates the line in "Perpetual Change.") It is a completely understated line, and yet the whole song depends upon it—indeed, one could imagine a version of the song with just this bass line and voice. And again one hears Jon Anderson as song stylist. There is a live version of the song on the *Yesyears* album where his voice is even jazzier. It seems to me that Yes has often achieved paradoxical effects, no more so than in the work of the musicians at the core of the band, Chris Squire and Jon Anderson. "Then" and "Everydays" are good examples: I've never known a voice with more clarity than Anderson's, and yet, on these songs there is simultaneously a throatiness, like the sound of paper being torn very slowly and carefully.

One line in the song has it that "Saturday's child stays home," but, traditionally, we know that "Saturday's child has to work for its living." "Drive away from here, forget your fear, getting it out of second gear" (again, you have to hear this in context and with the proper cadence)—there is definitely an existential feeling here, only relieved by "sweet dreams," perhaps.

Actually, there is another relief, if you can call it that, in the form of yet another bombastic instrumental interlude. I'm afraid that this one does not work as well as the interlude in "Then," because there is just not enough of a relationship between this interlude and the tone that has been established in the first, vocal part of the song. There is not enough of a contrast either; in other words, the interlude does not make enough sense in the context of the song, and, furthermore, there is a section of "wide-open" guitar and organ jamming that is just a screechy mess. Perhaps this is meant to be representative of a big night in the big city after a gloomy day, but then that undermines the whole thrust of the song.

Both "Then" and "Everydays" are strongest in their bass, percussion, and vocal lines, and would have been better if leaner in their guitar and keyboard parts. But it is important to listen to music for what is potentially there in the basic structure ("potentially there" could also mean potentially "less," sound-wise, than what is actually in the recording) of the musical work, apart from what the musicians actually did with "it." This sounds Platonic, philosophically speaking, as though there are musical works that exist as pure forms, which then may be more or less perfectly embodied (and the embodiment could never be as perfect as the form itself, which is why the greatest music would not actually have sounds in it). While this way of thinking is both appealing in general and probably appealing to Jon Anderson, I tend to be more of a materialist, though not a materialist who wants to rule out the role that *ideals* play in any attempt to achieve something great. What is imperfectly realized in some pieces of music is something that composers and musicians strive for but, for one reason or another, do not entirely achieve. This fact should not keep us from trying to hear—with our minds, in our heads—what might have been achieved.

With this understanding, "Then" and "Everydays" are the real gems of *Time and a Word.*

Of course, there are at least two broad categories of the failure to achieve the ideal that we will have to consider by and by: the "failure" that comes from striving but not entirely making it, and the "failure" that comes when record company executives and media conglomerates do everything to bring art fully within the logic of the commodity. The first "failure" is what makes great art possible, the "making love toward perfection" that is part of the core conception of Yes music. The second "failure" isn't a failure at all, unless the marketing survey turns out to have been off-target and the music shaped under its imperative doesn't make the big bucks after all. How much this second "failure" has affected even Yes's music is something that we will consider in part 3.

What else comes closest to being a gem on *Time and a Word*? Musically, "The Prophet" is very strong—there the band uses its full force (what I've been calling "bombast") to the best effect. The song is an integrated whole in a way that "No Opportunity" is not. At the very beginning, incidentally, we hear the Hammond B-3 percussion effect I mentioned earlier. The introduction is powerful, achieving a synthesis of both rock and church organ. Again, as soon as the rest of the band kicks in, it is the bass guitar that is out front, with a galavanting, galloping pattern. As the vocal part begins, the organ once again comes to the fore, with a surging Amaj7 to Bm movement each measure. (Another thing that Hammond B-3's are very good for is *surging*.) There are also bass lines moving throughout this part at an exhilirating, breakneck pace, especially punchy with the three-chord pattern that follows each pair of vocal lines. Yes is rarely content to just play each verse the same, so, on the third verse of the song ("Prophecy within your mind, and you will work it out"), the bass guitar, having just given us one of those long rows of rapidly played notes that Chris Squire seems to peel off effortlessly, suddenly drops out. (And there is a real sense of a "drop" or "plunge," creating a suspension effect; incidentally, that line of notes just before the plunge is especially reminiscent of John Entwhistle.) Remarkably, what then carries the song—and not to sound like a broken record, but I find it fascinating—is Bruford's play on the bell of the cymbal.

The instrumental section of the song uses strings effectively. Although one of the reasons Peter Banks left the group was the use of an orchestra on the album, one of the good things about the strings in "The Prophet" is that they displace room that might have been filled by another ragged, overcranked guitar solo. Toward the end of the instrumental section there is an interesting bit of bass guitar/percussion interaction that has a Middle-Eastern flavor to it, perhaps more in the sense of the way that "exotic" music is adapted for films about "Old Testament" times than in some more "authentic" sense. One catches a glimpse of Moses in an epic confrontation with Pharoah.

So, what's not to like in "The Prophet"? This song is one of many Yes works that deal with wandering holy men, religious seekers, and prophets. A comparison with what is probably the best such work of Yes's, "And You and I" from *Close to the Edge,* would show that the lyrics for "The Prophet" are a bit hokey and immature. Actually, these lyrics confirm too much the one-sided view of Yes that many people have, including many fans of the group who only want to affirm this one-sided view. That is, everything works out in such an overwhelmingly *nice* way in "The Prophet": "[S]eeing things in different lights his life was redeemed." Certainly an aspect of redemption is the breaking out of mental cages, seeing the world in a new light. But breaking out of cages, including mental cages, requires struggle, and there is no sense of this in the song. "And You and I," which we will be discussing at length in the next chapter, is the much more mature song in conveying that redemption, the path to utopia, is struggle and work and not simply solitary enlightenment on the model that many Westerners want to read into Eastern philosophies of transcendence. I'm afraid this goes for many Yes fans as well. In the early Yes corpus, "The Prophet" is balanced by "Harold Land," where a young man's soul is destroyed by war and everything doesn't work out nicely, and the destructive impulses that interrupt nature's cycles in "Survival," and even just the oppressiveness of the humdrum as spoken to in "Everydays." And even "The Prophet"'s musical counterpart from side one, "No Opportunity," invokes a key aspect of the seeking soul: "I know your cross grows heavier with every step, every step."

But of course the truly remarkable thing is that Yes did mature, and Anderson, whom again many critics and fans of the group simply want to see as a musically sophisticated but ideologically simple flower child, comes to write lines such as, "political ends, as sad remains, will die." I would not want to over-interpret this line from "And You and I," but part of the maturity that we see only two or three years after "The Prophet" involves understanding that seeking, and even finding, is not simply a triumphalist movement from success to success, with no one bloody, wounded, or defeated along the royal road to enlightenment (or at least no one we should remember or care about, because everything worked out in the end). Nor *should* this movement be such, for reasons that are fundamentally ethical.

Inasmuch as "The Prophet" is too much a triumphalist celebration—though certainly not in a mean-spirited way, but rather in a way that is fundamentally naive, or at least the song comes across as such—it is flawed. But, with twenty-twenty hindsight, hearing the song in light of Yes's more mature music and vision, I cannot help but affirm "The Prophet"'s celebration of the seeking consciousness. And, the last thing that I want to convey here is that I in any way, shape, or form agree with those "critics" of the band who claim that Yes's problem is that they are not jaded and cynical. If the choice is between blissed-out flower-child mentality and the faux-existentialist "been there, done that, got the tee-shirt" approach of most rock critics, I suppose I would prefer the former. But this isn't the choice, nor are these categories of consciousness adequate to understanding what Yes has been about.

"Clear Days" is a pleasant love song, a bit more sweetness stirred in with a spoon. The musically interesting feature of the song is that its instrumentation is simply piano and orchestra. Jon Anderson's voice has a little too much air in it on certain phrases, but there is a disarming simplicity to the song. This would have been even more effective if the song had been simpler still, with just piano for instrumentation.

With "Astral Traveller," Yes achieves an interesting synthesis of science fiction/space travel and mystical themes. The opening guitar chords create a feeling of a late-1950s, latenight spooky radio report of strange things in the skies, Sputnik perhaps. The vocal track is electronically altered in an eerie way as well. Yes has been so connected to advanced musical technology over the years that a connection with science fiction seems natural. And there are moments here and there where the connection seems clear enough, but these are relatively rare. When such moments do occur, the connection is more to a fifties version of science fiction, with a Cold War overlay, than to any sort of up-to-date version of fictional futuristic utopia. "Starship Trooper" is also the title of a novel by Robert Heinlein, who couldn't have been more of a Cold Warrior. What Yes was doing with the title is another question, and we will take that up in the next part. I suppose an argument could be made as to whether "Sound Chaser" (*Relayer*) and "Machine Messiah" (*Drama*) are more fifties dystopia or emerging Philip K. Dick–style cyberpunk (and there's a meta-argument riding along here as to whether or not the cyberpunk trend is simply a revamped, microchip-encrusted version of the fifties dystopia). "Machine Messiah" seems more clearly in the fifties category, an early space-age Frankenstein; in this same category is "Big Generator" (from the album of the same name). "Sound Chaser" is more ambiguous on this score (and possibly the craziest piece Yes ever created). Perhaps it does simply sit on the fence. The most recent Yes album (as of this writing), *Talk,* seems to me to be the most "science fiction" of all of the group's recordings, and to be the most clearly cyberpunk. (It is unfortunate that many of the hipper critics are apparently too hip to see this.)

An "astral traveller" is also a hovering soul, one that is having an out-of-body experience. The lyrics are disjointed, as might be the experience of the novice astral traveller, "wondering when . . . to do it again . . . of another flying to the sky . . ." The sense is of one caught up, caught by, an experience that is not entirely voluntary. Thus we have an ambiguous mysticism, again not amenable to a straightforwardly trippy interpretation. No, this is an experience that is both warmly fulfilling ("Once in the air, we could expect a great respect in being") and spooky. Our astral traveller is pulled up into the sky, acted upon by some force, and yet, once in the sky is solitary: "Astral traveller, leaving without her." These words are not sung in a spirit of joy, but more with dread. It's not all peace and happiness up there. After all, the song begins, "And in the ruins, caught in the noose around me, glasses tell lies," certainly invoking a strange incident that has occurred in the midst of a war-wrecked urban landscape.

All of this is further emphasized by the instrumental section in the middle of the song, with its surging march cadence and a well-developed guitar solo that is by far Peter Banks's best on the album—because it is the best thought-out. The solo begins with an "underground" feeling that is—again a paradoxical effect—somehow both warm and devious. It is hard to know whether one is being invited into a pleasant living room with a comfortable chair by the fire or lulled into the sleep of reason that gives birth to monsters. When this sweet and harmless earthworm comes above-ground, it seems that all doubts are dispelled, for at this point the guitar cuts like a knife, with a vengeance. And yet, in a third development, this knife is partially tamed, as it works into a cooperative weave with the organ, leading finally to a restatement of the radio static from the very beginning of the song and a final verse and chorus.

Perhaps this is the place for a final word on Peter Banks. I've perhaps given the impression that I think his guitar playing with Yes wasn't very good. I don't know that his playing with Yes was *always* on a high level, but then, it must have been very hard to fit in with the new things that Chris Squire and Bill Bruford were bringing to rock music. Their presence is so strong on the first two Yes albums that what would ordinarily have been thought of as the lead instruments in the band—guitar and keyboards—are relegated to a secondary role. This isn't to say that the "rhythm section" was "out front" in Yes, the way that it is in, say, the cool, understatedly intense funky music of James Brown or the more in-your-face funk of the Red Hot Chili Peppers or Fishbone, but rather to say that the whole concept of "rhythm section" was already significantly transformed in the early Yes. Thus Tony Kaye and Peter Banks often seem to be overplaying, even though, when you think about it, you hear that each is not really playing all that much. This goes double for Banks, if you take him to be the musician with more in the way of raw chops. Indeed, perhaps Kaye fit in better because there was less that he had in mind to do with any given song. Banks often sounds like a trapped tiger clawing at the bars of his cage—he's constantly trying to cut through, and the sound can be kind of obnoxious. In "Astral Traveller" this energy is better channeled, and the results are exemplary.

But have no doubts: Banks is an excellent guitarist. To say that he is perhaps not on a level with Steve Howe, or as versatile, should not be taken as a put-down. A musician could be half as good as Howe and still be awfully good, and Banks is subtantially better than that. It was undoubtedly for the best that Banks moved on. In the context of the three Flash albums and his excellent solo album, *Two Sides of Peter Banks,* Banks gave a better showing of what he was capable of. Of the Flash albums, the one I find myself listening to the most is the second one, *In the Can.* To me, Flash sounds like a cross between early Yes and The Who, because of the guitar-bass-drums instrumentation and because of their singer, Colin Carter, whose voice is quite similar to Roger Daltrey's. I like this combination. The opening song of *In the Can* is "Lifetime," a tune wrapped around some interesting wrap-around chords from Banks—they seem to turn in on themselves. The middle of the song is a long guitar jam where Banks can finally do what he's obviously wanted to do—stretch out. (He even throws in the main lick from "Hocus Pocus," in homage to his friend and fellow violin-effect master, Jan Akkerman.) The first Flash album (*Flash*) opens with "Small Beginnings," which features a "Roundabout"-like closing section with some very good vocal harmonies. The third and final album, *Out of Our Hands,* is a rock opera of sorts, and though it is a little hokey in places, I would certainly keep it on a list of good progressive rock albums. Using many different guitars, Banks achieves some very rich textures. (I should say that I find the cover art for the first two Flash albums pretty obnoxious—though also indicative of the fact that Banks wanted to be a rock'n'roller more than Anderson, Squire, or Bruford did—while the cover for *Out of Our Hands* is quite interesting.)

Two Sides of Peter Banks is a well-balanced and also richly textured album, and though the guitar is at the heart of it, it is not by any means simply a "guitar album." There's some fine composition and orchestration here, and definitely some virtuoso playing. The thing that I love about the record is that, by this time Banks is a much better guitarist than he was on the Yes albums, *and* he has much deeper insight into what to do with his abilities. As well, he has the confidence here to share much of the record with Jan Akkerman, and Steve Hackett from

Genesis even appears on one tune. The whole first side of the album, though divided into many parts, is a masterpiece of continuous development. Perhaps the high point, and also a masterpiece of orchestration, is "Knights (Reprise)," which features two electric guitars (Banks and Hackett), two bass guitars (Ray Bennett from Flash and John Wetton, then with King Crimson), and Phil Collins playing some monster drums.

Peter Banks's work with Yes was far exceeded by Steve Howe's. It is an interesting irony, therefore, that Howe has not yet made a solo album as good as *Two Sides of Peter Banks*. I also cannot close this discussion of Banks without wondering, wistfully, what has happened to many of the great musicians of the heyday of progressive rock, many of whom have not been heard from in too many years.

Time and a Word closes with a fairly straightforward pop song, the title song. Although the song has the same general spirit that pervades the lyrics of all of the early Yes songs that are in a hopeful vein, musically the song is not especially remarkable. Most of all "Time and a Word," as an album-closer, reminds me of "All You Need Is Love" as the album-closer for The Beatles' *Magical Mystery Tour*—except there is an undercurrent in The Beatles' farewell statement that is missing from Yes's final pitch.

As we have discussed, this undercurrent *is* present in many of Yes's songs, and even the early songs are not quite the flower-power anthems that some would make them out to be. The undercurrent is not one of cynicism—as I suspect it is in "All You Need"—but rather a recognition that accomplishing something in this world, especially creating significance itself, requires hard work and commitment, and there is no simple, straightforward road toward a redeemed world. In the first two albums, Yes recognizes this in places, much less so in others. Of course, inasmuch as "Time and a Word" is one song that is part of an album, it is not absolutely necessary that this song by itself demonstrate the emotional and ideological range that the album as a whole attempts to embody. And, as I have already argued, it does not hurt from time to time to present an unambiguous affirmation of life and its possibilities, even at the risk of too much sentimentality. This is the note on which Yes closes *Time and a Word.* I'm afraid that I do think the song, especially with the horn arrangement that recalls World War II–era British dance halls, is simply too sentimental, and does not, in any case, end the album on the strongest musical performance. Perhaps it would have been better to have opened side two with "Time and a Word" and closed with "The Prophet"; another possibility would have been to open side two with "Astral Traveller," followed by "Clear Days," then "Time and a Word," closing with "The Prophet." With programmable CD players, of course, this becomes almost a moot question, and it is certainly the case that, with *The Yes Album,* the group took a giant leap in considering the album as a whole as the basic unit.

So, we close this discussion of Yes's earlier music where we began: Exactly what do we hear in this music? It is a question of potential. With their first two albums, Yes had already established some things: their musicianship, their compositional adventurousness in developing new structures out of and on the basis of the rock music context, and their visionary, messianic, and utopian outlook.

Listening, say, to "The Prophet," could we have predicted that this group of musicians would go on to create the larger structures and the far greater range of feelings and ideas that are already much in evidence in pieces such as "Perpetual Change" and "Yours is No Disgrace"? Can we trace a line from "The Prophet" to that wonderful breakthrough work, a song that really transformed the terms of what was possible in rock music, "Roundabout"? Well, not a straight line: the development from quality to quality is *never* a straight line. Some of the elements were there; some of the elements were *not* there; some of the elements were there but had to be transformed by the catalytic action provided by additional elements. With twenty-twenty hindsight, I think it is possible to say that Chris Squire and Jon Anderson were the core, that their musical and intellectual vision was there at the beginning and it has been there throughout. But it is in the very nature of the phenomenon of the visionary that one could not have predicted what might have come about, and there are questions not only of possibility, but also of contingency, that must be explored further.

Part 2

Perpetual change: The "main sequence," from *The Yes Album* to *Going for the One*

With *The Yes Album,* and with Steve Howe joining the group, the Yes that had begun two years before really began again. Something new emerged, music and vision on a whole new level. Words often fail in the attempt to capture and give insight into what is happening in music; this is especially the case when this sort of leap has occurred. Call it the underdetermination of the unprecedented, an underdetermination that still echoes close to twenty-five years later.

Where to begin, then? (Philosophers from Plato to Marx to Derrida have marked this problem of "genesis" as possibly the most difficult.) Here is a first approximation, the outline of a methodology: We know that Yes music represents a synthesis of many elements. Let's begin with the important elements that play into the new Yes music as it began to unfold with *The Yes Album.* Analysis of any synthesis into its components cannot tell the whole story; there is also the question of how the elements come together and how they give rise to something new, something that was not seen in the elements taken individually or even taken in a merely arithmatic (sum-over) combination (except, at most, in hindsight). With this understanding, however, we might still gather some insights by examining the ingredients that went into the first Yes music of the "main sequence." I propose to do this under four headings, focusing closely on Yes and peripherally on other musical and cultural developments of the early 1970s. As a preliminary sort of analysis, the aim is to sketch out these elements in a cursory way, developing these and many other themes at much greater length when we turn to a more extended analysis of the musical works of this period themselves.

The time of progressive rock

Yes's main sequence opened in a time of great creativity and experimentation in rock music generally, and one might roughly define the progressive rock period as running from 1968 to 1978. Certainly there were progressive rock artists and albums before 1968, and many progressive rock artists, including Yes, continued with their work beyond 1978. But those years define the period in which progressive rock was at full strength as a musical trend and as a force in culture more generally. Perhaps for a year or two, around 1972 or 1973, this was even the dominant trend. I'll leave for part 3 speculations on why this major trend seems not to have left an enduring mark on either the mainstream of rock music or on the various avant-gardes that exist today (and I'll discuss ways in which this impression is true and ways in which it is not true), but I can't help but emphasize at this juncture that there is more to looking back to that exciting period than mere nostalgia. Indeed, one of the central arguments of this study will be that understanding this period of music is crucially important for generating real possibilities of a redeemed future—for music, for culture, for "politics," for life.

When *The Yes Album* appeared in 1971, progressive rock was already in full swing. An interesting argument to be made about some of the albums that were clearly among the first works of progressive rock is that, although at the time these albums were understood to be a part of the experimental trend, in subsequent years, after the time of progressive rock, these albums have been disassociated from the trend. The examples I have in mind are *Abbey Road* by the Beatles, *Tommy* by The Who, *Their Satanic Majesties Request* by the Rolling Stones, *Anthem of the Sun* by the Grateful Dead, *A Saucerful of Secrets* and *Ummagumma* by Pink Floyd, and possibly *Volunteers* by the Jefferson Airplane. (I'm sure there could be a more complete list, and it would be an interesting exercise to put it together, to really trace out the complete lineage of progressive rock.) To state the absolutely obvious, it goes without saying, for example, that no one now, or even for more than a very brief period surrounding the release of the album in question, ever thought of the Rolling Stones as a "progressive rock band." And yet, "Satanic Majesties" was clearly a part of the visionary trend of the late sixties that saw rock music extending itself both structurally and in terms of lyrical content.

What was that "trend," what were its contours? In terms of the musical lineage of the trend, there is something to be said that is perhaps too simple and neat, and yet absolutely true and recognizable as such: all of the developments that became progressive rock proceed from and come through *Rubber Soul* (1965), *Revolver* (1966), *Sergeant Pepper's Lonely Hearts Club Band* (1967), and *The White Album* (1968; officially this album is titled *The Beatles*). Of these, perhaps *Sergeant Pepper's* is the album that really gave rise to progressive rock and, again, although there is more to the story than this, the mark of these four albums and especially *Sergeant Pepper's* is all over the emergence of progressive rock as a trend and remains all over a great deal of this trend's subsequent development. Certainly this is the case with Yes, all the way through.

Giving examples of a thing or a trend is not yet, however, to give a definition. I have thought a great deal about the definition of progressive rock, thinking, of course, about the works and artists who make up the trend, and I present the following with some degree of confidence but also with openness to further refinement. "Progressive rock" is visionary and experimental music played by virtuosos on instruments associated with rock music.

Although I would like to save extended examination of the issues raised by this definition for another study, it is important to the project at hand, that of understanding Yes, to at least enumerate some of these issues.

1. Crucial to understanding the emergence of progressive rock from what had previously been a deepening trend in what I've called "experimental rock" is the idea of an *avant-garde* arising from and on the basis of the elements of rock music. Just as European classical music continually gave rise to vanguard movements, especially in the Romantic period and leading up to the avant-garde of Schoenberg, Webern, John Cage, and so forth on the one hand, and the influence of Stravinsky, on the other, and just as jazz has given rise to avant-gardes from Charlie Parker, Dizzy Gillespie, Thelonius Monk, Max Roach, and the other originators of be-bop, and later to Miles Davis, John Coltrane, Ornette Coleman, Cecil Taylor, Sun Ra, and Anthony Braxton, so has rock music since the late sixties given rise to avant-garde movements.[1] Besides progressive rock, we might associate another avant-garde with the New York (for example, Velvet Underground) and San Francisco Bay–area (for example, Grateful Dead, Santana) scenes. However, the label "progressive rock," over time, came to be more exclusively associated with English bands such as Yes and King Crimson, and, in fact, it was bands such as these who persisted the most in pursuing the avant-garde idea.

2. This avant-garde trend, as it developed out of rock music, continued to develop in terms of the specific language of rock music. This can be seen even if defining this particular musical language is difficult or even impossible. Thus it might be useful to coin (or borrow, as I imagine others have used it before) the term "avant-rock" as another name for progressive rock. The distinction between avant-rock and what, as an offshoot of the European classical music avant-garde is sometimes called "contemporary music," is hard to frame, but the attempt helps demonstrate the way that avant-rock is itself an offshoot of rock music.

If one considers contemporary chamber music, especially, it would seem that the main difference between this music and avant-rock is that the former generally involves the use of instruments such as electric guitar, electric bass guitar, and trap drums, and perhaps multiple keyboard instruments, including synthesizers, themselves also electric or electronic, and the use of voices that are not classically trained. That much is obvious, but the point is that, if one were to transpose the structures of a number of important avant-rock pieces for the standard instruments of European classical music, it seems that the difference between avant-rock and "contemporary music" would largely disappear. Imagine King Crimson's "Larks' Tongues in Aspic, Part One," scored for, say, two violins, flute, cello, trombone, tuba, and two percussionists. This isn't very hard to imagine (and it would be great fun to hear), and, in this version, it would seem senseless to try to hold to a distinction between avant-rock and contemporary music.

Indeed, at a later stage of the game—that is, in the eighties and nineties—it becomes silly to talk about the different avant-gardes; but this is because another factor has entered into play, namely, the difficulty of distinguishing an avant-garde that is readily identified as separate from the various "mainstreams" of European classical music, jazz, rock music, or what have you. We will return to this point when we take up the issue of the cultural developments that led to the eclipse of progressive rock as a major trend in music.

Despite these similarities with contemporary music, and despite the similarity between, say, the improvisational work of groups such as Soft Machine or Henry Cow (or King Crimson, for that matter), and some developments in avant-garde jazz, avant-rock remains rooted in the language of rock music for the following three reasons.

First, avant-rock comes out of a certain "tradition," even if it seems overreaching to refer to something as a tradition that had only been around for about fifteen years (that is, from the early fifties to the late sixties) at the point when progressive rock emerged. That tradition continues to mark everything that came out of progressive rock, which is to say everything that made the transition from experimental pop to avant-rock. Again, I would especially emphasize the role of The Beatles, but then we would also have to emphasize everything that went into their music, for example, Chuck Berry, Little Richard, Jerry Lee Lewis, and the other early giants of rock'n'roll, as well as the various folk singers who inspired the Beatles' early songwriting (for instance, Pete Seeger, Bob Dylan).[2] Now, it isn't easy to hear the connections between "Johnny B. Goode" and "Larks' Tongues" or "In Praise of Learning" (Henry Cow), or "Tarkus" (Emerson, Lake, and Palmer), or "Close to the Edge," but, if one traces out the actual lines of influence, always aware that new things happen that are not fully determined by what came before, it seems clear that, for example, Yes and King Crimson and the others are a development of the music that began with the early rockers.

This tells us something very important, by the way. As much as groups such as Yes and King Crimson may want to claim the influence of, say, Stravinsky or Sibelius or Schoenberg, and as much as this influence might actually exist in their music to some degree, their music is not of the line of these European classical composers, nor should it be judged according to the standards of this line. This point needs stating another way, for I am not trying to argue—and I would not argue—that, for example, "Yes is great as rock (or avant-rock) music, but it wouldn't hold up as European classical music or contemporary music." My belief is that works such as "Close to the Edge" and "Awaken" are great music, period (that is, regardless of the "kind" of music—I realize this is a problematic thing to say, given that I'm involved here in defining a "kind" of music, progressive rock). What I mean, instead, is that Yes could actually be better as a kind of rock music than Stravinsky is as a kind of European classical music, even despite whatever the former may have drawn from the latter.

Cross-genre comparisons are difficult, if not impossible, to make. What counts as "originality" in one genre may be old hat in another. For instance, a work such as Stravinsky's *The Rite of Spring* is rhythmically innovative as far as the tradition of Western classical music is concerned, but it has little in that department that can compare with the average performance in Indian classical music, or with the master drummers of Africa.[3]

The second reason why avant-rock *is* rock is that progressive rock continues to emphasize the beat, even if in time signatures other than the standard 4/4. In other words, in avant-rock, there continues to be a strong rhythmic center. In the work of almost all avant-rock groups this center even continues to coalesce around the rhythm section, meaning especially the trap drums and bass guitar. One very significant aspect of Yes music, especially of the main sequence, is that the work of the "rhythm section" is displaced and distributed around the group, so that it is difficult to associate the center with particular players. This development, which makes Yes virtually unique among even the most avant of the avant-rock groups, and for which the group is rarely credited by either music critics or even other progressive rock musicians, will be discussed in detail. However, even in the case of Yes, there is a kind of rhythmic center that is generally absent in European classical music and its "contemporary" offshoots.

One of the interesting elements of the music of Yes, as well as some of the other progressive rock groups that have been perhaps more associated with European classical music than with jazz (for example, Emerson, Lake, and Palmer, Genesis, Gentle Giant), has been the commitment to harmonic invention, which is seen by many theorists as the heart of classical music. This commitment relates to the third distinguishing feature, not unrelated to the first, namely the continued association of even the most developed works of avant-rock to song form. We will return to this point, but little needs to be said about this form as the standard structure for just short of everything in rock music. What remains to be said is how this form might be developed in a way that remains "true" to the form, and what the defining features of the "song form" are.

Having said all this, it is still the case that there are no absolutely hard and fast boundaries between avant-rock and contemporary music, other than perhaps institutional ones. And why should it matter in judging the quality of music that some musicians or composers went to Julliard while others pursued other sorts of "schooling"?

3. With the basic definition given above, I set out virtuosity as a dividing line. On the face of it this may seem silly, and we need an explanation for why it is not silly. Perhaps one way to explain this is to say what a virtuoso is and is

not. A virtuoso musician is not necessarily one who is creative, though the great virtuosos of rock, jazz, and European classical music are almost invariably creative.

Perhaps virtuosity in jazz and other forms of music where improvisation plays a central role is a special case, for it is not clear how it would be possible to be both a virtuoso at improvisation and yet not creative. But then, it is also a narrow definition of virtuosity where annotated music is concerned that brackets creativity, for written music must also be interpreted. There is an additional problem that arises around the question of "composition" because in rock music composition may take the form of "writing" music by playing it into tape recorders (or, recently, computer chips and disks). There is improvisation in annotated music and composition in improvised music (a term that gained some currency in jazz criticism is "spontaneous composition," recognizing that the "spontaneity" of a virtuoso such as John Coltrane or Cecil Taylor, for example, concentrates many years of musical and life experience and practice).[4]

My point here, however, actually concerns something far less complicated. There are musicians, especially in rock and European classical musics, who have "chops" galore, and yet little creativity. Having these chops is what I'm calling virtuosity at this point. The concomitant point is that, especially in rock music or other kinds of music where song form is foundational, there is much that is creative that does not require chops or virtuosity.

I only care about music, of whatever kind, that is creative—at least insofar as aesthetics enters the picture (all kinds of uncreative expressions might be interesting from a more sociological or anthropological point of view). If the music is not creative, it doesn't matter how "good" the musicians are who are playing it. For example, I wouldn't care how great a guitarist Steve Howe is—and he is one of the world's great guitarists, of that I have no doubt—if he was not using this ability to play great music. Perhaps it is indicative of something that, as much ability as Steve Howe has, you will never find him using this ability to show off. This says something important about devotion to an art and to a vision, as opposed to almost exclusively male fixations with masturbating with an instrument (I'm thinking of the whole trend of wank-off guitar players of the Edward Van Halen "school," and *not* of Jimi Hendrix who, appearances to the contrary, was doing something else with the sexual aspects of his creativity). A useful way to think about this is that there are "guitar players," "drummers," and so on (violinists, saxophonists, and so on), and then there are *musicians* who play the guitar, drums, and so on. I place Steve Howe in the latter category.

In the narrow sense, then, who or what is a virtuoso? A virtuoso is someone such as Alan White. He may or may not be as "creative" as Bill Bruford—and this is a question that we will get into at length—though he is definitely a very creative percussionist. What makes Alan White a virtuoso (and I choose him as my example at this point because he is often overlooked when it comes to the great drummers of rock music) is that, if you need a piece of music played, regardless of the difficulty, he can play it. Whatever you ask him to play, he can play. Even among virtuosos there are levels of ability, although, when one considers the level of musicianship of a John Coltrane or a Ravi Shankar or a John McLaughlin, it would be exceedingly difficult to say how anyone could possibly be any "better." So here is the technical definition of "virtuoso" that I propose: a virtuoso has great ability on her or his instrument, the ability to play music at any level of difficulty, and therefore a very broad and deep *vocabulary* with his or her instrument (or voice).

But, if creativity and vision are the thing, what difference does virtuosity make? In a word, this is a question of *vocabulary*. If an artist (or a group of artists, a band) has creativity and vision, then greater vocabulary with instruments (and with voice(s) and lyrics) should allow creativity and vision to develop all the further. Focusing primarily on creativity and vision should also encourage the artist to avoid falling into the trap of virtuosity for its own sake.

One of the major issues raised by the emergence of avant-rock is the question of whether or not the content of a music that has emerged from rock music is really up to the task of supporting virtuoso works. After all, if it is true, as I argued earlier, that progressive rock is a form of rock music in part because it emerges from and on the basis of the language of rock music, then we have to confront the fact that the lyrical and other thematic languages of rock music have typically concerned, shall we say, adolescent issues and difficulties. Sex, cars, parents, sex, perhaps surfing, and mostly sex. Perhaps an analogy might be made to a highly skilled artist whose medium is comic books. (Art Spiegelman's *Maus* is perhaps the most difficult example, a comic book that deals with the Holocaust.) The question is whether or not the comic book is up to the task of dealing with subjects that have outgrown adolescence. Is the attempt simply a sad display of "playing grown-up"? Or is it, on the other hand, a failure to set aside the things of our youth? If rock music is an *essentially* adolescent, teenage medium, then I would have to conclude that its greatest achievements are *Tommy* and *Quadrophenia*. In fact, I do think that these works of Pete Townshend and The Who are great achievements (and not only for teenagers, but for anyone who has ever been a teenager), but the real question here would have to be whether or not there is something in the very nature of rock music that means that it cannot develop into an "adult" art form, one that is capable of giving rise to an avant-garde and a set of important experimental works. By "important" is meant pieces that can stand the test of time and be considered significant alongside other major works from other genres of music.

Whether or not Yes music has achieved this status cannot be divorced from the question of whether or not this status is to be achieved in rock music. The answer to this major question can only be developed in what follows, in an extended analysis of Yes music. But it is important to recognize at the outset that to achieve such status has been the aim of Yes music (and the music of other avant-rock artists).

Of course, for those who think such an aim is either unattainable or simply silly (and who would also think, I would imagine, that the stretched form of popular music I have labeled "experimental pop," was already bad enough, and therefore avant-rock is completely over the edge), the progressive rock trend has broken with its "roots" and gone off into musical pointlessness. The analysis presented, even though it is meant to show how progressive rock is a valid avant-garde development from rock music, has also to recognize that such pointlessness is indeed a real danger, one that progressive rock groups have sometimes succumbed to. That danger is one of overloading adolescent content with pointless, even if also impressive, virtuosity, as well as overblown arrangements, not to mention pretentious attitudes.

For sometimes (to some, always) succumbing to this danger, the claim that "that ain't rock'n'roll" is often directed at avant-rock, especially from critics of the Lester Bangs or Robert Christgau schools. The problem is that such critics could be right, I suppose, about progressive rock (again, we have to get into the extended analysis before leaping to judgment), and yet they don't seem to want to take stock of the consequences of their claim. If "real rock'n'roll" is forever and essentially tied to adolescent content, then shouldn't it be abandoned by those of us who have at least the pretense of having entered adulthood?[5]

There is a further issue here that is quite important, an issue that should haunt the critics of the "that ain't rock" school. What is the fixation on the adolescent nature of much rock music, especially when this fixation is reenforced by critics who are themselves long past adolescence (age-wise, at any rate), other than an acceptance of the adolescent terms of our consumer society? We might say that these critics don't want to give up their Christmas toys. At the same time, another irony here is that the progressive rock groups of the seventies, and this goes just as much for Yes and the few other groups who were also quite popular, were the alternative music of their day, especially eschewing commercial values.

One final comment on the whole issue of "progressive rock," namely that the milieu, as it developed in the early seventies, was at that time far broader than critics today construe it to have been. In the early seventies, there was definitely the sense that groups as diverse as Santana, Chicago, or Traffic (and albums such as *Abraxis, Chicago Transit Authority, John Barleycorn Must Die,* and *The Low Spark of High Heeled Boys*) were part of what was meant by "progressive rock." That the label has subsequently been narrowed to include mainly a certain kind of English group is interesting, but neither necessary nor insightful. For, if one takes the definition I argue for, it is clear that groups such as those just named are well-described by it. It is also clear that groups that had previously not played progressive rock can start playing it, and that groups can also stop playing progressive rock. Indeed, in this study we are interested both in how Yes became an avant-rock band and in whether or not Yes at a certain point stopped being a progressive rock group and went back to being an experimental rock group.

Whatever the answers to all of these questions, it was undoubtedly against the background of such questions that Yes developed and defined itself as a force in avant-rock.

An avant-garde from somewhere else

Although the emergence of avant-rock may seem to take part in the distinction between "high" and "low" art/culture that is often discussed in aesthetics and cultural theory, the roots of this particular avant-garde are quite different from those of the avant-garde in European classical music or other "high" culture, though perhaps these roots are quite similar to those of the avant-garde in jazz. In other words, many of the avant-rock musicians did not, for the much greater part, come from privileged backgrounds, but instead almost exclusively from the working class or the lower middle class. This is certainly the case with the fellows from Yes. While biographical matters are not the subject of this study, it is a fascinating question, one rooted in biography but running quite beyond it, how it came to pass that fellows ("lads," as they say in that milieu) from the less-privileged or positively marginalized sectors of English society came to want to play avant-garde rock music influenced by the avant-gardes of other genres. (In this case, whether or not musicians such as Jon Anderson or Chris Squire, or Robert Fripp for that matter, really were influenced by Stravinsky or Schoenberg, in any real and deep sense, is not as important as the question, Why did they want to be so influenced?)

For the record, then, we might state in simple terms the class backgrounds of some of the members of Yes, recognizing that class, as a form of life, is never a simple matter, and also that there is a danger of stereotyping these backgrounds which must, at all costs, be avoided. All biographical information is taken from *Yes: The Authorised Biography,* by Dan Hedges. (At the end of each portrait are the page numbers for all of the material contained therein.)

Jon Anderson was born on October 25, 1944, and comes from Accrington, a mill town in the North of England. Such towns, like their counterparts in the American South, tend to be, as Hedges puts it, "grim, dead-end places" (p. 12). Anderson's mother worked in a cotton mill. His father was a salesman who also did the occasional show as a comedian. His parents participated in dance competitions, and won a trophy or two. "The Andersons lived on the edge of town." When Anderson was a boy and teenager, he worked as a farmhand at a local family farm, at first part-time, later full-time, until he was seventeen. He was raised in the Roman Catholic Church, and attended St. John's Catholic School. His daydreams were of becoming a professional soccer player; they were, in Anderson's words,

> the rock stars of that time, in the sense that being a footballer was the only way to get out of town. You'd be in a group, a team, and that team travelled the country. So, the appeal of being in a football club was (a) because I liked football, and (b) because it was a travelling experience. It was escape. I didn't want to get tied down. A lot of my friends at school were married by the time they turned eighteen, and I said to myself that I wouldn't get married for a long time. I'd try to find out a little more about life first. See what's going on. (Hedges, p. 13)

As Hedges reports (and as any Yes fan knows), Anderson is a bit on the small side for professional soccer (though, as Spudd Webb and Mugsy Bogues have shown, anything's possible).

After completing high school, Anderson worked as a truck driver, "delivering bricks to exotic ports of call like Manchester and Liverpool, forty miles away" (p. 13). Anderson: "Up to that time, to travel ten miles to Bolton or Blackburn was an event. You talked about it for two days before you went and a couple of days after" (p. 13). As Hedges reports,

> It was during a trip through Liverpool that a passing street scene later proved to be something of a vision of the future. "I saw all these people coming out of this club called the Cavern," he remembers. "I wondered what was going on, because it excited me—the fact that *they* were excited. I didn't know what they'd been hearing down there, though, as it turned out, the Beatles and the Merseybeat thing was just starting out at that time. That's what all those people were excited about, and I suppose that made a pretty strong impression on me." (p. 13)

Anderson was already inclined toward music, somewhat following the lead of his older brother, Tony, who had already formed a group called The Warriors. Jon stepped up as the lead vocalist when his brother quit the group to get married (pp. 11–13).

Chris Squire was born on March 4, 1948; he grew up in the Wembley/Kingsbury area of North London, described by Squire as "a bit of a rough place" (p. 18). His father was a cab driver, while his mother was a homemaker. Squire's main experience with music as a youngster was with the choir at St. Andrew's Church. This was a serious endeavor; the choir, under the leadership of Barry Rose, was one of the best in England. As a young person, Squire was most interested in church music, and most rock music "left him cold" (p. 15). Apart from his involvement in the choir, Squire claims, "I had no ambition about what I wanted to do" (p. 15).

> I had no thoughts of being a dentist, a lawyer, or even a singer once I left school. In fact, I was quite an anti-system sort of person. Therefore, music was something personal to me that I didn't even consider as an occupation until the emergence of the

Beatles—the whole Northern Beat Boom that happened when I was about sixteen. That was the catalyst, which I suppose interested me as a developing teenager, and also because it was something that I could apply my love of music to. (p. 15)

Besides playing in bands, the one post-school job that Squire had was working in a guitar shop. He describes himself in this period as not having a lot of friends, a bit of a loner (p. 19; pp. 14–19).

There is a certain experience and a certain attitude that Jon Anderson and Chris Squire had in common, and it seems likely that having these things in common helped cement the bond that made them the nucleus of the early Yes. The experience is that both of them were associated with churches and religious experience from an early age. Although it is not reported, in the Hedges biography or in other sources that I have seen, that Anderson was an especially devout young fellow, he did attend Catholic school, and Roman Catholicism is a minority religion in England, with, to some extent, its own culture. (A good portrait of this culture in the post-war period is found in David Lodge's novel, *How Far Can You Go?*) And, for Squire to have been a committed member of one of the very best choirs in the whole country, under the direction and tutelage of perhaps the best choir director in the country, must have been a heady and formative experience. As well, to be committed to church music as a young person, when all of your mates and the other lads are listening to rock'n'roll, is expressive of a certain sensibility. Again, none of this may equal religious devotion as this is typically understood, but it does evidence a certain commitment that cannot be separated from a religious sensibility.

The attitude Squire and Anderson had in common concerned the value of hard work, and the value of working hard together with other people. As Anderson says of his experience as a farmhand:

> It was a good upbringing in terms of knowing and appreciating the values of life, in terms of what you put in you got out. Everybody's different. Some people don't want to work, and some people don't need to work on that kind of level, but I always thought that I *should* be working. You learn a lot more about life, and there was always a *group* of people working together—the farmer, his wife, my brother, and me. (p. 12)

Perhaps it is significant, too, that Anderson goes on to say that, "We used to sing a lot together. Everly Brothers while we were milking the cows, while we were haymaking" (p. 12).

Squire reports that

> Barry [Rose] actually had a large influence on me in terms of the skill and the amount of effort he used to put into that choir. He made me realize that working at it was *the* way to become best at something. The whole standard of it was so high. I suppose the actual understanding of, and spiritual feeling towards, music that I got from that is something that's stayed with me. . . . (p. 15)

It goes without saying that "working at it" in a choir is collective, cooperative work. Whatever one thinks of particular religious traditions, or of any sort of religious sensibility, it is also important to note that Squire's formative experience with music was in working collectively to give expression to deep and profound thoughts. Perfect preparation, I would say, for creating the main sequence music of Yes.

Anderson and Squire had one other thing in common; neither of them, apparently, had any thoughts of going beyond high school, to college or professional school. (Indeed, Anderson would have been in the minority of young men in his town even in finishing high school.) This is not primarily a matter of ambition—both of them believed in hard work and lived according to that belief—but rather a matter of one's life experiences, especially one's class experience. It is typical of much working class experience that the idea of going to college simply does not enter the picture. There is a sense that "the better things and opportunities are not for us," even as there is also an anger and rebellion against this restrictive feeling. Although the stereotypical picture of the working class viewpoint is that it is limited, for the fact of being unschooled and narrow in experience, the ironic thing is that, when people from the working class start to reflect on their experience and give more systematic expression to their feelings about this experience, the breadth and depth of commitment, and power, if not always the artfulness, of expression makes the schooled, privileged perspective look very weak by contrast. An interesting comparison might be made between the raw power of the Sex Pistols and the, to my mind, middle-class suburban angst of, say Nine Inch Nails or other current stars of the "alternative" or "college rock" scene. Let's just say that the former makes much more of a statement, where the latter just seems to cop an attitude. When this commitment and power is developed through great artistic ability, then amazing things become possible.[6]

There is no guarantee, of course, that in every case these amazing things will become actual, and here we find ourselves again in the quandary concerning a rock-based avant-garde, with the attendant problems of virtuosity. I should add, too, that the argument here is not that nothing good can come from people who come from some other class than the working class; instead it is a question of where one's commitments lie. The commitments formed on the margins of life, especially when they achieve some degree of self-understanding, tend to be deeper, to give rise to a more powerful vision. As Pete Townshend has it in "Substitute," there *is* a difference between plastic spoons and silver spoons. This isn't to argue that silver spoons might not find something good to say, or even that plastic spoons *automatically* have something good to say. In either case there has to be struggle and transformation. Gaining the ability, the skills, the training, the language, to say something valuable, something that speaks to the condition of life on our planet, generally involves a great deal more struggle for working class people (or proletarians, propertyless wage-laborers) than it does for people who have had these opportunities handed to them. The latter may have the tools to say more, but not the experience that would actually give them much to say. They may find this experience in trying to understand how it is that we live in a world in which many, many people are marginalized (and not only in terms of class, but in a crucial way regarding class, as well as gender and nationality/ethnicity/color/"race"), but this can be very hard, and the question of "speaking for the other" (what social and cultural theorists call the problem of "representation") is a very difficult one.[7]

And, indeed, given the quite obvious fact that hardly anyone would identify the music of Yes and other avant-rock artists as "working class music," especially in the way that there is a whole tradition in rock music from England that is identified this way, from The Who to the Sex Pistols, a good deal of explaining is needed to show how deep-going links to marginalized classes, genders, peoples, as well as marginalized nature, exist in the music of Yes and not just in their class backgrounds. In other words, given that the core initiators of Yes came from working class backgrounds, what does this have to do with the music they later came to play?

In light of this analysis, it would seem that Bill Bruford was the odd-man-out among the original core. As Hedges reports, Bruford came from relatively comfortable circumstances. His father was a veterinarian. Unlike Anderson and Squire, and more like many middle-class young people, Bruford had "the automatic pilot set for university and the highway to success beyond" (p. 21). What set Bruford apart from the majority of his middle-class schoolmates was his love of jazz. Again, it is a question of commitment, for there are many from the middle class who imagine that they have an affinity for Charlie Parker or Miles Davis—or for Friedrich Nietzsche or Jean Genet, for that matter—and they feel safe in their dreams as long as they are only voyeurs of marginalization and lives of physical and emotional suffering. In other words, many want the risk-free version, they have some records or books, perhaps some pictures on their bedroom walls, and perhaps they even hang out at the clubs where the aforementioned themselves might have hung out in years past. Perhaps a few even pursue the lifestyle for a little while, knowing however, that there are other possibilities, other "options." This is called "slumming." A very few from this social milieu, however, really go with it, and although it will always be true that, *because* they have come from a background that encourages one to think of oneself as having "options," these folks do in fact have some options that others do not, the perceived or desired affinity over time becomes a reality. The affinity becomes a force that shapes one's life in such a way that it becomes unimaginable that one could ever simply walk away from this life.

In the process of identity formation, it is perhaps impossible to determine the points where wanting to have an affinity crosses over to having an affinity, and where the latter crosses over to becoming one's life. What does a middle-class, white, English fellow have in common with Art Blakey or Max Roach? Very little, but it is the desire to have something in common that counts. Bill Bruford wasn't slumming, he committed to the long haul; he went for the gig, the music, not the money. (His commitment was especially apparent when he left Yes, which by that time had become a very lucrative gig, after *Close to the Edge,* to join Robert Fripp in a new version of King Crimson.) Although Bruford has certainly done well for himself, it is abundantly clear that worldly success has not been his prime motivation. He was a dropout from middle-class opportunities who never dropped back in. (Perhaps he came close, in that Bruford did go on to Leeds University for a short period to study economics, but his real love won out.) The fact that he's a bit younger (born May 17, 1950) than the other fellows (and that Jon Anderson is a very strong-willed person) probably also meant that he would be very much under the influence of Squire and Anderson.

The ironic thing is that Bruford has not, at least as of this writing, ever really broken into the jazz scene per se. Groups under his own leadership have tended to play "jazz-rock fusion," of the Return to Forever variety. Certainly in joining Yes Bruford knew he was not joining a jazz group (and, significantly, the versions of King Crimson that he has participated in were formed after Fripp's period of interactions with very good English jazz musicians such as Keith Tippett). But, as he notes, the late sixties were a period in which the categories were quite fluid, and the idea of a "jazz drummer" in a rock band was not especially strange (see p. 22).

The other core musician who was crucially important to Yes's development as a real force in progressive rock is Steve Howe. He was born on April 8, 1947, and grew up in Holloway, North London. Howe attended the Barnsbury School for Boys. I'm told that this area of London was well known for its women's prison—and thus I'm assuming that this is not an especially high-class part of town. Howe's father was a chef (this is from other interviews, not Hedges). As with the occupation of Squire's father (taxi driver), it is perhaps difficult to call the occupation of chef a "working class" job in the more standard sense of "industrial working class." However, in both cases we are talking about working people, and we are definitely not talking about the "solid middle class."

Although it is unclear exactly how to—or, perhaps, why we should—relate this fact to Howe's class background, the other aspect of his life that people are quick to remark on is his "fastidiousness." Most likely this does relate in some way to Howe's strong work ethic and general perfectionism. But there also seems to be something deep in Howe's psychological makeup that requires order. Hedges relates the interesting story:

> As a child, Howe was plagued with nightmares, and found that listening to Chet Atkins's *Teensville,* played softly on his kiddie record-player, was the only thing that could lull him to sleep.

> The experts in Child Psychology can figure that one out, but it meant that Steve's everyday life was linked to guitar music, if not dependent on it, almost from the beginning. (p. 42)

On the one hand, Howe "couldn't stand sitting in a classroom day in and day out," and he describes his childhood as "pretty boring" (p. 42); on the other, "When I actually started learning how to play [the guitar], I found the whole process was abstract enough to keep my attention for more than three minutes" (p. 43).

My hypothesis is that we have here someone who was one of those beautifully awkward creatures, a working-class reclusive "egghead." I have come to know this type well, for my wife, Kathleen League, is such a creature herself. It is always a dangerous thing to try to speak for or represent others—there are limits to how much this can or should be done, and the attempt to cross these limits can do violence to the other—*but,* my understanding of this situation is that the working-class artist or intellectual feels a good deal of the time as though she or he does not fit in anywhere, either with his/her class or with the class that most artists and intellectuals come from, the middle class. Certainly Kathleen's experience as a graduate student in art history and philosophy bears this out, and there are more general studies that attest to this phenemenon as well.[8] Feeling a sense of belonging in no world, feeling doubly alienated, one attempts to create a world of one's own, quite often a very private world. This certainly describes Steve Howe:

> . . . Howe goes out of his way to be barely visible when he's not on stage. He lives quietly with his wife Jan and sons Dylan and Virgil in a nice but in no way ostentatious houseful of rare guitars on the edge of Hampstead Heath.
>
> He frequents classical guitar recitals, checks the label carefully before eating anything new, runs up outrageous long-distance phone bills when he's away on tour, reads books like *An Introduction to Medical Radiesthesia and Radionics* on airplanes, . . . spends most of his off-the-road hours hidden away in a small upstairs room, playing solo guitar pieces to his tape deck. Music that may never be heard by anyone else. . . . Although chaos amuses him for the first twenty seconds, he's got a precise image of the way things *should* be—on tour, in the studio, and on a day-to-day level. Neat, orderly, and done the right way. (p. 42)

It would be reductivistic and wrong to try to go beyond a merely "atmospheric" reading of the way that Yes's music relates to the social backgrounds of the core members. In addition, while there are class characteristics that are somewhat universal (in broad outline), there are certainly more particular aspects of the class and general social situation in postwar England that need to be taken account of, as well as the general sensibility among youth that grew worldwide in the late sixties, from Shanghai to Prague to Mexico City to Paris to Chicago, that everything was possible. "Be realistic, demand the impossible," as students in Paris put it; or Mao, "Nothing in this world is hard, if you dare to scale the heights." Anyone could be or do anything—and this "Woodstock" anti-essential-ism, though it may have been connected to a certain amount of mere libertinism (with sex and drugs, especially), was not at all reducible to that (even if this is the aspect that we mainly hear about today). As Jon Anderson was to put it later, in the song "Big Generator,"

> I have heard it said to someone,
> or maybe it was me,
> there is a reason to experience,
> psychedelic so we can see.

The word that is crucial here is "so"; in other words, for the sake of another aim, in order to "see." I have wondered many times, in this jaded, cynical world of postmodern capitalism, whether or not the machinations of the culture industry, the antidemocratic media, and the powers-that-be in general, would ever be able to completely obscure the utopian moments of that time, the moments that gave life to Yes. Jon Anderson continues to speak to and with these moments of tran-scendence.

Clearly, it was the generation of such moments that allowed a group of young working-class and lower-middle-class fellows to create an avant-garde out of the language of rock music—and to believe that they were as entitled to do this as anyone. To stay with the subject of class, however, and once again think-ing of the tradition of English working-class rock, we might ask if what issued from the late sixties and early seventies "of Yes" (and some of the other progres-sive rock groups, whose backgrounds I have not yet investigated), from their specific experience of utopian possibilities, was at the same time a negation of class background, perhaps even a betrayal of these backgrounds. Sometimes I think this is what is behind the oft-heard claim that Yes is pompous, pretentious, "not rock'n'roll."

There is more than one side to this accusation, however, as it is just as often heard from critics whose own backgrounds are middle-class; the implication is that these English lads don't know "their place," even if there also seems to be an affirmation of that "place." Perhaps the affirmation is more one of voyeurism (I affirm your place because I enjoy seeing you in it), than of solidarity.

On the other hand, Yes comes out of a cultural-historical moment when the fundamentally ethical relation of solidarity came into view, when people united across all kinds of barriers in the name of a better society. Considered in the light of this moment of "suspension" (Marx speaks of a society "sprung into the air") there is a sense in which it is quite clear that they became somewhat detached from their social backgrounds in becoming popular and somewhat wealthy rock stars, as well as simply becoming accustomed to moving in a dif-ferent milieu from that of working people. This is just as true, it must be noted, of the members of bands that have been more traditionally associated with the working class, from Roger Daltrey to John Lydon. In other words, this is a complicated question: the only way to be "purely working class" is to not become an artist or intellectual in the first place. And then, wouldn't that be convenient for those who do not want marginal voices to be heard in the cultural arena? (People who like to argue that Bruce Springsteen or The Clash "sold out" because they became very popular could stand to think about these issues, and again I have to wonder if the "sell out" argument is mainly heard from middle-class critics who only have a voyeuristic solidarity with the marginalized.)

For the working class artist or intellectual, then, solidarity remains an ethical relation, one of "keeping faith with" and "remaining true to" one's background of marginality, "not forgetting where you came from." We've established that the progressive rock music of Yes is an avant-garde that came from somewhere else, but it remains to be explored exactly where Yes went from there, in terms of their cultural politics.

"There is something very English . . ."

In discussing the original breadth of the term "progressive rock," I included in the list of possible members of this set bands from both England and the U.S. A more complete list would include groups from all over the world, and certainly groups who were making eclectic music that draws on music of the whole world. This list would include such continental European groups as Focus, Magma, and Can. Nowadays we have this interesting category, "world music." Although the idea is problematic in some ways (or, at least, the marketing strategies that cannot be completely disassociated from the creation of the music itself are problematic, in that these can quite often be a form of cultural imperialism), I certainly appreciate the spirit in which musicians such as Peter Gabriel and Bill Laswell and others have attempted to learn from many sources and create a new synthesis. In some ways this music is the inheritor of the spirit of progressive rock (and I hope this point will be better established by critics, by and by, breaking the present embargo on saying anything good about progressive rock). But it also should be recognized that much progressive rock, and first of all the music of Yes, was already very multicultural. As will be demonstrated when we get into the actual music of the main sequence, Yes's synthesis was the broadest of all.

And yet, there is something very English about Yes, as Steve Howe has remarked here and there, and there is undoubtedly something very English about most of the English progressive rock groups. As much as this statement is completely circular, it is still more than just trivially true. A comparison of progressive rock groups from England, such as Emerson, Lake, and Palmer, King Crimson, Gentle Giant, Henry Cow, Caravan, and Hatfield and the North with their

U.S. or Continental counterparts shows some marked differences. What remains quite difficult is specifying just what these differences consist in; for all that there is more to the "Englishness" of English avant-rock groups than just the fact that they are from England, it is hard to pin down just what makes for the "something very English."

Not being English myself, perhaps I am not especially well-equipped to go into this subject; inasmuch as an outside perspective may be useful, however, I think it important to have a go at it.[9] I trust that others with inside perspectives will fill out this picture elsewhere. What interests me most here is simply the discussion of what made these bands and their music different, as opposed to a detailed examination of the "national psyche." I find the latter notion somewhat offensive and, if nothing else, certainly overdone these days in the various attempts to promote the idea that human beings are incapable of getting beyond nationalistic loyalties and sentiments. I believe strongly in the manifold necessity of getting beyond nationalism, so the "national psyche" will only play the role, if even this, of setting a certain scene from which cultural and musical materials might be taken. Although I accept a certain sense of Hegelian "spiritual geography," in the sense of the influence of one's surroundings on the thoughts that one has, and the cultural productions that one might create, and therefore a sense of thought and production as both embodied and "located," I see no reason to place the restrictions of a particular kind of class rule, namely that of the bourgeois nation-state of political modernity, upon such an analysis.

Of course, the easiest explanation for the Englishness of Yes and other English progressive rock groups is that they had the Beatles as a forerunner and primary influence, whereas other influences were predominant elsewhere. But that simply begs the question of the difference that emerged with the Beatles. This is a good question to ask, however, as the Beatles were the beginning of the English difference, because the music that fundamentally influenced them came from the U.S.: Chuck Berry, Little Richard, Jerry Lee Lewis, Motown, Buddy Holly, the Everly Brothers, Elvis Presley, Bob Dylan, and so on. Perhaps most crucial were the Beach Boys, and then one must ask how it is that this fundamentally "sunny" music from the most fundamentally sunny of all places, Southern California, came to have such an attraction for working- and lower-middle-class lads from the run-down, war-wrecked industrial town of Liverpool. When the proposition is put this way, it isn't hard to see the attraction. Perhaps growing up in the "Sun and Fun Capital of the World" (Miami, Florida), I had a similar interest in what seemed opposite, as well as what seemed heavy, serious, by comparison to a local economy based in tourism and, later, drug distribution (and money laundering, paralleling a similar shift in Southern California) and not much in what one would ordinarily call "production." On one level, what the Beatles did was to take the sun and fun (that we were supposed to have until Daddy takes the T-bird away, but then we'd just go on a surfin' safari and dream about well-tanned California girls and how it would be nice if we were married so that we could say goodnight and sleep together—all of which must have seemed a utopia, or at least a tropical paradise, to our lads from Liverpool) and make it heavy, by refracting the musical structures of the Beach Boys through their own experience of dark, gritty, industrial England, where one also lives an island life, but of a quite different sort, among Satanic mills, and where the post-war mood was a good deal more existential and less triumphalistic (as evidenced again by Yes's "Harold Land," or by the numerous spoofs on Churchillian and aristocratic pomposity provided by Lennon and McCartney).[10]

Brian Wilson, the genius of the Beach Boys, had a side that was far from sunny, as we now know. Perhaps the Beatles had an intuitive sense of this and brought it out in their music—a subject for further speculation.

In addition to Southern California, and perhaps "America" in general, as the utopia of English rock music, there was another utopia closer to home, the pastoral vision of the English countryside. Ever since the rise of industrial capitalism in England (and in Europe more generally), there has been a Romantic response, one of the best and best-known examples of which is William Blake's poem, "Jerusalem."

And did those feet in ancient time
Walk upon England's mountain green?
And was the holy Lamb of God
On England's pleasant pastures seen?

And did the Countenance Divine
Shine forth upon our clouded hills?
And was Jerusalem builded here
Among these dark Satanic Mills?

Bring me my Bow of burning gold:
Bring me my Arrows of desire:
Bring me my Spear: O clouds, unfold!
Bring me my Chariot of fire.

I will not cease from Mental Fight,
Nor shall my Sword sleep in my hand
Till we have built Jerusalem
In England's green & pleasant Land.

Many listeners to progressive rock know this poem first of all from its rendition by Emerson, Lake, and Palmer (from *Brain Salad Surgery*); this is the hymn version, with music by Church of England composer Parry. The expression, "satanic mills" also pops up in Yes's "Machine Messiah":

Cables that carry the life
To the cities we build
Threads that link diamonds of light
To the satanic mills . . .

Perhaps the most interesting thing here is that this lyric is not by Jon Anderson—*Drama* being the only Yes album on which Anderson does not appear. Perhaps, however, Blakean reference is a nod to Anderson, who has almost continually exemplified the strong influence of Blake.

Literary theorist Terry Eagleton has argued that,

> William Blake, writing before the emergence of historical materialism [that is, Marxism], cast his critique of industrial capitalism in theological terms. For all its consequent limits, no materialist artefact has ever exceeded its power. (*Walter Benjamin*, p. 177)

In England, and significantly, *nowhere else,* there has arisen an entire school of radical social critique that has joined the agrarian, ecological, and communitarian concerns of English Romantic poetry to historical materialism's critique of commodity production. Although there are "red/green" alliances elsewhere, there is nothing like this attempt to take account of what Raymond Williams—perhaps the most important of these "Romantic Marxists"—called "the green language" and its contemporary significance.[11]

In terms of integrating the actual musical language of the English (and Scottish and Irish) countryside, as well as the more idiomatic expressions of English folk, the award probably has to go to Jethro Tull. *Thick as a Brick* is a tour de force (and, as they say, farce) in this respect ("Where the hell was Biggles, when we needed him last Saturday?").[12] In terms of thematics, philosophical-poetic affinities, however, I daresay that Yes has been most in the spirit of the "green language." (The mind wanders to the cover art for *Close to the Edge* in this connection, and why resist?) Perhaps the essence of the green language is the idea of living human minds and bodies immersed in a world that is itself living. (Again, one thinks of the theme of Roger Dean's album art, from *Fragile* to *Close to the Edge* to *Tales from Topographic Oceans.* These covers show a world breaking up into spores, which take flight through interstellar space and ultimately set down on another planet, giving rise to new life. Dean captured well this affirmation of life that is a constant theme in Yes music, to the point where his graphic depictions then inspired Jon Anderson to write *Olias of Sunhillow.*)

(As an aside, we might note that there were various transplantations of the green language to North America, as seen especially in the philosophies of Ralph Waldo Emerson and Henry David Thoreau, and the poetry of Walt Whitman, in New England, as well as in the hermetic and magical doctrines of many of the new religious movements of that region in the first half of the nineteenth century.[13] In some respects this magical world view has taken up residence especially in California—as has Yes since its *90125* incarnation. At this point, all of this is no more than a bit of free-association, but perhaps there is an interesting parallel to be drawn: from Blake to Yes, on the one side, from Emerson to the Grateful Dead, on the other. Ah well . . .)

In describing the green language, Raymond Williams, in *The Country and the City,* discusses "[t]wo principles of Nature" that can "be seen simultaneously":

> There is nature as a principle of order, of which the ordering mind is part, and which human activity, by regulating principles, may then arrange and control. But there is also nature as a principle of creation, of which the creative mind is part, and from which we may learn the truths of our own sympathetic nature. (p. 127)

This "active sympathy"—which seems to me to be in great evidence in Yes's music of the main sequence, and we will encounter examples of this quite soon—Williams calls

> the real change of mind, the new consciousness if only in a minority, in the very period in which the willed transformation of nature, not only of land and water but of its raw materials and its essential elements was to enter a new phase, in the processes we now call industrial. The agrarian confidence of the eighteenth century had been counterpointed, throughout, by feelings of loss and melancholy and regret. . . . (p. 127)

Williams argues that Wordsworth's poetry represented the "powerful assertion" of an "alternative principle": "a confidence in nature, in its own workings, which at least at the beginning was also a broader, a more humane confidence in men" (p. 127).

It is a commonplace of dismissals of progressive rock music to label the lyrics of same, "bad Romantic poetry." On a generous reading of this unthinkingly ungenerous claim, we might take the argument to be that progressive rock lyrics are often bad imitations of Blake, Wordsworth, Shelley, and so forth. Assuming that Yes lyrics are perhaps the closest in spirit to the green language (and ethos) of English Romantic poetry, we could then conclude that Yes's lyrics must be the absolute worst offenders against this purportedly anti-Romantic "critical" sensibility that would suggest that the naive lads ought to get with the modern world and adopt an appropriately cynical attitude. Yes's lyrics have to be examined in their own right, of course. But one reason for going into these "framework" questions at some length is to show that, if there isn't an understanding of what Yes and some of the other progressive rock groups were trying to do in the first place, a sense, that is, of Yes's self-understanding of its project, then any "criticism" is likely to fall short of its intended object and therefore not be very critical in any significant sense. I realize that it is quite presumptuous to think that one can give a philosophical (or otherwise theoretical) description of an artist's work that may involve terms that the artist him- or herself would be unlikely to use in describing his/her work. But this is indeed the task of the thoughtful critic, to make such a presumption, and to hope that he/she captures and further illuminates what the artist is actually doing.

Yes's (or any artist's) lyrics would indeed be nothing more than "bad Romantic poetry" *if* they are nothing more than mere imitation. This holds true even if the imitations are good ones. But there is another criteria that has to be applied. English Romantic poetry was a part of its time, and even if it is appropriate to invoke this time in some respects, it would be merely a form of "Romantic reaction" (as Marx put it), mere nostalgia, to do no more than to harken back to the days of Blake. Indeed, given that the emerging capitalist order that Blake was willing to call "Satanic" has, through many twists and turns, undergone at least several qualitative developments since the late eighteenth century, any "good Romantic poetry" would have to be more up-to-date, even if it continued to borrow from the tradition of invocations of the English countryside as *one* of its utopian sources.

Is there a place for some kind of Romantic poetry in the contemporary world of an industrial capitalism that has become postmodern imperialism? Are the lyrics in Yes's music—understood, I hasten to add, *as lyrics,* an integral part of a complete work, and so therefore having a somewhat different status than an independently standing poem—up to the task of being good Romantic poetry in this contemporary world of global capitalism and the commodification of everything? Again, we cannot—or we should not try to—answer this question until we consider the lyrics and their musical contexts themselves. It may be that there is a principled argument to the effect that Romantic poetry, no matter how good, is simply not appropriate today. The argument would have to go on to show that this poetry is not radically inappropriate either, for sometimes the most radical artistic gesture is precisely the one that is *untimely, contretemps,* "against-its-time" (and out-of-place). It is from making this gesture, for instance, that Glenn Gould's performances of canonical works of European classical music get much of their power—that and Gould's consummate musicianship. No one ever thought that the members of Yes lacked for musicianship. Gould has been called "Bach in the electronic age" (Richard Kostelanetz). Whether Yes's music can be legitimately understood as "Blake in the age of imperialism and cyberspace" remains to be seen. On the larger question, which concerns whether, in any case, this is a good thing to be (fin-de-millennium Blake), perhaps the best answer will also have to be Yes's lyrics and music themselves; if Yes can make a good case for itself, then we'll take that as an answer to the question of principle.

Perpetual change

We are a good deal closer now to discussing the actual music of the main sequence. As a final preparation for this discussion, let's consider four elements of Yes music in rapid succession, only for the purpose of setting out themes that will be developed at greater length.

I realize that these preliminary discussions may have tried the patience of the reader who wants to get on to the discussion of Yes in particular. I hope that, as the reader gets further into the discussion of the main sequence, she or he will understand that these preliminary arguments are crucial to understanding what Yes is all about. Indeed, on the principle that an analysis that could potentially stretch into infinity must fit into the confines of a book, there will come a point where the reader will simply be encouraged to apply this framework her- or himself. (As it happens, this point comes in the analysis of *Close to the Edge;* because *so* much more could be said, I will have to say less.) But I have another hope, as well. As I said in the introduction, I have deep and longstanding feelings about the music of Yes. I imagine that many readers of this book will share these feelings, if not always my analysis (though I do aim to convince). I also said that I see Yes as very much a part of the kind of utopian aspirations that need to be affirmed in this world, including their negativity against the world as it is. We need strong arguments for the good things, and we need to make these arguments (and to write music and poetry) against the fashionable cynicism that is urged upon us by the culture industry and, significantly, by most of the music critics who are dismissive of Yes. This is indeed a remarkable fact, that with very few exceptions (I can't say that I've actually seen even one exception, but I'm willing to allow that there might be a few), articles or comments that are dismissive of Yes are almost always dripping with cynicism. This fact makes me want to not only love the music of Yes, but to go beyond this, (1) to defend Yes music as a good force in the world, a force that *should* be upheld and promoted, and (2) to demolish the cynicism that would not only tear down the music of Yes but that also works to tear down any possibility of hope for a redeemed world. For Yes and others (in various ways) to keep on creating works that show us some fragment of redemption—and to not give in to the pervasive cynicism—is perhaps the best way to stand against this cynicism. For all that the critical endeavor may be secondary to this work, it is still absolutely necessary: the work of this endeavor is to expose the ethical, political, cultural, and aesthetic roots of the present cynicism (and its material basis in a social form that is fundamentally debasing of human capacities), and to show how artists such as Yes combine structure and vision to present an alternative to a jaded world.

Four elements, then.

1. With each of the first four albums of the main sequence, Yes made a qualitative leap in synthesizing structure and vision. As I hope to show, to experiment with musical structure is itself representative of vision. This is probably obvious to any serious listener of Yes music, as is the fact that the leaps that made possible *The Yes Album, Fragile, Close to the Edge,* and *Tales from Topographic Oceans* are really quite extraordinary, especially when one considers that all of this took place in just three or four years. The point is that we shouldn't allow the obviousness of this fact obscure its extraordinariness. One is tempted to say

that there were giants in the Earth in those days. Our task in what follows will be to try to understand what "internal" factors—internal to the band—and "external" factors—external in the larger culture—created the opening for these developments.

Incidentally, my argument will be that *Relayer* and *Going for the One,* while they are excellent works, represent for the most part a further development of the approach opened up by *Fragile* and *Close to the Edge.*

2. Integral to understanding these leaps is especially the part played by the entrance of Steve Howe. I have already argued that the core aspects of what Yes was doing with both structure and vision were in place with Jon Anderson and Chris Squire. Clearly, however, a lot of musical ground was covered between *Time and a Word* and *The Yes Album,* and it makes sense to argue that Howe's joining the band was what made for the leap to the main sequence. However, explaining precisely what sort of role Howe played is another issue. My argument will be that he played the role of a catalyst, bringing an instrumental virtuosity and an encyclopediac stylistic eclecticism that allowed Anderson and Squire to take their vision to a higher level.[14]

The addition of Rick Wakeman can be similarly associated with the leap to *Fragile,* which represents a more sure-footed consolidation of the main sequence. (*Fragile* definitively showed that what Yes had begun with *The Yes Album* was no fluke.) But there are important differences as well. Wakeman brought more instrumental viruosity to the band, and in that respect was again a catalyst in the band's development, but he was arguably a good deal less a part of the development of the group's vision than Howe was. If this is the case, then we might have a clue to understanding why instrumental facility is not in itself an unqualified good.

3. This has been remarked upon already, but let us set out as a theme, and an idea to be played off of, the possibility that what remains key to Yes's musical development is the qualitative extension of song form. This proposition is not nearly as straightforward as it looks, for there is no absolute definition of what counts as a "song" (and what doesn't). There are certainly pieces of progressive rock music that would not appropriately be called songs, such as King Crimson's "Lark's Tongues in Aspic, Part 1." On the other hand, it seems as though Yes's "Siberian Khatru" is still in some respects a song, even if song form here is radically stretched, and even if the Yes piece is just as long as and has just as many different parts as the King Crimson piece. There are lyrics in the Yes piece, and not in the King Crimson piece, so that is one major difference. But "Close to the Edge" has lyrics, and yet it does not seem appropriate to call it a "song." "Close to the Edge" has "songs" in it, perhaps, but it does something with these songs that is also a qualitative development of song form. "Siberian Khatru" might be understood as a "song," much as "Roundabout" could, in that you could imagine a "reduced" version of it involving only piano or guitar and voice. I suppose that

"Close to the Edge" or even *Tales from Topographic Oceans* could be made into "song cycles" on this model. Steve Howe performs a guitar/voice version of "Roundabout" on his solo album, *Not Necessarily Acoustic,* and this version holds up pretty well. In other words, one can see the relationship between the guitar/voice version and the more orchestrated Yes versions.

If it is indeed the case that song form remains at the heart of Yes music, then we might wonder at the paradox that is created when we have pieces that might be understood and performed as "songs" in the ordinary sense and yet at the same time have their musical material extrapolated into avant-rock territory. We find in Yes music both remarkable directness and simplicity as well as very difficult complexities. The paradox is that we sometimes find both of these elements in one and the same musical moment.

4. Anyone who has seen Yes live, or who has heard live recordings of the group, knows that the "that ain't rock'n'roll" charge is not exactly true. Yes can *rock,* and their version of avant-rock remains an extension of rock music. They may incorporate all kinds of elements from other kinds of music, but what they incorporate these elements into is a kind of rock music. (For example, Steve Howe may play a jazz-inspired guitar solo that borrows heavily from Wes Montgomery, but the music he's playing isn't jazz.) My real point here, though, is something different. It seems to me that the "real rock'n'roll" claim always has an underlying machismo to it, and to the extent that Yes confounds the idea of "rock'n'roll" in this sense, they are making a statement that has to be understood in terms of gender dynamics. There is something very "feminine" about Yes, if by this is meant not an essentialist definition of "the" feminine, but instead that which resists androcentrism, the definition and valorization of the world in masculinist terms. If "real rock'n'roll" is a form of masculinist assertion and rebellion against the feminine, then it's true, Yes "ain't" that; to the extent that Yes is instead a resistance to and a rebellion against this masculinist mainstream of rock music, we find another sense in which Yes is coming out of rock music but also taking rock music to new and uncharted territory.

And finally . . .

The Yes Album

In many ways, *The Yes Album* is somewhere between experimental pop and avant-rock. While the album is framed with expanded pieces, in the form of "Yours Is No Disgrace," "Starship Trooper," and "Perpetual Change," each of these works remains an expanded form of rock that is not exactly avant-garde. Indeed, it is the length of the pieces that itself comes closest to being "avant," while tonality and rhythm remain somewhat conventional. In between these longer songs we find the country flatpicking–inspired acoustic guitar classic,

"Clap," by Steve Howe, the two-part folksong-into-rocker, "I've Seen All Good People," and the much underrated "A Venture." There's no question that *The Yes Album* is very solid and a wonderful album of rock music, but, in terms of the main sequence as a whole and the more experimental directions that Yes was to pursue, the album is transitional.

In fact, one of the main differences between *Time and a Word* and *The Yes Album* is that the latter is a good deal "cleaner" than the former. Perhaps it was necessary to simplify the structures a bit before making them more complicated again on *Fragile*.

Let's take a look at the individual pieces one at a time, and then try to get a sense of the whole and the album's relation to Yes's development as a force in progressive rock.

"Yours Is No Disgrace"

Interestingly enough, "Yours Is No Disgrace" opens with chords and a rhythm very similar to the beginning of Yes's version of "No Opportunity Necessary, No Experience Needed." Bill Bruford describes this as "Big Country" music. I have to think that, in the case of "Yours Is No Disgrace," there is an irony implied in using this "Western," "cowboy" music, for the song concerns the Vietnam War. The shifting point of view in the lyrics is fascinating. I don't have any independent confirmation of this, and so I cannot claim that my interpretation is anything more than speculation, but it seems to me that the lyrics begin with a Western, perhaps American, point of view, but then shift to the viewpoint of the Vietnamese people who have been invaded by the West. Certainly there is also the possibility that the song is meant to express the idea that war is tragedy for all who were involved, and this would be in keeping with Jon Anderson's approach to the subject elsewhere. It is also clear from other lyrics, however, that Anderson understands the fact that, while war can be hell for both armies, this does not necessarily erase the differences between imperialist aggressors and those who are the targets of aggression. In the lyrics for "The Gates of Delirium," Anderson provides his most sophisticated view of this subject, but "Yours Is No Disgrace" is already quite sophisticated.

With its chunky opening chords to launch *The Yes Album*, and especially with its long and varied guitar solo, "Yours Is No Disgrace" served well to mark Steve Howe's presence in the group. The introduction makes a powerful statement, without being overbearing, as Peter Banks could sometimes be. Really, these opening chords are quite conventional, E, A, and D major, and give little indication of what is to come, as far as album openings are concerned, during the main sequence. Tony Kaye's Hammond part at the beginning of the song is also quite conventional, still very much in the mainstream of rock organ playing, à la Jon Lord of Deep Purple. What really makes the structure unfold is the incredibly dynamic bass playing of Chris Squire. Significantly, the bass line here is also similar to the opening line from "No Opportunity." The line there was plenty out-front and propulsive; in "Yours is No Disgrace," the line is not necessarily more propulsive, but it is more in the front of things. Indeed, in one of the middle sections of the song (before the guitar solo), Squire carries the entire instrumental burden, with harmony vocals and just a little guitar on top. Here it can be readily seen how large a contribution Squire makes to the music. We'll come back to this bass line in a moment.

Following its opening instrumental sequence, the lyrics arise out of a swirling organ, a choir-like harmony. Once again Yes is playing with church music, though not irreverently. As lyrics go, "Yours is No Disgrace" begins with words that many would call "stream of consciousness." But this term was always meant to be (in the work of philosophers, psychologists, and poets, such as William James and Sigmund Freud and André Breton) the beginning of understanding, not the end. For, although there are definitely limits to the activity of interpeting lyrics and poems, there is nothing definite about where the limits are. If we are presented with a lyric taken from the "stream of consciousness," we still know two things. We know that the stream is one not only of consciousness, but also of language, and the latter is something that is socially created and shared. And we know that the lyrics came from one stream and not another; in this case mainly from Jon Anderson's stream. Of course, consciousness is the meeting point of many streams, of language and experience. Knowing this does not yield certainty regarding what Jon Anderson was thinking when he wrote,

Yesterday a morning came, a smile upon your face,
Caesar's Palace, morning glory, silly human race,
On a sailing ship to nowhere, leaving any place,
If the summer change to winter, yours is no disgrace.

But these are words, they can be understood; and, if this is poetry, then we might expect to understand these words on many levels. With this in mind, it might prove useful to enter into a brief excursus on the interpretation of lyrics.

To say that these words came from a particular stream called Jon Anderson may sound a good deal like an "intentionalist" understanding of art. In this view, what it means to understand the artwork is that the interpreter has grasped the intention of the artist in producing the work. With verbal works, such as poems and lyrics, this interpretive activity can seem deceptively simple. The intentionalist view holds that the interpreter must attempt to find out what the artist "meant" by the artwork. Literary artworks (poems, novels, and so on) are made out of language, obviously enough. And language seems to be *the* place where it is most clear what meaning *means*. (It seems a much more straightforward proposition to ask what a poet meant by her words than to ask what a sculptor meant by his sculpture; even much more difficult would be the question, What did Beethoven "mean" by his Fourth Symphony. Indeed, it is because literary works seem too much open to the straightforward attribution of intention that writers such as Bertolt Brecht and the Russian Formalists created "defamiliarization" effects.) But intentionalism, with literary works as much as with any other artworks, has two basic problems: (1) We do not have direct access to the artist's intentions, and (2) the artist could never have complete control over how his or her intentions map onto artworks that must necessarily consist in socially generated and socially understood meanings.

To reject the intentionalist theory is to reject Humpty Dumpty's claim that "a word means just what I say it means and nothing else." None of us individually has control over the meaning of even a single word (with the possible exception of a word that is coined by a particular individual, but, even then, this new word will take its place in a fabric of meanings that individuals do not control, and this fabric will play the primary role of assigning meaning), much less over language as a whole. (One reason why this is the case is that language is never a finished "whole" that one can get a grip on.)

At the opposite end of the spectrum from intentionalism is the theory of the "verbal icon," a view associated with the New Criticism. This view holds that the poem is, in a sense, a complete world in itself. The poem must be dealt with as a found object, completely apart from who the author of the poem is or was.

Interestingly, the intentionalist and verbal icon theories have common ground, in that both eliminate the richness of context.[15]

On one level—but only one—the intentionalist theory is insightful. If I know that you have a certain way of saying things, because I know you (the idea being that the two knowings here are linked), then I have a better chance of understanding what you are saying than someone who doesn't know you. If I am interested in understanding what someone has said, then why would I ignore what I know about the person?

On the other hand, on another level—but again only one—the verbal icon theory is insightful. If we are concerned with understanding a work of art, then what we have to focus on is the work of art. Otherwise, we would have to say that anonymous works (as long as they remain so) cannot, in principle, be understood. Now, it may indeed be very difficult to understand such a work if not only the artist but the artist's culture, is unknown to us (in fact, it may be very difficult to even know if what we are dealing with is a work of art—archaeologists have on occasion mistaken toilets for altars, and the modern Western conception of "art" or "music" or "dance" is not always an appropriate lens through which to understand activities that may play certain ritual functions in other cultures that are not paralleled in the activities of artistry in the modern West). But this also tells us something useful: if we know the language, culture, society, and other generally *contextualizing* facts about an artist, we already know a great deal about what "goes into" his or her art, and we know this quite apart from knowing the intentions of the artist.

To return to the earlier discussion of the idea that progressive rock is an avant-garde based in rock music, and therefore we must be careful with comparisons to other avant-gardes that have grown out of other traditions of music, the point is that we understand a kind of music, or a work that is an example of a certain kind of music, first of all in its own terms. This seems to take us back into the problems of intentionalism, in the case that the previous claim is taken to mean that a work can only be judged according to standards that are set by the artist's expectations—that is, by what the artist was trying to do. (And, how do we know what the artist's expectations are, when these are no different than his or her intentions?) And, this claim runs against what I and many others would also like to think, that the best kind of music is that which belongs to the following "kind": *good.* There is a good deal more to be thought out concerning this tension—for example, could there be a kind of music that, in itself, is incapable of producing anything good, because the kind itself is bad? There are some who think this about rock music in general, and many rock music critics who think this about progressive rock. At the other end of the spectrum, the question is, Is it appropriate to judge one kind of art by the standards of another?

My answer to this question, and my way of coming full circle on the interpretation of Yes lyrics in the main sequence, is "yes and no." No, it makes no sense to compare an apple to an orange. If we're having an apple pie–baking contest and you bring a pie made with oranges, we shouldn't give you a bad score, but instead no score at all. But there might be an overlapping pair of contexts in which we would welcome all pies from the fruit family (I can't imagine that orange pie would be too good, but I'm willing to try a piece). It is especially hard to see how Cecil Taylor might be "compared" with Glenn Gould or John Cage (or some other appropriate figure from the European classical tradition—but that's the question); to compare these individuals would be to compare genres. Then we would have to ask if we have an overarching genre, called "music," in which it is appropriate to make such comparisons. Of course, some people claim that there is such a genre, but they go on to claim that the "true" or "good" or "serious" part of the genre is represented by only one kind of music—as the reader might suspect, the claim is most often made for European classical music.

One of the main aspects of progressive rock is that it creates overlapping contexts, bringing traditions and formal innovations together on the basis of the language of rock music. This is one of the things that makes progressive rock inspiring and even educational. Indeed, there is something to be learned from the "multicultural" aspect of much progressive rock, not only as regards music, but also as regards that most difficult set of "genre" questions, the ideas of universal humanity and history that have been debated extensively in modern Western philosophy, from Kant to Derrida.[16] As one of the most multicultural and "open" (I mean by this something more than mere "eclecticism," almost that "absolute hospitality" of which Derrida speaks in *Specters of Marx*), I think that Yes could help us with these musical, philosophical, and otherwise *human* questions.

Finally, back to the more immediate question: How should we understand the lyrics of Jon Anderson and the others who contributed to Yes lyrics, especially at the point when these lyrics became more abstract and obscure (in other words, in the main sequence)? (Although I must emphasize that Anderson is not the only writer of lyrics for the group, it is quite easy to forget this, because his stamp—perhaps his stream of consciousness, if you will—is all over Yes lyrics, even, as I discussed earlier, lyrics that were written when Anderson was not even in the group.) I think that we should avail ourselves of all accessible contexts. Among these contexts would be the biographical and the intentional. In the latter case, it would seem that we would be ahead of the game if we simply got on the phone (or whatever) and asked Jon Anderson himself what he meant when he said, for instance, "Dreamer easy in the chair that really fits you." But not only do I not find this either very practical or very desirable in a book that means to be a critical study of the music of Yes, I also think that such an approach, even when interpolated with other investigations into the contexts of Yes lyrics (and then into the lyrics themselves, of course), violates the power and integrity of poetry. If the "just ask him"–approach is applied, the expressed intention of the poet will tend, come what may, to dominate the interpretation of the poem. Any great poet or lyricist will say more, a great deal more, than even he or she knows to say. A great lyricist will set into play numerous contexts, stir up a motion that gets out of the poet's control even while not becoming completely chaotic. Therefore, the last person who should be asked for "all the meanings of the song" ("Heart of the Sunrise," *Fragile*) is the songwriter (that is, the poet).

And yet, we can go a good deal beyond simply saying that Yes lyrics are "stream of consciousness" word chains that concern general themes such as conflict and harmony. This is true only on the most superficial level. Now, back to our regularly scheduled program . . .

"Silly human race," indeed! The first four lines of "Yours is No Disgrace" cover a great deal of ground. Indeed, every line functions on the level of more-or-less concrete representation, as well as on the level of an ironic turning back on themselves. "Silly human race"—human folly is simply the way of things, and, if the good times turn bad, then it isn't your fault, or anyone's fault, alone. "If the summer change to winter"—well, the summer does generally change to winter, so why say this? Not, surely, for the reason of simply reiterating what is naturally determined in every cycle of seasons. Note that this statement is not simply "stream of consciousness" either. Indeed, as with "Survival," the ironic twist is against mere fatedness, and against the interpretation of going to war as only tragedy without responsibility. Caesar's Palace, on the one hand—the ultimate in human folly, the wretched casino-"culture" of Las Vegas, spin the wheel, take your chances; Morning glory, on the other—these flowers that are also "folly," they only play, they do not "work" ("Consider the lillies of the field, they neither sow nor reap").

(Just to take one last jab at the "stream of consciousness" interpretation of Anderson lyrics, and then to leave this point alone, assuming that it's been made well enough: Sure, one could say that these strange-sounding lyrics just popped into Jon Anderson's "stream of consciousness," and then onto the page. But why "morning glory" and not some other kind of flower? Why "Caesar's Palace" and not some other example of human folly and wastefulness? To understand that the functioning of these terms within the song does not require that Anderson "consciously knew what he was doing" with these lyrics is not to also necessitate that we see him as just saying whatever pops into—or out of—his mind.)

A sailing ship is somewhat—and ultimately—at the mercy of the four winds. So, again: Is the idea that, if someone is simply blown by the winds of time, history, and society, from summer to winter, from peace to war, then that is the end of responsibility? Is war, then, simply "tragedy," not in any deep sense as understood by the ancient Greeks, but instead in the trivial sense presented on a daily basis by the culture industry, where there's no sense looking for the causes of bad things that happen?[17] But, if one is susceptible to being blown about by winds, and one *knows* this, then isn't one obligated to do what one can about the fact—for example, to avoid being blown into another ship, if that is possible?

"If the summer change to winter, yours is no disgrace" seems as much a question as a statement of fact—an ironic question. "So that is what you think, eh? Well, isn't that convenient for you?" The viewpoint shifts with the next verse—or does it? The next verse attempts to capture the Vietnamese point of view, beginning with the line, "Battleships confide in me and tell me where you are." This is clear because only the Americans, and not the Vietnamese, had battleships. But, why not read the first verse as also coming from this point of view? It could be that, from a Third-World standpoint, "Caesar's Palace" is as good and well-known a symbol of first-world excess, corruption, and imperialism as any other (for example, Coca-Cola). Still, the first verse as a whole seems more an expression of first-world moral ambiguity ("a sailing ship to nowhere"—that's "the good life" in the U.S.) than of Third-World accusation. But then, in the image of Caesar's Palace, there is also the question of aggressive invasions into Third-World countries as mere "gambles" of imperialism, a spin of the wheel to see what "we" come up with. After all, isn't this still the dominant rhetoric in the first world? The irony in what I am calling the "question" expressed by the first verse seems to be generated either by conflict within the aggressive, imperialist population as a whole, or perhaps even within the soul of a single first-world soldier sent off to war in the Third World (perhaps a working-class soldier for whom the lights and glitz of Las Vegas seem to be a utopia). This issue is especially complicated when we get to the final verse (before the recapitulation of the first verse):

Death defying, mutilated armies scatter the earth,
Crawling out of dirty holes, their morals,
their morals disappear.

Who is "they," here? If, at this point in the narrative, the death and destruction of war have played the role of great equalizers, does this cancel any distinction between imperialist aggressors and Third-World people who seek independence and national liberation? I would say that such "equality of the battlefield" is not at all where this song takes us; but then, I'm not convinced that the "they" in this verse refers to either both armies or to the U.S. military alone. To some relatively small extent, the U.S. Army in the last years of the Vietnam War was "death defying" and "mutilated," but to a relatively very small extent when compared to the Vietnamese. And, "mutilation," by means of carpet bombing and napalm (what was called a "scorched earth" policy), was the explicit objective of the U.S.—forms of warfare that included torture at every step and that revealed that there never was any moral purpose to the U.S. invasion. The U.S. (its economic and political system, represented by its army, which carried out war as politics by other means) never had any morals in Vietnam that could "disappear." This is not to say that individual soldiers in the U.S. military were necessarily completely immoral. Indeed, many, when they came to see that the invasion itself was immoral, did the moral thing and opposed the war.

However, what I believe Anderson is really after with this verse is the true tragedy of a war in which the aggressing side has weapons of enormously destructive capability and the invaded side has only its people that it can rely on. "Only its people"—the Vietnamese people managed to defeat an invasion by the most powerful military machine on the planet. But, as Marx once said, one of the ways that oppressors take revenge on the oppressed is in what the latter are forced to become in attempting to throw off the former. "Crawling out of dirty holes, their morals disappear."

What, then, is the recapitulation of the first verse in both the middle of the song (where the bass guitar does most of the instrumental work), and at the end? Is this simply irony upon irony, an ironic portrayal of an attempt to get some ironic distance on the death and destruction that came before? I don't think so. Instead, each repetition of the first verse moves away from irony and denial, toward the acceptance of responsibility; away from mere fate, toward a combination confession and accusation: "Yours is no disgrace!"

There are four statements of the basic musical theme that supports the verse lyrics. Considered from a purely melodic and harmonic perspective, the song retains so much consistency throughout that it would appear almost monotonous. Significantly, this goes for the other longer pieces on *The Yes Album* as well, "Starship Trooper" and "Perpetual Change." Although there is complexity to these pieces, it is not a complexity based on having a lot of different musical parts, as say, "Roundabout." In "Yours is No Disgrace" there are only verses, with no real chorus (the "Death defying . . ." part follows the same melody as the verses, and it leads into a recapitulation of the first verse). The real musical work of the song takes place with the rhythmic variations and the combinations of different tone colors—which is to say, the song's orchestration. (That some critics wanted to call this sort of thing, "orchestral rock," however, seems silly to me. No one calls the Beach Boys' *Pet Sounds* "orchestral rock," but it is plenty-well orchestrated.) Essentially, the timbral complexity and variation of the four statements come from the alternation of dominance by a single instrument with very driving statements from the whole band: organ, band, bass guitar, band, acoustic guitar, band. (Just count "band" once and you have the four statements.) With this alternation comes a great dynamic range. And, in-between the second band part and the acoustic guitar that supports "death defying," there is an entire orchestra of guitars, with Steve Howe's extended solo.

The *Yessongs* live version brings out additional possibilities of the song. I'll go into these at length when I discuss that album in part 3, but it is interesting to note that, at the end of Howe's solo, there is the feeling of being completely drained. The live guitar solo is truly outstanding, and it is draining just to listen to it, but the feeling created by this is perhaps more appropriate to the "death defying" part. Here, instead of acoustic guitar, it is Jon Anderson's voice that is central, and, instead of sounding a bit too much like a folk song (too much for what is being said), as in the studio version, Anderson sounds much more like the "still small voice" that "cries in the wilderness." The combination of heroic-but-wearying instrumental part followed by a voice rising from the ashes also foreshadows the instrumental middle (the battle scene) and vocal end ("Soon") parts of "The Gates of Delirium."

Two things stand out about the "band" parts. First, there are Steve Howe's frenetic yet felicitous guitar fills. The pace of these fills is dizzying, and yet there is never a hurried feel to them—this is the mark of a virtuoso, that one never gets the sense that Howe is straining to put every note in the right place. Instead, there is a wonderful ease to his playing, one that allows Howe to express musical urgency and intensity without letting the guitar get in the way. (This goes back to what I was saying about there being guitarists, on the one hand, and musicians who play the guitar, on the other.)

Second, there is the pulsing propulsiveness of Chris Squire's Rickenbacker bass guitar, and the playfully light touch of Bill Bruford's percussion syncopations. In combination, this "rhythm" work is similar to what Howe is doing with the guitar fills: there is no heaviness or strain to any of it, and yet the band sections really rock. What is perhaps more important, however, is that these sections begin to *reinvent* rock, by completely changing the hitherto designated role of the "rhythm section." Yes was beginning to show that it was possible to play rock music without the bottom-heaviness that seemed the necessary anchor for most bands, even most progressive rock bands. This transformation was foreshadowed in the first two albums, but Steve Howe's warmer sound (especially from the Gibson ES-175 electric guitar, and the acoustic guitar parts on *The Yes Album*), as well as the cleaned-up structures of the extended pieces on the album, seemed to take this concept into a whole new territory. Again, without being "heavy," without crashing and bashing away, with soaring, propulsive, trebly bass lines and jazzy, syncopated drums, Yes was playing a new kind of rock music that incorporated many levels of emotional and intellectual sensibility. And, they could be intense and they could rock.

A few final observations on "Yours is No Disgrace."

First, the music of the opening vocal section of "church organ and choir" stands in ironic counterpoint to the lyrics of the first verse.

Second, the new role of the bass guitar is underlined by the first repetition of the first verse, where Chris Squire plays a jazzy walking-bass part that accompanies the vocals. Squire's ability with contrapuntal lines stands out nicely here, and one gets the sense, deepened with the rest of the albums of the main sequence, that many of Squire's lines could stand as pieces of music in their own right. The interesting comparison might be to Bach's Sonatas for Solo Cello. I will return to this idea of the "Squire variations."

Third, with the extended guitar solo we see the beginnings of what Steve Howe will develop, using a large array of different instruments, with guitar orchestration throughout the main sequence. Readers who play guitar or bass guitar know well that different instruments give you not only different tone colors to experiment with; in addition, different guitars and bass guitars seem to urge upon one different styles of playing. Of course, this has to be handled carefully, and not everyone finds this approach fruitful. Indeed, Chris Squire remains quite identified with the Rickenbacker 4001 bass guitar, and, when he plays another kind of bass guitar on a song, this playing clearly has the character of a departure—though often a good one, to be sure. Even so, Squire remains rooted in his work with the Rickenbacker. (I saw Yes perform on the *Talk* tour in the summer of 1994; when he wasn't playing his Rick, Squire always had the instrument on a stand to the front of stage-left—instead of in the back, with his other instruments—seemingly as a kind of symbol of where his playing comes from.) While Howe has a special place in his heart for his Gibson ES-175 (which he attests to in the preface to *The Steve Howe Guitar Collection*), he often uses more than one guitar on a single song, and many guitars on a given album, as well as a good many tone-altering effects. While many rock guitarists do this, the point is that there is a thoughtfulness behind Howe's symphonic approach to the guitar that is generally missing from the work of the many guitarists who simply found themselves with more money than sense. Again, "Yours is No Disgrace" is a very nice forum for introducing Yes's new virtuoso to the world.

Finally, moving from "Yours is No Disgrace" to the rest of the album, there are some parts of this first song that significantly parallel parts of the other two extended pieces on the album. The solo bass part with harmony vocals is paralleled by the solo acoustic guitar part in the second section, "Disillusion," of "Starship Trooper. And, the guitar solo in "Yours Is No Disgrace" can be heard as merging into the final part of "Perpetual Change." Sometimes, when I'm just running "Yours Is No Disgrace" through my head, I accidentally "skip tracks" into "Perpetual Change"; it seems to me, though, that the sense of unity from beginning to end of the album is not an accident.

"Clap"

   Almost universally mistitled as "The Clap," even on *Yes Album* CD reissues and in the *Yes Complete* Deluxe Edition music book, this solo guitar tune is much more innocently named "Clap." In *The Steve Howe Guitar Collection* (p. 73), Howe says that "Clap" is probably his best guitar piece, and that, if he never writes a better piece, he would be satisfied with this one. When Howe writes solo pieces, they seem mainly to be in one of two styles: either in a classical style, as with "Mood for a Day," or in a country flatpicking–style, as with "Clap." This piece owes a good deal to the style of flatpicking that developed in the Appalachian ("hillbilly") country of the southeastern U.S., itself a derivation from English, Irish, and Scottish folk music. In that respect, "Clap" might be an example of the "green language" coming full circle, with a nod, as well, to the American backcountry guitarists, such as Doc Watson and Norman Blake, who added another dimension to this language. There are basically four solo guitar pieces by Howe that appear on Yes albums: "Clap," "Mood for a Day," the "Along without You" piece from the end of *Tales from Topographic Oceans*, part 3, and, though it might be stretching the point a bit, the truly strange Fender Telecaster solo from "Soundchaser" (*Relayer;* only part of this is solo, while part of the performance is backed by bass guitar, tympani, and mellotron; still, the guitar is featured throughout in a way that makes the performance something different from what we would ordinarily call a "guitar solo"). Each of these will be discussed in turn, but it might be interesting to note that, of these four, the first and fourth are quite raucous, while the middle two are much more subtle and sweet.

   "Clap" is raucous, jangly, chicken-scratch music, in some ways a strange piece to follow "Yours Is No Disgrace." There is no studio version of the piece, the version on *The Yes Album* being a live recording (as is the more recent performance on Steve Howe's *Not Necessarily Acoustic* album—where the correct title was finally given). In a way, this live romp, following the intense but very clean "Yours Is No Disgrace" is a good release, a changing of the channel, so to speak. Played on a six-string steel acoustic (a 1953 Martin 00-18), "Clap" is almost the backwoods version of thrash, as Howe eschews almost all delicacy here, in favor of chords that are really "hit" and two-string open chord splits that stretch sonorities to the point just before they become outright irritating. This isn't for any lack of delicacy on Howe's part, but instead an exuberant example of the Appalachian style.

I don't know if "Clap" makes sense as a piece of "Yes" music (certainly the piece makes sense in itself), as part of a Yes album. In some ways it is too much of a showcase of the new guy, who was already showcased to great effect in "Yours Is No Disgrace," but in a way that made more musical sense. As a bit of fun between the longer works on the album, "Clap" is paralleled by "A Venture" on side 2 (a phrase the meaning of which is either transformed or destroyed in the CD age—probably the latter). "A Venture" is, however, a group effort (though the musics and lyrics are by Jon Anderson alone), and, although it is a short song, it is not in any way "light," as "Clap" might be said to be. "Clap" is in any case a very good bit of guitar composition and performance.

"Starship Trooper"

There is a science fiction novel by Robert Heinlein (perhaps best known for *Stranger in a Strange Land,* a novel that I imagine would appeal to Jon Anderson) called *Starship Troopers.* I have always wondered if the Yes song of the same name has any connection to this novel. In any case, one sees here once again a preoccupation with military matters and war, a preoccupation that runs throughout the main sequence and that was already prevalent in Yes's first two albums. What's interesting about this, and the reason to emphasize it so much, is that this preoccupation runs completely counter to the ordinary (un-)critical portrait of Yes, which has the group always singing about flowers and sunlight. The band does sing about these things often enough, but not at all in the purely "happy," "everything is beautiful" way that many rock critics portray them as doing. Indeed, the title "Starship Trooper" reminds one of the old saying, "Ad astra per aspera": "To the stars, through adversity." This is a better description of Yes's affirmation, not the facile reading that has them taking the easy road to bliss.

But then, when did that group ever take the easy road?—say whatever else you will about them!

"Starship Trooper" is in three parts, "Life Seeker," "Disillusion," and "Wurm," each part written by one of the principal composers of the band, Jon Anderson, Chris Squire, and Steve Howe, respectively. Other than the Coda from the first part, which comes in at the end of the second part, the three parts seem somewhat independent. And yet the parts function together very well. What we hear in "Starship Trooper," in fact, is a good example of musical minds that are thinking both independently and together in creative ways. The effect here is not unlike what we find in John Lennon's and Paul McCartney's collaboration on "A Day in the Life," where the former wrote the "I read the news today oh boy" sections and the latter the "Woke up, fell out of bed" part. The contrasts in style and general approach are what make the song work (and the contrast of Lennon and McCartney, it goes without saying, is the main force that made most of the Beatles' albums work), but notice that, while Lennon is his usual acidic self here, he is also a bit dreamy, and McCartney, though playful as always, has a bit more of an edge.

In other words, they remain independent musical minds, even while also working together toward a common goal. The old saying in rock music is, "the group's the thing." To have something to contribute to the group, while aiming toward a collective project, this is the ideal in rock music. Going back to the idea that individuals, all alone, create the art, this is nothing more than a legal fiction—and it is the place where lawyers insert themselves and destroy the music. We'll come back to this topic in part 3 and the conclusion. However, the point here is that, in this magical period before the lawyers and business executives and artists and repertoire people took full charge of the music, Yes was perhaps the perfect example of collective musical effort.

Each of the three parts is fairly simple in its basic structure, continuing the generally "clean" approach of *The Yes Album* as a whole. In fact, once again, the "hardest" instrumental parts of the song are the bass guitar lines, especially in the "Speak to me of summer" part, and the guitar picking during "Disillusion." "Life Seeker" is framed by a progression of two major chords (E-A), recapitulating and even streamlining somewhat the opening chords of "Yours Is No Disgrace" (E-A-D). For most of "Disillusion" the entire accompaniment is acoustic guitar, while "Wurm" is basically a guitar jam over the major chords G, E♭, and C. (As it turns out, the chords for "Würm" were previously used by Howe in the song, "Nether Street," with his pre-Yes band, Bodast.) What makes the song more interesting is its vocal and lyrical content, its mixture of disparate styles, and the propulsiveness of the bass lines in the first part.

Note, not incidentally, that there is a logic to simplicity and complexity in music, and perhaps especially in progressive rock music. This logic might be thought of in terms of Gödel's theorem, which says that, in a logical system, there is a trade-off between basic rules and the length of a logical proof. If there are fewer basic rules (in principle, a system for deduction could function with only a single rule, that of noncontradiction), then the proofs carried out with the rules will be longer. If there are more rules, which allow steps to be taken that combine a number of operations, then proofs can be shorter. At either extreme, things become cumbersome: either you have simplicity of rules, but the proofs become too long to handle, or you have short proofs, but too many rules to remember. Most devisers of logical systems aim for an in-between point that philosopher and logician W. V. Quine describes as aspiring to the aesthetic ideal of "elegance." The analogy to music might be that, if the underlying harmonic structure is fairly simple, then something complex can take place on top of it—for example, Steve Howe's guitar solo in "Würm," or the harmony vocals in "Disillusion." If the underlying structure is quite complex, as, say, with the middle section of "Gates of Delirium" or the opening development of "Awaken," then it is likely that what comes on top of this needs to be more simple and clear in order to be effective. (Gödel's theorem goes on to show that logical systems face another trade-off, that they can be either complete or consistent, but not both at the same time. The ramifications of this argument for music might be an interesting subject for another discussion.)[18] "Starship Trooper," and most of *The Yes Album,* is both a demonstration of this general principle and a choice for simpler harmonic structures that allow other structures to be developed in a more complex way.

In the first part of the song, as I've indicated, the more complex parts are the lyrical allusions and the bass lines. Taking the second of these first, the interesting thing is the way that Squire provides a line during the "Speak to me of summer" part that is, paradoxically, very driving but also following a contrapuntal logic. Perhaps this is best heard in the feathery turn-arounds that we hear under the line, "Setting up of other roads." Squire is simply amazing in the way that he can create lines that seem to go in two contradictory directions at once: both "forward," in a driving, propulsive way, and in circles, doubling back on themselves. The best image that I can think of for this effect, especially when heard on the very trebly Rickenbacker 4001, is that of a spring uncoiling. The spring leaps forward, but it also continues to consist in its coils. "Amazing," I realize, is hardly a term of music criticism or analysis, but the fact is that I've never heard anything else like it—and, frankly, I think Squire is the only bass guitar player that I can say this about. There are other originals, of course, but it is easier to see where they got some of their basic ideas from and what they were building on. Jaco Pastorius, for example, certainly knocked the heads off a lot of bass guitarists and other musicians when he appeared on the scene in the late seventies, especially with his brilliant use of harmonics. Not to take anything away from his accomplishment, but it is much easier to trace the influence of (jazz contrabassist) Ron Carter on Jaco Pastorius than it is to assemble the elements that went into Chris Squire's mature style. Or, perhaps the point is, we can list the elements, but what comes out of the elements is qualitatively distinct. I'll have much more to say about this, because Squire's bass guitar transformations are absolutely essential to understanding what Yes accomplished in the main sequence.

(Incidentally, perhaps Squire's most "circular/forward-propulsive" line is the main bass line in "Hold Out Your Hand," from his solo album, *Fish Out of Water.* More on this in part 3.)

If anything, the lyrics for "Life Seeker" would have to be considered a critical response to Heinlein's novel, *Starship Troopers,* in that the latter has to do with a young man who joins an intergalactic militia that travels to far-flung planets, whipping alien species into line. Although there was a bit of a new-age aspect to Heinlein's writing, probably best seen in the classic *Stranger in a Strange Land,* this was always mixed with right-wing populism and U.S. nationalism of the Newt Gingrich or Ross Perot variety.[19] Perhaps Jon Anderson's lyrics are not a response to Heinlein's title at all, but they cannot help but resonate with the title; both "Starship Troopers" are out there in the world, after all.

The references in the song, however, seem to be more to something like Native American spirituality. The juxtaposition in the lyrics, of "sister bluebird" with "starship trooper" is interesting. As Thomas Mosbø argues, the words concern an inner journey and an inner discovery (*Yes—But What Does It Mean?*, p. 41). The message is not unlike that of Jesus of Nazareth: "The kingdom of God is within you." However, the picture is more complicated, for three reasons. First, one can understand the image of "sister bluebird" as a kind of soul messenger, as a voice within one that calls out. But why the image of the "starship trooper"—why the starship, why the trooper?

Second, Jon Anderson conveys the sense that looking into one's soul is not a matter of mere or pure transparency. What is understood there cannot be understood whole, nor can it be told to others. Significantly, there is also a recapitulation of "summer/winter" themes in the middle section of the first part, conjoined with a return from the solitude of the soul, to the world:

Speak to me of summer, long winters,
longer than time can remember,
Setting up of other roads,
travel on in old accustomed ways.

There is a strong sense, however, that this is not simply a return to the world, but instead perhaps a conversation with ancestors:

I still remember the talks by the water,
the proud sons and daughters that,
in the knowledge of the land,
spoke to me in sweet accustomed ways.

The rolling, propulsive bass lines I mentioned earlier, accented nicely by Bill Bruford's beboppish use of the bass drum (that is, as punctuation, rather than as simple beat-keeper), convey the feeling of an ease of mind. This is appropriate, of course, to the "sweet accustomed ways," but it is also in marked contrast to the starkness of the main musical theme of "Life Seeker." The understanding that is found in solitude may or may not be knowledge, and thus is not to be spoken of; the final words of "Life Seeker" trail off, "What I don't know, I have never shared." If this solitary moment that is, simultaneously, one of self-knowledge *and* self-doubt *and* experience of finitude[20] is contrasted to "the knowledge of the land," then we seem to find two orders of discourse, as well as a point of radical underdetermination. (To the skeptical reader who might ask, "Does Anderson really *know* all that?," the answer is, Yes, on some level he does—and on some level he doesn't [this recapitulates the general point here]; and the same goes for the critic and the listener).

This leads us to the third point. Whatever "Life Seeker" may be about in itself, it is part of a larger piece of music, in which the solitude and underdetermination of "What I don't know" leads into Chris Squire's "Disillusion." Therefore, the picture presented by "Life Seeker" is also complicated by this association.

Incidentally, in considering the authorship of "Disillusion," we might remind ourselves of the general discussion of progressive rock presented earlier in this chapter. Virtuosity-with-vision (which some musicians or critics would argue is simply the deeper meaning of any real virtuosity—it has to have "virtue") does not simply show off digital dexterity. Here we have a perfect example: Chris Squire writes "Disillusion" not only as not a vehicle for his own bass guitar skills, but without any bass lines at all.

It might be said that "Disillusion" portrays the other side of the solitude of "Life Seeker." Even when one withdraws into a spiritual solitude, where one listens for the "still small voice," this is a withdrawal not only *to*, but also *from*. "Loneliness is a pow'r that we possess to give or take away forever." This could be interpreted in numerous ways, but perhaps it makes the most sense, in light of "Life Seeker," to understand this line and those that follow as a warning that one who has undertaken a spiritual quest can seem to others to have disappeared into one's own navel. Furthermore, the understanding that one reaches in such a quest is open to misinterpretation: "Take what I say in a diff'rent way and it's easy to say that this is all confusion." Interestingly, a much later Yes song, from a quite different band (or so it would seem), also speaks of confusion: "I want to be all of you, and that's the confusion" ("Love Will Find a Way," by Trevor Rabin, *Big Generator*). The possibilities of miscommunication are immense when the subject is something deeply felt. This is perhaps the deepest paradox of philosophy, that it seems the most important things cannot be said—a problem spoken to across the history of Western philosophy, from Plato to Wittgenstein and Heidegger. Squire seems to bend the gist of the first three lines on "Disillusion" in a very different direction in the fourth and final line, when he goes in a much more "Andersonian" direction: "As I see a new day in me, I can also show if you and you may follow." But then, let us take into account the triple entendre of Squire's title: (1) to be disillusioned, to be set free from pleasant but mistaken beliefs (*OED*); (2) a "disillusion" as an anti-illusion, going beyond mere disillusion; (3) the near homophonous but implied sense of "dissolution," that is, of something being dissolved. The first and third meanings are invoked in the first two lines of the song. Perhaps the third meaning is implied by the third line. And the second meaning, as the pathway to something deeper and higher than pleasant illusions, is invoked in the final line.

In its return to the "Speak to me of summer" part of "Life Seeker," this last line makes sense, for now it is once again a matter of "you and you," neither the me who has momentary, secret wisdom nor the me who is wrapped up in the pessimism of disillusion. And, speaking of "skipping tracks," I think that most anyone who is immersed in all of the Yes music of the main sequence will see the connection of "Disillusion"'s "follow" with "the teacher travels, asking to be shown the same" from "And You and I" (besides the thematic unity, they are in the same key, E), as well as of the "you and you" with "You seekers of the truth accepting that reasons will relive and breathe and hope and chase and love for you and you and you," the closing line of "The Revealing Science of God," part 1 of *Tales from Topographic Oceans* (also in E). This is all after the fact, but the lyrical and musical threads are there to be traced, showing that there is an immense vision at work. (And all of the "you"s just show that Yes's vision is very inviting and inclusive!)

The musical contrast in the first two parts is significant as well, going from the anthem-like opening chords to the folky guitar-picking of "Disillusion." It is difficult, perhaps, to think of the latter as having much to do with the reflective sensibility of the lyrics. But I would place this middle part of "Starship Trooper" in the "old-time religion" category, indeed, within the category of that anabaptist religion from Appalachia that is also an expression of the green language, as well as the radical reformation of Northern Europe. For what follows the coda (recapitulation of "Life Seeker") is basically a choral and church organ arrangement—which then leads into "Würm."

And how to make sense of this transition, when, for one thing, the name of the tune is the German word for "worm" (and there is also consonance with "warm"), and when, for another, the tune sounds a good deal like a funeral dirge (even more so in the *Yessongs* live version, with the deep, dark Mellotron voices coming in at the end). The guitar solo is more than a little devilish as well. Returning to science fiction themes, with its big guitar sound and big chords, the worms I think of aren't our cute friends who turn the topsoil (working alongside the magnificent ants). Instead, I think of the giant, unstoppable sandworms of Frank Herbert's *Dune*. In any case, as "Würm" winds down, everything that was either hopeful or at least thoughtful about the first two parts of "Starship Trooper" seems to be simply ripped apart in a ritual of destruction and, ultimately, doom. At the very end, one can almost see the torn, shattered, burning metal of our starship, looking too much like the crash of the Hindenburg. Honestly, I don't know if this works, even if I like the idea of the song not ending simply with happiness and hope. It all seems a bit cynical, rather than tragic.

What perhaps gives a larger context to this, however, is that the next two songs also deal with the struggles of solitude and a cynical world, but without themselves simply confirming this cynicism—which is the last thing anyone needs (which doesn't mean that there aren't legions of artists and critics who are more than willing to supply this "service," and to think that they are awfully hip for doing so).

"I've Seen All Good People"

The theme of moral ambiguity, and, what's more significant, the idea of moral ambiguity as a crucial form of moral irresponsibility, runs through much of Yes's work. I see progressive rock as a whole as an idealistic response to a cynical world—or, I should say, I see progressive rock as the expression of a time when idealistic social and cultural currents were expressing themselves powerfully, and I see the more recent dismissals of progressive rock as themselves mainly an expression of the dominance of cynicism in this postmodern capitalist world. What better captures this cynicism than the ironic opening of the next song on *The Yes Album:* "I've seen all good people turn their heads each day so satisfied I'm on my way." "Even the good people turn away from responsibility, so I can certainly be satisfied in doing so." Indeed, one thinks of the cynical critics' response to Yes, where there is the sensibility of finding any little handhold for finding fault, always pursuing failure rather than the ideal. The opening line to "All Good People" captures perfectly the cynical irresponsibility of this course.

Both "Starship Trooper" and "I've Seen All Good People" begin as anthems, the latter perhaps even more powerfully for the fact that it begins a capella. But, whereas the former then becomes a powerful rocker that leads into a folksong, the latter becomes a very gentle folk song from the outset, "Your Move." It is a folk song that seems to be about chess and relationships, with a bass drum that marks the beginning of every measure, and a gently surging bass guitar that comes in with the second verse, but still, it's a folk song. Indeed, as such, "Your Move" is perhaps more like a song, in the ordinary sense, than anything else on *The Yes Album.* In other words, with acoustic guitar or piano and singing, you could perform your own "home version" of "Your Move," and have something not entirely unlike what we hear on the album. This brings out something about Yes's relation to song form, a topic I remarked on earlier. When I argue that Yes, even in their most developed works, remains rooted in song form, I mean that much of the music is built around songs. "Close to the Edge" and any of the movements of *Tales from Topographic Oceans,* however, are not songs. Songs could perhaps be extracted from these works (more from *Tales* than "Close to the Edge," where there isn't a whole lot you could do with just guitar or piano and voice), but the point is that these works are extensions of song form to some extent (again, "Close to the Edge" is perhaps less so than any other Yes work). But "Your Move" simply remains a song—and a very good one.

"Your Move," in its chess imagery, is written from the perspective of the black pieces. Black begins at a disadvantage, as white always has the first move. Chess, like many games and sports, is an analogue to war: the point is to defeat the opposing forces, ultimately to topple the king. One disadvantage of playing black is that there is a tendency to fall into a purely reactive, defensive posture—I've seen what everyone else does (even the "good people"), so I'm satisfied with just going on my way." And, "if the summer change to winter . . ." Whereas "Yours Is No Disgrace" seems to wrench us out of our purely personal frame, toward the theater of real war ("shooting wars," as they say), "I've Seen All Good People" is much more straightforwardly personal, except that the song reminds us that even the scene of interpersonal relationships is a scene where ethics and politics are enacted.

In chess, if you are playing black, and if you hope to win, there has to come a point when the initiative is taken away from white. This may be a dramatic moment, where it is obvious that the initiative has passed from one side to the other, or this turn of events may be seen only in retrospect—say four or five moves later.

Chess represents a particular kind of war, what is called a "war of position." Such a war does not depend for its overall shape on a single, frontal strike, but instead on a series of guerrilla-style incursions. The three basic rules of chess strategy are usually said to be, (1) control the center of the board, (2) protect your king, and (3) advance your pawns. Of course, the overall aim is to capture the opponent's king, but this is something more than a rule or strategic principle—this is the whole point of the game. Now, one way to protect your king might be to "surround yourself with yourself." This strategy will protect the king up to a point, but, if overdone, will result in the failure to do any damage to the opposing forces and to get anywhere in capturing the opposing king. Ultimately, the "surround yourself with yourself" strategy is simply defensive, and this allows the opponent to pick off your pieces one by one, until the barrier set up around the king is destroyed and the king is defenseless.

Now, what does this have to do with personal relationships? Plenty, as a matter of fact, but "by negation," as it were, in that the strategies of warfare are not what most of us would call good rules for building healthy relationships. It is this negation that "Your Move" plays with. Up to a point, the king is safest in a corner: "Take a straight and stronger course to the corner of your life." The queen on either side is the most powerful piece, and, after the king, the most important. The queen is the next most important precisely because of its power, and not because it is absolutely necessary for winning the game, as is the case with the king. (Many games are finished without queens on the board, but, of course, once the king is gone, that's the game.) One way for black to gain initiative is to threaten the white queen: "Make the white Queen run so fast, she hasn't got time to make you wise." Well, this is fine for chess or war, but the point is, any relationship that is structured this way has lost the dimension of friendship (or love), of something that goes beyond my mere personal *interest,* and has become no more than that socially contained form of warfare that Thomas Hobbes calls the "social contract." Then the aim is not for all of us to "capture the gold," but instead for me to try to capture to the exclusion of you. How do I justify this move to myself? Simple: "I've seen all good people turn their heads each day, so satisfied I'm on my way."

Love and war, the possibilities of mutual flourishing, of utopia, and the negation of this, sometimes the necessary negation of these possibilities, paradoxically in the very name of these possibilities: these themes are constant with Yes. Even what seems to be a simple song, a straightforwardly beautiful song such as "I've Seen All Good People" shows how very complicated and difficult these issues are. The fact that Yes deals with these issues in their complexity also shows that their utopianism is not simply flower-power bliss, but instead is both complex and revolutionary.

Again, keeping with the idea that the entire song, "I've Seen All Good People," is part of a larger whole, then we can see the irony implied in having the meditative "Your Move" resolve into the rocking chant of "All Good People." "Your Move" is as close to a basic folk song as Yes ever came, while "All Good People" is perhaps as close to basic "rock'n'roll" as we're going to find from Yes. Playing these two simple structures off of each other, however, gives us something other than "basic"—there is a statement made with the music here. Among other things, the music goes from the folkiness of the countryside and the green language to the electricity and hustle-bustle of the city. In "Your Move" there is a moment of meditative suspension in every other verse, for example, the moment in the middle of, "'Cause it's time, it's time in time with your time and its news is captured . . . for the Queen to use." There is no such meditative moment in "All Good People," any more than there is a meditative moment, a moment to consider the morality of what one is doing, when one is "satisfied" and "on my way." Indeed, the city hustle is inserted into the final suspended moment of "Your Move." (In this respect, I find the drum fill of the live version of the song more effective than the studio version for precisely the reason that it makes the point of a violent disruption of this moment of ethical consideration—and then we're "on our way.")

As with "Starship Trooper," "I've Seen All Good People" has a first part by Jon Anderson and a second part by Chris Squire. This time Squire doesn't hold back on bass. Indeed, the bass line *is* the song, but not in the way that many punk or funk songs might also be described this way. Instead, the line is a complex structure, one that combines a kind of jazzy walking bass with a blues progression that has an interesting bend in it, all refracted through the metallic sound of a Rickenbacker bass guitar with Rotosound round-wound strings. The bend in the blues scale comes when Squire plays a major third rather than a minor third. (This is helpfully explained by Squire on the "Master Sessions with Chris Squire" instructional video.) This bent scale is also heard in the pedal point section toward the end of "All Good People," when Howe takes over the bass line on guitar. The interesting contrast is between this rocking good-time music, evocative of the honky-tonk, and the lyric, which sounds "carefree"—and it is, but in the sense of irresponsibility, not ease of mind.

At the ends of both parts of the song there are vocal parts that recede into the background. "Your Move" has the line from John Lennon sung at an almost subliminal level, "All we are saying, is give peace a chance." (Another irony is that Alan White was the drummer with Lennon's Plastic Ono Band on this recording.) Listeners can readily understand that this seems like a nice gesture, but the point is that it is also a point of contrast to the war of position that is described in the main body of "Your Move." At the end of "All Good People," the lyric gets both deeper (moving down the scale) and lower (in volume) as it seems this statement of thoughtlessness recedes in the distance—or perhaps sinks down the drain, or is blown into the desert. In any case, there is once again a contrast: the forceful rock of the main body of the part gives way to a sound shrinking into the distance. This brilliant use of musical contrasts underlines the irony of the lyric, in a fashion similar to the repetition of "Yours is no disgrace" at the end of the song with the same title.

"A Venture"

Like "Clap," "A Venture" is set between the more extended works of *The Yes Album,* and is easily overlooked. The song, however, is a little gem and not to be ignored. Once again the theme is the ongoing struggle against cynicism and disaffection, though this time in terms of the temptation to run away from the world. The music and lyrics here are both by Jon Anderson.

"A Venture" is perhaps the most Beatles-like of the songs on *The Yes Album,* with its crystal-clear yet mysterious-sounding piano at the beginning and end reminding me especially of "Magical Mystery Tour" (in the latter song, the piano I'm thinking of only comes at the end). In either case, there is something very magical and mystical about how these songs seem to rise out of and fall back into a mist, like a dream. Many songs fade out, but "A Venture" also fades in—and it sneaks up on you a bit for, all of a sudden, the guitar and piano give way to the stabbing thrust of the bass guitar and drums and Jon Anderson's storytelling voice. Indeed, the opening electric guitar part has a furtive quality to it, with the piano playing a series of gentle, single-note scales in the background, evocative of a waterfall—not a big, crashing waterfall, but something quite pleasant, just beyond the village proper. The piano also sneaks up on you, for these scales, which seemed not to contain the least bit of tension, all of a sudden develop into chords that seem filled with warning.

The lyrics are practically declaimed, as in a kind of fierce sermon, even if the story is once more one of reflection. The tension here is that, on the one hand, the lyrics speak of a man who could control "horses with a handclap or a whisper," therefore of a man with a sense of power, and yet, on the other hand, there is no "action," to speak of, in the song. These are the thoughts of a man who goes down by the river to think, to sort out his life.

Of course, there are many rivers and other bodies of water in the music of Yes. In fact, the song "Wondrous Stories," from *Going for the One,* seems to return us to this same river. "A Venture": "Once a peaceful man laid his old head

down by a river; Thought about his childhood life, his father and forgiver . . . ."
"Wondrous Stories": "I awoke this morning; Love laid me down by a river.
Drifting, I turned on upstream bound for my forgiver." Perhaps some of the references to bodies of water in Yes are less directly spiritual (for example, "In and around the lake . . ." from "Roundabout"), but it seems clear enough that the references in "A Venture" and "Wondrous Stories" and in many other songs *are* spiritual, in the sense of having to do with an interrelated set of themes: baptism, redemption, cleansing, immersion. I have tried to stress that there is an ethics and politics of these redemptive themes, that Yes is not simply after "spiritual" escapism. "A Venture" underlines this point: it is a sermon, or a parable, concerning the necessity of not giving in to the forces that wear one down, emphasizing that hiding away is a form of giving in.

(It would be interesting to trace out the water theme in rock music, from Al Green's "Take Me to the River"—better known to some in the Talking Heads version—to The Who's many references in *Quadrophenia* and beyond. At least in these two cases—Al Green, Pete Townshend—there is no doubt that the songwriters are seeking the waters of redemption.)

In playing on the terms "a venture" and "adventure" in the context of the river, the song also invokes the idea of the advent—which is, of course, the advent of the forgiver, the redeemer, the messiah. But in sermonizing against the temptation to hide away, the song takes a particular position on the messiah, a position that theologians and scholars of religion refer to as "postmillennial." I am not attributing any complex theory of the apocalypse to Jon Anderson here, at least not in any studied, scholarly sense, though Anderson has a complex understanding of these things, and he has gone on to study religious and philosophical ideas somewhat systematically. The point, instead, is that Anderson has a grasp of the issues involved in making a distinction between postmillennial and premillennial views of the world, and this distinction colors Anderson's world view and artistic production generally.

The premillennial view, which is common to many mainstream as well as fundamentalist Protestant and Catholic forms of Christianity, holds that things in the world will just get worse and worse, until the messiah returns and sets things right once and for all. One should try not to be dragged down with the world, but, as for the world itself, there's little or nothing to be done about its steady and inevitable decline. Therefore, religion and spirituality are best understood as a "hideaway," an attempt to protect oneself from the corruptions of the world (with the help of God, of course, and ultimately through God's saving grace alone) until the messiah returns.

While it is always dangerous to make quick comparisons between thought-systems, we might note briefly that non-Western religions also have their other-worldly variants. I mention this only because Jon Anderson draws on a wide range of sources, including many non-Western sources, in his ethical-spiritual vision—and because an otherworldly ("acosmic") view is often attributed, *wrongly,* to Anderson.

In a song from one of his solo projects, "Some Are Born," Anderson sings of "trying," and he says, "Trying harder seems the only way to go." The point here is that this way of looking at things is fundamentally at odds with the premillennial view.

The postmillennial view has it that redemption will come after we have done the work to make the world ready for redemption—"trying harder seems the only way to go." Redemption, in this view, is not something that comes from the "outside" (the "wholly other") regardless of, and despite, what we have tried to do in the world. If this were redemption, we would do best to hide away—but, "A decent man would realize that alone is no adventure, just to hide away."

Considered in light of themes from "Yours Is No Disgrace" and "I've Seen All Good People," it is very clear that Jon Anderson is a postmillennialist: the fact that the world does indeed seem to be going to hell is no excuse for hiding away, or turning one's head because even the good people do it, or simply saying that this is the way of the world ("if the summer change to winter"). On the contrary: "Trying harder is the only way to go." This seems as central a message as anything in Yes's work, and, again, for the "critical" establishment in rock music to trash this message seems to me to be nothing more than a reflection of the pervasive cynicism in the world at large.

(Again, not to move too quickly here, but perhaps the "postmillennialist" strain in Western thought and religion is paralleled, for instance, by the *bodhisattva* idea in Buddhism.)

"A Venture" ends with two fades, to be precise. First the exhortation to not "just [to] hide away" fades out, then the piano chords that had developed just prior to the vocal part takeover. The piano playing here is nothing very complex or requiring tremendous virtuosity, but it is exactly right—and you can't trade mere chops for that. This is Tony Kaye's best playing on the album, and it is part of an instrumental section that could have been effectively extended for a good deal longer. As the song fades out, in fact, one can hear the beginnings of a swirling guitar solo from Steve Howe, and it would be interesting to know how things develop from that point. Again, this reminds me of the ending of "Magical Mystery Tour"; even though the tempos are quite different, there is a jazzy feel to both endings, and, what's more significant, the endings create an overwhelming feeling that the music leaves this plane, headed for worlds beyond the fields we know. Perhaps this is why both pieces *need* to fade out, in order precisely to allow our minds to proceed further on this voyage.

"Magical Mystery Tour" is a very interesting song, in that it seems to be rather light-hearted and even trivializing in its take on the world, and yet it takes us, perhaps, to the sort of carnival that we find in the film, "The Circus of Dr. Wu." Dr. Wu also "fades in," and ultimately delivers a message of apocalypse before fading out. While "Magical Mystery Tour" does not, on the surface, seem to have such prophetic overtones, "A Venture" certainly does. Both are "prophetic," however, in the sense that they seem to call to us from another world. As I said, "A Venture" is an underrated gem. As a masterwork, "A Venture" is "minor" only in the sense that it is not one of Yes's extended works.

"Perpetual Change"

A larger symphonic splendor is hinted at in all of the songs leading up to the last piece on *The Yes Album;* with "Perpetual Change" this splendor comes into full view. This is not, as many critics would have it, because Yes starts to let loose the "orchestral rock" that almost every progressive rock group is accused of aspiring to. Rather, "Perpetual Change" is "symphonic" music in its expansiveness, its range of instrumental colors, and its range of harmonic and rhythmic expressions. If pursuing this sort of range is representative of "orchestral" aspirations, then so be it, but it seems to me that what Yes was trying to do here was simply to create a large-scale, visionary work, using the talents and sensibilities available to them. And this goes retrospectively for *The Yes Album* as a whole, with "Perpetual Change" as both its final statement and its gateway anthem, looking toward everything Yes would go on to do in the main sequence.

There is something about sustained 4th chords that is especially inviting. "Perpetual Change" begins on Gsus4, as does the Beatles' "Hard Day's Night." No one can hear that solitary guitar chord, which just resonates while everyone holds their breaths, without the feeling that something immensely exciting is about to take place. There is no other chord that creates such anticipation: just play the chord on a guitar for some friends, without even announcing what you're going to do, and, involuntarily, everyone is transported to a magical time, to Shea stadium, the Ed Sullivan show, screaming teenage girls, picture phones, rockets to the moon, and so on. This seemed to be a time of immense possibility —an illusion, perhaps, but there was something to be said for the illusion.

Rhythmically, the beginning of "Perpetual Change" is quite different from "Hard Day's Night," rushing right along with the opening chords played by electric guitar and organ, moving from Gsus4 to Asus4. But that sense of magic and anticipation is still captured on some level, and perhaps updated for an even faster-paced time.

There is a great deal packed into the opening measures of "Perpetual Change." It isn't hard to see how a great orchestral version of this piece could be arranged. First the violins and violas begin with one series of the Gsus4 to Asus4 progression. On the next progression, the cellos, basses, tympani, and cymbals come in with stabbing crashes at the end of each chord sequence. Third progression, these instruments, plus trap drums, play the percussive bass and drum patterns that cut across the original guitar and organ like a fast locomotive speeding across the green and wheat-colored fields of Kansas. Finally, a pair of trumpets enter in with a soaring, almost raucous solo and the bass and drums have changed once again, to a pattern that seems to surge locomotively ahead, even while the second half of the pattern is actually backing down the scale. The percussion is subtly understated, demonstrating Bruford's keen awareness that a well-placed silence can be just as powerful as hitting another drum.

Perhaps someday we'll hear this version, as played by some fine orchestra—it is great fun listening to this version in my head, in any case, and I can see the conductor (it's me, of course) raising his arms and bringing them down for the bass and drum crashes at the end of the second progression. What is interesting is that "Perpetual Change" is a good example of the even more "symphonic" (in the sense I specified earlier, of employing a broad range of tonal, harmonic, and rhythmic possibilities) turn that Yes began to take with *The Yes Album,* and yet the other half of this richly orchestrated work is something like a country-western song. This is not a case of the sublime to the ridiculous, however, but a statement about the immense possibilities of music itself—and the possibility of crossing all kinds of borders.

So, we go from the lush, broad chords—again, something like the plains of Kansas, the green countryside of Devonshire, or perhaps the unending blue of the Atlantic—to a burning, country-rock guitar solo, from the ostentatiousness of the European classical scene to the humble working culture of the American South, musically foreshadowing lyrics that have everything to do with human possibilities, limits, hubris, and ultimately an understanding of where we fit into the world.

But first, even as we can hear the afterburn of full-tilt country-rock Yes fading into the distance, there is that wonderful bass guitar figure that introduces the song proper: D-C-B-C-B-G-F#-G-A-A-D (the last D is an octave below the first). The "hook" here is very reminiscent of Paul McCartney's bass lines, reminding me especially of "Fixing a Hole" from *Sergeant Pepper's.* Listen for the slightest hesitation between the first and second A's at the end of the figure; this tiny moment of suspension opens into an effortless glide that works from the simplicity of the opening measures of the vocal part of the song back into the two-chord progression that opened the song. This anthem, "Perpetual Change," presents itself in the form of a circular structure that also develops in a forward motion. This is significant for three reasons. First, this structure mimics the form of many of Chris Squire's bass lines. Squire wrote the song, along with Jon Anderson, so this is not too surprising. Second, in developing many of the materials that were first brought into rock music by the Beatles, Yes was announcing that they would build on that legacy. If it also makes little sense to say that Yes were *the* band who took off from the point where the Beatles left off, this has more to do with transformations in the larger culture than with what Yes were trying to do as experimental rock musicians. Finally, as I've already indicated,

the song announces the band's outlook toward creating experimental rock—
namely, "perpetual change"—and it does so with both the lyrics and the musical
form of the song.

The vocal part of the song is at first accompanied by electric piano, sounding
a good deal like a country-western song, even bordering on the schmaltzy—you
can almost see the grey wooden floors and walls of a Southern roadhouse, the
sort where guys from the Allman Brothers Band would hang out, decorated with
neon tube signs for various beers popular with working people. Whether or not
this was the image in Jon Anderson's and Chris Squire's minds for this part of
the song, there is definitely a homey warmth to this opening vocal section. The
irony, of course, is that the first image that Anderson gives us is one of cold: "I
see the cold mist in the night." As with the opening progressions of the song,
there is a quick evolution. By the third vocal line, the instrumental background
has become very rich, threatening to erupt into the foreground. Just as this erup-
tion is about to occur, the instruments back off, and the process repeats itself,
culminating in a recapitulation of the opening instrumental section.

This back-and-forth, but always with development, with something new, is
captured in the signature line of the lyric, "inside out, outside in, every day." In
subsequent repetitions, "every day" is replaced first by "perpetual change" and
then by "all of the way"—thereby emphasizing the basic point. How to sum this
up? "Dialectic and difference," we might say, with a strong emphasis on the
question of "appropriation"—appropriation *of what (or whom)?, by what
(whom)?;* these economical lyrics bring us into a debate that ranges from Hegel
and Marx to Heidegger, Gadamer, and Derrida. I say this mainly to pique the
reader's interest in systematic philosophical discussions of these issues;[21] but the
more relevant point is that there is a very sophisticated understanding of these
issues compressed in Yes's music here, and this understanding plays itself out in
both the lyrics and the instrumental music and, most significantly, in the interaction and integration of lyric and music. All of these elements make up music that
is, I think, *profound.*

This difficult and perhaps confusing word is brought into the discussion at
this point for a reason. Yes set out to be profound, or at least this aim seems fundamental to what Anderson and Squire were doing from the start. They wanted
to make important music, music that worked on many different levels, and, most
significantly, music that speaks in a deep and powerful way to the human condition.

Ah, that's where they—and most other "progrockers"—went wrong, some of
the hip-chic critics say. Groups such as Yes can never create a Ninth Symphony,
or even a Third—this just isn't in the nature of rock music. As I said earlier, if
this were definitely true, then why haven't these critics packed away the things
of their youths, and moved on to more important pursuits? Why wallow in perpetual adolescence? My argument is that the "critical" approach of these critics
is in fact tied to the valorization of adolescence—and therefore they have an a

priori reason for rejecting the attempts of some rock musicians to develop beyond this adolescence. As I argued earlier, this development, "progressive rock," took many different forms. It would be very difficult to see, for example, the music of Carlos Santana as tied to adolescent themes. Critics of progressive rock have especially focused on a certain kind of "English" progressive group because of the very wide array of influences, especially from European classical music, that goes into their music. The interesting paradox is that this criticism amounts to a kind of absolute valorization of European classical music, and of its supposed purity—no one else, from some other field of music, can approach what the European *masters* have done; to even try is tantamount to blasphemy! Yes then is the worst offender and their music is therefore, in the words of an article in the English music magazine *The Wire,* "irredeemable." Groups such as Santana are let off the hook because, if critics were to go after them for not accepting "rock music as limited to adolescent reflections on adolescence" (as opposed to mature, provocative, possibly profound reflections, as with *Quadrophenia),* then they would have to sort out their whole critical approach, as well as deal with the problematic status that would have to be assigned to jazz, blues, and other non-European classical forms in their framework—and this approach cannot be sorted out. Or, it can only be sorted out under the category of valorizing perpetual adolescence.

In his book, *Music Alone: Philosophical Reflections on the Purely Musical Experience,* Peter Kivy explores the idea of "profundity" in art. Kivy focuses, at first, on two particular questions. First, he points to the fact that the general listener is more likely to find works of art, including musical works, profound, if they deal with the "darker, more serious" emotions (pp. 203–4).[22] However, Kivy points out, this claim requires more justification than simple intuition. For, Kivy argues, the fact that a piece of music may be *about* something profound does not in itself make the piece profound. If this were not the case, then one could set, for instance, one of Shakespeare's tragedies to any kind of music, and because the music is "about" something profound, then the music would be profound, too. As this is most certainly not the case, Kivy is interested in what makes music, in itself ("music alone"), profound.

Second, then, he turns to the question of form; in particular, he turns to the question of counterpoint, working through the example of J. S. Bach. Kivy takes up Albert Schweitzer's famous analysis of Bach's music, especially of Bach's last composition, which the composer wrote on his deathbed:

> I think it requires no argument to convince the reader that Schweitzer thought Bach's last composition "profound". . . . And it seems obvious too that the profundity has something to do, to his mind, with the "contrapuntal art . . . so perfect that no description can give any idea of it." . . . (p. 206)

In Schweitzer's analysis, "[t]he harmonies of the spheres were already echoing round the dying master"; "over the whole" of this final composition "gleams the word 'Transfiguration'" (p. 206). Assuming, as I do, that "transfiguration" is a profound subject (and not unrelated to themes taken up in many Yes pieces), the point would still have to be that Bach's music itself does not become profound simply in being "about" this subject. "For Profound subjects can be botched as well as beautiful, bungled as well as splendidly brought off" (p. 203). Kivy, then, considers the formal qualities of Bach's composition:

> Counterpoint itself, since time out of mind, has been associated in the thinking of musicians with the profound and the serious. And in the modern musical era, com-posers of instrumental music have continually turned and returned to "learned" counterpoint, always in the interest of "deepening" their style. Is the association of counterpoint with profundity merely a psychological association, like the layper-son's association of profundity with serious emotions? Or is there a real connection . . .? That is to say, is there some rational justification for thinking that contrapuntal music is profound in virtue of being contrapuntal? I do not mean to suggest that con-trapuntal music might be the only profound music. But if we can discover just what it is about counterpoint that so frequently elicits the judgment "profound," perhaps—if indeed that judgment is rationally justified—we may be able to generalize from that to all profound music properly so-called. (p. 207)

I will leave off from Kivy's analysis of counterpoint for the time being. We will return to this analysis, however, because much of Yes's music is, broadly speak-ing, contrapuntal. Perhaps Kivy can shed some light on what Yes is doing with counterpoint and why this is a good way to describe Yes's music. At this point, however, what is important is that we see the way that Kivy has developed a schema for understanding what can be profound about music. Kivy goes on to argue that profound music is music that is able to be about a profound subject matter: "a subject of abiding interest to human beings." This music is "about" its subject matter by being, so to speak, "up to it." This music must be "up to" its subject matter by virtue of its form. Finally, the form of a piece of music serves profound subject matter through "supreme musical craftsmanship." Such "con-summate craftsmanship" is "the common denominator between counterpoint and other instances of musical profundity." Kivy goes on to argue that, "[c]raftsman-ship is a relative notion"; "[e]very major style or idiom will have a concept of craftsmanship defined relative to it" (p. 211).[23]

In the book that I have been quoting from, Kivy is interested in defining musical profundity for "music alone," that is, instrumental music. The "subject matter" of such music, as Kivy sees it (and I agree), is the form of the music itself—"music alone" is about "the possibilities of musical sound" (p. 214). "[A]s musical sound appears to be, for many people, of abiding interest and supreme importance, that condition too seems to be satisfied by at least some musical works" (p. 214). Here, obviously, we run into a snag in applying Kivy's definition to Yes's music, or any music that is not "music alone." But it seems that we can remain faithful to Kivy's general argument if we take it that the instrumental component of the music (and this would include the shapes of the vocal sounds, as sounds, though not the lyrics) in music that is not "music alone" now has to meet *two* conditions. First, for music that is not "music alone," apart from the lyrics presented in such music, the purely musical component of a particular work must itself be profound if the work itself is to be profound. And this means that the purely musical component must be about the possibilities of musical sound, in a way that displays consummate musical craftsmanship. Second, if the lyrical content of such a work is itself profound, then the purely musical component, in addition to fulfilling its obligations under the first category (that is, as though it really is music alone), must also "support" the lyrical component. In a moment, I will return to showing how this is done in the case of "Perpetual Change," but it seems to me that this "support" could take a variety of forms. Most obviously, one might expect the music to "represent" the lyrics,[24] but such "representation" could seemingly take a variety of forms.[25] My suspicion, however, is that one way that the form of music might be sufficient to the tasks of profundity in its purely musical form and in the forms it takes on to support lyrics has once again to do with counterpoint.

It may be that, in order to hear music with lyrics *as* music alone, we would have to imagine the lyrics as if they were being sung in some language that we do not understand. This way we could simply hear the singing for its formal character, as sound, as another instrument in the ensemble. This is certainly a difficult thing to do in the case where we have come to identify strongly with the lyrics. Paul McCartney may have originally written "Yesterday" as "scrambled eggs," but it is doubtful that the song would have been very powerful in the latter version. At first glance, this would seem to tell us something about the limitations of the song ("Yesterday," that is). But, just because the song might not hold up as "scrambled eggs" doesn't mean that "Yesterday" is not a good song—we know what "scrambled eggs" means, after all, and it would be difficult to not think about this meaning if we heard that version. A more useful example might be of the music of Christian Vander and his group, Magma. All of the "lyrics" to their music are written in a "language" of their own invention (I'm not sure if it is an actual language, or simply a system of sounds).

I hasten to add that these characterizations of Kivy's argument are my own, especially this last part where I try to apply the argument about music alone to music that is not music alone.

This diversion into possible definitions of the profundity of music was itself a diversion from a discussion of the typical rock critic's view of Yes and other progressive rock groups. So now we have some criteria for musical profundity, and Yes's music (or various works by Yes) either meets the criteria or it doesn't. But one more thing needs to be said about the kind of rock music criticism that takes it for granted that any attempt to achieve profundity working out of the language of rock music will necessarily fail—and fail in an embarrassing way. It may certainly be the case that no work of rock music—avant-rock, experimental pop, or what have you—has yet achieved profundity. But what would be entailed in the claim that (it is necessarily the case that) rock music (of whatever sort) cannot be profound? What is entailed, whether rock music critics like it or not, is that rock music cannot be art, but instead only entertainment. There might still be a critical approach to entertainment, but now the approach will only have to do with either (1) the sociological status of the work (for example, an analysis of rock music, or some part of it, as a social phenomenon), or (2) consumer-oriented reports on the "pure entertainment value" of various songs, albums, or musicians. Inasmuch as the rock critic is concerned with the music itself, the cynical type of criticism tends in this latter direction. Music reviews then become little more than reports on how this or that album sounds like some other album that you might have liked ("if you like R.E.M. and 10,000 Maniacs, then you'll probably like Lobster Boy"), or how this or that album is good to party to, or how this or that musician has a spunky attitude. And, if you read the pages of *Spin* or *Rolling Stone* or *Musician* or even *Option,* this is pretty much what you'll find. Now, keeping with this analysis, to negate the claim that something is necessarily not the case (that is, is impossible) only tells us, at most, that something is possible. Therefore, it might be possible, if the cynical anti–progressive rock critics are wrong, for there to be some profound works of rock music. But this doesn't mean that there *necessarily* are any: the proof, as always, has to be in the pudding, there have to be particular cases proposed and tested. And, it also has to be said, the fact that the approach of the anti–progressive rock critics leads to some consequences that I and others find unsavory does not mean that this approach is *necessarily* untenable. In other words, wishing that there could be works in rock music that are profound does not make this so. And wishing that rock music could do more than supply the background for a declining postmodern capitalist social order does not make this so. On the other hand, if we can demonstrate that there are particular works based in rock music that are profound, then we might recommend that the cynical entertainment reporters rethink their approach—or, better, just keep to their own areas of expertise and keep quiet about the rest.

Let's get back to the music; we won't take up the issue of the general state of rock music and rock music criticism again until part 3, where we'll deal with the effect of the cynical bleat on a visionary group such as Yes.

So, my argument is that, with "Perpetual Change" as its crowning piece, and with *The Yes Album* as a whole, Yes is at least on the verge of musical profundity. Let's stay with "Perpetual Change" for the moment, then we'll come back to the big picture, what Yes had accomplished with its third album.

When we broke away from this discussion, I was linking the lyrical theme and musical form of "Perpetual Change" to the work of some major names in modern and contemporary philosophy. My point is not that Yes is giving us "heavy" philosophy in "Perpetual Change." They aren't giving us "philosophy," in the more narrow and proper sense, at all, but instead some important ideas. Keeping with Kivy's arguments concerning profundity in music (or at least my variation on those ideas), it seems to me that Yes is treating a profound subject matter in what *may* be a profound way. My addition to Kivy's argument, concerning music with lyrics, was that this kind of music must demonstrate two levels of profundity. This means that we actually have to ask *three* questions. In the present case, we must ask if "Perpetual Change" (1) deals with the possibilities of musical sound in a way that demonstrates consummate musical craftsmanship; (2) in its instrumental content deals with its lyrical content in a way adequate to the latter; (3) has lyrical content that concerns issues of "abiding interest or importance to human beings." And, as a matter of fact, there is a fourth question: are the lyrics, *as lyrics* up to the profundity (if such there is) of their subject matter?

This is asking a great deal. I'm not absolutely sure that "Perpetual Change" delivers, but I am quite sure that it is trying to deliver, and that it comes awfully close—it's "getting there." If Yes didn't quite make it to the supreme heights here, they were certainly on the way. But let's not take anything for granted—let's break it down and see how we come out.

Taking the third question first, it seems clear to me that the lyrics for "Perpetual Change" have to do with some profound issues. Perhaps first of all the song concerns human hubris with regard to the natural world—and even the greater cosmos. "Even in time we shall control the day"; "And there you are, Saying we have the moon, so now the stars." Anderson is emphasizing the kind of human arrogance and audacity that brings about "near disaster, gazing down on you and me." Indeed, the line that occurs in the first chorus, "And there you are, Making it up but you're sure that it is a star," stands as a critique of the epistemological relativism that is somewhat typical nowadays, that holds that truth is whatever one makes up in one's mind. ("It all comes down to what you believe"—my answer to this is, when I hear it in the classroom, is [1] If the world is just what I make up in my mind, then I think I would make up a better world than this, and [2] This seems to work with questions of value—ethical, political, aesthetic, but would anyone care to try it out on, for example, gravity? And, if this approach doesn't work for gravity, we might ask about its other limitations.) Do the lyrics to "Perpetual Change" hold instead with a physicalistic determinism? Not at all. It is true, the response to hubris seems to be, "Deep inside, the world's controlling you and me." And, in fact, in the dialectic of human subject with the world, Anderson does give primacy to the world. This also speaks to the question of "appropriation"—is it a matter of a human appropriation of the world, or an appropriation of humanity by the world? But the viewpoint presented in the song is not mere fatalism or determinism; the lyrics present a dialectic: "As truth is gathered, I rearrange, inside out, outside in, . . . perpetual change"—"every day," "all of the way." There is dialectic and there is difference: what is described here as dialectic is not simply the continual unfolding of a process that is always the same, but instead a process that involves something new being brought to the world precisely through the process of gathering truth in and "rearranging."

There seems little question to me that these are issues of abiding human interest, as attested to by the work of the philosophers mentioned previously. "Perpetual Change" is not meant to be a systematic philosophical exploration of these issues—nor could any piece of music or other work of art be such an exploration and remain an artwork, so no apologies need be given, either, for what "Perpetual Change" actually is and what its authors are trying to do. Looking to the fourth question set out above, what we would need to ask is, Do these lyrics do justice to the profundity of these issues? The answer is, Yes. These lyrics represent a high-level application of craft to the issues treated, much in the way that the poems of W. B. Yeats or Wallace Stevens treat modern philosophical issues. Which is to say, in the present case, *economically.* The sensibility of the lyrics for "Perpetual Change" may be Romantic (or neo-Romantic), but the formal structure of the lyric has more in common with the shorter poems of Yeats or Stevens than with even the shorter poems of Blake, Shelley, or Wordsworth.

Now, turning to the first question, it may be that "Perpetual Change" is just short of profound. That is, if we were to treat the song as a work of "pure music," I don't know that we could sustain the argument that "Perpetual Change" pursues the possibilities of musical sound in a way demonstrative of consummate musical skill. It seems to me that Yes comes close to this with their final song on *The Yes Album,* and indeed with the whole album, and that they are on the way to something quite profound—but this last point is telling, because the fact that they used *The Yes Album* as a springboard for yet another qualitative leap tells me that consummate musical skill was still to come. Perhaps, too, if "Perpetual Change" were simply an instrumental piece, with some instrument playing the vocal line, this point would be further borne out—I just don't know if such a version would be that interesting to listen to.

But perhaps this is simply to say that such a version would not be true to what "Perpetual Change" is, which is to say a piece of music with lyrics and a vocal line as an integral part. What's the point of judging the piece according to standards for what it is not? (One might as well judge human longjumpers by the standards set by gazelles.) I am not sure whether this causes problems with Kivy's conception of "music alone," but surely he does not mean to privilege instrumental, nonprogrammatic music, but instead to use this kind of music as a way of isolating what makes a piece of music profound *purely by virtue of its musical elements.* Again, one way of making the point is that a great poem set to music does not necessarily make a great piece of music—if the music itself is not good. But the music must be more than good "in itself" in this case; the music must also be appropriate for what not only the lyric but rather the piece as a whole is meant to accomplish.

This is where question two comes in, and I have already attempted to demonstrate that the interaction of instrumental music, vocal line, and lyrics in "Perpetual Change" works very well. *How* it works is perhaps the key question, but first we might ask, To what *end* is this work done? This seems a very Aristotelian question to ask—about the "final cause" of a piece of music. But what I also have in mind is the fact that some music seems to "work" fine in its internal structure, and to deal in an interesting, perhaps "profound" way with the possibilities of musical sound, but it does not seem to exist for any greater end. Perhaps this is the point of "music alone," and Theodor Adorno makes a powerful argument for valorizing the "autonomous work of art" for precisely this reason. In a world where everything (and everyone) is forced into servitude as a means to an end, art can best give us a glimpse of utopian possibilities when it seems to not be a means to anything other than itself.

But Adorno did not mean by this argument that music cannot be the music of ideas. It is overwhelmingly clear that Yes's music is inextricably tied up with ideas—ideas in a philosophical sense, ideas in the sense of explorations of musical possibilities. Indeed, as Yes explored the visual and theatrical possibilities of creating total works of art—through album covers, stage design, and so forth—they were clearly aiming for a very broad philosophical-aesthetic range. But a "music of ideas" can be unsatisfying "as music," just as some "novels of ideas" can be unsatisfying "as novels"—I have in mind some of John Cage's music in the former respect, and, for example, *Foucault's Pendulum* by Umberto Eco in the latter respect. Even virtuoso displays of craftsmanship can seem pointless or silly—this is one of the problems I have with much of Frank Zappa's music (much of it seems like the employment of an enormous talent in order to make a junior high school–level joke). (The work of recent academic "avant-garde" composers would be another important example.) The question for any "music of ideas" would have to be, what does this music do with its idea that is interesting, provocative, perhaps profound, *as music*. Returning to the first question, then, I would have to say that, looked at as a complex whole, "Perpetual Change" comes close to being profound. Looked at in the pure terms of the first question, the song comes a little less close. This latter point tells us something important, and certainly Yes was to go on to create much more innovative explorations of musical form. But this latter point perhaps also tells us, once again, that what we ought to be interested in is the whole.

So, once again, I have found Kivy's categories useful for reflecting upon, but we also have good reason to modify these categories somewhat.

Now, taking "Perpetual Change" as a whole, what we need to consider is the complex functioning of its parts, as defined by the four questions. Taking this as a question of "form," we can return to one of Kivy's proposals for finding profundity in music alone, namely to consider counterpoint. As with some of the other categories discussed here, counterpoint turns out not to have as narrow a definition as it might first appear to. Kivy argues that "[t]he challenge of counterpoint . . . is, most simply stated, to juggle successfully a complex function of two variables: the number of melodies combined together, and the intrinsic, melodic interest of each of those melodies" (p. 207). Although "Perpetual Change" takes up this challenge in a fairly straightforward way, we might wonder if "counterpoint," as a larger musical category, might take in the possibilities for theme and variation with all of the elements of music: rhythm, coloration, and so on. Of course, in some sense, this is already included in the definition Kivy gives us, in that variations on melodies include stating the melody in different registers and with different instruments, as well as mixing up the rhythm. (The way that orchestration is the key aspect of Ravel's "Bolero" is an example of the former, while the different statements of the initial melody in "Close to the Edge" demonstrates the point about rhythm.)

What I'm driving at is that, with a work such as "Perpetual Change," that is not a piece of music alone, there is something like a counterpoint of the whole that has to do with the logical interaction of all the song's elements. And, on this most important level, "Perpetual Change" is a very good piece of music, approaching profundity.

Summary

Getting all of these elements of analysis on the table may have seemed—all right, it was—a tortuous task to the reader. Rest assured, however, that it is important to have some elements of systematic analysis and that, because we now have in our possession a systematic approach, we can proceed without repeating some of the technical-philosophical aspects of the analysis, and work more economically.

With *The Yes Album*, Yes created their first fully integrated work, framed by three pieces that stretched song form into a new kind of extended rock structure. Yes would come back, here and there, to song form in the ordinary sense, either in the form of actual songs, or in the form of "songs" that are imbedded in expanded structures. But now, in the main sequence, it would be these expanded, extended structures that would set the tone for Yes's musical explorations, with songs as anchors or, occasionally, interruptions perhaps, but not as forms that set the parameters for the more adventurous works. And, in fact, the actual level at which any given work by Yes would now come together was the album as a whole.

Perhaps the claim is overreaching, but in discussing *The Yes Album* I claimed that we might make an analogy from Gödel's theorem to music. Regardless of the plausibility of this argument, it is clear that Yes went in for simpler, less busy, cleaner, clearer structures on *The Yes Album,* with everything else working "around" the structures—everything from the rhythmic contributions of each instrument to the lyrics to the instrumental solos (everything that cannot be absolutely separated from "the structure," that is)—bringing the complexity. When I say, "less busy," I mean, of course, less busy than with Yes's first two albums. In retrospect, it seems that Yes did something absolutely essential to their subsequent development with this simplification of structure.

This is a point that could perhaps only be seen with twenty-twenty hindsight. It seems that, however, if Yes had continued with the often very busy contrapuntal exercises of the first two albums, their sound would have become much too "trashy." Perhaps the latter quality is what gives the first two albums a closer relation to "rock'n'roll" than anything that was to come in the main sequence. The irony is that, even though the transition in Yes's music from the initial period to the main sequence owes a great deal to Steve Howe, it isn't as though Peter Banks was any more of a "rock'n'roll" guitar player (in the sense that, say, Keith Richards or Pete Townshend are) than Howe. Not to underestimate Howe's enormous abilities at all, but there is also that crucial element of a fresh face, a fresh start, and the ever-growing sense of possibility that was in the air.

And, if anything—another great irony—it was Tony Kaye's limitations as a keyboard player that also encouraged the employment of more straightforward structures on *The Yes Album.* If you think about it, the basic chord progressions in the three more "epic" pieces (Thomas Mosbø calls these "sub-epics," in comparison with the truly epic works such as "Close to the Edge," which is fair enough; see p. 92) are quite "chunky," "block" structures. Such structures suit Kaye's playing and his instrument of first choice, the Hammond B-3, very well. Although we will come back to Tony Kaye, at the point when he joined the reworked Yes of the eighties, it is appropriate that we say something now about his work in the early years of Yes. While Kaye's playing is not up to the sort of creativity that Yes would require for most of the main sequence, he was and has been a perfectly good keyboard player for the experimental rock work that the band has done. And, while his blocky style of B-3 work would have led any other group of talented musicians in a heavier direction—the natural comparison would be with Jon Lord of Deep Purple—the rhythmic innovations of Chris Squire and Bill Bruford allowed Kaye to make a somewhat different contribution on the Hammond. Finally, in some ways Kaye's simpler approach is more suited to experimental rock, if not avant-rock, than the approaches of Rick Wakeman or Patrick Moraz (who don't really know what to do in the more pop-inflected side of the experimental rock setting); this is not meant to be a backhanded compliment, given that each kind of music has to be judged according to its own internal logic. After Yes, Kaye went on to form Badger. I've only ever listened to their first album, *One Live Badger.* It's a gutsy thing to record your first album live. *One Live Badger* is a pretty good album in the way that organ-heavy experimental pop albums were in the mid-seventies (there's an interesting

"Jesus rock" song that closes the album, reminiscent of the Doobie Brothers' "Jesus is Just Alright with Me"), and it has a very nice Roger Dean cover. Kaye also played on the first Flash album to good effect.

Again, in retrospect, *The Yes Album* plays a crucial transitional role into the main sequence, with one foot in and one foot out. If Tony Kaye was, in a sense, the foot that remained out, this does not detract from the solid effort put in by everyone on the album; it just means that Yes was making the transition from experimental rock to progressive rock. They achieved a greater level of integration than ever before; this integration included the overall packaging of the album. Although the cover of *The Yes Album* was not done by Roger Dean, still, the green-tinted photograph of the group conveys the sense of a total work of art: cover, production (Eddie Offord came aboard for *The Yes Album),* songwriting, and simply the general mood. (Interestingly, the "bookends" of the main sequence, *The Yes Album* and *Going for the One,* are the albums from this period without Roger Dean cover art.) Certainly *green* came on in a big way; besides being Chris Squire's favorite color (perhaps it is the favorite color of other band members as well, I don't know), it symbolizes perfectly the vision of the group in the main sequence—the concern for the Earth and ecology, the concern for bringing fresh sounds and ideas to music.

In sum, I do not find every moment on *The Yes Album* to be "profound," but, what Yes showed with this album is that all kinds of moments could be integrated into a larger vision. I would say that this vision, as presented by *The Yes Album,* approached profundity, often achieving it. The dynamic range of the album is remarkable, as is the ethical vision demonstrated. *The Yes Album* is a very good album in its own right, approaching excellence; the album was an important statement for Yes, but, what's more, and more significant, it was an important statement for progressive rock.

Bill Bruford *(Yesyears* video) compared Yes to King Crimson at the point when the former made *The Yes Album* and the latter made *In the Wake of Poseidon.* He found Yes wanting, and was especially unenthusiastic about the vocal harmonies that one would, of course, never find on a King Crimson album. We'll get more into the comparison of what are arguably the two most important progressive rock groups in due course. But, taking stock of Bruford's point for the moment, we might consider the fact that perhaps King Crimson was more musically adventurous even with its first album *(In the Court of the Crimson King)—* or at least more "out"—than Yes was even by their third album. But we have to look at the whole. Whereas lyrics, and to some extent even singing (please don't get me wrong, Greg Lake is a fine singer with a very "noble" voice, clear as a bell), were almost an afterthought for King Crimson (which is to say, for Robert Fripp), these things were a major part of what Yes was doing, and Yes presented lyrics and singing that were several levels above what Crimson was doing. (Yes, some of Pete Sinfield's lyrics were good—or amusing at least—but there was no vision there, and it's clear that Fripp didn't see lyrics and singing as important as other elements of Crimson's music.) Even on the purely instrumental level, we might consider that, while the drumming on all of the Crimson albums has always been first-rate and innovative, the interaction between the bass guitar and percussion has very rarely been as interesting as what we find on all of the Yes albums (the exception for Crimson would be the interplay between John Wetton and Bill Bruford), and this would include the first two, and certainly *The Yes Album.* To leave off the comparison for now (and it is a comparison of great with great—and, fortunately, no one is forcing us to only listen to the one or the other) and to stick to the positive assertion I'm interested in making here, with *The Yes Album* we see Yes coming into a visionary maturity. They were beginning to achieve what Jon Anderson and Chris Squire set out to accomplish. Propelled by their own ideals and talents, as well as the utopian energies of the time, they were on the verge of another quantum leap.

Fragile

For readers of this book who were born in the mid- to late-fifties, and who grew up in the United States, the spring of 1972 was an important time. That was when many of us heard Yes for the first time, because "Roundabout" was a "hit" on commercial radio. An amazing and very unlikely hit: the very classical-sounding introduction, strange, high-pitched vocals, esoteric words that were oddly poetic for a top-forty radio song, that weird "bonking" sound from the drums, and a bass line that sounded like nothing ever heard from the bass guitar before. That spring I was fifteen going on sixteen. I can still remember very well sitting in the car in the spring heat of Miami, Florida, listening to that magical sound. It just seemed to draw one in, and to speak of new possibilities. I asked for, and received, *Fragile* for my sixteenth birthday, and I can honestly say that my life was changed—and not just my life as a musician or as someone who loves and thinks about music. My guess is that many readers in the U.S. have similar stories to tell. Perhaps the stories would be slightly different for readers who are slightly older or more hip than I was in 1972 (or now, for that matter), who listened to FM radio in the early seventies (I started listening to FM soon after, and "underground" stations such as WBUS—the "magic bus"—would play tracks from "Close to the Edge"), who already knew about *The Yes Album* or even the first two albums. But I would guess that these readers have their own tales to tell of a magical moment when the possibility of Yes came into view—and younger listeners have their stories of discovering Yes at a later time. By the time of *The Yes Album* and *Fragile,* Yes were certainly making music of discovery and music to be discovered. One had the feeling of discovering a whole new world.

"Roundabout"! I intend to provide an analysis in a moment, but first, What a song! Like many admirers of Yes, I must have heard that song at least a thousand times—possibly many more, I'm not actually counting—and I have never grown tired of it. I sing or hum it to myself constantly (I live near a very big lake, Lake Michigan—one of the great ones, you know—and I walk along this lake almost every day, so you can imagine what line of "Roundabout" I often find myself starting with), and I could certainly go into the living room right now, put on the record or CD (there's something about listening to the LP, the warmth, the sensuousness of the album cover, . . .), and take emotional and intellectual sustenance from the song on many levels. "Roundabout" is an extraordinary piece, one that really turned a great many heads around, certainly mine. With "Roundabout," Yes made a clear statement that rock music, this "medium of our generation," was not in any way inherently limited as to its range of structural or lyrical expression. "Roundabout" was "serious" music that could also rock.

The hip critics have forgotten this—even though a great deal of what came after "Roundabout," including the alternative or experimental rock of more recent years, was inspired by Yes's experiment. But forget about these "critics"-cum-entertainment-reporters, and instead talk to the musicians. They'll tell it to you straight: when "Roundabout" became widely popular, that changed the whole musical scene, completely changed the sensibilities of rock musicians. Some musicians were less than enthusiastic, and even sharply opposed to what Yes was doing with rock music, to be sure—but this only underlines the point: what Yes was doing was *important,* their music demanded that musicians and engaged listeners take a position. Indeed, with "Roundabout" and *Fragile,* Yes quite forcibly put three issues on the table: musical structures, poetic visions, and, most straightforwardly, *musicianship.* It is not an exaggeration to say that, on a most basic level, a great many rock musicians really started to work on their playing after they heard "Roundabout," to get serious about being musicians, even if without buying tuxedos and getting all stuffy about it. Were there some bad side-effects of this movement? Undoubtedly—there was excess of virtuosity for its own sake. But, overwhelmingly, the inspiration of "Roundabout" has been to the good, and the effects remain with us in every piece of rock music that aspires to use an enlarged musical vocabulary to do something innovative and serious with rock music. The hip-chic critics won't recognize this—to hell with it, talk to the musicians!

(I say to hell with "it" rather than "them" because I want to believe that all people are in principle redeemable—certainly a constant theme in Yes's music—but what is not redeemable is cynicism.)

As with *The Yes Album, Fragile* is built around three longer pieces: "Roundabout," "South Side of the Sky," and "Heart of the Sunrise." However, with these longer works, the "chunkiness" is gone, replaced by a much more developed counterpoint. And, although each of these pieces has moments of great subtlety and gentleness, each also has moments where the music cuts like a knife and where the rhythm is very jagged. As before, with a certain amount of hindsight it is possible to see where the elements of *Fragile* were already somewhat in evidence in the earlier work, but it is also clear that Yes reaches a qualitatively new level with their fourth album. With *Fragile*, Yes consolidated their position as a major force in progressive rock.

An undeniable but, paradoxically, somewhat intangible role in this consolidation was played by the addition of Rick Wakeman to the band. Certainly, with the coming of Wakeman, Yes was finally a group composed completely of virtuosos. The level of musicianship was such that, with creative vision, Yes was now capable of doing anything. Fortunately, they had this vision. Furthermore, besides sheer "chops," Wakeman was interested in using a greater array of keyboards than was his predecessor in the band. To my mind, a certain fetish with "multiple keyboards" arose in the mid-seventies that at times gave priority to the instruments and the technology over the music. This approach is in evidence on some of Wakeman's solo albums, I'm afraid. However, within the collectivity of Yes, priorities were generally kept in proper order—that is, music first—and Wakeman's keyboards brought a wonderful array of new colors to the music of Yes. Just as "Roundabout" as a whole had a significant effect on many musicians and on rock music quite generally, so did even the smallest parts of the song. For instance, Wakeman's synthesizer fill at the end of the first verse (in the little break before the second verse comes in), which lasts only a measure or so, is striking on several levels: in its pure sensuousness, its creative use of tone color, its delicacy in inserting something not uncomplicated into the song without at all making the song too "busy."

Although synthesizer was used to a small extent on *The Yes Album*, Wakeman was the one who really brought its use, as well as the use of the Mellotron, to Yes.[26] In addition, Wakeman used electric piano, electric harpsichord (later he used a "real" harpsichord), and Clavinet.[27] Wakeman became well-known as the person who was "stacking keyboards one on top of another," and he even played a major role in designing the multiple keyboard racks that are very common today. He was literally surrounded by keyboards. But, of course, the important question concerns his use of the instruments, and the crucial thing is that his musical creativity was expressed through this technology without being overwhelmed by it. More will be said on this point in a moment.

In search of his own possibilities, Steve Howe began at this point to use a good many different guitars. As with the use of multiple keyboards, this multiplication of instruments and accumulation of technologies can become gratuitous and gimmicky. Some guitarists are very closely identified with a certain guitar, as Jimi Hendrix was with the Fender Stratocaster, for example, Roy Buchanan with the Fender Telecaster, or Robert Fripp and Martin Barre (Jethro Tull) were for a long time with the Gibson Les Paul. Steve Howe is at the opposite extreme. Although he still says that his "ultimate guitar" is the Gibson ES175 D that he bought back in 1964 (the beautiful deep-box hollow-bodied electric with the tobacco sunburst finish), Howe has become internationally famous as not only a great guitarist, but as a great collector of guitars. As shown in *The Steve Howe Guitar Collection,* (a book that provides some interesting material on the use of Howe's guitars in making the music of Yes and other projects, as well as, of course, much of interest on guitars themselves) Howe has more than a hundred guitars. This is a bit excessive, to be sure, but I take Howe's word for it when he says in the book that, "I'm constantly discovering fresh musical areas to investigate as instruments surface in the collection, providing new voices through which my music can speak" (p. 3). In the music of Yes, at least, this point is well demonstrated, and *Fragile* marked the beginning of a great expansion in guitar colors in the group's music. Howe said somewhere that part of his aim as a musician was to master a great many different styles and use many different sounds and colors, and yet at the same time to produce something distinctively in his own musical voice. Again, in Yes, and with varying degrees of success in his other projects, Howe accomplished this goal.

Perhaps you have to be a guitarist or bass guitarist to be aware of this point (I don't know how this question plays out for drummers or trombone players, for example), but playing different instruments, with not only their different sounds but also their different *feels,* can indeed open up new possibilities for playing. The different instrument, its *character,* asks you to and perhaps even forces you to play it in a way peculiar to that instrument. I have a little experience with this as both a bass player and a guitar player. For instance, at present I have a bunch of different bass guitars; each has its own character that has to be responded to—and learned and respected. And, when this is done, each opens up new possibilities, in combination with whatever creativity can be brought to playing them. (At the expense of sounding like an old fogey, there is something about the "classic" guitars and bass guitars—the Gibson ES-335's, the Stratocasters or Telecasters, the Rickenbacker 12-string electrics, the Gretsch Chet Atkins Country Gentlemans, etc.; that is, they have this quality of "character." This means that they can be a bit temperamental and cranky sometimes, too. Not all things are possible with each of them; sometimes only *one* thing is possible, but it can be one thing that is musically significant. The old fogey part is that I often don't find this character in some of the more recent instruments that are in fact quite versatile. On this point, of course, I'm not an expert, but Steve Howe is, and a look through his *Collection* seems to bear this point out.) Steve Howe has multiplied this respect for instrumental character to a truly extreme degree, and the amazing thing is that he has managed to stay on top of this—which speaks of great devotion and dedication.

The larger point is that, for both Howe and Wakeman, rather than get caught up with instruments and technologies in themselves, music and vision led in the employment of these new sonic possibilities. Given the role that these questions, of technologies and musical priorities, played in the emergence of Yes as a major force, and with *Fragile* as a qualitative leap, let's take just another moment to set out the issues.

Around the early seventies, when people were trying to figure out what bands such as Yes, King Crimson, and the other progressive groups were doing, among the labels that were tossed around was "techno-rock." This label was applied to Yes as much as to any group. Obviously, the presence of the synthesizer was a major factor in attracting this designation, but so was the use of lots of different instruments and sounds, the very sophisticated production of Eddie Offord, and increasingly elaborate stage sets. The accepted wisdom was that the music of groups such as Yes was somehow *about* the technology and crucially dependent on the technology. I think it's worth taking the time to argue the point that this was *never* the case for Yes. Certainly, they not only used the most advanced musical and production technology, they even played a crucial role in the development of this technology. On the purely musical side (leaving aside here the stage sets and other components of the complete Yes presentation), with perhaps an exception here or there (I would point to some of the synthesizer technology and bass guitar sound modifications on *Tormato,* although even these are not especially egregious examples), Yes only ever used technology to create more sounds, not to present technology as a gimmick or an end-in-itself.

The crucial question might be put this way: Would the music of Yes be possible without electronic (or even electric) instruments and technology—and would this music hold up? I think the answer is yes, absolutely. As a thought experiment, I don't have any problem at all replacing the aforementioned synthesizer fill in "Roundabout" with a flute or bassoon or viola. (As I've said, this is a thought experiment I enjoy immensely—and I think this says something about the structure and vision of Yes's music.) The whole aim of the technology was to achieve a broad range of colors—again, a "symphonic" range, which has nothing to do with the clichés about "orchestral rock." Think of the similar question that might be asked about Beethoven's piano music. After all, the development of the piano involved a good deal of technology that didn't exist in Johann Sebastion Bach's day, especially the development of the cast-iron frame (the part that holds the strings). Without this frame, the tension required for the strings so that the piano can be as loud as it is would have simply caused earlier keyboard instruments to implode. Now, Beethoven's piano music, quite obviously, is very much involved in the character of the piano itself, as an instrument and as a technology. Significantly, piano technology today has created instruments that sound a good deal different from the pianos of Beethoven's time. Although there are a few people who want such "authenticity" that they demand to hear Beethoven played on a period instrument (what's perhaps inescapably inauthentic about this is that these folks, try as they might, will never be able to hear this music with period ears), no one seriously suggests that Beethoven shouldn't be played on modern pianos. Indeed, only a few would suggest that it is musically invalid to perform Bach's harpsichord music on a modern piano, although it is quite nice to hear this music on the original instrument as well—in other words, because the music is profound in its structure and vision, what we hear with the different instruments is simply two different versions or dimensions of this profundity. I think that we would hear the greatness of Beethoven's great piano sonatas even if there weren't any pianos (which is not to say, either, that any instrument would do in every case; it's not likely that the Hammerklavier sonata would work very well with a quartet of oboes).

I would even allow that it can be valid for a composition to be *completely* identified with a particular instrument. It's kind of hard to imagine "Foggy Mountain Breakdown" without banjo, or possibly John Coltrane's extended improvisations without tenor and soprano saxophones. But this could not be the rule for music in general, which is perhaps to say that timbre is integral to musical creativity. What if we were limited to only a handful of colors? What if we only had, for instance, the piano? Then "Close to the Edge" would be in no different a situation than Sibelius's Seventh Symphony. The point is, however, that we do live in a world of many colors, and this is what Yes has chosen to use in a very creative way (and with five people rather than a hundred); technology is secondary to this.

The other point that needs stressing here is that, with *Fragile,* Yes was evolving a process of group composition the likes of which had really never been seen before anywhere in music. One aspect of this group composition was that individual temptations to run wild with instrumental dexterity for its own sake were brought into a group project that subordinated egos to structure and vision. Indeed, with *Fragile,* rock music came as close to an egoless band as it ever had—and this in the midst of a musical scene where big egos were the norm. Group composition is typical in jazz—sometimes this is called "spontaneous composition." But what Yes was doing was different—and it was something both akin to and yet quite beyond even the ideal, to say nothing of the reality, of what John Lennon and Paul McCartney had accomplished in the Beatles. Furthermore, the egoless aspect of Yes's group composition set them apart from the other main pillar of avant-rock, King Crimson. Robert Fripp had (and has) a great genius for putting the right people together and letting them develop as a group *up to a point.* To Fripp's credit, this point is generally when the group started to get stale, but there is something to the fact that King Crimson is really a succession of groups, built around Fripp. (Perhaps the most interesting parallel would be to Miles Davis.) Yes, arguably, has remained one group throughout its history. I say "arguably"—when we come to albums such as *Drama,* and especially to the version of the group with Trevor Rabin, we will obviously have to make the argument in its own right. My point now, however, is that, with the addition of Rick Wakeman to the group, Yes not only had the right people to play a very sophisticated and visionary form of rock music, they also had the elements for changing the nature of creating complex compositions. As with all of the other arguments presented here, the proof has to be seen in the music, so let's return to a more direct discussion of *Fragile.*

As the reader undoubtedly knows, *Fragile* is organized around four group works (including the aforementioned three extended works, plus the shorter "Long Distance Runaround"), and five works representing solo efforts by each member of the band. Do the solo works detract somewhat from the group feel of the album? I would have to say, "yes, somewhat," when this is thought about analytically. Looked at in the abstract, one would tend to see only the group works as really belonging to the album-as-a-unified-work-by-Yes. But, in actuality, while some of the solo efforts are a good deal stronger than others, they generally play the role of providing balance to the intensity of the extended group works. Such balance is important: unrelenting intensity does not always add up to overall intensity, but instead to boredom and disaffection. (About the only exception that I can think of that has even a small chance of escaping its time frame is *Never Mind the Bollocks* by the Sex Pistols. But that's the exception that proves the rule.) In addition, these solo efforts helped to demonstrate, by contrast, what the process of group composition that Yes was developing was all about. This may sound like a backhanded compliment, but that's not my intention. However, having said all of these things, I find that the best way to get into the analysis of *Fragile* is to consider the solo works first, and somewhat apart from the rest of the album, and then to turn to what is the real heart and soul of the album, the group works. At the end of these discussions, I will once again return to looking at the album as a whole.

Not to keep the reader in suspense, my plan is to go from the least interesting of the solo works to the most interesting. The order that will be followed, then, is: "Cans and Brahms," "Five Percent For Nothing," "We Have Heaven," "Mood for a Day," and "The Fish." In turning to this last solo work, I also want to provide a fairly detailed portrait of Chris Squire's musicianship in general. My aim will be to demonstrate the thesis that Squire's approach to the bass guitar is absolutely central to the development of the music of Yes.

"Cans and Brahms"

Rick Wakeman's performance of part of the third movement of Brahms's Fourth Symphony is reminiscent of other experiments in using electronic keyboards to perform classical music, of the *Switched-On Bach* (Walter Carlos) or *Snowflakes are Dancing* (Tomita) variety. Wakeman provides an alternative orchestration, using acoustic, electric, and electronic keyboards, of an excerpt from a work often performed in the orchestral repertoire of European classical music. Such efforts can be clever, fun, and pleasant enough, but I'm not sure that they add much to our understanding of the music in question. At most they might demonstrate what the use of different voices does for a work that was written for some other instrument or set of instruments. In some ways I prefer Wakeman's exercise here to some of the more heavily synthesized experiments, because the pianos and harpsichord have some "bite" to them. However, this reorchestration does not really rise to the level of an interesting reinterpretation. My understanding, in any case, is that the reason Wakeman's solo spot here did not consist in an original piece was that he was contractually obligated to another record company for all of his solo compositions. Fortunately, this was only the tiniest foreshadowing of what can happen to music when lawyers get involved—something that would trouble not only Yes, but indeed all of music, starting around the end of the seventies. (As we will see, this phenomenon is not unconnected to the general social dynamic that brought the era of progressive rock to a close.) Given the legalities involved, however, I think that it would have been more interesting if Wakeman had performed a classical work simply on piano or organ, aiming at creating an interesting interpretation. Such an interpretation would have been that much more interesting if it could have had some connection to the larger album. "Cans and Brahms," fortunately, does not really hurt *Fragile,* but it doesn't especially help, either. We might say the same thing about Steve Howe's "Clap," from *The Yes Album,* but at least in this case we have an original piece that stands on its own. Both works, "Cans and Brahms" and "Clap," demonstrate skill and cleverness, but the former doesn't do much more than that, while the latter does. As for the role that either plays in the larger and more significant context of their respective albums, both are harmless enough—but of course we're not interested in Yes as a group of harmless musicians. But, again, I'm happy enough to blame the lawyers and record company execs for this.

Wakeman's skills at keyboard orchestration play a major role in Yes's music more generally, and in some of his solo albums, especially *The Six Wives of Henry the Eighth.*

"Five Per Cent for Nothing"
The thing about Bill Bruford's solo contribution is that, at 35 seconds in length, it seems simply inconsequential, whereas its "idea" is both interesting and possibly significant. Had the piece been developed at greater length, "Five Per Cent for Nothing" could have done for rock-based percussion what "The Fish" did for bass guitar. In particular, what seems important about "Five Per Cent" is the way that Bruford puts the drums and percussion up front, leading the group interplay, without playing anything that sounds like a drum solo. (Isn't it a great irony that Bruford has generally stayed away from the "monster drum solo" sort of thing made popular by John Bonham, when the former certainly

could play a far more interesting solo than the latter?) "Five Per Cent" is a very small foreshadowing of the music that Bruford would go on to make on his solo albums, especially the first one (*Feels Good to Me*) and the King Crimson of the eighties (with Robert Fripp, Tony Levin, and Adrian Belew). Because the entire group plays on the piece, "Five Per Cent" flows well enough into "Long Distance Runaround." The piece adds to the album, just not a whole lot.

These first two solo efforts, in other words, are hardly fatal flaws for *Fragile,* but they aren't integral to the album either. This is important in the context of progressive rock, where the album as a whole is the basic unit of the artwork. For this reason, too, perhaps it doesn't make that much sense to put solo works in the midst of a group effort. At the very least, the solo works should be carefully integrated into the group effort, as is, for example, the classical guitar solo at the end of *Tales From Topographic Oceans,* Part 3. For various reasons, which we will take up in turn, the other three solo works on *Fragile* do fit better into the album concept.

"We Have Heaven"

It isn't hard to see why Jon Anderson's solo piece seems much more part of a Yes album—as opposed to a momentary break from the album—given the fact that his voice, his composition skills, and his personality are so much part of everything the band does. "We Have Heaven" also anticipates some of Anderson's solo albums, none so much as the first, *Olias of Sunhillow.* I don't know if, at least in rock music, I've ever heard anything else like "We Have Heaven" and the related pieces on *Olias.* Anderson creates something akin to a round, but with choirs (of his own multitracked voice), with cymbal flourishes every now and then, and a steady, driving rhythm underneath. There's something almost "Christmas-y" about it, reminding me of "The Carol of the Bells," an eerie *English* Christmas song. This is appropriate to the Blakean messianic theme of the piece, encapsulated in the line, "Yes, he is here." In the spirit of the Radical Reformation of which William Blake was a part, this announcement is made to the animal kingdom: "Tell the Moondog, tell the March Hare." Anderson is moving toward the idea of a rejoicing of all creation, a celebration of an absolutely universal redemption. No theme could be more utopian. At the same time, in the "We have," Anderson is evoking the idea that "the kingdom of heaven is within you." Some of Anderson's conceptions undoubtedly came from the reading on various religious and philosophical traditions that he was beginning to undertake. But I also have the feeling that Anderson was reinventing hermetic lore for himself. In this lore, as known in Western and non-Western traditions since before Socrates and Buddha, one of the central ideas is "as above, so below." The work of redemption is a work for both the heavens and Earth. "We Have Heaven" is most significant as the most basic fragment of Anderson's redemptive utopianism, which we will see develop into something akin to a philosophical system in later works.

In some sense of "pure music," "We Have Heaven" is not especially innovative, though it does demonstrate Anderson's ability to put whole pieces of music together by himself. Instead, it is as a concentrated, dramatically simple statement that the piece has its charm.

"Mood for a Day"

In his solo contribution to *Fragile,* Steve Howe created a work for classical guitar that stands as a fine example of craftsmanship. Leaving for just a moment the perspective of each solo work as a solitary piece, we might also contemplate the way that "Mood" operates in juxtaposition to the work presented just before it, Chris Squire's "The Fish." The latter is very electric, very "steely" one might say, as befits a work made up of layers of bass guitars, especially trebly Rickenbackers fitted with Rotosound Roundwound strings (on which, more in a moment). From this metallic model of scientific (and science fiction) musical efficiency, we turn in a much more warm, Mediterranean direction.

To the best of my knowledge, "Mood for a Day" is unique among works composed by rock musicians for having entered the repertoire of "classical music" for its instrument. The irony here is that, among Howe's enormous output of guitar music (I include here not only independent guitar works, but also the many guitar solos and orchestrations that are part of larger works; the solos at the end of "Roundabout," for example), "Mood" is not an especially innovative piece. (Compare "Mood" to the solo guitar section from "Sound Chaser," for instance.) However, if "Mood" had been avant-garde in the way that much of Yes music is more generally, it is doubtful if the piece would have caught on with classical guitarists. (Significantly, part of the way that the piece has caught on has been in inspiring young people to take up the classical guitar in the first place.) Another approach to the question, however, might be to argue that "Mood for a Day" is, so to speak, "avant" as a piece of "classical music" that has been integrated into an album of rock music.

Be that as it may, "Mood" is fairly "conservative" in its tonality (the piece is in the key of D throughout) and, even though there are several time changes, there's nothing in the rhythm of the work to throw your spine out of joint. I'm being facetious, of course: at the same time that "Mood for a Day" is warm and pleasant, and seemingly conservative, it is also a subtle and sophisticated demonstration of the kind of baroque counterpoint that made its way into Spain and what became "classical guitar." (This instrument was a latecomer to respectability among classical musicians, the key figure being Andres Segovia.) In a much more quiet way, "Mood" is not unlike "Clap" in the way that it works out a series of loosely related themes. Whereas "Clap" recapitulates the opening material at the end, however, "Mood" is a bit more rhapsodic; at the close of the latter, there is a final theme that, though also related to the others, is yet another new line. And, whereas "Clap" pushes forward in a kind of straightahead hill-billy romp, "Mood" has a more subtle flow, even though its gentle rocking is in fits and starts. In its final line, "Mood for a Day" becomes something of a lul-laby. This is very sweet, the kicker being that naptime is over a half-second later when the charging bassline of "Heart of the Sunrise" leaps out!

Ignoring once again the context of the larger album of which it is a part, however, one of the subtleties of "Mood" is the way that it *empties* itself of its harmonic material. Instead of going for the "big finish," "Mood for a Day" is a remarkable model of restraint in the way that it begins with sweeping chords and ends with just a pair of notes. This kind of elegance gives the lie once again to the well-worn idea that Yes's music is just a lot of bombast. "Mood" becomes less and less dense, not because its thematic and harmonic material is in any way played out or exhausted, but instead in the manner of a crystal that is polished to perfection.

"The Fish," and a portrait of Chris Squire

The discussion of *Fragile* opened with some incantations regarding the remarkableness of "Roundabout," the way that this work made a statement on many levels. Going back to the opening bars of "Roundabout," one of the most jarring aspects of the piece was its positively weird bassline. What Squire was doing was strange in every respect—perhaps most noticeably, at first, just the tone of the bass guitar (if that was the instrument we were hearing—that's what the tone made us wonder); but, on repeated listenings, there was also the incredi-ble springiness of that line, and the way that it seemingly unfolded in a direction opposite to that of the rest of the song—not only melodically, but rhythmically as well.

Chris Squire was, as mentioned above, one of the co-founders of Yes, along with Jon Anderson. As we've discussed before, there is an interesting question as to what made Yes more than the sum of its parts. To return to terms set out many pages ago, what made Yes different from all the other Strawberry Alarm Clocks and other vaguely experimental, quasi-psychedelic post–*Sergeant Pepper's* groups from the late sixties? In this study, I've continually stressed the inter-weaving of two factors: the utopian vision that was perhaps more the contribu-tion of Jon Anderson (who, however, "channeled" the vision from what was in the air at the time and what had been in the ground for hundreds of years), and innovations in musical structure. From the beginning, everyone in the group made contributions on this latter score. It seems to me, however, that there was one magical element that drove this structural innovation and took Yes places that not even other progressive rock groups were going, and this was the bass guitar artistry of Squire. In particular, Squire's unique approach to the bass gui-tar brought about a redefinition in the idea of a rock group's "rhythm section" (meaning, generally, the bass guitarist and drummer, perhaps a rhythm guitarist—this last term has mostly gone out of use, but some readers will remember the days when people said, "Oh, you play guitar? Lead or rhythm?"). In a purely analytic sense (in other words, this is not a description of how things necessarily happened in real time), Squire's style had an effect, first, on Bill Bruford's playing, and then a ripple effect on how the rest of the band configured itself; in the final analysis, the very idea of the rhythm section is undone, and a whole other matrix for taking care of the traditional role of the bass guitar and drums is generated. At the same time, new roles are created for the bass guitar and drums.

There have been many innovative and talented drummers in progressive rock, and some (but fewer, I would say) innovative bass guitarists, but Squire and Bruford went further than anyone else. Again, I think the impetus came especially from Squire. Bruford was doing something other than what most rock drummers did in the context he found himself in—that is, he was bringing jazz stylings and a keen sense of spacing and syncopation to a group that, in other respects, was more oriented toward harmonic innovation. Bill Bruford has deservedly received attention and accolades for his contributions. More than twenty-five years into the career of Yes, however, I still don't think anyone has caught up with the brilliance of what Chris Squire has been doing—with the bass guitar, with music.

Of course, many people (especially other bass guitarists) will tell you that Squire is a great "bass player," but his contribution really goes far beyond that. He has simply done things with the bass guitar, and with music, that are unlike what anyone else has done. For this reason, Squire's overall contribution is missed—no one knows what to compare his work to, or what scale of comparison to place it on.

(It may be, unfortunately, that any crucial contribution to a larger musical picture that was initiated with the bass guitar would be missed, because of expectations of what the instrument is about. More recently, in large part because of the influence of both Jaco Pastorius and, in a different way, certain ultra-funky bassists such as Bootsy Collins and Flea, the contribution of the bass guitar has been noticed. Especially in the latter cases, however, this has been where the role of the rhythm section as such has not been transformed but has instead moved to the forefront of the music—the "bottom" has moved to the top, you might say. I have mixed feelings about this, but that's a discussion for another time.)

As discussed earlier, Squire's early musical experience was as a chorister at St. Andrew's Church in London, whose choir was quite likely the best in England at the time. As every fan of Yes knows very well, Squire's voice is an integral part of the vocal harmonies that distinguish the group; on his solo album, *Fish Out of Water,* Squire demonstrates that he is more than capable as a lead vocalist. What also stands out is the role that this choral experience must have played in Squire's development as a bass guitarist, in his sense of melodic development, harmony, and counterpoint, and in his sense that the bass voice could be the equal of all of the other voices in the "choir." (So as to not cause confusion, I should note the obvious—namely that, as a singer, Squire is not a bass.)

Given the general atmosphere, in the late sixties, of experimentation in rock music (and most every other sphere of human activity), it was probably unlikely that a person of Squire's musical background would turn out to be just another bass player who laid down the bottom. In particular, we should note the influence of two bass guitarists whose groups were in the forefront of innovative rock music: Paul McCartney and John Entwhistle had already carved out a large role for their instruments.[28] Squire has remarked that he wasn't interested in pop music at all until he heard the Beatles, "who changed [his] life." Around 1965, Squire "saw the Who, and John Entwhistle became a major influence." "I had always played with a pick because I hated the dull, boomy tone most bassists had. John was using a pick then—and his massive, cutting sound and integral parts were inspirational."[29] Significantly, the vehicle for much of McCartney's and Entwhistle's work in the late sixties was the Rickenbacker 4001 bass guitar. Squire obtained one of the first few of these instruments to be sold in England, and it seemed this pairing of musician and instrument was a marriage made in heaven. Despite the fact that Squire has played other axes over the years, he is clearly identified with the Rickenbacker—as well as with the use of a pick, Rotosound Roundwound strings, a very trebly tone setting, and full coverage of the fingerboard.

These elements contributed to a style that, even from the first Yes album, was both unique and controversial. It has certainly been common for some to say that anyone who plays with a pick all of the time is probably "not a real bass player"—notice how this feeds nicely into the "that ain't rock'n'roll" claim made about Yes more generally—and possibly a "frustrated guitarist" as well. On the other side of the equation, the uniqueness of Squire's style is possibly most seen in the fact that Squire has many admirers but few real imitators.

To be fair, while Squire, especially in the main sequence, rarely played what might be thought of as a "conventional" bass line, there is no doubt that Chris's ever-unwinding spring provided something like a groove, or, even better, what might be called a feeling of *propulsion*.

One of the fascinating aspects of the music of Yes in the main sequence was the way that the division of musical labors in the band was very unconventional. Seeing this is, again, integral to understanding the way that Squire's bass lines functioned in the music. In almost all rock music, even that of a fairly experimental sort, there is generally a groove that is continually set down by at least one musician, a kind of anchor for the music. In almost every case, this role is reserved for the rhythm section, or, barring that, the bass player. For instance, even in the case of very creative and experimental groups such as King Crimson or the Mahavishnu Orchestra, the bass guitar is usually playing a fairly conventional line, sticking fairly close to the root of the chord. (Perhaps it is significant that both of these groups were led by guitarists. We might also note that Crimson changed somewhat on this score when they had John Wetton as their bassist—but then, the percussionist in this period was none other than Bill Bruford!) Yes did something quite different in this regard, something quite fascinating to listen to: in most of their songs and extended pieces from the main sequence, the "anchor" function was distributed *throughout* the band, so that, even though there is a strong center, it is rarely located in the playing of just one of the musicians. Returning to the earlier description of the analytic structure of this distribution, my guess is that this is something that evolved in the band, but that Squire's emerging style was the spur. Bruford noted (in the *Yesyears* video), for instance, that Squire's tendency to play high on the neck caused him to find different drum sounds that could cut through the high frequencies of the Rickenbacker—apparently this was the origin of the distinctive "bonk" heard in "Roundabout," which is produced by lowering the snares on the snare drum (so that the drum in effect becomes a very high-pitched tom-tom). And from there we get the ripple effect throughout the band, to the point where the term, "rhythm section," no longer applies.

(Later on we will take up the question of how this ripple effect worked in a different way when Alan White came into the band. For now, suffice it to say that, whereas Bruford brought a previously unknown level of jazziness to Yes's synthesis, there is a kind of "orchestral" feel to White's playing that is original—and, to my mind, much underrated—in its own right.)

Even listening to songs from the first two albums one can hear the elements of the more mature style. This may seem a strange comparison to make (and I doubt that there was any direct influence), but the thickness of Squire's lines from songs such as "Survival" and "The Prophet" remind one of John Coltrane's "wall of sound" approach to the tenor saxophone (give a listen to *Giant Steps,* especially). The neat trick here is that Squire could play so many notes without sounding muddy, a feat much aided by the trebly, cutting tone of the Rickenbacker. (In this connection it is interesting to note that, on some songs with more conventional bass lines, such as "Sweet Dreams" or even "To Be Over," Squire played a Fender bass guitar.) With the closing part of "The Prophet," as well as "Astral Traveller," Squire developed a very punchy, almost "stabbing" sound that would be used to good effect on subsequent albums.

To carry the Squire-Coltrane analogy just a little further, we see in both cases a radical departure from the "blues orthodoxy" that has reigned for large parts of the histories of both jazz and rock. (However, at least in jazz there is more the understanding that the music is entitled to develop an avant-garde, whereas critics have almost universally condemned such a development in rock music.) In both cases there is a radical redistribution of the rhythmic center, and therefore a seeming break with what counts as "real" jazz or rock. Both Yes and Coltrane were accused of taking their respective musics into the stratosphere—the idea being that one could not go there and still retain a vital connection with the majority of music listeners. Unfortunately, John Coltrane's life was cut short before he could see whether or not he could retain or rebuild the mass audience for his music. It's true, in the last couple of years of his life a good many people were questioning his direction. But Coltrane didn't live to see the late sixties, in which experimentation was more the *popular norm,* when musicians and artists and, for that matter, political theorists and activists and people in the streets were *expected* to take an experimental approach to life, the universe, and everything. ("Be realistic, demand the impossible!" was a popular slogan of the day.) Yes, on the other hand, were very active during this period, and they were also very popular. But this gets into questions and themes that I would like to save for later chapters. However, we might simply restate the point that the music of Yes, spurred by Squire's bass guitar innovations, were a decisive and radical refusal of the blues orthodoxy. We will have to come back to the question of whether this refusal extended to the very spirit of the blues and therefore, some would say, the spirit of rock music as well.

With the group that created *Fragile,* Yes was made up entirely of virtuoso musicians. Most bass guitar players, undoubtedly, would have lost their way in all of this. After all, so much is already going on in the group pieces on *Fragile,* why not let the bass fall back to a more conventional position? As I've said, this is precisely what happened in most progressive rock groups. But, for once and in an entirely singular way, the contribution of the bass player on *Fragile* and subsequent albums in the main sequence was absolutely crucial and in every way the equal of all the other parts.

Indeed, of all of the Yes albums, Squire probably pushed the Rickenbacker bass to its "trebliest" and "springiest" (it's only appropriate that we make up some new words to describe this new style) on *Fragile.* As mentioned before, with "Roundabout," Squire's "spring" seems to be unwinding in the opposite direction to that of the rest of the group, while "Long Distance Runaround" is built around the bass figure.[30] (It is interesting to compare the versions of "Long Distance" on *Fragile* and the *Yessongs* live album with an acoustic version of the song that the band played on the *Relayer* tour—there is a snippet of this version on the *Yesyears* video. Without the bass line we have an almost completely different song.) In "South Side of the Sky" and "Heart of the Sunrise," the songs that close sides one and two of the album, respectively, the bass cuts like a knife, and the pace of the line is dizzying.

These general strategies, the stabbing knife, the wall of sound, the contrapuntal spring, and even a kind of propulsive, syncopated repetition (for example, in the instrumental "war" section of "The Gates of Delirium," from *Relayer*) served Squire well during the main sequence. With *Relayer* yet another element was added to the arsenal: funk. Not that Yes became "funky"—there was little likelihood that the thoroughly English lads (even with the inclusion of the Italian-Swiss Patrick Moraz) were going to encroach much on the territory of the Ohio Players or Iseley Brothers (or even the Average White Band!). But there were moments of jazz-funk fusion on *Relayer* that seemed unlikely for the group and yet were, as with many other influences, incorporated seamlessly into the larger whole. Despite not being a "real" bass player to some, Squire practically waxed funkadelic (Everybody say Bootsy!) in the synthesizer-jam section of "Sound Chaser," and there is a funky part in the instrumental middle section of "Gates of Delirium" that takes syncopation to a whole new level.

Comparing *anyone* with John Coltrane will get you in trouble in some circles, as will comparing anyone with Jimi Hendrix (in the first case, and even in the second one, I have to admit to subscribing a little bit to these musical theologies myself). But there is a comparison to be made: the only other musician who seems to have had Squire's ability to sing a line that was completely independent of the line played at the same time on his respective instrument was Hendrix. Generally it is hard enough to play bass and sing—it's quite a bit easier to play rhythm guitar and sing, because then both lines are going in the same direction. Hendrix would play lead guitar or very angular chord progressions and sing over that, and Squire does something similar—both to an uncanny degree.

Going for the One is a fine album, overall, and "Awaken," which takes up most of side two, is one of Yes's best extended pieces. Significantly, however, it seems that Squire and Alan White, while not exactly tame in their contributions, play something more like a standard rhythm section role on parts of the album. At least they are closer to this role when compared to their own earlier contributions to Yes albums (even if, when compared to what most bass guitarists and drummers are doing on most rock albums, Squire and White are still pretty "out"). Perhaps this is only apparent in retrospect, but, with twenty-twenty hindsight, one can see the beginnings of a turning point in the development of the band and Squire's basswork. We will pursue this question, of a turning point in progressive rock, indeed, of the end of the progressive rock era, in greater length starting at the end of this part. What I want to emphasize here, however, is that this end was foreshadowed by a change in the innovative style of Chris Squire.

Before we take up this latter question (as part of understanding what Squire was up to in the main sequence), however, let us turn to a remarkable piece of music, "The Fish."

Squire's solo contribution to *Fragile*, "The Fish," is one of the singularly interesting moments in the development of the bass guitar. While the piece includes percussion and vocal harmonies, the heart of the piece is a kind of "orchestral arrangement" of multiple bass guitar tracks. "The Fish" is based on two main themes, the first being the familiar harmonics at the twelfth and seventh frets (EADG, BEAD), the second a melody based on the latinate scientific term for a kind of fish, "schindleria praematurus." As the music is printed in the *Yes Complete* (Deluxe Edition) songbook, the first set of harmonics is played in one measure of 4/4, while the second set is in a measure of 3/4. I don't know if the music is written this way just to be cute, since it seems that this could also be written as a single measure of 7/4. All the same, Squire continues Yes's long-standing avoidance of 4/4 rock rhythms.

The development of the piece depends on the Bach-like extrapolation of the harmonic material generated in the interplay of these two themes. Ultimately there are seven or eight themes running through the piece (depending on what counts as a theme), each one representing a different possibility of the bass guitar's range. While this description may make "The Fish" sound like an exercise of sorts, like Bach's many "exercises" (for example, the Suites for cello, which, until taken up by Pablo Casals in this century, languished in obscurity), Squire's piece rewards repeated listening. I have often wished for an entire album of works such as this.

"The Fish" is also a nice feat of record engineering by Eddie Offord and Gary Martin. Multitracked bass guitars can easily get very, very muddy after about the third or fourth track. "The Fish," which has many more tracks than that (I don't know how many, exactly, but the group was using a thirty-two track studio at that point), is a model of clean sound. Given that careful engineering is an integral part of this bass guitar orchestration, and given the "early classical" flavor of the composition, one might expect "The Fish" to sound more machine-like. Certainly there is that aspect to the work—it can be heard as a smoothly running, very metallic machine. And yet there is a friendly and warm undercurrent to "The Fish," which erupts to the surface at the end when the vocals come in.

The live "Fish," from *Yessongs,* opens a whole other universe in its own right. Along with the performance of "Yours Is No Disgrace" from the same album, the live "Fish" raises an issue that is close to the heart of many bass guitar players, namely a musician's ability as an improviser. Squire is not much known as a "jammer," and there are not many recorded (or, at least, released) bits of his improvisational playing. The live version of "Yours Is No Disgrace" features a guitar jam that, driven by the alchemy of Howe's inventiveness and ferocity (a fine answer, indeed, to those who think of Yes as "prissy"), is all the same the sort of jam that only Yes would or could do. The basslines seem a bit stiff, at least at first. When it comes to jamming, it might be said that Squire is no Jack Bruce (check out Cream's *Wheels of Fire*) or Jaco Pastorius.

On the other hand, even in jamming, Squire remains Squire—the result is not always or completely satisfying, but, when the style works in this context, we hear something we haven't heard before. In this light, the reader might give a listen to Squire's playing in what would seem to be a competely foreign context, side two of jazz saxophonist Eddie Harris's *E.H. in the U.K.* (Atlantic, 1974; copies still turn up in used record stores occasionally). Even though he is joined by familiar bandmates Alan White and Tony Kaye, it is clear that, about half the time, Squire doesn't quite know what to do in this setting. But then, about a third of the way into the side's long track, "Conversations of Everything and Nothing" (which clocks in at about sixteen minutes), something clicks, and Chris starts to make his own sort of jazz—to be sure, a weirdly metallic, springy sort. Again, a singular moment.

In some ways, the live "Fish" is simply a showcase for a bass guitar solo. Needless to say, long bass solos are probably even less popular than most long drum solos, and deservedly so. But there are a very few cases where one would like to know what a bass guitarist would make of the opportunity to play a long solo, and I would certainly have an a priori feeling about this in the case of Chris Squire. "Fish" live is an absolutely thorough exploration of the range and power of the Rickenbacker, everything from the quietest, most subtle passages, to pure bombast—and often very startling turns from one to the other. I prefer the soft, subtle passages, especially when Squire does some nice things with transformations on chords.

There is a great deal more to be said about Squire's crucial contributions to the music of Yes, and we will turn to these points as we take up other albums (including Squire's solo album, *Fish Out of Water*). However, I thought it would be a good idea to take a moment and simply begin to specify how these contributions work. There was a time, back in the seventies, when musicians and listeners did a great deal of serious talking about music. There were a few musicians whose work forced people to take a stand—for or against—and this is one of the things that stands out about Chris Squire's style. This strikes me as the highest praise one could offer an artist, that his or her work makes people take a position one way or the other. I talked with many people who hated it and thought that it was not even "real bass playing." There was a point at which Squire was definitely *the* bass guitarist of the moment, winning *Melody Maker* polls, appearing in all the rock magazines, and so on. (Notably, Squire was the first musician after Paul McCartney to win the *Melody Maker* poll for best bass guitarist.) And yet, discussion of Squire has waned, disappeared practically, even as other major contributors on the instrument from the last twenty years or so have remained influential, for example, Stanley Clarke, Jaco Pastorius, Larry Graham. Furthermore, apart from Geddy Lee, perhaps (and less so in recent years), one does not hear the influence of Squire in many bass players. Why is this? The reason is that Squire's classic style requires—and propels the making of—a certain kind of music, and the time when this music was a major style has, at least for the time being, passed.

Perhaps this assessment is not entirely accurate, however—Squire's influence operates on many levels that are just below the surface: the more trebly bass line, the bass line that carries an independent melody, the bass line that does a great deal more with harmony than just emphasizing the root, and the general emancipation of the voice of the bass guitar, making this voice an equal with every other voice in rock music. Many bass players are influenced by Squire's playing without really knowing it (just as many of today's "slappers" may not be able to tell you who Louis Johnson or Larry Graham are), and, I fear, this influence is sometimes unacknowledged because of the way that just mentioning Yes or other progressive rock groups has become very uncool in many circles.

There is one other aspect of Squire's contribution that bears further study. Listen to any Yes album from the main sequence, and you will hear a good many bass lines that are practically complete works in themselves. It seems to me that there is an interesting set (or more than one) of "Squire variations" for bass guitar to be derived by some enterprising musician/arranger.

To be sure, Squire's work on the post–main sequence Yes albums, especially the albums with Trevor Rabin, is also interesting: in some sense, Squire's work there represents a streamlined version of what he did in the main sequence, synthesized with a rapprochement with a more rock'n'roll sound. Significantly, this also goes for the sound of Yes in the Trevor Rabin period. All of this will be discussed in part 3.

The point I've wanted to emphasize, however, is that the synthesis and synergy of structure and vision that drives the music of Yes exists in microcosm in the musicianship of Chris Squire.

Now, without further delay, let us turn to the group pieces on *Fragile.* Perhaps I've delayed this long because I find entering into this period a very daunting task. If Yes provisionally entered the main sequence with *The Yes Album,* which still has one foot in experimental rock, there was something completely *decisive* about *Fragile,* which simply takes things to a whole other level and from which, seemingly, there is no looking back.

"Roundabout"

"Roundabout" challenged and transformed conceptions of music and even conceptions of life for an entire generation of musicians and serious listeners. After "Roundabout," a lot of us got a good deal more serious about making music and grappling with music. Recently, I was looking at a guitar magazine in a bookstore, drawn in by a cover feature on "Fifty Albums that Changed Rock Guitar" (or something to that effect). I opened the magazine with some hesitation, because I had remembered a feature from a couple of years before, in *Musician* magazine, on the "100 Best Guitarists of All Time." Among these 100 was not to be found the name of Steve Howe. But then, as I've said, Ask the musicians. I was pleased, then, to open this guitar magazine and see *Fragile* toward the top of the list (I think it was in the top five, along with The Jimi Hendrix Experience's *Are You Experienced?*, which I think was number one—and I won't argue with that). A little justice, finally! I would wager that any similar feature for any instrument played by the members of Yes would yield similar results— the fact is, just the first ten measures or so of *Roundabout* changed everyone's conceptions of rock guitar, bass guitar, drums, keyboards, and even vocals. What's especially wonderful, then, is the fact that all of this instrumental ingenuity by itself doesn't even begin to add up to the brilliance of the song as a whole.

The opening of "Roundabout" is one of the hooks on which the idea of Yes as "classical rock" is hung. It isn't hard to see why this is the case, for clearly the whole conception of the opening is meant to evoke the sort of structural framework that is typically associated with classical music (especially of the "classical" period, before romanticism). The funny thing is that the "classical guitar" opening is not in fact classical guitar, but instead steel-string, and the piano chord heard in the background of the opening harmonic E (played at the twelfth fret of the first string) could not have been produced "naturally," but only through studio technology (as pianos cannot by themselves well up in volume).

The *brightness* of "Roundabout" from the very beginning heralds a general warmth and celebratory spirit in the song and for *Fragile* as a whole. Certainly this bright side was more evident in the AM radio version of the song many of us first heard in 1972, so that hearing the album version was its own revelation. There, as with almost all of Yes music, the celebration is a bit more complicated. The music does seem to begin in the pastoral England that is never far from the heart of Yes music in the main sequence. Or at least this England is evoked, but from a distance—"twenty-four before my love you'll see I'll be there with you." The opening lines of "Roundabout" are about music, what music can do for the soul, and about personal relationships. Even in the first line of the song, all three common meanings of the word "roundabout" are evoked: the idea of news coming to one in a roundabout way, a merry-go-round, and a traffic circle (the second two meanings are more peculiarly English). Also evoked is the musical idea of the round. Perhaps what this all adds up to is the idea of being drawn out of oneself, by these swirling processes. These processes are in a sense impersonal—as evidenced by the fact that there seems to be no reference for the "they" in "The music dance and sing, *they* make the children really ring." And yet the sensibility here is one of the world that is not simply a thing or an "it," but instead a world that can be celebrated in a personal way, a living world. "I'll be the roundabout"—or, as Yeats said, "How can we know the dancer from the dance?" "The words will make you out 'n out"—the round will draw you out of yourself, toward something larger.

There are four basic parts to "Roundabout": the opening guitar sequence (with a little bit of piano), which is taken up again just before the main instrumental break (here with organ) and at the end of the song; the Em-F#m-G progression that undergirds the opening verses of the song; the chorus, where the electric guitar comes rocking in—this chord sequence also is the basis for the instrumental solos toward the end of the song; and the middle part (coda) of the song, where the flavor of the piece seems to change almost radically. I've called the totality of these parts a "song," though we're obviously dealing with something pretty complicated here. In every part of the song there is the feeling of a cycle, a round, although there is also linearity and progression—both in the succession of rounds that make up the song, as well as in the forward movement of the chord structure in the opening vocal part. Significantly, this forward movement is what stays with the listener when she or he first thinks of the song, even though the lines that partake of this movement are the shorter part of the whole. In other words, the "spirit" of this movement hovers over the whole song and gathers the other parts into a progression—certainly, listening to the song one feels that one has been on a journey, and yet one also feels a sense of home. The recapitulation of the opening line at the end of the coda reinforces this feeling, as does the repetition of part of the opening guitar figure at the end of the song.

With so many different things going on in this song, it is a wonder that none of it sounds forced or contrived. I suppose that some people hear the song this way—it's true, it's not "rock'n'roll"—but the song has a wonderful sense of flow and, in fact, it does rock. Indeed, there are many "Roundabouts," many songs on Yes albums where the idea is to do a piece that stretches the boundaries of rock music while still rocking: "Siberian Khatru," "Sound Chaser," and "Going for the One" would be the other examples from the main sequence. "Sound Chaser," takes this idea to ridiculous and amusing extremes, but then, so does "A Day in the Life." If the opening vocal section of "Roundabout" bends the definition of rock music a good bit, the chorus section ("In and around the lake") brings the song back from the brink. The electric guitar chords cut in like a chainsaw, and everything that was moving in different directions—bass guitar, drums, keyboards—is suddenly lined up, as though a magnet had swept over iron shards. To suit this change, Jon Anderson sings the vocal line in a slightly lower register. This chorus, then, serves as a bit of grounding for the song, even if it too has the character of a round: G-C-F-C-F-C-G.

In fact, there is more going on in the chorus of the song, and indeed in each of the parts, than this sort of description indicates. The feeling in the chorus, of things being lined up, is something of an illusion, a feeling relative to what comes before and after. Another way to come at this is that the chorus is more clearly built up from a guitar chord sequence, with embellishments from the other instruments, and therefore seems more a bit of rock music. The feel of "guitar rock" comes in again during the instrumental section. Even with this chord sequence, however, the drums and bass guitar are working with a complex syncopation that moves the beat around more like erratic tennis players—sometimes hitting the ball after one bounce, sometimes on the fly—than by pounding it into the ground. (Actually, about the only time I can think of where this sort of pounding takes place on a Yes album is "Machine Messiah" from *Drama*. Even the albums with Trevor Rabin, though they have some *heavy* work from the drums and bass, are not heavy-handed in the way that most guitar rock albums are. "Machine Messiah" uses this heaviness as a special, foreboding, effect.)

The idea of an interweaving of personhood with natural processes is perhaps best captured in the new line found in the third verse of the song, "I will remember you, your silhouette will charge the view . . . of distance atmosphere." This is the beginning of a turn in the song toward nature and, more generally toward the *organicism* that informs the music of Yes from this point forward in the main sequence. What may be significant is that "Roundabout" is the only song from *Fragile* that maintains this organicism—the idea of a living world and a living cosmos, with human beings as co-participants in a larger process—throughout; each of the other three group works on *Fragile* have substantial parts and end with the idea of separation from and great difficulties with nature and with other people. We will return to this question when we discuss *Fragile* as a whole.

Despite what some commentators (pro or con) on Yes seem to think, however, even Jon Anderson's most deepfelt hermetic organicism does not simply translate into bliss, pure universal harmony, or ethical neutrality.

This point is amply demonstrated by the middle section of "Roundabout" ("along the drifting cloud . . ."), which represents a major change of mood. The guitar and bass form a strong backbone for the section, with major chords that, played with a different emphasis, might have easily been the basis for a heavy metal tune. However, because of the metallic tone of the bass (oddly enough), and the wiry, slightly strained tone of the guitar, the passage maintains a tenuous, ungrounded feel, the precipitous sensibility of one caught in a storm, one who might be blown over at any moment—"as weather spins out of hand." Moreover, the storm is focused in the drums and the keyboards. Bruford once again contributes some remarkable cymbal work, and the beat is all over the place, puncturing any sense of stability to be gained from focusing on the backbone chords. If the drums are a hard rain, Wakeman brings the swirling winds with synthesizer. In the midst of this storm there is an attempt at a valiant stand, with guitar, bass, and organ playing a rising sequence of major chords that, although the chords come back down a few notches from their highest point, do not come back down to the ground—the major E chord that begins and ends the backbone—established by the backbone sequence. The drums do not let up at all, and the bass seems about to spin out of control as well (in one of those passages that earned Squire the reputation as the bass player who "played so many notes"). All of this reminds me of a Chinese saying that Mao Tsetung was fond of quoting: "The trees may prefer the calm, but the wind will not subside." Whether Yes's music "ends" in infinite peace (the "bliss" interpretation) or infinite struggle (à la Mao's view of things) I'm not prepared to say at this point, but the common view that we can easily settle on the former of these possibilities is beyond easy, it's a cop-out.

The musical and lyrical references of the middle section take us far away from the English countryside (or even a Scotland where "mountains come out of the sky and stand there," as per Mosbø's interpretation; p. 95). In these winds there is both a tropical and a prehistoric feel, or perhaps the idea that humanity is now in no less a prehistoric situation than it was in the time of the pterodactyls: "we stand to lose all time . . . next to your deeper fears we stand surrounded by a million years." When the refrain, "I'll be the roundabout, the words will make you out-'n'-out" comes in, this does not necessarily indicate that the sailor tossed on the roiling sea has reached calm and security. On the one hand, eagles are "searching down on the land"—and eagles, though they are beautiful creatures, are more than capable of dealing a fatal blow to small mammals, including human children. And, on the other hand, going closer to the land, in an attempt to "hold" the land, we find that we are "no more than grains of sand." Danger on every side, or, better said, contingency. This is no straightforwardly blissful organicism.

Rising out of this storm is a return to a seemingly far less dangerous body of water, surely one of those mystical Scottish lochs (and we know that that particular "monster" means no harm), and to the majesty of mountains that, for all that they may overwhelm us, do not seem intent on immediate harm—they are a moment of stillness. But perhaps this is a little dream, a small respite from the storm, because the instrumental solos then come upon us with a vengeance. Then again, it is more likely that we're hearing some proud, celebratory human bombast—yes, for once, this can be admitted, but there is a purpose to it—and yet this is a joyful noise in the wake of a terrible storm and at the foot of the mountain. The celebration is, accordingly, frenzied, with traded licks between Howe and Wakeman reemphasizing the back and forth of the round. If anything, the bridge in between the solos is *scarier* as a demonstration of virtuosity than the solos are themselves. (Yes, it was definitely time for rock musicians to get more serious!)

We have been on a journey to many places, and through many moods. The music in "Roundabout" is an extraordinarily complex fabric—seemingly brittle in places, but perhaps this is only because the multitudinous fibers of the song each have such clarity. If there is a lesson here about contingency, still, there is no denying that "Roundabout" concludes on an upbeat and then a peaceful note. There is no denying, either, that the harmony vocal section at the end of the piece is very beautiful, something very sweet to the ears after the ordeal of the second half of the piece, from the beginning of the middle section on. Perhaps there is another creature present in the song, a creature not as ostentatious as the eagle or as bombastic as humans who have survived the storm might be, but a fellow creature who works away with fine craft all the same, perhaps a more patient fellow. The spider who weaves first from a single strand gives rise to a magnificent matrix and then, having done a fine day's spinning, slips out once again on a delicate line.

"South Side of the Sky"

The storm and travail motifs of "Roundabout" are continued in the second group effort on *Fragile*. Indeed, "South Side of the Sky" might be seen as a kind of inversion of "Roundabout," in that the harsher side of nature is given the predominant place here, with the moment of relief—and more angelic harmonies—coming in the middle of the song. "South" begins with the sound of thunder, wind, and rain, out of which emerges something that could almost be considered a parody of the standard drum intro (the paradigm for which would be one of Keith Moon's long tom rolls). Bruford begins haltingly, a fitting prelude to what has to be one of the most jagged lines ever heard in rock music, even in progressive rock. Indeed, heard only as an instrumental track, it would be hard to see what holds "South Side" together. Clearly, what carries the song and makes the jagged sections somewhat coherent is the vocal line, which somehow drives through this storm while the drums, bass, and especially guitar flail about. Where the mood of the middle section of "Roundabout" is ominous and foreboding, almost resigned, "South Side" opens with a skitterish desperation—again, heard especially in the frantic, out-of-control guitar lines. (Of course, what this means in reality is extraordinary control by Steve Howe.) Occasionally the organ comes on strong to give a feeling of stability ("around the south side so cold that we cried"), but this quickly gives way to a roller-coaster ride in unisonous guitar and bass lines: "were we ever colder on that day a million miles away." In fact, though, we aren't on a roller coaster, but, at best, a white-water raft—but no, even that suggests more stability than is found in the song, and if the vocal line seems more determined, this is the grim determination of people reduced to the pure tactics of mere survival. "Move forward, was my friend's only cry." To make a long story short, and respond to the "bliss" interpretation, the tactics don't work and the people die.

But there is more to it than that. "South Side" is the story of a group of people who get caught in a snow storm and freeze to death. The "million miles away" resonates with the "million years" with which the seafarer is surrounded in "Roundabout," and both speak of an earthly and cosmic immensity beside which humanity pales. After two of the four verses, the respite comes in the form not of real bodily warmth—"of warmth of the sky of warmth when you die"—but instead a heavenly delusion presented in a mode of irony but not skepticism. In other words, the delusion of warmth at the end (of life) does indeed create real warmth in the heart. Musically this warmth is provided by an intervention into the electrically charged, jagged storm by Rick Wakeman's (acoustic) piano. What begins as an extended arpeggio resolves itself once again as a series of cyclical single notes, the mystical round, joined by very understated drums and bass. The rhythm (at first 3/4, then 5/4) and flavor of the whole trio at first seems jazzy (and that is certainly the influence that Bruford is bringing to this section). Once the vocal harmonies come in, however, we are once

again in that familiar Yes territory that defies categorization (and therefore famil-
iarity). There's jazz here, there's a very classical counterpoint, and there's something almost Mediterranean, possibly Italian in its lyrical romanticism. Again we
have an inverse of "Roundabout," where the tropics were the place of the dangerous storm and hovering predators. Now the warmer climes are a delirious
dream, a final feeling of peace before the end.

This middle section represents such a fine use of dynamic contrast; and, it is
nice, too, that a group with one of the world's great guitarists can also have the
wisdom to have the guitar lay out for a bit. In the midst of the unrelenting storm,
the gates of heaven seem to open up: angels come to carry us away, and their
wings are the voices of Jon Anderson and Steve Howe, with Chris Squire's voice
taking the lead over their harmonies.

But this precious moment ends all too soon: the wind will not subside. The
sense of time itself is lost in "all the noise" of the snowstorm. The first two
verses end with the line, "It seemed from all of eternity"; the final two verses,
following the interlude of heavenly warmth, substitute "we" for "it," a significant
change. If the warmth was no more than pure delusion, then this change is
toward mere resignation. Instead, one has the sense of what Wittgenstein called
"the feeling that I am absolutely safe, that no harm can come to me." There is
calm in the midst of the storm, but there is also calm within the storm. For the
"it" to become "we" here is not resignation, but instead both an identification
with the cosmos—"we seemed from all of eternity"—and the expression of a
will to persist. The very idea of the "south side of the sky" might be read as
referring to "this side of the veil," so to speak, beyond which are the mysteries.
But the final line, "we seemed," asserts that the veil cannot be an absolute.

Again Yes has expressed the idea that cosmic vision does not equal mere
neutrality or a quietistic acceptance of whatever fate has in store. This expression is not without a hint of bitterness, however: "South Side of the Sky" begins
with "a river . . . to be crossed," and comes toward the end to the river that "can
disregard the cost." If there is a moment when the wind takes on a heavenly personality, it is also the case that this personality has no words, but only a pure
beauty that may also be without content. (An interesting comparison might be
made with the opening choral section of Ravel's *Daphnis and Chloe.*) Still, the
guitar persists in the end, the jagged voice of the intrepid wanderer—until even
that voice is once again overtaken by the wind.

"Long Distance Runaround"

We begin with a mixture of the swirling winds and the personal relationships
that draw us out, into the roundabout; we then find ourselves confronted with the
overwhelming powers of nature, obscuring even the struggle to hear any human
voice (and the only voice that can be heard can say no more than "move for-

ward"), on the south side of the sky. Feeling already somewhat drained, we turn the record over, and now we are decisively in the realm of the social and the interpersonal.

(I don't want to get back into the issue of LPs versus CDs, but the fact is that the organization of experience is quite different for each, and the space that exists and physical activity required at the end of side one of the *Fragile* LP is a good example of this.)

The playfulness of the instrumental music of "Long Distance Runaround" is very much in contrast to the irony and bitterness of the lyrics. In rock music it is typical to give the writer's credit to the person who composed the main themes of a piece and the lyrics, and Jon Anderson is credited here. Anyone who has heard the acoustic version of the song (mentioned earlier, in the portrait of Chris Squire) knows that this is almost a whole other piece than what appears on *Fragile;* I assume that the acoustic version represents what Anderson wrote, and the fleshed-out *Fragile* version represents the group composition process. This is a useful demonstration of what group composition is all about—quite often what is involved is a theme that one person contributes, and a set of elaborate parts that the other group members integrate into this theme. In the process, it is often the case that the original theme is substantially transformed. (A much bigger example of this sort of thing would be "Gates of Delirium," also credited to Anderson.) There is another significant aspect of this process that especially needs pointing out here. One of the stark differences between the acoustic version of "Long Distance" and the *Fragile* version is that the latter has an amazing bass line. I assume that this bass line was written by Chris Squire (just as I assume that the guitar lines in "South Side of the Sky" were composed by Steve Howe, though the song is credited to Anderson and Squire). It is standard practice that the composition of a bass line does not enter into the credit for the composition of a piece of music. (This has changed a little bit in recent years, both because of the more liberated and up-front role of the bass guitar in recent rock music, and because there are more lawyers involved these days.) In the case of Squire and his approach to the bass guitar, however, clearly an expanded definition of composition is called for. I'm not saying any of this to take credit away from Jon Anderson, but more to point toward (1) an amazing bass line that is a representative example of Squire's general approach, and (2) the fact that there is a point in most of Yes's music where the individual contribution gives over to group composition. Indeed, Bill Bruford has referred to the group's composition process in this period as "democratic to a fault." (Clearly, too, this is the school where Bruford himself learned about composition.)

Ahem . . . back to the playfulness. The two main instrumental melody lines in the song are found in the guitar and electric piano, on the one side, and the bass guitar and drums, on the other. Each line in its own right seems to fold back in on itself at a dizzying pace, like those squirrels who can't seem to decide whether they want to run out in front of the car or scramble up the tree. The bass line is about as unexpected as any you will ever hear, and the opening and middle instrumental sections of song are great examples of Yes's rethinking of the rhythm section. Somehow the whole thing stays anchored—if barely—but the anchor is not to be found in the activity of any single instrumental line.

Even in the vocal part, where the bass guitar and drums are the main instrumental underpinning, there is only one little section where the rhythm is "pounded home," and that is almost a teaser—the part underneath "Did we really tell lies, letting in the sunshine." Otherwise the bass, especially, circles around the area where a more typical bass line would find itself.

As with the chorus of "Roundabout," when Jon Anderson comes in with the vocal line in "Long Distance" there is a feeling—which from a more coldly analytical stance is once again something of an illusion, a trick-of-the-ear—that things have momentarily fallen into line. Anderson's lyric then becomes both a declamation—and Jon can certainly declaim, as we will see in other examples— and a reflection, basically on a relationship that was a lost cause, a relationship that went sour sometime in the past. There is a sadness and bitterness over this: "I still remember the dream there." There is also the sense that everything in this relationship was either topsy-turvy or impossibly hard: the summer is cold, anger melts to stone—if that's the best that can be achieved, then there isn't much hope here. Patience has run out: "Did we really count to one hundred?"

What to make of the contrast in lyrical and instrumental content? In the context of the lyrics, I take the playfulness of the instrumental lines to bespeak a certain wistfulness, the feeling that something good could have happened—but ultimately didn't, and, again, a certain bitterness. This is captured especially in the last lines of the song, when the questions, "Did we really tell lies," "Did we really count to one hundred?" are repeated, before the last line, which asserts that this was done out in the open, under the shining sun. In other words, How could we have done this? But, we did.

Of the four group pieces on *Fragile,* "Long Distance Runaround" is less an "epic" (with Yes, of course, we have the "mini-epics," the epics, and the epics of near-Wagnerian proportions) and more like a song. But, at the expense of sounding pretentious, I think that we can assert with some confidence that an adequate reduction (one that captures the complexity of all of the lines) of the song for, say, piano and voice, would yield what in classical music is called an "art song" (or *Lieder*).

"Heart of the Sunrise"

Of necessity, the first album by Yes that has both feet in the progressive rock arena, an album where Yes aimed to make a definitive statement about what it was doing with music, with structure and vision, had to have a dramatic finale, and "Heart of the Sunrise" is indeed dramatic. The cycle is completed, the spheres are fully set out: "Roundabout" is persons and nature in the large; "South Side of the Sky" is more focused, primarily on nature; "Long Distance Runaround" is also more focused, almost entirely on the interpersonal (with the slightest ironic reminder that the sun continues to shine while we are up to our machinations). Now we return to the more panoramic view, and consider the sphere that has thus far been underrepresented: the social.

And yet this is the social arena from the standpoint of alienation. After the warmth and fibrousness (if that is a word) of "Mood for a Day," we are quite suddenly and rudely plunged into what sounds like the world of a person gone nuts. The bass-heavy opening line of "Heart" charges along with the frantic delirium of someone who is screaming, "Let me out of here, let me out of here!"—only to stop and realize that he doesn't really know where "here" is. This moment is captured by the warped organ sound that Rick Wakeman provides at the end of the opening line. Run. Stop. Run. Stop.[31]

This initial alternation of frenzy and stasis is interrupted by what seems to be a momentary solution to the madness, in the form of a knife-edged groove provided by Squire. The alienated but driven soul has come to a modus vivendi of sorts, life as a sly character of the underground. The bass line is furtive, searching, slightly smarmy. Bruford's syncopation thickens the atmosphere of the demimonde. Along with his work in the vocal harmony section of "South Side of the Sky," this is perhaps Bruford's best work on the album. He really establishes here what has become his trademark, the ability to create spaces that are felt just as strongly as a sharp strike of the snare drum—the absence that is felt as a presence (as Derrida once put it). In this Bruford is different from almost every other rock drummer, and it is this sort of finesse that has earned him his well-deserved reputation as one of the world's best percussionists. Obviously there is a synergy between Bruford's use of contrasts and group composition that integrates such contrast. Bruford is one of the composers of "Heart," along with Anderson and Squire. But the element of spacing that is used to such great effect in this opening section of "Heart" wonderfully foreshadows the most dramatic aspect of the vocal part of the song, namely the spaces immediately following Jon Anderson's emphatic "Sharp . . . Distance . . ." Emerging from some dark alley, Howe's snaky guitar fills out the cast of characters, while minor chords from the string setting of Wakeman's Mellotron provide an ominous backdrop of towering skyscrapers.

Throughout this second introductory section, the music is dominated by the bass guitar. This could be heard as a solo by Squire, and, in concert performances, this section is presented somewhat as though it is a solo. This is not a bass solo, however, but instead a piece of music that foregrounds the bass (and to a slightly lesser extent, the drums) as any equal voice in the ensemble might be foregrounded in any given section. While on the subject of bass guitar, though, let me mention that this section does provide a good example of where the trebliness of the Rickenbacker, which might undercut the strength of the bass voice, is balanced by the instrument's sustain and thickness of tone.

Even as the scene is set for questionable characters living on the edge, there is a buildup toward a repetition and extension of the frantic opening section. The pressure coming especially from the drums and guitar is palpable, even if also subtle, until the very end of the "underground" section, where Bruford gives the signal, in the form of two sets of four beats each, and our lost soul is running frantically once again. This time there are only very short moments of relief, although these are more playful than disorienting, as they were before. When real relief finally comes, there is no more energy for the marginal existence of the demimonde, but instead the feeling of being completely drained.

Out of this state comes a purely reflective moment, Jon Anderson's plaintive and fragile singing presented with the minimal accompaniment of fingerpicked chords on the guitar. In some sense the theme of the lyrics continues the question raised at the end of "Long Distance Runaround," in that the singer asks how his life could have gone in the direction that it has. In "Long Distance" the question is asked of a "we" that no longer exists. In "Heart," there seems to be no "we" to begin with. But this is not quite the case: "Love comes to you and you follow." There is someone—or is this only the illusion of a someone that turned out to be only some*thing*?—that drew our protagonist into the city, only to abandon him. The refrain, "on to the heart of the sunrise," might be interpreted as a signal that even those who feel lost and alienated in the city can still "find spiritual fulfillment" (Mosbø, p. 115). That interpretation is glib and unwarranted: the emphatic statement, "Sharp. Distance," even when stated more as a desperate plea (as in the first verse) rather than a bitter declamation (as in the last three instances), is the expression of one whose world has been shattered. This is the expression of a person who doesn't have any answers to the questions that his own life raises: "How can the wind with its arms all around me"? This person has found three supposed alternatives to this state of disaffection, and all of them are found wanting: the all-too-cool world of the clever character (the character who is so cool that he says nothing); abdication to illusion—"Lost on a wave that you're dreaming"; and abdication to glibness and superficiality—"Dreamer easy in the chair that really fits you." I take this last line as a comment on the possibility of just giving up on any kind of personal depth or committed grappling with the world, and just trying to find a comfortable place from which to ride out the whole sorry affair.

In the end, the protagonist refuses to trade his alienation for any of these false solutions. The mood of "Heart" is sometimes momentarily playful. Sometimes the protagonist can at least tolerate his alienation, as when a purely phenomenological description is given in an almost wistful, amused tone: "Lost in their eyes as you hurry by." What could be more alienating than to know that, to the great mass of the people around us, as individuals we are no more than another bit of light striking the surface of the retina? And yet, for a moment one could step back and see this merely as an interesting philosophical problem. But only for a moment. These themes, both instrumental and lyrical, alternate and intertwine, but in the end our lost soul sings his anomie with defiance: "I feel lost in the city"!—better this than to be "found" and "at home" with the cool, the glib, or the illusory. Better this, and then to run, frantically, once more.

If there is a more affirmative point to be made regarding the condition of urban alienation, of anonymity and anomie, of sheer disconnectedness in the midst of "so many around me," the group does not make this point within the confines of this song, but instead perhaps with *Fragile* as a totality. Let us turn, then, to that level of analysis.

Summary

Certainly the standard conception of Yes is not of a group that deals very much in tragedy and despair. By its many fans, the group is seen as a great well of hope and affirmation; by its many detractors, the group is seen as a bunch of blissed-out hippie throwbacks who haven't learned the great lesson of cynical realism. In emphasizing what may seem to be the more depressing themes of the group works on *Fragile,* my aim is not at all to dispel the idea of an affirmative, indeed utopian, core of what Yes has accomplished, but instead to show that this picture is more complicated than is often understood and, still more, to show that Yes's utopianism has great depth and richness. Only a very superficial "affirmation" would hold that there is no crying in heaven, that things look bad for awhile, but then, somehow, everything is really all right and everything works out in the end. This is the "affirmation" of what Herbert Marcuse called "affirmative culture"; this is the affirmation of the three-minute pop song and the TV sitcom, where nothing bad ever really happens—at worst there might be some mild embarrassments, and the rest of the time we're in la-la land and on the way to McDonald's.

This affirmative culture is a false utopia, as most people realize when they turn off the TV and go to bed. If there is a *real* utopian core to what Yes has done, it does no service to that core to interpret it under the categories of affirmative culture (including the more recent category of New Age bliss).

How is it that most of the themes from the group works on *Fragile* could testify to tragedy, alienation, bitterness, contingency in the face of the overwhelming largeness and impersonality of nature and of mass society, and so on and yet there be an underlying current of hope?

The whole of *Fragile* is a set of musical works, produced for the most part through a process of collective composition, arranged in a certain order, and presented in a certain way—namely, wrapped in artworks by Roger Dean. On the front cover of *Fragile,* one sees the Earth whole and connected, obscuring the dark, unfathomable depths of space. The continents are connected, even, by a white road, one might even say a shining path—which is a potent symbol from Native American mythology.[32] (I'm not saying that the use of such a symbol is entirely intentional.) However, hovering over the Earth is a space-faring ship. I put it this way because this wooden-looking contraption is hardly the gleaming metallic spaceship of most science fiction adventures. We are suspended here in a world between science fiction and magic, a blending of the organic and the technological. This ship is surely wondrous—but would we risk our lives in a voyage on this ship? What would compel us to take such a risk? Tucked into the record sleeve there is a booklet of photos of the group members with their families, instruments, dogs, and a long list of thank-yous from Rick. On the front of this booklet is another work from Roger Dean, this time of some quasi-reptilian creatures who are kind of cute and vaguely creepy. Do you want to pet them, to have them running around in your apartment? They live on "our" planet, too, you know. On the back cover is a painting of a single mountain climber struggling up the sheer, thin face of a rock formation that goes straight up, seemingly without limit. Finally, on the back cover of the album, the Earth is coming apart, with one piece flying into space—and with dark blue space seen in the place that this piece had previously inhabited, a catastrophic hole in the previously round (about) sphere.

Where, then, is the space for hope? For one thing, there is hope in the practice of meticulous craft at the service of formal innovation. To do something original and to do it very well, this tells of a possible future. "Nothing is hard in this world if you dare to scale the heights" (Mao). But it is not the case that the formal innovation of *Fragile* overwhelms the tragic or desperate element and in doing this achieves a pure affirmation. "Pure affirmation" is not affirmation, or even a good dream. In Yes's organicism, connections are contingent, connections can be shattered, and meaning is difficult to find. The world that must be affirmed and transformed is a *fragile* world, where risks have to be taken and real loss is inevitable and not to be wished away.

In their group works, Yes achieved something great with *Fragile*. This greatness is not diminished overly much by whatever problems there might be with a couple of the solo works, or with the idea of having such works interpolated into the album in the first place. My reservation only has to do with whether or not each of these works really contributed to the album as a whole. Roger Dean's artwork does make an important contribution, not only to the album, but to the idea of a "total work" (what highbrow-types call the *Gesamtkunstwerk,* the total work of art, for which Wagner's operas are the paradigm). With so many instrumental and vocal lines at play, the music could have gotten awfully tangled up. The production work of Eddie Offord is a crucial contribution to the clarity of *Fragile* and subsequent albums—Mosbø rightly compares Offord's contribution to George Martin's work with the Beatles (p. 19). Following in the footsteps of the Beatles, and expanding on their innovations with the help of greater instrumental skill and more advanced technology, Yes was expanding the idea of the "rock group," even the progressive rock group. And yet, in contrast to much of the Beatles' history, the focus remained on the creation of music, and Yes remained a group of fellows who were making music, a band. Taken as a whole, *Fragile* approached perfection.

Close to the Edge

And then perfection came . . .

Nothing prepared listeners for *Close to the Edge*. There had been experiments with odd rhythms, polytonalities, atonality, thematic and lyrical visions, and sheer complexity before, frcm *The Rite of Spring* to *Sergeant Pepper's* to *Bitches Brew* (Miles Davis) to *Lizard* (King Crimson). In rock music, however, no one had achieved such an extended integration of these elements before. And, in more general terms, *Close to the Edge* as a totality was and is an original and moving work.

Close to the Edge does present one large problem as far as music theory and criticism goes, at least in my own case: there is nothing that I would change about this piece of music. In all of the Yes albums up to this point, there are pieces here and there that might have been done differently—perhaps a bit better, or better not done at all. If one way to define perfection in a work of art is in terms of a certain completeness, where everything fits together in the right way and there is nothing lacking, then *Close to the Edge* is perfection, to my mind. This definition of perfection perhaps makes it sound as though the music is "workmanlike," a term generally used to damn with faint praise. Instead, *Close to the Edge* is music that takes risks, it is music that is infused with great craft, and it is music that has a sophisticated vision that works on many levels; and this is music with passion.

Well, actually, there is one thing that I would change: the order of the pieces as they are presented on the album. I always felt that the album should have led off with "Siberian Khatru," followed by "And You and I," building up, finally, to "Close to the Edge." That is the way that I hear the pieces, as a kind of complete concert program (perhaps I am influenced, too, by the fact that Yes performed the works in this order on their concert tours). From the standpoint of putting out a record, there might have been other priorities—for example, the fact that, in the days of LPs, what was on the first side made a big impression on people. If someone didn't like what was on the first side, he or she might have been disinclined to flip the record over. But there is a certain flow to the music in the order that I have proposed, beginning with the rocking and playful "Khatru," as a rousing jump-start to the experience, then taking up the more introspective "And You and I," and finally presenting the pièce de résistance, "Close to the Edge." I beg the reader's indulgence, therefore; my plan is to discuss the pieces in my preferred order. (I will again ask the reader's indulgence when we discuss *Relayer,* where I have similar preferences. For what it's worth, I think the fellows got it right on *Going for the One.*) The additional logic to this order is that, to begin with "Close to the Edge" and end with "Siberian Khatru" may lead to the impression, with regard to the whole album, that the mountain has brought forth a mouse.

Close to the Edge is in many ways a progression, in terms of both music and lyrics, from what the band had been doing from the very beginning, and certainly since *The Yes Album.* Certain lyrical themes remain, but come through even stronger: the general concern for the Earth, for ecological issues; the anti-machismo portrayal of women; the possibility of what might be called a radical togetherness, a utopian-communitarian perspective; an engagement with religious traditions and teachings, East and West (as well as the theme of a crossing of East and West); and everything that threatens these concerns and renders them dangerously fragile. This is also the case for the musical material that makes up the total work: the displacement of the traditional rock rhythm section, the use of odd time signatures and keys (sometimes verging on the atonal and certainly entering into the polyrhythmic realm), the use of a very large array of tone colors, and the development of large, complex, extended structures. All of these elements were there in the beginning, even with *Yes,* but each of these elements is now taken to a qualitatively higher level and flawlessly integrated. It is as if some omniscient being had been given these elements and told to bring out the greatest possibility inherent in them. The elements were plenty good to begin with, and stirring Steve Howe and Rick Wakeman into the mix didn't hurt either! But *these* elements of Yes music have led to something very important: a speaking of the green language rarely seen since the time of Blake and Whitman. And we need that.

"Siberian Khatru"

When progressive rock first got going around 1968 or 1969, the longer "song" was more the stock-in-trade, rather than the "epic," which came later. In experimental rock more generally, as well as in progressive rock, one of the first barriers that had to be broken through was the idea of the two-minute-thirty-second song for top-forty radio play. The Beatles and then the Moody Blues and Pink Floyd led the way, followed by that great opening blast of the progressive rock era, "21st Century Schizoid Man." The aim was to stretch out, to take up musical ideas that required six to ten minutes for their proper elaboration. Within this sub-genre there is yet another subset of works that are distinguished by the fact that, for all that they clearly may be works of experimental or progressive rock, they did indeed rock—as did Crimson's scary heavy-metal Schizoid jazz, Yes contributed to this sub-genre from their first album, with songs such as "Survival." With "Roundabout" Yes perfected their work in this sub-genre, and went on from there to create additional works that pursued this possibility.[33]

The song begins with what might be taken as a trademark of rock guitar, a bit of the old "chicken scratch." Now this doesn't sound very *graceful,* of course, but Howe does signal quite nicely that we're in for a romp. Indeed, the short guitar introduction demonstrates very well the way that, in the larger scheme of his playing, Howe recapitulates the whole history of the guitar—not only rock guitar, but classical, jazz, country, Appalachian, and so on. Here he takes a figure that strikes one with its raw immediacy, and yet he also immediately begins to fold it around and appropriate it to a new synthesis. (A similar, but more extended, example of this is the steel guitar opening on "Going for the One.") Things get complicated awfully quickly in "Khatru," so, by the time you realize that Duane Eddy has already entered and left the stage, there seems to be an entire orchestra playing. Actually, there is one other crucial introductory element to this build up, namely, Squire's stabbing bass notes, accentuated by Bruford. Then comes the "orchestra," but one made up of players from both the classical and jazz worlds: Wakeman's grand, sweeping strings on the Mellotron, Bruford's splashy swing drumming (and, as always, very precise cymbal work), tied together by an enormously *big* bass line—a "walking line," that would be the standard term for it, but there is nothing standard about this particular walk. No, this is an animal that is both substantial and yet quick and nimble. In any case, in these opening bars we find in microcosm the kind of complete synthesis of styles that is a trademark of Yes—and it all flows beautifully.

Just as quickly as the complicated synthesis emerges, there is a pulling back, a simplification. The core stands out: a very hard, thick bass line, understated drums, with guitar and vibes (played by Wakeman on the Mellotron, I think) circling around. The vocal line follows this pattern as well, with the first two lines of the verse sung in harmony and the third line simplified into the singular voice of Jon Anderson. The first verse presents two startling images, the "bird of prey" and the "gold stainless nail." In each case, ironies abound. The bird of prey is beseeched to become instead a songbird. (Remember, too, that we know at least one bird of prey from "Roundabout.") And what nail is it that has been "torn through the distance of man," other than the blood-stained nail that held Jesus to the cross, at the summit of Golgotha? Even the coldest inhabited climes on Earth partake of this motion—but this is a hidden motion. The bird of prey become songbird is the transformation within one creature that is sometimes represented by two: the lion that lies down with the lamb. And the lamb is present, if not presented as such, in the next lines: the "holy lamb of God" (Blake) sacrificed. But the motion is hidden, we hide it from ourselves—"hold down the window"; "hold out the morning that comes into view"—and the machinations of power, the supposedly stainless nail, hide it from us: "Cold reigning king, hold all the secrets from you." We don't allow ourselves to experience the movement: "River running right on over my head."

Even as Blake is once again invoked on the purely thematic plane, there is also an invasion of the empirical, in terms of some of the words interjected in between the main lines of the verses: "Out bound, river, blue tail, tail fly. . . ." The phenomenological cast of these lyrics is slightly reminiscent of Wallace Stevens's poetry (I'm thinking, for example, of his "Anecdote of the Jar").

The comparison is a bit overreaching, admittedly, but consider: Stevens presents us with a bewildering mixture of everyday objects, including the seemingly trivial, but there is something much larger (even ominous) going on. In "Khatru," Anderson (who wrote the lyrics) is also creating a mixture, of the everyday with Romantic themes. "Stainless steel" wouldn't and couldn't have been found in English Romantic poetry, but the nail and the lamb are there in abundance; "steel" is not what Anderson, Squire, and Howe sing, but you hear it all the same—cold steel, stainless steel.

In the midst of this "chorus" ("Even Siberia"), as the vocal harmonies turn to the background lines, "out bound, river, blue tail, tail fly," Howe provides a subtle, warm segment of orchestration with the acoustic steel-string guitar. Such segments often pass so quickly in Yes's music that it is easy to forget that they are there. But this forgetting is itself an artfully generated response. When one concentrates closely on the music, one sees that there is so much there. But what Yes does so skillfully, at least in their best moments, is to weave this great amount of material into something that remains first of all *music,* and not simply a demonstration of complexity or instrumental virtuosity. Eddie Offord must again be given all due credit for his masterful production work; the group recognized his contribution by placing a picture of him on the album cover, giving him equal billing with the other members of the band. This moment should be marked, as well, for its demonstration of Steve Howe's ability to orchestrate with different guitar voices. In this, there are very few others in his league. Howe is perhaps overshadowed in this by the presence of Rick Wakeman and by expectations of what the guitar is all about. Truly, in all of his work on *Fragile* and *Close to the Edge,* Howe uses colors masterfully, and extends the possibilities of the guitar—he approaches the instrument first of all as a complete musician.

In the instrumental bridge that follows, and almost as if in answer to Howe's guitar work, Chris Squire provides a nimble bass passage that trips through four notes to the measure like clockwork, against the background of majestic Mellotron strings. This, too, is true symphonic orchestration, the employment of many colors. The vocal harmonies that follow, in the "How does she sing?" verse, are very bright.

The first longer instrumental passage is indeed a wonder, the sort of thing that could come off as completely contrived but instead flows in a way that doesn't call attention to its weirdness. What I'm thinking of in particular is the electric sitar solo by Howe followed by a harpsichord solo from Wakeman. Whereas most other post-Beatles groups, inspired by the Fab Four themselves, would probably highlight the contrast (I'm thinking especially of Gentle Giant here), Yes seems to be making a kind of multiculturalist statement: Why draw attention to the crossing of two different musical cultures? Why not proceed as if there's no big deal about hearing a sitar and harpsichord together? All of this is followed by an electric guitar solo that generates a further synthesis, but here the real action is in the bass and drums, especially Squire's alternation of a cascading line that seems to go up and down at the same time (he is the fish swimming upstream, but he also seems to be the stream itself) with a very heavy pedal-point.

There is yet another interesting coupling in "Khatru," and that is in the extended "words" section—"blue tail, tail fly, Luther, in time," and so on. At first the main support for the vocals here is a very gentle, very beautiful line played by Wakeman with Mellotron flutes. In the background the rest of the group creates a subtle buildup, led especially by Bruford's precise paradiddles on the snare drum. There is something almost military about this, and Wakeman's and Bruford's contrasting parts generate a tension that remains just under the surface. This tension returns and breaks through the surface in the vocal part that interrupts the final instrumental section, but there is also a partial release of that tension into Howe's last guitar solo, where the guitar, bass, and drums simply cook. As this part fades to silence, one is certainly left with the feeling that "something goes on"—the movement, the river. Musically, this is effective, but I actually prefer the ending the group uses on the *Yessongs* live version of "Khatru," where Howe recapitulates the opening guitar figure, the bass and drums drive powerfully as if to hammer home a point, and the singers add the period with what sounds like "bop." I've heard that certain flying saucers, anyway, can move at great speeds and then come to a sudden and complete stop!

(Of course it is problematic to use the term "hammer" in the vicinity of the nail that has been under discussion here, but there's no other word for what Squire and Alan White do at the end of the live version.)

In concluding the discussion of "Siberian Khatru," there are three issues that remain to be raised.

First, we need to somehow square the idea of the "cold reigning king" who "hold[s] all the secrets from you," with the idea that this king also somehow "shelter[s] the women that sing, as they produce the movement." Please—it is no answer to say, "Well, this is *just* a song." Either, for whatever reason (something like intention or something like carelessness), there is a kind of contradiction at work here, or at least a tension that is integral to the lyric, or the "hiding" and "sheltering" functions of the king (or perhaps kingdom) are not really at odds with one another. My interpretation lies somewhere between the "tension" and what might be called the "resolution" view. Even oppressive regimes can "shelter," in the simple sense of "house" or "contain," voices that are in opposition to their oppressiveness. In the same light, we have already heard that the secrets themselves produce the movement, even though the king "holds" these secrets. Then again, the line might be read as an invocation, provocation, or command to the cold reigning king. But there surely remains a tension: a cold reigning king and women that sing are moving in different directions. Indeed, the cold king and gold nail (who else would control the gold other than the king?) are like forces, working against the movement, while the women who sing produce this movement. He who possesses the gold and the nail may feel that he possesses all power, but there is a secret power that erupts from within this very regime.

Second, we see a thematization of gender in "Khatru" that will develop even more as Yes moves further into the main sequence (and, in fact, beyond this sequence). Not only are those who produce the movement of the female sex, but so, apparently, is the wondrous Khatru itself: "How does *she* sing?"—I take it that "she" is a reference to the Khatru. And though the singing women may be imprisoned in the tower of the cold king, there is a warm side of this tower, which the Khatru visits. On this side of the tower, the green language is heard: "green leaves reveal the heart spoken Khatru." The green leaves spread despite and against the cold, the very definition of which is absence of movement.

The thematization of the feminine as secret, sheltered, and the masculine as "reigning" cannot help but play off of longstanding masculinist traditions of the public and private spheres. Mary Wollstonecraft argued that locking women into the private sphere brings about "civil death," the obliteration of women as far as public space is concerned. "Khatru" should be read as a feminist subversion of the reigning system of "sheltering" and secrets—in other words, we'll see who holds the secrets, and also who will sing against the cold.[34]

Finally, What should we make of what I referred to as the "words" section of "Khatru"? While there is clearly a playfulness at work here, one that selects words as much for their sound as for their meaning (but what else have poets ever done?), some of these words are clearly not here by accident. We begin with a bird, and then we come around to "blue tail" and "tail fly." We are concerned with movement, and we come around to "river," "mover," "changes," and "glider." But most significantly, we are concerned with the nail that is "torn through the distance of man," a distance that can be read as both humanity's history and humanity's alienation from itself and the movement, and we come around to "Luther," "in time," "heart gold," "soul mark," "Christian," "changer," "called out," "saviour," and "turn round"—to say the least, and the complete chain of references here is undoubtedly even more complicated. Clearly, Jon Anderson's sense of "Christian" is very complex, indeed very difficult. Without getting too deeply into psychobiography—often dubious terrain, especially when viewed from a distance—we might still wonder what it is for a person raised in the Roman Catholic tradition to invoke Luther. I take it that the invocation is affirmative, because it fits well with the generally this-worldly cast of the larger chain—the turn round (the roundabout again—"the children really ring";

"ring, and you will find me coming") that must take place "in time," not in any glibly "transcendental" frame. And yet the "heart gold," whose value cannot be measured on the scale of the king's gold, constitutes a "soul mark," a secret identification that is not immediately manifest to the reigning, cold world. By the same token, the gold nail *is* stainless, so far as it's cold, antigreen, anti-woman language is concerned: some radical Jew nailed to a tree on the periphery of the empire—so what? How could this conceivably have any significance? Such is the cold arrogance of power, of the nail. But, between the king and the women in the tower, "who holds the ring?"

One very important indicator of what Yes has accomplished is the fact that the analysis I have just presented achieves, I hope, a degree of complexity and depth, and yet it only scratches the surface. In other words, great art invites extended exploration on many levels.

"And You and I"

Divided into four parts, with various recapitulations but also rhapsodic departures, with great dynamic range moving from the folk song to the symphony, and with a sweeping vision in the lyrics, "And You and I" is an epic work in miniature. The story here is one both of individual pilgrimage and utopian dream.

As with "Roundabout," "And You and I" begins with a solo guitar part, this time with twelve-string guitar. Indeed, the beginning of "And You and I" is very tentative, something that it is easy to forget when the piece has built up into a larger-scale orchestral work. In the movement from the initial, crystal-like notes of the twelve-string to the thick tableau of Wakeman's strings, we see the development of "a moment's answers to the dream" into an entire vision. At the heart of this vision is the idea of a togetherness that lies beyond "political ends" which, "as sad remains, will die." Here we may seem to encounter a kind of purely (some would say "merely") utopian fantasy that hopes for a postpolitical space. Certainly this vision is present here, but there is greater sophistication here than the merely middle-class desire that political conflict cease. The vision might even be called "Kantian" in its affinity with the second and third formulations of the categorical imperative: treat others as ends, not as means only, and act so as to bring about a universal kingdom of ends.[35] As persons come into their own, in other words, political ends, whereby persons are means rather than ends, are transcended. "And You and I," therefore, presents a journey of individuals within a society as well as a development of society itself.

It would be tempting to say that, as with "Close to the Edge," "And You and I" seems to emerge out of a musical space that is undefined (the latter leaves this space much more quickly than the former). But, other than a little bit of tuning at the very beginning of the piece, and Steve Howe's signaling to the recording engineer that he is ready to begin ("Okay"), the guitar itself gives form to the beginning. Howe's opening chords are bright and warm, like a kind of blessing. Still, where is this going? This question is answered when Squire comes in with the famous pedal-point line, a succession of D-notes, which functions as a "call to order" or invocation, capped off by the ritual element of Bruford's triangle. Howe's twelve-string with the basic chord structure of the first part of the song, "Cord of Life," along with a brief synthesizer solo from Wakeman, set the essentially "friendly" and reflective tone of the entire piece. It is not hard to hear the continuing interruption of the bass guitar and triangle line as the "heartbeat" of "And You and I," but, in more purely musical terms, this line also provides an interesting counterpoint to the other lines. This counterpoint is perhaps the only underlying tension in a song that is otherwise remarkably free of such tension.

When Jon Anderson comes in, there is an alternation between an ascending line that climbs note by note up an imaginary staircase (or terraced waves, climbing "over the sea to the valley), and a line that at first climbs but then descends to a lower point on the scale. In a way similar to Allen Ginsberg's poetry, the vocal line seems measured to the breath. (Ginsberg credits William Carlos Williams and Bob Dylan as important influences on this matter. We know, of course, that the latter influenced at least Steve Howe a good deal—he named one of his children "Dylan"—so perhaps this influence is manifest here.) This is appropriate to the spirit of the piece, which begins very much as an episode of storytelling with musical accompaniment. (Perhaps the larger frame is that all of the folks mentioned here owe something to the tradition of romantic poetry and therefore romantic balladeers.) In the surging—albeit slowly—movement of the vocal line we have both the wavelike motion of the sea and the development of a spiral, and both images are present in the words of the first verse.

As we discussed in the case of "Siberian Khatru," and indeed with most of Yes's works under discussion here, there is simply too much poetry here for there to be a complete unfolding. The precedent that I aim to establish from this point on is simply that of a sketch and a beginning, an opening of a longer discussion that I hope will be taken up by thoughtful readers of this book. In the longer discussions of pieces from the main sequence that we have undertaken already, I have begun to establish some of the main themes and poetic devices that Yes was working with in *The Yes Album* and *Fragile*. There is more to come: new themes, even greater skill in lyric writing, and a continued and sometimes qualitative development of what was already present. However, with this greater sophistication comes the need for even more extended analysis—and the fact is that not all of this analysis can take place within the finite confines of this book. This goes for the analysis of purely musical form as well. So, again, I hope that I have begun to establish a certain kind of framework for this analysis and discussion—and that you and I, dear reader, will continue to carry on this discussion in other forums.

Having said this, let us note that the first and last lines of the first verse of "Cord of Life" speak of a kind of completeness, albeit in embryonic form—"a moment's answers" (and I take it that a "moment" is necessarily fleeting), "all complete in the sight of *seeds* of life" (my emphasis). This momentary vision of completeness is not yet the achievement of such, however, which requires going out into the world and encountering all that would sever the cords of life. "Life" here is used as a kind of overarching category, something akin to an all-enveloping force that, however, must be actively embraced by that which is within it. There is much here that might be discussed in terms of the "process theology" inspired by the philosophy of Alfred North Whitehead and taken up by Charles Hartshorne and others. This vision, too, is very much present in the novels of Orson Scott Card. In this work, there is a real sense in which the world as a whole could be said to be *alive* (this comes through in a very strong way in the *Tales of Alvin Maker* and *Ender's Game* series of novels by Card). But this does not mean there is an end to striving; instead, this understanding tells us something about the character of striving—that, if anything, the aim of striving is to overcome that force within us that is set against the world.[36] As the first part of "And You and I" turns to the impediments to an active embracing of life, the music becomes a swirl of lines, both vocal and instrumental. Indeed, the first line of the second verse of "Cord of Life" presents a fundamental opposition, "coins and crosses." Only one can win out, but this is not simply an intellectual problem. The process that must unfold is well-captured in the final line of this verse, "watching the world, watching all of the world, watching us go by"—we are watching the world, the world is watching us. But this interactive process has become a mere tangle, a mere confusion, because the cords of life are "broken, locked inside the mother earth."

In the midst of this confusion we find two responses that contrast in tone but unite in purpose. The first of these is the heavily orchestrated theme, led by Wakeman's strings, that sounds out an anthem. (This is the theme that opens "And You and I" in the live version.) The second response, on an appropriately more humble level, is the voice that says, "and you and I reach out for reasons to call." The anthem, symbolic of Mother Earth and the ocean maid—and, in its development, perhaps more evocative of the latter—calls out to individuals who find themselves in the midst of confusion, of the cynical time when the cords of life lay broken, subordinated to political ends. This calling out is almost pure feeling, symbolized very well by the larger-than-life orchestration of this theme. In the midst of the cynical time itself, our seekers reach out for reasons—reasons to believe against the time, reasons to call out to the possibility of completeness in this broken time.

We should note that the idea of the "call" is an important theme in Judaism and Christianity, especially insofar as ethics is concerned. (The most important contemporary philosopher who has dealt with this theme is undoubtedly Emanuel Levinas.) The question might be, What calls us out of the world as it presently exists, toward greater possibilities? Whether from a "schooled" or more "naive" perspective (in some sense, the latter lends even more credence to the vision), these thematics are an integral part of "And You and I."

There are some significant gender thematics present once again—as they are present in all of the works on *Close to the Edge*. "Emotion" is "revealed as the ocean maid"; the Earth is female; the male seekers in the song, soon to be named as "the preacher" and "the teacher," reach out for reasons. How is this more than a replication of the entrenched dichotomy that associates women with emotion and men with reason? In this regard, the song responds on two levels. First, if anything, the traditional Western valorization of reason and knowledge over emotion and care is reversed. Second, the search is ultimately for an intertwining of these aspects of a whole life.

In the second part of the song, "Eclipse," the "anthem" develops in a great wash of strings and steel guitar—one wants to invoke the German, "grosse," for "great," as there is a romanticism here that comes very close to going overboard. What saves this movement is that, before it goes on at too great a length and with too much pomposity, it gives way to the crystal clarity of the twelve-string guitar and then to an unexpected change of direction, a folk song. Here, in part 3, we finally meet the man who "conceived a moment's answers to the dream," as well as the "you" of the work's title: the "preacher" and the "teacher," respectively.

And, once again (or for the first time, if you stay with the order of works on the album), we encounter the nail: "Sad preacher nailed upon the coloured door of time." Interestingly, there may be another play on Luther here; he was famous, of course, for having nailed his theses (his theological claims, which disputed the theology of the Roman Catholic Church) onto the door of the monastery that he was in the process of leaving. What does it mean to be nailed rather than to do the nailing, to be nailed to the door of time? If one is crucified on this door, then is one inside or outside of time—or perhaps in some state that is both and yet neither inside nor outside? The preacher is sad; the teacher is *insane*—one is beat down, the other has lost his mind. The three verses of "The Preacher The Teacher" do not sort out all of these difficulties of finding oneself against the world as it is, of being both inside and outside and feeling oneself to be neither. The folk ballad builds up into a rock song, which builds up into a symphonic work. In the first transition, as Jon Anderson intones, "oo-ooh, oo-ooh," there is an amazing bass line that gathers into itself and releases all the power required to go from the folk guitar to the full band, beginning with a nimble set of notes climbing the scale and then crashing down, ultimately plummeting, with tones as broad as the ocean's horizon. This is appropriate, as the transformations spoken of in the lyrics are simply too large-scale for the participants to get a grip on: "I listened hard but could not see life tempo change out and inside me." But now it is becoming clear, the outside is the inside, the inside is the outside.

It is ironic that the fourth part of "And You and I" is called "Apocalypse," for, in a pretty substantial sense, it is here at the end of the third part that the real apocalypse is occurring. As the music builds up once again to full symphonic strength, the singers (Anderson, Squire, and Howe) join together to sing,

> Coming quickly to terms with all expressions laid,
> as a moment regained and regarded both the same,
> emotion revealed as the ocean maid,
> a clearer future, morning, evening,
> nights with you.

This last word, "you," extends out into the "anthem" musical theme, which itself is drawn out, with some especially dramatic, apocalyptic drumming from Bruford (one of the few times he emphasizes the "bottom kit"—the bass drum and tom-toms—rather than the "top").

When all of this becomes "clarified" into the twelve-string guitar one final time, it would seem that the "apocalypse" has come and gone, despite the title of the final part. We are finally, without knowing entirely how we got here, in a postapocalyptic world, a new world of endless searching and endless calling and being called. Of course, we are already in this world, indeed a good deal more urgently in the world where one must reach out for reasons to call; the utopian vision of the ending of "And You and I" is of a world where we are finally clear on the necessity and goodness and beauty of this reaching. (We might note that the imagery here is quite similar to that at the end of "Close to the Edge.") We no longer seek to avoid this reaching by remaining mired in cynicism and confusion. And yet this vision is not purely organic, and its sense of "completeness" is not one in which there will no longer be seeds of the new, but instead this is a vision of calling and being called "over valleys of endless seas." Contradiction and struggle are not finished, rather they are moved to a higher plane.

"Close to the Edge"

Yes's most developed work up to its time presents the greatest challenges. If *Close to the Edge* as a totality comes about as close to perfection as a set of musical works might hope to, the title piece comes that much closer.

I doubt that I am alone in saying that, when I first heard "Close to the Edge," I wondered what these crazy fellows were up to. Arising out of jungle sounds and a stream flowing nearby, the opening instrumental section of "Close to the Edge" seems out of control, completely chaotic. Instead, this part is *very* tightly controlled; the evidence is in the fact that this wild river of notes and rhythms and timbres has its own discrete parts and intersections, its own underlying logic. There are points where the whole group has to come to together—this stands out especially in the live performances of the piece. In the *Yessongs* film version of "Close to the Edge," for instance, when Steve Howe finally reaches the signature melody that leads into the first vocal section (G-F#-D-E-F#-D-E-F#-D-E-A-A-A-A-A), there is a moment when Jon Anderson gives him a look as if to say, "Well, we pulled that off again!" But still: the opening instrumental section plays with extreme chromaticism bordering on atonality, and with extreme rhythmic variation bordering on polyrhythms, to a greater extent than anything in rock music had before. In a time when originality was valued in rock music, we knew that this opening section was introducing us to something that was going to be very original—and, on first hearing, I imagine that many listeners felt as I did, not knowing whether we were going to be able to wrap our heads around this one. Another way of putting it is that the leap from *Fragile* to *Close to the Edge* was an even bigger one than the leap from *The Yes Album* to *Fragile.*

Howe's opening lead guitar lines are snaky, devious, and devilish sounding, an appropriate introduction to what might be thought of as an extended pagan hymn. But, if such it is, the "paganism" exemplified here is not of the "Satanic" sort, but related instead to the tradition of Wicca and other nature religions. If "Close to the Edge" is to rock music what Stravinsky's *The Rite of Spring* is to Western classical music, we might note an interesting thematic parallel that underlies the formal innovations of each with regard to rhythm and timbre. Both "Close to the Edge" and *The Rite of Spring* seem to come out of an African, specifically a Black African, "non-Western" setting. This element is in fact present in both works. (And one might say that this element is more "authentically" present in Yes's music, as an offshoot of rock music, than it is in Stravinsky's, where there is more than a little mere exoticism.) But both works are also doing something more complex with regard to non-Christian sources, in that *The Rite of Spring* is also subtitled, "Scenes from Primitive Russia," and "Close to the Edge" is appealing to traditions in the British Isles that predate Christianity. However, there is an important difference between these works in this regard as well: whereas *The Rite of Spring* never departs from this "pagan" experience, "Close to the Edge," we might say, works in and through the Christian experience, transcending this experience but not necessarily negating it. (At the expense of being too clever by half, we might say there is a "total mass retain.") Indeed, Rick Wakeman's organ, which is thoroughly frenetic throughout the opening instrumental section, takes a decidedly "churchish" turn in the last measure or so of that section.

Streaming through this apparent chaos, it should be added, is a "bass line" that has nothing in common with this concept as previously understood, accompanied by the primary propulsive element of the section, Bill Bruford's cymbal work and odd, "spaced-out" drum fills.

Out of the seeming chaos comes "order," with the presentation of the chords that support the first vocal lines. Apart from Bruford's disarmingly harmless tom-tom role leading into this presentation, however, there is no let up in intensity. Steve Howe plays these chords on the electric sitar, making that instrument postively *shred*—there has never been anything remotely like it, before or since.

(For a picture and explanation of the Coral Electric Sitar, see *The Steve Howe Guitar Collection,* pp. 68–69.) As the verse begins, Chris Squire gives us one of his most interesting lines, made up of two sets of the note "A," alternating between octaves (three low, then one high, and one low, then three high). Very simple, certainly, but the charm is in the rhythm—the whole business is in 12/8 to begin with, and the bass line plays against the center of the beat. Recalling the earlier discussion, introduced in the analysis of "Perpetual Change," of profundity and counterpoint, there is no question that Yes has both in spades here.

The first of four parts, "The Solid Time of Change" is perhaps most of all about the greatest of paradoxes, transubstantiation and transfiguration. There is so much here that I can only gather together a few of the themes and hint at their intermotivations. Perhaps we should take a moment to remind ourselves of what Raymond Williams said about the green language, present in abundance here and drawn out at even greater lengths in *Tales from Topographic Oceans*—I hope that the reader will engage with these ideas and take the discussion further than this poor, finite book will be able to. In the green language, Williams argued, there is nature as a principle of order and nature as a principle of creation, with the creative mind as part of the latter. In many ways, the music of Yes tells us that this creativity is always interactive, and that it goes "all the way down," so to speak—or, as the physicist Freeman Dyson put it, this creativity is "infinite in all directions." In short, "a dewdrop can exalt us like the music of the sun."

A close reading of the first two verses of "Solid Time of Change" reveals a hermetic intertwining of themes both "pagan" and "Biblical." (Henceforth I will dispense with the scare quotes.) While we are immediately introduced to an experienced ("seasoned") witch, which would seem to be a pagan reference, we are also shown the fallen state of humanity, as it is manifest in our own disgrace, which would seem to be a Biblical reference. Both themes come together under the standard reading of gnosticism, but this standard reading generally has with it a denegration of matter, of time and space—and this we do not find in "Close to the Edge" or, indeed, in other Yes works. Instead, we find a hermetic view that does not separate spirit from matter; human fallenness and disgrace is primarily an ethical-political question, only secondarily a metaphysical or ontological question. The music with which the seasoned witch calls us to transfiguration is "from afar," but it is not from "nowhere." Indeed, our fallen state consists in following "points to nowhere." Why is it the *liver* that must be rearranged? Because this is the organ responsible for removing the poisons from our bodies. With the first presentation of the "chorus" (if we can call it that), "Down at the edge, round by the corner, . . . ," we find that we are not only caught up in the prehistory and early history of humanity, but that we are also walking down the city streets ("round by the corner" is not an expression of preurban life) of the present era. We are the beneficiaries of a kind of visitation, and this is both frightening and exhilirating. We are transfigured, even as we continue to walk down these familiar streets. The poisons are cast out by a call: the word is made flesh. The visitation is by a "witch," but I would venture that this female siren—and there is no question but that this is a woman—is the angel of history: "Then taste the fruit of man recorded losing all against the hour."

In a piece of music that, at times, seems unrelievedly *heavy,* there are in fact a few playful moments. Between the chorus and the third verse ("Crossed a line around the changes of the summer") there is a deliciously angular guitar fill that snakes its way around some nearly arhythmic, intermittent bass notes. The third verse then proceeds with a much lighter feel, now in the trippy, skipping cadence of 3/2; the key has changed as well, from D to C. It seems that everything has dropped down a bit, in register and intensity, until the very last lines of "Solid Time," "Now that it's all over and done, now that you find, now that you're whole." Despite what seems to be the meaning of these words, however, "Solid Time of Change" does not end on a celebratory note or even with a feeling of closure or completion; indeed, the first part slides without obvious change of direction into the second part, "Total Mass Retain."

At first it is not clear in what way this is a "new part," it seems such a continuation of what has come before. And it is, but "Total Mass Retain" is also a subtle transfiguration of "Solid Time of Change." "Total Mass" continues in the key of C, on the one hand, but returns to 12/8 time and reintroduces the sitar, on the other. And the wholeness that is announced at the end of "Solid Time" is nowhere in evidence in "Total Mass," except perhaps in a more developed exposition of what is involved in humankind's having its liver rearranged. Biblical themes are also present here—manna from above, crucifixion—but, if anything, there is a bitterness to Jon Anderson's voice in this part, as if the "Christian episode" of humanity, the total mass, has found itself in fundamental impasse: "passing paths that climb halfway into the void." The vision from "Solid Time of Change" is not the end, but rather the beginning: against the poison of our disgrace we have received the *grace* of the angel's call, but the *work* of redemption remains.

We are "close to the edge"—of the corner, the turning point, and the river, where the waters of redemption flow. And yet, in this prefiguration of transfiguration, we remain who we are, or, at least, our new experience does not cancel the experiences that have led us up to this moment: "Sudden call shouldn't take away the startled memory." (This is a remarkably insightful comment on the ontology of redemption.)[37]

One of the most interesting aspects of "Total Mass Retain" is what goes on with the bass guitar, drums, and Mellotron strings. As usual, Squire's line is thoroughly unusual, developing a reptilian tension and then dramatic release; however, the release is conditional, as it plays off against the tension and bitterness that Anderson and Howe are creating with voice and electric sitar. Squire's line consists in two pairs of four notes, which slither slightly downward, then slightly upward, giving way to the lowest note in the group: C-B-G#-A; G-F#-D#-E; E; E.[38] This last pair of E notes is accompanied by a cymbal and bass drum punctuation that allows the cymbal to ring out for just the briefest instant (an effect achieved by hitting the cymbal and then stopping its vibration by hand), and a swelling of Mellotron strings for each note. As "accompaniment" for the vocal line, this is definitely out there; it is counterpoint of a profound sort.

After inverting and problematizing the message of "The Solid Time of Change," "Total Mass Retain" wanders off into a swamp in its final measures. In the *Yessongs* film version of "Close to the Edge," this part is filled out with images of Venus's flytraps and a luminous jellyfish—the bass and guitar play a diligent marching theme in the low notes, while the organ intones a high-pitched anthem (a variation on the G-F#-D-E-F#-D-E-F#-D-E-A-A-A-A theme from "Solid Time"): Onward, denizens of the deep! However, this march of the swamp beings means us no harm, but merely serves to remind us that, underneath the folly of the human drama, the little creatures of the Earth continue about their hourly routines. Perhaps this break from the more developed metaphysical ideologies, whether neo-Christian or neopagan, is necessary to prepare the ground for a scene of great delicacy, "I Get Up, I Get Down."

This third part of "Close to the Edge" is clearly a dramatic scene: "You can clearly see . . ." Is this the return of the seasoned witch, or is this a kind of female Christ-figure who is new to the narrative? Or is there a difference? It would be wrong, I think, to presume to give a straightforward interpretation of the lyrics to "I Get Up, I Get Down." Still, there are certain elements that can be spelled out. There is a woman who is willing to "take the blame" for some sort of disaster that has occurred—"the crucifixion of her domain." She has responsibility for a "world" (of some sort), it seems, and this world has been lost. At the same time, the speaker who is identified by the "I" of the lyrics is also confessing to failure: the deception of millions, and the deception of one's self—"Do I look on blindly and say I see the way?" If the first two parts of "Close to the Edge" play Christian and hermetic themes off of one another, leaving us at the river's edge at the end of "Total Mass Retain," "I Get Up, I Get Down" continues this interplay, but now fully in the realm of the tragic shortcomings of humankind. Among these are the present inability to welcome the messianic in female form. This shortcoming is felt on scales both cosmic and intensely personal: "How old will I be before I come of age for you?" Again, not to force a too straightforward interpretation, but this seems a comment on the fact that, at a certain age, girls and women leap beyond boys and men in terms of maturity, and the men never seem to catch up. In all of these struggles, there is a ceaseless motion, "a foundation left to create the spiral aim" (in the words of "And You and I"), forward and back, upwards and downwards.

The instrumental part of "I Get Up, I Get Down" is disarmingly simple, a fine demonstration of the way that Yes, with all its virtuoso musicianship, has the wisdom to let the music and the vision guide what's being played. Here we find just a few notes from the keyboard and a little ornamentation from the cymbals; the rest is done with vocal harmonies, with some very fine intertwining lines from Howe and Squire.

I have never been entirely sure whether the instrumental solo section that follows belongs to the third or the fourth section of "Close to the Edge"; I assume it is the third, because it makes sense to see this moment of understanding, where the understanding is of failure and shortcoming, as giving way, finally, to the transformations that bring about the New Church. When we arrive in the fourth section, then, we have a retrospective view of the world as it was before.

The instrumental section is a marvel. Jon Anderson has spoken on many occasions to the way that this section represents the dissolution of the old church and the emergence of the New. As Anderson sings "I get up, I get down" for the last time, his voice is caught up in the organ of the old church, which is also making its appearance for the last time—giving way, after a momentary burst, to synthesizers. The rest of the group comes in with a raucous version of the original theme from the first section of the whole work. Steve Howe shreds through this progression, adding harsh notes to make dissonant chords out of the original theme. Bruford and Squire also cut loose here, with the former playing many more of his actual drums than are heard throughout the rest of the entire piece. The original chaos that begins "Close to the Edge" seems natural and primal; the chaos here is more that of large-scale social upheaval, revolution. Out of this chaos emerges an astounding organ solo, one of Wakeman's finest works: the old church is gone, the New Church is established. Seemingly, there is a New Heaven and a New Earth, as foretold in the book of Revelation.

Supporting this solo is a variation on the bass, drums, and Mellotron part from "Total Mass Retain," except the surging-yet-spacy Mellotron is replaced here by some very aggressive guitar chords, which basically follow the same pattern as Squire's line. Everything is speeded up here, of course, as the organ charges ahead, reorganizing life, society, and consciousness. Although I am attaching (perhaps wrongly) this instrumental section to the third part, for sure this section runs full steam into the fourth part. The bass-drums-Mellotron part returns, but now at this quickened pace.

In some sense the perspective portrayed in "Seasons of Man" is almost alien, declaimed as if by someone in a position to survey all of human history (and prehistory) and pronounce judgment upon it. Perhaps the most significant line here is, "A constant vogue of triumphs dislocate man so it seems." This seems to speak to a kind of triumphalism endemic to a certain version of Christianity and to a certain version of Enlightenment progressivism. If anything, it is the downfall of humanity to believe in the straight line of "progress," without twists and turns, failures and defeats, and irreparable loss. The true progress of humanity involves both the getting up and the getting down. It involves not a "pure time" which unfolds mechanically, but instead a human time, developed through "song and chance."

The "alien" perspective is one from the other side of the river of redemption, and, rather than being a triumphalistic perspective, this view is somewhat wistful. "The man" who "turned around and pointed revealing all the human race" could hardly be any other than the Ancient of Days, in the form of the Lamb of God. He points backward, to the way things were. "On the hill we viewed the silence of the valley, called to witness cycles only of the past." The response of the "I" is somewhat unexpected: "I shook my head and smiled a whisper knowing all about the place." The "alien question" concerns the form of this "knowing"—is this an experiential knowing or a merely conceptual knowledge? In other words, is there something more here than just knowing that a great deal of suffering came before the time of redemption, the New Church/New Heaven/New Earth that has now arrived? Again, there is the basis here for some difficult reflections on the ontology of redemption, and "Close to the Edge" seems to conclude with a deep ambivalence with regard to these questions. On the one hand, there is the "now that it's all over and done." On the other hand, the piece closes not with images of eternity, but with a reaffirmation of the ongoingness of time and struggle: "Seasons will pass you by. I get up. I get down." Perhaps the new church will someday itself be an old church. After all, even from the standpoint of *this* redemption, we are "called to witness cycles only of the past"; the future remains yet unwritten.

The vocal cadences of the final lines of *Close to the Edge* are a hymn, really, but one that trails off, in the end, to the forest and the stream once more.

"Close to the Edge," and even more so the album of which it is a part, scales the heights. It is one of the truly significant works of rock music. To the extent that it is right and coherently reasonable to say that *Close to the Edge* transcends its genre—even as it expands and redefines its genre and helps to create a new genre—*it does:* this is supreme music that deserves to have a place in the history of great music.

With *Close to the Edge,* Yes said farewell to Bill Bruford as a regular member of the group. He does reappear for a short time in the late eighties and early nineties, with Anderson, Bruford, Wakeman, and Howe (the self-titled album and *Union,* which will be discussed briefly in part 3. Bruford went on to do great things with King Crimson and with his own groups, quite arguably establishing himself as the best percussionist to come out of rock music. One has to admire his musical integrity in jumping ship from Yes at a point when the group was reaching its time of greatest popularity and financial success. While Bruford learned to work with and participate in the creation of large-scale musical structures with Yes, clearly he needed to give more free rein to his jazz and improvisational inclinations. I suppose that one of the most remarkable things about the musical career of Bill Bruford is that he is the connecting point between what are arguably the most important progressive rock groups. To have played a major role in the development of each is a singular contribution. Not many musicians could have answered that call.

Perhaps his most important contribution to Yes's development was to always generate a kind of space of rich potential that made Yes cook too hard to just be a psychedelic band and yet kept Yes up in the air enough that the music never became "heavy" in the sense of being merely sluggish and thick. In my view, Bruford has never quite been a "jazz" drummer—though he hasn't really performed in contexts that are more purely jazz, either, without fusion inflections (and I wouldn't begin to compare him to some of his inspirations such as Elvin Jones, Buddy Rich, Max Roach, and Art Blakey). It's not a matter of quality, either, but instead the fact that Bruford is, when all is said and done, a rock drummer who has brought a jazz sensibility to rock music. He has inspired countless rock drummers, and many musicians who play other instruments besides. Now what we need is more music that can make use of this inspiration and really run with it. Although Bruford's work with Yes has been overshadowed somewhat by his work with King Crimson (at least in terms of the group that most listeners identify him with), the "model" that he created, for how to work with large structures where most of the parts are set out in advance (that is, "composed," as that is ordinarily understood), still has plenty of room for development.

With Yes's next studio album, the era of Alan White began. Indeed, in some sense one could say that the main sequence is divided between the Bruford and White periods. What effect the coming of Alan White had on the development of Yes is something that we will take up in the discussion of *Tales* and *Relayer.*

Tales from Topographic Oceans

Having taken things to an extreme with *Close to the Edge,* and, in the face of certain critical reactions, Yes took things even further with their next album. At least, this is the case as far as the size and complexity of the structures involved is concerned. This is also the case regarding the breadth of their vision. After receiving a certain amount of criticism for daring to take on questions of profound and cosmic significance with *Close to the Edge,* Jon Anderson, especially, went into the next project with a bit of a chip on his shoulder. If this led, to some extent, to some excess on *Tales from Topographic Oceans* that went beyond musical justification, it also led to the creation of what is probably progressive rock's biggest and most difficult work. Unlike *Close to the Edge,* I wouldn't call *Tales* "perfect"—it has its imperfections, which will be discussed.

But, the *audacity!* It seems to me that, when the music is all wrapped up under a single heading, this should be it. The group was asking itself, How far can we take this experiment? *Tales* was really a big risk, and not only with the critics. Around the time of *Close to the Edge,* Yes was the most popular English band in the United States, and they had a huge following worldwide. With *Tales,* the group was saying that they were willing to put all that "on the table," so to speak, and to risk losing it all. Everything that some critics said about the "pretentiousness" of *Tales* has to be weighed against this.

In rock music, the only complete works that were on the scale of *Tales* were the great rock operas of Peter Townshend and The Who, *Tommy* and *Quadrophenia.* Not to take anything away from these terrific albums, but they consist primarily in a series of interrelated songs, many of which have a fairly simple structure, whereas *Tales from Topographic Oceans* consists in four interrelated movements, venturing into the vicinity of song form here and there, but generally staying at the level of a complete, and very complex, work. In other words, *Tales* is indeed unique (perhaps that is why it has been uniquely despised by some). Of progressive rock groups, perhaps Yes were uniquely situated to attempt such a work. King Crimson's greater emphasis on improvisation didn't lend itself to the composition of an eighty-minute piece. Emerson, Lake, and Palmer were not thematically inclined to such grand visions—even their own grand visions were interrupted, here and there, by a silly song of some sort. Genesis went in for the long form with *The Lamb Lies Down on Broadway,* but they had a theatrical side that kept them away from big philosophical themes. Yes had not only the grand thinkers but also the musical inventiveness to sustain a work such as *Tales.* One might even say that, *if* such a work could be brought off, Yes was the group to do it.

A sense of anticipation had built up around the release of *Tales.* No one knew what to expect. Not only was there the departure of Bruford and the arrival of White to wonder about, but there were also strange things coming out of interviews with group members, in *Melody Maker* and other print venues. Jon Anderson said that Yes was going in a more "earthy" and "funky" direction, and those of us who were really into the group wondered exactly what that meant—especially the "funky" part, given that this was a time of some pretty heavy funk, from the Isley Brothers, Ohio Players, Parliament/Funkadelic (of course), Kool and the Gang, etc., and we couldn't exactly see Yes doing that kind of stuff! So, Yes fans were even a little worried. I will come back to these questions, especially in relation to how the members of the group responded to the controversy. First, though, let's focus on the music and the vision.

As with *Close to the Edge, Tales* was conceived as a complete work, including the album cover art and the subsequent stage presentations. With "Roundabout" and especially "Close to the Edge," Jon Anderson and Steve Howe had cemented a partnership in composition that ultimately gave rise to the general structure of *Tales*. Thematically, the origin of the work is almost "postmodern," in that Anderson attributes the chief inspiration to a footnote. Perhaps the work *is* a kind of postmodern multiculturalism; in the largest sense, *Tales* takes its inspiration from a description of some Hindu scriptures in Paramhansa Yogananda's *Autobiography of a Yogi.*

Analyzing such scriptures is quite beyond my competence; perhaps others will develop these themes at more length, deepening the context of the Shastric scriptures and Yogananda's text. Thomas Mosbø argues that the "ultimate goal" of *Tales* is to evoke "total unity with God" (pp. 223–24). Surely this is the case *in some sense;* there is no denying the engagement of *Tales* with Eastern (or otherwise non-Western) traditions of enlightenment. But there is a grand historical—and even prehistorical—sweep to this topographic view that places the work in a different tradition than that of religious contemplation. This is not to say that one of the motivations of the work is not "religious"; indeed, in a profound sense, the religious vision is the fundamental motivation. But this point has to be understood in broad terms. As Mosbø also points out, this vision is global and inclusive, not restricted to a particular *religion* (p. 224). Furthermore, this religious vision is representative of a complete philosophy; it is not "religious" in the contemporary secular sense of a set of beliefs that can be compartmentalized in the form of a metaphysical creed. The vision of *Tales* concerns difficult questions of society, gender, ecology, and the possibility of being at home in the cosmos. Its sense of making progress with these issues is neither purely meditative or otherworldly. Its notion of transcendence is not presented in a mode of denial; the vision here is one of *working through,* not a contemplative leap beyond. As with "Close to the Edge," there is a complex intertwining in *Tales* of "Christian" and "pagan" themes.

Tales from Topographic Oceans is in four parts, which I will now take up in order.

"The Revealing Science of God"

More than twenty years later, the opening measures of *Tales* still seem pretty outlandish. With only minimal instrumental accompaniment, Anderson leads an invocation that is part chant, part hymn. As other voices enter in, and the synthesizer and percussion become more intense, we are told a story that intermingles Biblical and Eastern creation stories with more materialistic, evolutionary accounts of the emergence of consciousness—and all of this in the first few lines. All of life and consciousness is brought into a single chain, one that leads from the "dance from the ocean" to "endless caresses for the freedom of life everlasting." In other words, we are introduced to a long poem on *mortality* and *meaning.* The question might also be framed as one of knowing and being known, such that there was and is some point to our existence.

The cadences of the opening section are trippy, moving from 6/8 to 3/8 to 6/8 to 5/8 to 3/8 to 6/8 and finally to 4/8. As this section reaches a climax, the bass notes tumble down like polished metallic stones (hematite, say); there is the slightest moment of silence before Alan White introduces the first main theme with a strange, almost offhand splash of the hi-hat. Then we hear the theme that I have always thought of as a "triangle," based as it is in three-note figures that form a left angle when played on guitar or bass. (The interval is 1-3-4.) This theme is really quite "Squire-like," in that it mimics his style of playing lines that both loop around and move forward. As far as the scale is concerned, this particular line moves "backward," almost as a kind of "descent" from the sky to the ground (or even to the bedrock). (The swirling chords that open "Awaken" follow a similar pattern.) The music settles into a fairly rock solid 4/4, and there is even a bit of a loping feel about it.

Indeed, one criticism of *Tales* is that it seems to be dragging and lethargic in places, and it has to be admitted that there is some basis to the charge. Jon Anderson describes the album as, in some ways, a "meeting place of high ideals and low energy." Perhaps the real issue is that, for whatever reasons, the whole band was not as on board for this project as Anderson and Howe were, and sometimes this resulted in parts that could have been played more creatively if everyone had been more together. In particular, what had been touted as the greater "earthiness" of Alan White's contribution turned out, in places, to simply be fairly conventional rock drumming. As we shall see, especially when we discuss *Relayer,* this was not for lack of musical ability.

On the other hand, there is a basic beauty to the first verses of the "triangle" section of "Revealing." The vocal lines come across as very careful and caring. There is a skillful alternation between the generally rising, choral parts performed with harmony vocals, and the almost "lonely" solo voice of Anderson. Returning to the level of the whole for a moment, what might be perceived as a lack of *complete* forcefulness in the delivery of lines such as, "I ventured to talk, but I never lost my place" (which has a strong element of drama to be sure), has to be placed in the context of a work that develops and builds over the course of eighty-some minutes (81:14, to be exact). Some of the more spacy parts of the album also have to be put into this context. The ordinary rules for writing rock music either don't apply or are stretched much further than they ever had been before. This doesn't mean that the experiment was always successful or couldn't have been improved on—but let's try to come to terms with what the group (fragmented as it was over the project) was trying to accomplish.

These initial verses have to do with a kind of disorientation, perhaps summed up best by the line, "What happened to this song we once knew so well?" Here the music flows very well, and the vocals have already dominated the first parts of the album to a greater extent than with any previous album in the main sequence. Although Wakeman was not entirely happy with his playing on the album, he does contribute some very good Mellotron string work in the "What happened?" section, and the orchestration in general is both rich and tight. I don't know that the philosophical vision is entirely coherent through this part, or even if it is meant to be. When the question, "What happened?", flows into "We must have waited all our lives for this moment," we aren't sure if the moment has actually come or what the moment is all about. The cadence in this line is neat, though, with the pause just before "moment" and then the multiple, out-of-phase, vocalizations of the word from all three singers.

We then find ourselves in what might be taken as an archetypically "dragging" section, of the sort that Rick Wakeman probably thought of as "filler." (In the *Yesyears* video he called it "bluff.") The problem is that there have to be such sections if the whole is to be something other than simply a collection of songs. (The individual vocal sections, it should be added, with one or two exceptions, are not really songs by themselves.) The whole might have been tightened up a bit, however, and here I'll for once concede an advantage to the CD format—namely, that there is no imperative to compose or play to the format of four sides of approximately twenty minutes in length. (Just be ready to throw out the entire genre of album cover artwork for the sake of this advantage.)

From this slow-moving instrumental section we turn to a very much hurried vocal section, based on a set of sometimes disconnected terms, not unlike the "blue tail, tail fly" section of "Siberian Khatru." The synthesizer contributes an interesting sound to this movement, something between a "click" and a "squeak," and the drums seem to get more involved at this point. The overall effect of all of these lyrics, from "Called out a tune" to the rhyming of "seasons" and "reasons," is to create a context of searching and uncertain wondering rather than contemplative knowing. When this hurried section seems drained, and Anderson intones (in a way that echoes the "death-defying, mutilated" section of "Yours Is No Disgrace"), "They move fast, they tell me," the feeling is really one of alienation. If one were to put this spiritual quest in terms of the sort of unfolding experiment with mortality that is portrayed in some Eastern thought systems, as well as in some versions of Judaism and certain marginal forms of Christianity (for example, Mormonism), then we have arrived at a moment when our seeker is not so sure that the experiment was a good idea.[39]

Again, the music flows and builds artfully, first through a recapitulation of the "statement of terms" section ("Starlight, movement"; "Skyline, teacher"). The lyrics here are some of my favorites from the whole work:

> Getting over overhanging trees,
> let them rape the forest.
> They might stand and leave them

clearly to be home.

Getting over wars we do not mean,
we charm the movement suffers,
call out all our memories
clearly to be home.

Again, I find this to be a statement of ambiguity concerning the experiment with mortality—it's not all fun and games. In the midst of all this is the "And through the rhythm" section, which more forcefully introduces "Christian" material: the idea of "work[ing] out the story," which is really no part of purely *contemplative* Eastern traditions (even, I think, of the Bhagavad Gita, which comes closest to the idea of "divine drama"). Squire's bass cadences play an essential role here, and yet they are also very understated and unobtrusive. In this general vicinity, as well, is a spectacular synthesizer solo from Wakeman, with rocking chord support from Howe. After all of this activity, the closing section of "Revealing Science" is a bit disturbing, to my mind, in that it is too purely "devotional," in the manner of a religious cult devotee. Of course, in a secular and cynical society, anyone who ventures to actually believe in much of anything will be accused of cultic devotion, but I find this resolution too simple and pure, given the elements of struggle and strife and uncertainty that have been expressed up until this point. But there is another reading of this passage, wherein it is placed more in the context of the entire album. Thus, while the passionless (practically Moonie-like) tones of the final verse of "Revealing Science" recapitulate the cadence of the opening chant/hymn somewhat, but without intensity or enthusiasm, the whole of the first part of *Tales* will now enter into a series of more passionate explorations, in terms of the childhoods of contemporary individuals and the childhood of our species.

"The Remembering"

The beginning of the second part of *Tales* is much lighter than what has come before, an almost necessary relief. Although the orchestration issues primarily from the keyboards, there is almost a folk song feel to the opening lines of "Remembering." We have shifted from a strangely cold statement of a supposedly warm truth ("You seekers of the truth accepting that reasons will relive and breath and hope . . .") to a much more homey atmosphere. The initial lyrics simply evoke this atmosphere, and are a kind of homage to memory itself, without getting into particular memories. As the music develops, the guitar takes us into an inwardly curving pattern, a song that is warm and pretty.

There are a few moments of drama in what becomes a fairly long opening section, but they are relatively mild and fleeting: "And I do think very well" (the second time around "feel" is substituted for "think"). Just as this section has become a bit overdrawn and languorous, a subtle transition sets in. First, the

lyrics begin to turn to the particular—"we walk around the story." Second, an
acoustic guitar introduces a bit more bite into the music, just as we are "out in
the city running free." Obviously, this is a moment of seeming freedom, before
the urban alienation of being "lost in the city" ("Heart of the Sunrise") has set in.
(Recall, too, the line from "No Opportunity Necessary," "Listen for the sound
that city ears cannot hear.") With the line, "School gates remind us of our class,"
Yes gives us the only direct reference to the subject of class in all of their music
(to the best of my knowledge). When, two verses later, Anderson sings, "Don the
cap and close your eyes imagine all the glorious challenge," does this portend a
supposed transcendence of class? Is this because "We don't even need to try, we
are one?" I find this to be a rather large piece of escapism, especially in juxtaposition to a line such as, "All the passion spent on one cross." Crucifixion is a
grotesque, bloody, physical form of brutality. Despite some drama to this presentation, there is also an unbearable lightness to it.

Thus, the particularities are seen only at the edges, as if they need to be hidden. The leap to large themes obscures real suffering, and when this suffering is
invoked, it is so mired in contemplative spirituality that the invocation is an
insult to those whose pain is real; for example:

All the dying cried before you.
We've rejoiced in all their meaning.

There is a need here, as Marx argued, to *ascend* from the abstract to the concrete. The music itself is very strong in some places, including the place where
these lines are sung. And I especially like Howe's flowing use of an acoustic
twelve-string guitar in the section, "Force the bit between the mouth of freedom
. . ." Indeed, there is more drama in the line concerning the passion of Christ
than there is in the entire opening section of "Remembering." All of this can take
you in, for sure, but one longs for something of the kinds of memories that Pete
Townshend gives us in *Quadrophenia.* This isn't Yes's way, but without dealing
with the real struggles that people must confront, including those of "our class,"
transcendence is hollow, and the "alternate view" is merely a mind-trip.

"The Ancient"

The third part of *Tales* is, musically, the most experimental and avant-garde,
a primitivist excursion that ultimately concludes in a very classical mode.
Although "The Ancient" could also be criticized for meandering a bit too much,
I feel that, with this part, Yes finally gets on with something that is more musically important. Perhaps this is because, unlike the first two parts of the work,
the third part is finally not dominated so much by either vocals or keyboards
painting with a very broad brush. The percussion comes more on board here, as
well, and, though this may seem a strange thing to say, I'm heartened by the fact

that, finally, there is more to the music that is almost *irritating,* in the sense that
it bends your ears, and is not so overly melodic and pretty. (In places, part 2 is
just downright prissy.)

The main source of this ear-bending is the percussive work by Alan White,
both with drums and vibraphone, and what I would call Steve Howe's "pagan
guitar." Indeed, it is hard not to hear the latter as anything other than the serpent
which drags its tail over all. In some ways, the dissonance of part 3 is necessary
to redeem the melodicism and flow of the other parts. Where the other parts leap
too quicky to a redemption that has not been achieved, and thus becomes the
object of mere contemplation (which, ungrounded in experience, especially the
experience of struggle, cannot in any sense be real), part 3 is down in the
swamp, mired in materiality—and our overly topographic tales need this. If I say
that "The Ancient" meanders *too much,* this doesn't mean that the piece shouldn't
meander at all, for meandering is what it is about. Indeed, with its opening invocation of "the majesty of music," "The Ancient" reminds us that theology and
philosophy have their origin in music and dance. Rather than to emphasize
humanity's "savage" beginnings, perhaps what Cynthia Willett argues for the
infant child goes for the infant species as well:

> As a barely conscious, boundless happening of uncertain desire, the infant gropes
> for nourishment and attachment, not death and antisocial nihilism. Its rhythm is
> the rhythm of life. (p. 30)

Part of the message of *Tales* is that this time of minimal consciousness might
have also been, at least in some ways, a time of greater consciousness, an "asking for the source." It is in this context, but also Willett's, that we might ask,
"What happened to this song we once knew so well?"

Surely this is furtive meandering, as especially emphasized by Squire's subterranean bass playing. (I think he used a fretless bass guitar for at least part of
"The Ancient.") There are two interruptions to this primeval searching. First, the
crashing sound emphasized especially with guitar and drums evokes the fragility
of these first steps of life and consciousness—the spider's web sits atop a vol-
cano. Second, Jon Anderson intones names of the sun in various languages
(some of which are Native American). Occasionally Anderson's voice, used in a
purely instrumental way, as well as Mellotron strings, lift the music out of its
"primitive" state, but in that way emphasizing the primitivism all the more.
Finally, however, this lifting motion takes the music into another realm, an emergence from the primeval soup into England's mountains (or valleys) green. The
transitional verses are:

> So the flowering nativity of life wove its
> Web face to face with the shallow.
> And their gods sought out and conquered: Ah Kin

and

> Do the leaves of green stay greener through the autumn?
> Does the colour of the sun turn crimson white?
> Does a shadow come between us in the winter?
> Is the movement really light?

With this first verse, Steve Howe enters with the classical guitar, but the music is still somewhat oriented toward the harshness of the first half of "The Ancient." The full transition toward a more melodic and classical sound is made by what amounts to a gem of classical guitar composition (and playing, of course). This is a lovely guitar work that stands on its own. Does it work as a transition? To my mind, the starkness of its contrast with what has come before is indeed what makes it work.

When the music comes to the second verse quoted above, we find the one complete song in all of *Tales* (the only one that wouldn't have to be cobbled together from parts separated by instrumental sections). Perhaps this is a kind of answer to the question, "What happened to this song we once knew so well?" Here there are verses and a chorus, mainly accompanied by classical guitar, and minimal bass and percussion. The tone of the song is plaintive, and here, more than before, *Tales* seems to engage with the materiality and sociality of redemption. In the second verse of the song proper, Anderson asks, "Is the movement in the head?" This question correlates with another (from the chorus): "Does it all come out along without you?" To my mind, these questions have to do with the idea of reaching some sort of "redemption" or "enlightenment" in a solitary movement of contemplation, versus the idea that questions such as, "When does reason stop and killing just take over?" are fundamentally social and communal questions. Whereas this irreducible social dimension is, in my view, too quickly "transcended" in what has come before, now this dimension has come to the fore. Thus, when we reach the final part of *Tales*, "Ritual," there is some bite to having the lyrics in the third person. Perhaps the primeval character of "The Ancient" also requires us to read backward, so that we now see the first two parts of *Tales* as a search for the understanding that demonstrates there is no redemption without the perspective of the lamb and the child, and the "story" (the unfolding of history) cannot "come out" without "you," without the millions of voices singing.

At the conclusion of part 3, Howe's classical guitar morphs and melds once again into his pagan electric, perhaps demonstrating the episodic and fleeting character of the realizations presented in the "song." Some things, it seems, have to be learned again and again—at least until a certain flowering creativity of life reaches a critical mass.

"Ritual"

Where "The Ancient" ends with a harsh, electric crash and the spiral movement of primitive organisms in the "shallow," "Ritual" seems to make a decisive climb out of the swamp and into the contemporary city. Against a lead guitar line that has taken to the air, the cadence of the drums and bass guitar is grounded and substantial, a very noble sound. Toward the end of this long journey, it seems the instrumental parts have finally begun to click. There is also a passion and urgency to this part of *Tales* (something generally missing from the rest), especially as we approach the romping part where Jon Anderson uses his voice as an orchestral instrument. The synthesis of styles here is phenomenal and, on the face of it, quite unlikely. In the midst of some of the harsher sounds that have been carried over from "The Ancient," we have something like a Western swing dance from the guitar, bass guitar, and drums that are simply flying along, but in a syncopated pattern that is a million miles away from country music, and then a bass/vocal part that is something out of fifties rock'n'roll. Squire plays what might be called a "bass solo," but one with a solid logic that extends the harmonic and rhythmic picture that the whole group is developing. Just as the whole at this point blends divergent musical styles, it is difficult to come up with a single metaphor that captures what Squire is doing in his solo. There are a lot of notes, but they are presented with an unhurried feel. The solo stands out, but it drives the group as well.

Finally, even in the case of Wakeman's playing, this picture has become more together and group-oriented. If the chance to infuse a greater energy and group commitment to these high ideals ever comes along, in the form of an opportunity to rework *Tales,* "Ritual" provides the clear model on how to do that.

The opening romp gives way, for another moment, to the primeval soup—the elemental material, "magic of the source," and voice of the child out of which our musical ship for sailing topographic oceans is built. Against the backdrop of high, rapid notes from the bass guitar, and cymbal crescendos, a moderated pagan guitar wanders one last time, eventually meandering even through the signature theme from "Close to the Edge." But this reptile is finally ready to make its own way into the song, to transmute itself into a higher form. As the meandering guitar makes this subtle transformation into folkish chords, the music makes a sudden, and yet gentle, leap toward the "anthem" for not only "Ritual," but indeed *Tales* as a whole: "Nous sommes du soleil"—"We are of the sun." There is a tremendous *brightness* to this moment, bolstered by Squire's heartbeat line.

When, from this moment, one thinks back over the course of *Tales* up to this point, one sees that the movement of mind and materiality works through spirals—and some of the spirals take backward leaps, as it were. At the moment when everything seems completely clear, just at that moment all of the complications of life make a comeback. The rest of "Ritual," therefore, recapitulates the ideas given us in the work up to that point, in compressed form. One moment we have understood the essential unity of all the Earth's creatures, the next moment "life seems like a fight." *And it is.* Understanding how these two things, unity and struggle, form their own dialectic, is key to understanding the vision that Jon Anderson and Steve Howe are trying to present.

From "Nous sommes du soleil" forward, "Ritual" is filled with memorable moments—especially great singing, very much integrated with strong playing. The rest of the album consists in three parts: from "Nous sommes" to "at all"; the percussion ensemble; and the conclusion.

The first of these parts uses repetition of words and phrases to extremely good effect. For instance, there is not only the repetition within verses of, first, "Life seems like life seems like a fight/fight/fight," and, second, "Asking for, asking for the source/the source/the source," but these verses also play off of each other.

There is a beautiful *ease* to the vocal presentation of some of these phrases, especially given all of the musical transformations that take place in and around them. Consider especially the verse that begins, "As we try and consider." The lines in this verse take us in about four different directions, and these different directions are all stated with strength and not understated, and yet the whole has a terrific flow to it. My favorite "turn" within this verse is where, three lines after singing "We won't tender our song clearer, till we sail" (delivered with artful cadences), there is indeed a "nautical" harmony and rhythm that supports, "As clearer companions shall call to be near you"—this *is* sailing music, and yet for just a moment. It's a musically interesting moment, because, one expects in this brief time that only the most minimal impression might be left. But, as I've said, every mood here is stated strongly. In this one verse one sees all the talent and artistry that is Yes, and it is no surprise that weaving in and out of the vocals (especially at the end, "at all, at all") there is a most improbable bass line from Chris Squire. (This line is composed of sixteenth notes, and there are a lot of them in a short amount of time, and yet the whole thing is entirely unhurried and delivered with consummate ease, integrating smoothly and with seeming effort-lessness what would be a major piece of work for most musicians.) The weave takes us through all the changes of life; in a sense, whereas the element of "fight" and struggle seemed to be at odds with "asking for the source," now we see that one cannot be had without the other. On the plane of this understanding, the minor distractions of life "don't seem to matter at all."

Coming after the "Nous sommes" section, then, what is the meaning of the rocking guitar-bass-drums theme building to frantic, nervous intensity and then giving way to the percussion section that has Alan White at the center? Again, I think this is a recapitulation and further development of the theme of struggling consciousness and gathering unity.

Musically, this whole section is fascinating and weird. Although the percussion section features White's drumming, to be sure, this is not a drum solo, but instead a fairly large piece of percussion orchestration. White plays some frighteningly virtuoso rolls, but the point of this section is not to show off his skills. Instead, the point is to create a section of music that is based on percussive possibilities, but one that also contributes to the larger musical picture. The section plays off the idea that drumming—or, at least, banging on things—is the most primeval form of instrumental expression. Mixed in, though, are the quirky synthesizers that prefigure some of the "future primitive," "tribal" sounds that have become somewhat popular in more recent years. As with the entire portion of "Ritual" that stretches from "Nous sommes" to the end, the percussion section is in three parts: first, White charges around by himself, although there is the constant ringing of sleigh bells and the occasional inverted cymbal in the background; second, White establishes a heavy rhythm with the bass drum and tom-toms, with other percussion working along side as an accompaniment; finally, all of the percussion instruments (as played by Anderson and Squire, in addition to White) come into a unified pattern, one that is lifted by synthesizer and Mellotron string notes. The whole thing is exhausting and draining, but also fascinating and exhilirating.

In light of this intense percussion ensemble, too, and looking back over "The Ancient" and "Ritual" up to this point, we finally realize that White is not simply a conventional rock drummer—an impression created by the first two parts of *Tales*. Although he is obviously a good deal more heavy-handed than Bill Bruford—and the percussion ensemble in "Ritual" is nothing if not heavy—White also demonstrates that he is a fine percussion orchestrator. Once he finds himself in this music, White goes even further with his work on *Relayer.*

Although the musical effect of the percussion ensemble is not unlike that of the guitar jam in "Yours Is No Disgrace," where one feels a bit shipwrecked and stranded at the end, here this is the result of "coming down" from something that has to be called "religious ecstasy," rather than a "crawling out of dirty holes." Indeed, it is interesting to compare the two moments, and remember that both are part of the vision of Yes. This is made all the more clear when we consider a similar moment, once again in the aftermath of war and devastation, at the conclusion of "The Gates of Delirium." I would argue that *Tales* has to be understood in this larger context if it is *not* to be assimilated to apolitical New-Ageish otherworldliness. In the vision that became *Tales,* Anderson was certainly toying with *this* "utopia." Although he was not able to articulate this issue precisely, perhaps Rick Wakeman understood some of the essential ungroundedness of *Tales,* and perhaps this is part of what made him uncomfortable. For my part, I would argue that there is always an irreducible ethical-political dimension to these issues, even if they seem to get played out in other ways—for example, in supposedly purely musical or "personal" terms. I'll come back to this in a moment.

The concluding part of "Ritual" is quite lovely. As Mosbø remarks, Anderson creates a skillful juxtaposition of the playful intimacy experienced by two lovers with a larger, more cosmic intimacy—the warmth of the cosmos as "home." It's an iffy proposition, that we belong in this world, that we are "children of the universe." Most of our experience tells us otherwise. If the reality is more in line with a "real essence" that we have managed to hide from ourselves, I would still argue that we must have an active role in constructing this essence. I realize, of course, that in classical terms "essences" are not constructed; but Yes's is a vision of movement, potential, and possibility, not of eternal sameness. In keeping with this vision, even in *Tales* there are hints of the hermetic and material dimensions of "flying home." Even if the concluding vision of *Tales* is one where we are "lost on a wave and then after," we also have to account for the concluding musical section which, irony of ironies, features in its brief span the most fiery and intense playing on the album. Until, that is, this too makes a leap toward another plane, leaving behind only the trace of spirit. I wouldn't say that this resolution is simply "tacked on," there is a logic to it; but we can't say that this is the same sort of tranquil resolution that one finds in Indian music, either, even though the final guitar, bass, and synthesizer notes of *Tales* invoke this music. Instead, we are looking back upon a great journey from an even greater distance: "a picture of distance . . . revealing corridors of time provoking memories disjointed but with purpose."

Tales from Topographic Oceans should be considered as an experiment that needed to be attempted. So, what's all the *pressure?* Why were so many music writers not only critical, but seemingly *set against* the album? *Tales* needs to be considered in its time, when greater musical experimentation driven by the utopian spirit of the sixties was developing more and more formal complexity just as that spirit seemed to be waning. The radically utopian sense of "political ends as sad remains shall die" was in danger of giving over to a "lost on a wave"—transcendence of an apolitical sort. Furthermore, the forces of "accessibility," speaking a populist language but serving to promote cultural homogenization and, at bottom, crass commercial motivations, were gathering steam. (All of this is discussed at the beginning of part 3.) If Rick Wakeman was worried about the musical incoherence of parts of *Tales,* its lack of musical justification, he was also pulled away from Yes by the success of his first solo album, *The Six Wives of Henry VIII,* and by the fact that he was somewhat less idealistic than the other members of Yes to begin with. (Rather than make a separate point out of this, I would argue that Wakeman's acknowledged problems with alcohol in this period also have to be understood in this context; meanwhile the rest of the band were committed vegetarians in this period, as well as gaining a reputation for avoiding the rowdy side of the rock scene—to the point where one article compared them to Mormon missionaries.) In other words, complex forces were at work here. Two members of Yes—Anderson and Howe—had a strong conception of *Tales* as a complete project. Two members—Squire and White—had a less strong conception, though they came through brilliantly for extended parts of the album. One member, Wakeman, contributed some good parts, but, as for participating in the project as a full member, he might just as well have been replaced by a competent sideman. To his credit, he did the right thing by leaving the group at that point.

It is in the nature of any real experiment that it may not succeed on all fronts. If this is the case with *Topographic Oceans,* this has to be put into the context of the time and the audacity of what the group was trying to do, even as it was somewhat divided against itself. *Tales* isn't perfect—except in conception. Perhaps one day something more like this conception will be realized. Meanwhile, the visionary contributions of Yes were far from finished.

Relayer

Apparently, after *Close to the Edge,* some critics asked, sarcastically, if Jon Anderson's next project would be to set the Bible to music. Although *Tales* is a work of almost Biblical proportions, *Relayer* is more Biblical in spirit, especially in its epic-length work, "The Gates of Delirium." Although that work comes first on the album, I will follow the practice established in the discussion of *Close to the Edge* of considering the longest, epic piece in the final section of the album analysis.

The loss of Rick Wakeman was a difficult blow to the group. By the time he left, however, it seemed as though a break from the more negative energies he was bringing to the band was necessary. Furthermore, the music press, in the process of becoming even more focused on personalities and star-quality, made too much of this break. Of course, Wakeman made some very important contributions to the group, especially in that his work was crucial to the development of Yes into a full-blown progressive rock enterprise. But the core of the group was not only elsewhere, it became increasingly elsewhere with the making of *Tales* and the subsequent tour. The irony is that, with the departure of Wakeman, Yes took a turn toward the further development of the vision they had demonstrated with *Close to the Edge.* In other words, with Wakeman departed, the group made a record that he might have wanted to have been more a part of than *Tales.*

In more than superficial ways, *Relayer* is indeed a further pursuit of the ground that was opened up by *Close to the Edge.* In some ways, the former is just as perfect as the latter—as with *Close to the Edge,* there is very little that I would propose changing. Whereas *Tales from Topographic Oceans* has some great writing, playing, and singing, but is not *tight* and could use some editing and improvement and sharpening, *Relayer* is very together. If parts of it, especially "Sound Chaser," are "over the top" in the way that Wakeman was critical of, still, the musical logic of such pieces was more readily apparent. This is not to say, of course, that this logic isn't quite complex and more than a little weird in places.

With *Relayer,* two developments in the instrumental performance aspect of Yes stand out. First, and most obvious is the fact that Patrick Moraz joined the group. His keyboard abilities were and are comparable to Rick Wakeman's—in other words, the virtuoso ability to be able to play whatever needs being played. In not very sophisticated terms, I think Wakeman had a better sensibility with the synthesizer (on which more in due course) and possibly more facility with the organ, whereas Moraz's piano chops might have been better. In any case, one outstanding keyboardist was replaced by another one, the replacement bringing the sort of enthusiasm the band needed at that point.

Second, Alan White simply took his work with Yes to another level, demonstrating that he is a virtuoso percussionist capable of great creativity. I'll get into the particulars of this as we take up each piece in turn.

The order in which I would like to discuss the works on *Relayer,* then, is as follows: "Sound Chaser," "To Be Over," and "The Gates of Delirium."

"Sound Chaser"

I saw Yes perform live at the Omni, in Atlanta, Georgia, in the fall of 1974, a few weeks before the actual release of *Relayer.* I can still remember quite well the performance of "Sound Chaser" that opened the concert. To say the least, the whole thing was completely unreal! From the opening notes and drum patterns, "Sound Chaser" seemed *crazy.* As the initial chord sequence took off, the pace was too dizzying for reflection, until the song came finally to one of its weirdest moments, a mostly unaccompanied electric guitar solo, played on a Fender Telecaster set to maximum treble. "Sound Chaser" follows in the footsteps of other Yes works that attempt to push the envelope of the "rock song"—especially "Roundabout" and "Siberian Khatru." Needless to say, "Sound Chaser" goes even further than these two efforts, pretty much to lunatic extremes. The words and music here will definitely make you out and out. For a band that is often characterized as having no sense of humor, I can't imagine that there isn't a good deal of humor to this piece. But perhaps some critics don't see this because they can't understand that this humor can be intermingled with a number of other elements, including a serious attempt to see how far rock music can be pushed.

"Sound Chaser" begins with an alternation of three parts: White playing vibes, White playing drums joined by Moraz on electric piano, and Squire on bass guitar. Squire's riff is frightfully fast and razor sharp. Out of this matrix comes some monster drumming by White, with a swelling of Mellotron strings in the background. Finally a lightning fast line played in unison by the bass and guitar enters, caroming off of the drums and keyboards like steel balls in a pachinko (Japanese pinball) machine. The beginning sequence is in 5/4 time, first in the key of D, then F#. How Squire and Howe stay together at this pace I don't know, but I guess if they can do it live they can do it in the studio. (A video from the *Relayer* tour for a concert in Queen's Park, England, shows them pulling this off.) If anything, the difficulty of the line increases in the instrumental interlude after the first verse, which is a bass guitar and percussion tour de force. The lyrics are so cosmic that they are almost a parody—at the very least they are a humorous celebration of "electric freedom." In the midst of all this the key has changed to E and the time signature to 4/4, after the brief insertion of a measure of 2/4. Numerous other key and time changes follow.

Then we come to the bizarre guitar solo, where Howe explores the sonic possibilities of the Telecaster, the ultimate rocking country guitar, set at its trebliest, but playing passages that alternate between a classical and an avant-garde feel. Everything here is exceedingly metallic and completely unexpected. Some critics referred to this solo as "gratuitous." My sense of it is that it is meant to be a kind of *violation* or transgression on various levels. In the live setting, at the beginning of the concert, this solo seemed a striking announcement of the fact that this is a very experimental band; to open up with a full and intense sound from the entire group, and then suddenly to turn to the thinnest possible sound, is definitely out there. The other instruments that passed through this segment were interesting, too, especially the strings that seemed to have some sort of phasing or flanging effects on them, and Squire's broad sheet-metal bass, also refracted through some gothic electronic device. Toward the end of the solo, White adds tympani to the mix.

The final verse of the song, delivered in the wake of the solo, is ethereal and disembodied:

> From the moment I reached out to hold
> I felt a sound.
> And what touches our soul slowly moves as touch rebounds.
> And to know that tempo will continue lost in trance of dances.
> As rhythm takes another turn,
> As is my want I only reach
> To look in your eyes . . .

Despite the element of alien visitation here, the lyrics are not New-Agey, nor are they delivered in the sometimes glib meditative style of parts of *Tales from Topographic Oceans.* Instead, they are *avant* and fitting, precisely because of this alien element.

The instrumental section that then opens up is yet another study in extreme contrasts, almost a kind of "avant-country" music, with washes of slide guitar and galloping drums. In the midst of this steely ride, the music suddenly jumps to double speed—and not through any trick of the studio. It's an amazing and rather disorienting effect, as is the reverse motion a few moments later, when time is once again elongated. Our visit with the electronic cowboy is interrupted by the supremely weird "Cha-Cha" (and "Hum") vocal part, which then gives way to what might be the most unexpected section at all, where we finally get to hear the *funk* that Yes had been promising for a couple years at that point. And it really is funky, with great syncopated drums, a bass line playing expertly against the rhythm, and powerful chords from Howe. All of it works, to my mind, except Moraz's synthesizer solo, which is just too much in the vein of Return to Forever and other jazz-rock fusion units. But the rest of the band is definitely engaging in a hard funk, of a sort that might even make George Clinton proud. I should add that some of Moraz's note bending is interesting, even if his solo is perhaps the weakest point on the whole album—because it introduces a very conventional moment into a piece that otherwise fits no conventions whatsoever.

Even so, we might note that Yessified funk had its one brief moment in the history of the group, not to appear again—and this is obviously because of Moraz's presence.

Suddenly, this funk gives way to the initial bass and guitar theme once again; with a final "Cha-Cha" and one more speed race by the guitar, bass, and drums to the end of the street, the sounds have been thoroughly chased.

"To Be Over"

One thing that can be said about pieces such as "Sound Chaser" is that they emphasize the fact that Yes's music has to be worked at. To listen to the piece obviously doesn't require as much work as it took to compose it or play it, but this listening is work all the same. One is about ready "to be over," after chasing these sounds. Of course, in the original order of works on *Relayer,* the album itself is just about over, and perhaps we should keep this in mind in considering this song. "To Be Over" is very much in contrast to the rest of *Relayer,* where everything else is either a frantic breaking of all rock (and many other musical) conventions, or an intense drama of war and peace, or both. While "To Be Over" might be compared to "And You and I," in some ways it is a more conventional and restful song—as it is meant to be. Whereas "Sound Chaser" fits into no conventional category, "To Be Over" is simply good songwriting of a more settled-down sort. Perhaps this is seen most in the fact that Chris Squire plays a Fender bass guitar on the piece, and he and White play something more like a conventional rhythm section role. Not everything about "To Be Over," however, is as straightforward as I have characterized it thus far.

"To Be Over" once again visits a nautical theme, though for a much longer duration than the brief appearance of such a theme in "Ritual." The funny thing, though, is that this theme is played by Howe on the electric sitar, so this is a bit of seafaring India, apparently. As with the sitar/harpsichord section in "Siberian Khatru," however, the idea of this unlikely combination is understated, as though sailors in port always slap on some Old Spice and head down to the local bar for some ragas. "To Be Over" is another example of excellent guitar orchestration by Howe, even though he only uses three instruments—the Coral sitar, the Fender Steel guitar, and the Telecaster.

A note on the last of these. When I saw Yes on the American part of the *Relayer* tour, I was kind of shocked when Howe came out playing a Telecaster— and played it for the larger part of the entire *Relayer* album. When Howe became known to fans outside of England, especially with the release of "Roundabout," the guitar afficionados among us were especially impressed with the way that he played big-box Gibson guitars, especially his prized ES-175. This set him apart from most rock guitarists of the day, very few of whom were playing anything other than solid-body guitars, mostly Fender Stratocasters (e.g., Hendrix, Clapton), Gibson Les Pauls (Jimmy Page, Martin Barre), or Gibson SG Standards (Pete Townshend). (The only guitarists I can now think of who then played hollow-bodied electrics were Alvin Lee, who played a Gibson ES-335, and Ted Nugent, who played a Gibson Birdland—which is a big box instrument.) Telecasters were known at that point as "country-western" guitars. But then, Howe is unique among progressive rock guitarists for introducing country elements into the mix. (Howe discusses his use of the Telecaster in *The Steve Howe Guitar Collection,* pp. 42–43.)

The instrumental introduction for "To Be Over" is gentle and inaudacious, hardening for just a moment with a series of cascading notes that introduce the vocals. When Jon Anderson comes in, his singing is also very gentle, and there is a slight country feel to the song. Everything here is a model of understatement. Lyrically, the song begins as a straightforward love song, painting a picture as Yes often does, bringing together the calming streams and the possibility of healing. The second part of the song reminds me of the way that "Ritual" makes the turn from intimacy and the interpersonal to a larger, cosmic theme. As with the conclusion of "Ritual," the idea of belonging is stressed: "Don't doubt your part, be ready to be loved." This is a song of possibility, presented this time with deep humility.

In the instrumental section, Steve Howe begins with some flowing steel guitar lines, which operate as a string section as much as a they do a solo; he then makes a neat transition to the Telecaster, playing what he appropriately calls a "chicken scratch" solo. There's great bite to it. What Howe does in this guitar section, in fact, is to explore two sides of country music—the ballad, and "hard" country. The whole instrumental section is unhurried, but it doesn't drag. Moraz contributes a spirited synthesizer solo just before the last verse; the tempo picks up a little bit, but without disrupting the spirit of the song. There is a subtle build-up into the final verse, and then a somewhat long, gentle denouement, in which it sure sounds as if Squire and Howe are singing "Nous sommes du soleil" in the background.

This is a very nice song that is somewhat the mirror image of "Sound Chaser."

"The Gates of Delirium"

Yes's epic work from *Relayer* is right on a level with "Close to the Edge." If Yes had difficulties making the leap from an album side to four album sides, they didn't seem to have any problems going back to the "shorter format"—a funny thing to say, since "The Gates of Delirium" is an epic work that clocks in at nearly twenty-two minutes. Around the time of its creation, I recall interviews with Jon Anderson and Patrick Moraz where they both expressed appreciation for the symphonies of Sibelius. In a way, what Sibelius did was to take the chromatic innovations of late Romanticism and distill them down into their most economically expressed essences. To my mind, many late romantic symphonies, especially some of those by Mahler and Bruckner, are interesting in what they do with harmony, but they are simply too overblown. Of course, everyone in the late Romantic period was trying to produce another Beethoven's Ninth—an admirable goal. In the wake of the late Romantic period, a number of composers went very much in the other direction, toward "miniature" works, such as those by Anton Webern (a pupil and associate of Schoenberg's). In a sense, backing off from the "late Romanticism" of *Tales from Topographic Oceans,* Yes went more in the direction of Sibelius (a route also taken by Stravinsky, Ravel, and others, to be sure), aiming for a more economical expression of the tonal, timbral, and rhythmic innovations that they had already developed.

The argument might be made that King Crimson's direction was more akin to Schoenberg and his followers, including John Cage. In the case of either King Crimson or Yes, this was all refracted through the Beatles and the language of rock music.

In all of their works, whether they be songs or more song-like, or epic, symphonic works that go a good distance beyond song form, Yes seems to oscillate between two approaches to themes and subject matter. On the one hand, there are works such as *Tales from Topographic Oceans* or, for that matter, "Sound Chaser," that mainly present something like a set of philosophical or theological (or "spiritual") views. On the other hand, there are works such as "And You and I" and "The Gates of Delirium" that are involved with telling a story. Of course, many of Yes's works are some combination of the two, such as "Close to the Edge" or "Yours Is No Disgrace." In any case, many of Yes's works take a kind of "painterly" approach to music, with some sort of narrative at the heart of the enterprise. This comes across quite clearly in the case of "The Gates of Delirium," because Roger Dean's album cover art is clearly geared toward illustrating the story involved in the work. The predominant gray of the cover might be interpreted as a comment on the grimness of the subject matter of "Gates." On the cover, warriors are not only heading into battle, they are descending into the Earth. And it is quite clear that the trail of the serpent is all over this enterprise.

I have to wonder if the group itself didn't feel that they were going off to battle with this outing. True to form, however, they are carrying forward the fight with optimism, but not by falling into the "constant vogue of triumphs." Indeed, "Gates of Delirium" is an important statement about the necessity of militant action in certain circumstances, the risks involved in taking such action, and the imperative to not lose one's moral bearings in the midst of this necessity. Although I believe that *Tales from Topographic Oceans* is an important piece of music, it is the ethical commitment of works such as "Gates of Delirium" that allows me to place the more contemplative statements of Yes in a perspective I feel much more affirmative of. With this ethical commitment firmly stated, I can place the contemplative side in a different context than if this side were the complete vision of Yes. Because Yes creates works that put forward statements such as, "Peaceful lives will not deliver freedom/Fighting we know, destroy oppression," the more blissful and contemplative lyrics and music can be understood as prefiguring a redeemed world that is on the other side of struggle. This prefiguring can inspire us to struggle. Anything else is simple escapism, of the sort that leaves this unredeemed world the way that it already is.[40]

"The Gates of Delirium" opens with a very rich harmonic landscape, and one imagines a peaceful village going about its daily business. The cymbal work by Alan White is masterful, and Howe and Squire create some dense harmonics on their respective instruments. However, the predominant background sound is created by Moraz, a synthesized texture bordering on white noise, but out of which comes the occasional note or even melody. Into the midst of this peaceable realm comes the beginnings of a call to order and discipline, the need to prepare for dealing with a threat to the realm's freedom. Musically, this transition is presented as the emergence of a marching rhythm from the bass and drums (especially the rhythm of the bass guitar and bass drum playing in unison). The transition to a military footing is not made all at once; the gentle singing, with sounds that would ordinarily indicate a carefree sense of life ("La La"—which has to be understood in musical context, or else it seems more like the gesture of a mindless person, and not in any Buddhist sense) are intermingled with heightening intensity. This intensity, developed narratively, is especially built up in the guitar—the "sword of rock," after all. More and more the other instruments also become weapons, until there is a complete transformation of the scene and an army is assembled.

Here Anderson enters both as balladeer and as sermonizing preacher. The army is assembled on the field, and Anderson speaks to tell us why the army has been gathered and why it must "stand and fight." At first this ballad/sermon is delivered with only the accompaniment of an acoustic guitar, but this quickly builds up into a full scale orchestration that is, interestingly, somewhat *festive*. It is not difficult to see the banners unfurled, the trumpets all shined up, the horses ready for a good gallop. The lyrics do a very good job of showing how all of these things are bound up together—ethical necessity, a sense of pride about the preparations that have been made to face this necessity, and an almost joyous eagerness to dive into the task. That war can be both ethically and politically necessary and yet ethically ambiguous is perhaps the central message of this work. This goes even for a war that is for good things—for freedom, against oppression. Of course, it doesn't go at all for wars that are not for just causes, as with the case of wars of colonial or imperial conquest, where there is no "moral ambiguity" to assuage the souls who would prefer to say, "If the summer change to winter, yours is no disgrace."[41]

The music takes an enormous leap in intensity as the battle is joined. Squire's bass guitar pulses mightily, and the guitar is ferocious. The scene of battle is intense as well, and the moral cause of the war is swept up into the mere dialectic of opposing forces, one of which *may* win if both are not completely consumed. In this dialectic, the idea of justice is progressively reduced to mere vengeance, mere eye-for-eye: "Kill or be killing faster sins correct the flow." Interestingly, the music here alternates between 3/4 and 4/4 time. 3/4 time is traditionally known as "waltz rhythm," and there is a kind of slow dance undercurrent here, alternating with a more straightforward rock cadence. The dance rhythm is appropriate, for a war involves not only enemies, but in some sense "partners," in that each side comes more and more to gear its movements to the other—and all else is lost.[42] There are stages in the development of the war, and for a brief moment the preacher speaks, refocusing the army on the reason for this war:

> Surely we know
> In glory
> We rise to offer
> Create our freedom

Even in this statement of purpose there is the reminder that "Power spent passion bespoils our soul receiver"—even those with justice on their side may find themselves "crawling out of dirty holes, their morals disappear[ed]."[43]

Again the army pumps itself up, even if in light of the ethical ambiguity at the heart of war: "we fight the power and live by it by day." The rot and corruption of triumphalism begins to spread:

> Our Gods awake in thunderous roars and guide
> The Leaders' hands in paths of glory to the cause.

To be sure, this is the ultimate triumphalistic declaration, to claim that the gods are guiding the leaders in a path to glory. The marching music is bold here, especially in the confident bass line, and the almost carping reverberated octaves from Howe's knife-sharp Telecaster.

But again things become momentarily, indeed eerily, quiet; again, in camp one imagines, the army refocuses—and confronts its necessity with the grimmest determination. The two "Listen" verses are a great study in thematic development and dynamic contrast. The first of these verses asks, in a still small voice, "[S]hould we fight forever, knowing as we do know, fear destroys?" At the end of this verse, the guitar plays a very metallic, disonant chord, one that (electronically) echoes and multiplies itself—these are the swords of battle being unsheathed. The second "Listen" verse is played with a determined march cadence, with the bass guitar and bass drum driving the army into a lockstep progression. The lyrics speak of what has to be done:

> Listen, your friends have been broken,
> They tell us of your poison;
> Now we know.
> Kill them, give them as they give us.
> Slay them, burn their childrens' laughter.
> On to hell.

"Give them as they give us"—this is what the just cause has come to; and yet, this has to be done. For we have children as well, and there is no peaceful resolution that will bring justice (or even peace) to them: "The pen won't stay the demon's wings"—there's no getting around this conflict with talk, prayer, contemplation, or even flight. "The hour approaches": the stage is set for a final, manic, spasm of violence. "The fist will run, grasp metal to gun": wave upon wave of building intensity.

At first the battle seems to go well; forces are contending, represented by the guitar and synthesizer. Howe's guitar runs are both furious and tightly controlled. Moraz's synthesizer lines sally forth with confidence. The bass pulses with a slight hint of syncopation. There is a turn in the battle, and here the bass and drums take on an extreme and difficult syncopation. I'm not entirely sure how to count this, but I'll venture a guess that it is alternating measures of 5/4 and 7/4. Howe plays some steely yet thick harmonics that are reminiscent of those heard at the opening of the piece, alternated with springy, angular lines, very harsh, stabbing chords, and ultimately a line in unison with the bass guitar. Things are building to their most intense point. Moraz brings the storm, with swirling, hurricane-force strings and synthesizer wind sounds; he also creates the sound of true calamity, with an "electric slinky." The rhythmic center is absolutely everywhere at this point.

As intense as everything else is here, the most forceful part of this music is Alan White's drumming, which is nothing short of incredible. Even as it sounds as if he is simply flailing about wildly, there is no question but that this effect is created through virtuoso control. One does not associate such creativity and control with such extraordinary *pounding*—truly, I feel sorry for those drums! And yet, all of this is part of a complex orchestration, and contributes to the larger symphonic landscape—in a way that is, frankly, a good deal more interesting, musically and otherwise, than the cannons firing in the *1812 Overture* (tell

Tchaikovsky the news!). In other words, this isn't a drum solo, it is orchestration within and by the drum kit. I think if more people listened to White's work in this light, they would realize that he is one of the really great rock drummers.

Thematically, as the swirling strings and other cacophonous sounds are caught up in this percussive tour de force, there is the strong feeling of a war and a violence that has taken on a life of its own and that cannot stop. And yet, even this does not tell us that the struggle finally lost all purpose. An army that has to fight the just cause must both keep a moral perspective on what it is doing, and gear up to fight the war well and to completion. If the enemy is determined, and especially if the enemy is not held back by moral principles—as is the case with any army that is fighting not to overcome oppression but to extend or enforce it—then the fighters for freedom and against oppression have to deal with this. They can't just say that they didn't want to get into this battle and walk away. Although the group fleshed out "The Gates of Delirium," Jon Anderson provided the basic thematic and musical conception. In interviews concerning the composition, Anderson said that he wanted to deal with the question of "war and peace." I do not know to what extent he had Tolstoy in mind in creating this music, but I think of another important Russian battleground, where the invader was fought off at great cost: Stalingrad. The fighting there was some of the most fierce and brutal in all history, and there was no walking away from it, there was no mental escape, there was no divine deliverance. To my mind, this is the sort of scene that Anderson is trying to set here.

And then there is the aftermath. To fight the war, our village had to *become* war, and this is a horrible, scarring thing. The victory is celebrated with a theme that begins triumphantly, that carries over all of the energy of the battle itself, but now in a happy spirit. Again, the drums are at the center of this, not simply as rhythm section, but as orchestra leader. The lead melody is played on the steel guitar, in a spiraling dance in the village center. Finally, the celebration begins to play itself out—though it fades back in several (three, in fact) times. Realization begins to set in; war cannot simply be waged *externally,* there is an interiorization of the conflict that must be healed. The oppressor, Marx argues, wreaks one kind of vengeance upon those who fight oppression in what it makes the latter become in order to carry out that fight. "Soon," the final part of "Gates of Delirium," implicitly takes account of this, and perhaps goes a good deal further. The enemy army has a dual nature: it is fighting to uphold oppression, and therefore must be dealt with as an enemy, and defeated on the field of battle. But the enemy *army* is also made up of people who are much like "us," and even in the case where these people are slain—or perhaps *especially* in this case—there has to be a healing, there has to be a recognition that "there is no mutant enemy" ("And You and I"). "They" are like "us," and "we" are like "them," and the only truly just cause is to work and, if necessary, fight for the day when there is no longer any "us" or "them." Still further, the violence that has been wreaked upon the world soul and our mother, the Earth, must be healed. All of this we hope and work for "soon," for this cannot come immediately—the healing is a transformation, a work of redemption. Indeed, just as the "night" is endless, so might be this passing within of the light, this healing.

This is a view not unlike that argued for by Jean-Paul Sartre in his final interviews with Benny Levy, some six years later:

> . . . evolution through action would be a series of failures from which something positive, already contained in the failure and ignored by those who had wished to succeed, would result unexpectedly. This positive result would be these partial, local successes, difficult to recognize by those who had worked for them but, which, from failure to failure, would accomplish some progress. It is thus that I have understood history. ("Today's Hope," p. 161)

All of this has to unfold materially—which isn't to say that consciousness isn't a decisive factor in the form of this unfolding. Indeed, the essence of the struggle is to overcome oppressive determinations that prevent "the race" from inventing and reinventing itself consciously. To say, at the end of this, that the struggle shows us nothing more than the folly of struggle, is to do justice to no one, including to the enemy who had to be defeated. "Soon" is a plaintive cry for healing; it is not an invocation of theodicy, some theological scheme in which the struggles and wounds of humankind can be transcended by a god who makes everything work out in the end (the so-called "final harmony" argument). "Soon" is the aftermath that cannot be walked away from any more than the struggle to defeat oppression can be.

If there is one way in which *Relayer* does not compare to *Close to the Edge,* it is in the fact that the pieces on the former do not interconnect to the extent that those on the latter do. It is harder, therefore, to "totalize" *Relayer.* This is also the case for Yes's next effort. However, at least in the sum of its parts, *Relayer* is certainly a masterpiece.

Going for the One

Within the space of about five or six years, it seemed that Yes came full circle within the main sequence. Everything that had been opened up with *The Yes Album* and *Fragile* was explored at length and sometimes pushed to extremes. The membership of the group shifted somewhat, but throughout the main sequence there was the solid core of Anderson, Squire, and Howe. With *Relayer,* Alan White fully found his bearings within the Yes matrix. Rick Wakeman lost his, but then found them again; despite having said, in interviews, that he would never rejoin the group, there came a point when this seemed the natural thing to do. The communal spirit that had been Yes's in the earlier years of the main sequence, especially for *Fragile* and *Close to the Edge,* came together one more time. Appropriately, two main sensibilities permeate *Going for the One:* celebration and reflection.

Going for the One is a very *bright* album, starting with its album cover. Perhaps the fact that the cover is not by Roger Dean helps the album form a bookend with *The Yes Album.* The latter was also the only other album in the main sequence that had a photograph of actual people on the cover. This time, of course, we see the backside of a rather hunkish young man, who stands naked before those glass and steel monuments to the corporate world, skyscrapers. (I was working at a record store at the time this album came out, and one customer, a middle-aged woman, asked me if the frontal view was to be found on the inside of the album. Alas, no.) The man is being crossed and penetrated by various geometrical lines and shapes vectoring across the scene. The inside of this three-panel foldout cover, in contrast to the gaudy outside, is a serene photograph of a lake at sunset. I assume that the lake is Lake Montreaux, near where the album was made. Out in the lake, standing on a very small clump of land that may or may not deserve the honorific "island," stands a large and substantial tree, its leaves mostly shed. Here, too, are separate photographs of each band member, in natural settings. I read the whole cover as saying: "the corporate monster is out there, the music is *in here."* The photographs of the group are also crossed by the lines of cosmic rays seen on the outside cover. Are they a benign force?

Going for the One is also a less dense and less heavy album than the two that came before. Perhaps the group started to realize that some of their pieces were filling too many tracks. This is a problem that affected most of the progressive rock groups—and many other ordinary rock groups besides—toward the end of the seventies. As studio recording expanded to thirty-two and then sixty-four tracks, groups added additional layers of guitars, keyboards, and vocals. The technology buried the music, in many cases. This threat hovered over *Tales from Topographic Oceans* and *Relayer* somewhat, so "slimming down" for *Going for the One* was a good idea. Having said this, I should point out that the album is no less a virtuoso piece of writing and performance for the fact.

Just as *Relayer* had returned to the fields already somewhat plowed by *Close to the Edge, Going for the One* takes up the spirit of *Fragile* and even *The Yes Album.* The album certainly begins with more outright rocking than had been heard since "Yours Is No Disgrace" or the second part of "All Good People." In a way, there are two "Roundabouts" on *Going for the One,* the title song, as well as Chris Squire's "Parallels." Both are more straightforward than their *Fragile* predecessor or "Siberian Khatru" or, it goes without saying, "Sound Chaser." (Significantly, both also have the word "roundabout" in their lyrics.) The album also presents two works, "Turn of the Century" and "Wondrous Stories," that feature acoustic guitar prominently. Finally, the epic work on *Going for the One,*

"Awaken," is almost a pure hymn, both celebration and reflection. In all of this music, the elements from the main sequence are refined, pared down but not watered down, elegant.

The neo-Platonic philosopher Plotinus (205–270 C.E.) argued that all existence is formed from "emanation from the One."

> The One is that from which all else derives by a process of emanation, on which all else depends, and toward which all aspires to return. [The One] is above the realm of Being, lying beyond the possibilities of thought and discourse, and is to be attained only by a rare ascent of mystical exaltation.[44]

Plato had argued, in Book VI of *The Republic,* that the form of the Good is "beyond Being." Therefore, this One and the Good would seem to be identical. I do not know if the members of Yes were aware in 1977 or in more recent years of neo-Platonic philosophy; I tend to doubt it, but I also feel confident that this isn't the important thing. Clearly there is a neo-Platonic drive in *Going for the One* that goes beyond the title of the album. Indeed, in broad terms this drive sums up the general "Yes philosophy," if I can put it that way. This philosophy is monistic in outline; in answer to the ancient question of the one and the many, Yes answers, "the one." Although monistic conceptions can be either materialist or idealist in their ontology, it is safe to say that Yes's is more oriented toward the idea that there are higher values that are "past all mortal as we."

Some political theorists, Marxists especially, have attempted to argue that such an ontology, while it may be aligned for a time with a radical political outlook or even movement, is at root quietistic and therefore reactionary. Some theorists of a more "postmodern" predisposition, such as Paul de Man, might argue that the idea of "returning to the one," which is certainly a part of the Yes vision of the main sequence, belies an organicism that is, again, politically dangerous.[45]

Of course, as artists, the members of Yes (and obviously I am thinking of Jon Anderson most of all, but I think there is something like a group "Yes philosophy" of the main sequence, even if Anderson is the core of it) are not primarily concerned with shaping a metaphysical system. On the other hand, it is no stretch to say that they are involved in such systems. A work such as "Awaken" is practically a hymn to a monistic, organicist ontology. However, despite the fact that there is clearly a philosophically idealist side to Yes's myth-making, we ought to keep in mind the roots of this metaphysicalizing that were closer to home: William Blake and the English Romantic tradition, and the larger hermetic traditions of the Radical Reformation and figures such as Jacob Boehme.[46] These traditions were thoroughly engaged with what Marx called "sensuous" materiality, as well as with radical, communitarian politics. One might argue that rock music, in its very essence, cannot avoid sensuality—though, of rock groups, Yes has probably been accused of this avoidance as much as anyone. With perhaps a few exceptions (mostly in the vicinity of *Tales from Topographic Oceans*), in furthering the *ideal* of "going for the one," Yes paints a picture of the *mortal* surpassing of this *present* existence.[47] The momentary glimpse of a world where "kill or be killing" is not the norm (the ever-present war of all against all that threatens to break out at any moment) is a political gesture *against* the world where such killing *is* the norm.

In discussing the individual pieces on *Going for the One,* I now return to the practice of following their order of presentation on the album.

"Going for the One"

Two instruments stand out especially on *Going for the One* as a whole: the guitar and the church organ. Of course, any group that has Steve Howe as its guitarist is going to feature his playing. But there are places where *Going for the One* really has the guitar in the forefront, and the title track is certainly one of these. As it turns out, "Going for the One" is the first Yes song or work that features Howe on the steel guitar exclusively. Howe is a master of all forms of the guitar unlike any other player, and he is an accomplished practitioner of the steel guitar, an instrument that most rock guitarists don't even go near. (The closest some come is to play slide guitar.) The steel guitar (including the pedal steel guitar, which Howe plays on "Awaken") is usually taken up as a specialization in itself, most often by country musicians. (The country-rock group Poco had a pedal steel player, Rusty Young. In the early seventies, Poco toured with Yes, and Howe was exposed to the steel and pedal steel at that time; see *Steve Howe Guitar Collection,* pp. 40–41, 46–47.) Some of what Howe does with the steel guitar is country-inflected; almost all of it *burns,* and nowhere more so than in "Going for the One."

The neat thing about "Going for the One" is that it somehow combines a real rock'n'roll sensibility and edge—of a sort never heard before on any Yes album—with everything that is completely up to date about Yes's music. "Going for the one" is the "Good Golly Miss Molly" of progressive rock: a cool, light blue and white 1950s Chevy, as driven like a bat-outa-hell by the Road Warrior.

The initial verses of "Going for the One" are completely trippy; it takes getting to the third verse to see the point of this:

> Now the verses I've sang
> Don't add much weight to the story in my head.
> So I'm thinking I should go and write a punch line.
> But they're so hard to find
> In my cosmic mind,
> So I think I'll take a look out of the window.

Clearly, Anderson is having a little joke on himself, and on all those critics who think that there's no humor in his "cosmic mind." (Another aspect of this punch line is Anderson's use of slang and bad grammar—"verses I've sang," "N' should I really chase so hard.") Though the humor here remains more cosmic than, say, sexual or sensual, I think there is a connection between this trippiness and the sort of thing that Little Richard was doing with "Tutti Frutti."

The drums and piano also rock quite hard in this song, especially giving Rick Wakeman a chance to play some honky-tonk piano. Where these instruments drive rather insistently, Squire provides a walking bass line—though one that, as one might expect, walks a good deal further than most such lines.

Howe's solo between the second and third verses could be characterized as hard country rock. As Squire and Anderson sing without words at the end, there are a pair of stops and starts that again drive home the rocking nature of this piece. Finally, the steel guitar burns even more fiercely, rising into the stratosphere as if to say, "That's all, folks!"

"Turn of the Century"

As I have mentioned, *Relayer* and *Going for the One* are not as thematically tight as were *Close to the Edge* and even *Fragile*. "Going for the One" and "Parallels" form a pair, the first giving us a humorous parody of the more cosmic side of Yes, the second a more straightforward statement of themes that were central to Yes in the main sequence. Both are stretched versions of rock songs, played and embellished with vast skill. Thematically, "Awaken" is not unlike "Parallels," though it is musically quite different. In their more acoustic orientation, "Turn of the Century" and "Wondrous Stories" would also seem to form a pair; they are similar, too, in that they are the works on the album oriented more toward narrative (something almost entirely missing from the other works). However, whereas "Wondrous Stories" is more about the desire to hear a narrative, "Turn of the Century" is a rather developed story itself. In contrast to *Fragile* and *Close to the Edge*, *Relayer* and *Going for the One* present what might be called a "varied program." Indeed, the latter is even much more varied than the former in musical terms. (*Tormato,* as we shall see, "varied" to the point of somewhat falling apart.) We make quite a turn, then, in going from "Going for the One" to "Turn of the Century."

Indeed, it is hard to think of another of Yes's works to compare "Turn of the Century" to. There are a lot of words in its eight minutes; if this were Pete Townshend's song, "Turn" would be a mini–rock opera. Here, instead, Anderson, Howe, and White have written a very lovely and sensitive piece. The story concerns a sculptor whose wife dies. He tries to recapture her "form out of stone." Although there is some sentimentality in some of Yes's songs, there is no other that comes so close to bordering on an outright tear-jerker, at least when one pays attention to the lyrics. And yet, "Turn of the Century" is not mere sentimentality. In some ways, this song does a better job of crafting a sense of the sorts of human connections we all hope for than the more cosmic and thematically metaphysical works by Yes. This song will have special meaning for anyone who has experienced a deep loss. My argument has been that the sense of such experience needs to be brought to Yes's work as a whole, otherwise the listener may leap too quickly to a final harmony that is an egregious insult to real human suffering (or the suffering of other creatures, or of the Earth, for that matter). (So, go have your heart broken, if you want to understand this music—or any music or art worth a damn.)

"Turn of the Century" begins with some crystal clear guitar work on the Martin 00-18 acoustic. Howe's octaves are especially crisp and effective. The guitar parts for this piece are quite complex in the way they weave themselves around the narrative of the song. The sensitive playing by the guitar and piano allow Chris Squire to avoid anything that sounds like a conventional bass line here. Indeed, for much of the song, he shadows and elaborates on the vocal line; this works very well, as the bass becomes something like the spirit of the sculptor's wife—whose name we never hear. This omission occurs not, I think, out of any desire that her name not be known, but instead out of respect for the sculptor and his feelings of loss—there is the sense that the story will tell itself, and that the singers or lyricists are mainly involved in hearing the story told and repeating it. In any case, Squire does a fine job of barely being there, and yet doing quite a lot. It should be added, too, that, as much as "Going for the One" is a "real" rocker, "Turn of the Century" isn't rock music at all, except in the sense that it was written and played by rock musicians. So not only is there not a conventional bass line, there is no conventional drumming either. For most of the song, White plays vibes and other tuned percussion, including tympani. On either vibes or tympani, he's quite good.

Anderson's singing here is beautiful and heartfelt. It's nice to know that someone who thinks on the level of the cosmos is also attuned to the level of the hurting heart. The poetry of this song is understated, not melodramatic, and Anderson gives it the correct reading. Does the sculptor's wife really come back to life?

Now Roan, no more tears
Set to work; his strength
So transformed him.
Realizing a form out of stone, his work
So absorbed him.
Could she hear him?
Could she see him?
All aglow was his room dazed in this light.
He would touch her.
He would hold her.
Laughing as they danced,
Highest colors touching others.

The instrumental build-ups are subtle and powerful, especially around the questions, "Could she hear him," and so on, as well as the verses that begin "Was the sign with a touch" and "Was it sun through the haze." Howe switches over to electric guitar, and he shows how it is possible to play emotionally intense lines that are not blues-based (in any but the loosest sense).

I do not know if Roan's wife comes back from the dead. She lives in Roan's memory and work, at least—what more can be said? "Like leaves we touched"—does *Roan* really live, now that "time has caught" his life companion? They are both a memory, a photograph, from "all those many years ago." This is the other side of "past all mortal as we," this is mortality, past which is memory and those who go on.

"Parallels"

Chris Squire's compositional contribution to *Going for the One* is very much in the vein of "Hold Out Your Hand," from his solo album, *Fish Out of Water.* "Parallels" has a bass line that both propels from behind and leads from out front, while providing ornamentation as well. Furthermore, this song takes Squire back to his musical roots, in that it features the church organ. There aren't too many things to compare the employment of this instrument in a piece of rock music to, so almost anything that might be said about it will sound silly. Wakeman certainly knows how to play the instrument (I'd like to hear a whole album of compositions for church organ by Wakeman), and what he does with the organ is very lively, not at all lumbering (as one might expect). The low tones at the very beginning of "Parallels" are, I assume, from the organ pedals. (My understanding is that Wakeman has played the church organ since he was a young boy.) In any case, it is the organ and bass guitar that set up the framework for this piece, which allows a good deal of freedom for the guitar and drums. The vocals are very straightahead—strong and clear, for the most part featuring Anderson and Squire singing in unison at almost equal strength.

"Parallels" is very much an anthem of the spirit of Yes. The lyrics are perhaps not brilliant, in any poetic sense, but they make a clear statement, and there are some good lines. The best of these are, "Could be an ever opening flower," which is an expression various band members used during the main sequence to describe what Yes was doing, and "When we are winning we can stop and shout, making love towards perfection." In an interview, Jon Anderson said something to the effect that, "When we reach perfection, we'll quit." What he implied, of course, is that perfection is a regulative ideal which is never fully reached—but it remains the ideal, nonetheless. Squire's line reflects well the kind of "perfectionism"—the ideal of eternal progression—that is an integral part of the green language, as manifest especially in the poetry of William Blake and the philosophy of Ralph Waldo Emerson.

The song begins with some brilliant, soaring guitar from Howe. Whereas the Telecaster was Howe's Fender of choice for *Relayer,* here he comes up with yet another unexpected axe, the Stratocaster. His playing in "Parallels" is a model of clarity; Howe goes a long way toward "build[ing] a shining tower," with lines that unfold with impeccable logic and no bluffing.

The instrumental interlude before the final verse, where Squire and Wakeman play off of each other, is also remarkable. Squire's line seems quite simple, given that its basis is just two notes pulsing against one another, but the way he mixes up the rhythm is enchanting. Wakeman shows musical wisdom in keeping the organ in balance with Squire's line, and the whole interaction is at once playful, spirited, and substantial. (To be sure, recording engineer John Timperly should receive due credit here as well.)

The vocals, which were so bright already, simply light up in the final verse. It's a beautiful effect: Squire's voice is thicker, Anderson's higher—the former provides a boost to the latter. I can't help but remark, too, that the line "create a new dimension" is appropriate for a song by Chris Squire. When it comes to the bass guitar, that is precisely what he has done. Or, I should say, what he has done with his instrument has opened up a larger musical dimension.

The series of guitar lines at the very end of the song are frightening in their difficulty—and intense without being heavy, burning without distortion effects. Indeed, there is a great deal of music in the last few measures of "Parallels," with some well-timed stops and starts and, finally, those final three notes that are at one and the same time an ellipsis and a series of singular, hard, affirmative periods: Yes. Yes. Yes.

"Wondrous Stories"

As if again to provide yet another segment of the full circle, "Wondrous Stories" features Steve Howe on the "vachalia," an instrument he introduced on "Your Move." As Howe explains in his *Guitar Collection* book (pp. 64–65), this instrument is in fact simply an acoustic twelve-string guitar, of Portuguese origin and with a pear-shaped body. (A vachalia, as Howe explains, is something else altogether, though still an instrument in the guitar family.) In any case, "Wondrous Stories" is at root an acoustic ballad telling of a balladeer, with a glistening solo and set of embellishments from Rick Wakeman's polyphonic synthesizer. This instrument is used to good effect; it is the only keyboard on the song, and Wakeman is careful not to overdo it. As an advocate of keyboard restraint, I salute Wakeman's work here.

Chris Squire's lines for "Wondrous Stories" are artful and understated; he supplies a surging "bottom" for the main lines of the song, with some delicate, subtle high notes for embellishment.

As one might expect of such a ballad, it is the harmony vocals that are the highlight of the piece. These are especially strong in the "it is no lie" segment (final verse), and the way that Squire shadows Anderson on the line "imagine everything" is very powerful. A Yes motto, we might say.

In this brief song, Yes makes a statement about the importance of hearing and listening. Yes's music is a music of *respect,* in the Kantian ethical tradition of fundamental regard for the other—"our heart is open, our reason to be here." Good musicians are good listeners (and it is the inability or refusal to listen that keeps many instrumentalists from being real musicians—they do not listen to the muse). If anything, Yes goes beyond this truth to an even deeper one: that music that is "going for the one" must aim for the form of the good, and this is both an aesthetic and an ethical ideal—and this is a matter of being open, of listening.

"Awaken"

At last we come to Yes's final epic work of the main sequence. With "Awaken," an era comes to a close. Who can know if Yes had a sense of this when they composed and performed this piece? I'm not even sure that the group members knew or could have known this. And yet, "Awaken" is a hymn to the spirit of Yes and a very appropriate capstone to an extraordinary period of their music and of music more generally. While I have stressed the ways in which *Going for the One* comes full circle to the spirit and musical innovations of *The Yes Album* and *Fragile,* there is simply no precedent for "Awaken."

The whole idea of "Awaken" is also very much in the spirit of "going for the one," both in its lyrics and music. "Awaken" is a very complex piece of music, and yet running throughout is a crystal clarity, a sense of wholeness, and indeed a sense of holiness. Long ago, Thomas Aquinas argued that, "for beauty, three things are required: clarity, harmony, and integrity." "Awaken" is very "classical" in its approach to these values, perhaps more than any other work by Yes. Indeed, one might extend the comparison with Stravinsky here: just as Stravinsky went from a complex "pagan" and "primitivist" (especially with his three ballets for Sergei Diaghilev, *The Firebird, Petrushka,* and *Rite of Spring*) period to his later "neo-classical" period (for example, the *Symphony of Psalms*), Yes made a similar move from "Close to the Edge" to "Awaken." "Awaken" *is* harmonically and rhythmically complicated—in its twenty-four opening measures there are ten time changes, including a brief passage through 9/32 time, which boggles the mind—just as Stravinsky's later works are, but there is also a kind of *austerity* to both later compositional styles.

Another post-Romantic composer in the Western classical tradition whose work "Awaken" might be compared to is Carl Orff, especially his *Carmina Burana.* One reason the comparison suggests itself is that sleigh bells—as well as large percussive resources more generally—are featured prominently in both works. Another similarity is the use of chants.

Lyrically, "Awaken" is a hymn to clarity itself, to "ask away/that thought be contact/with all that's clear." Indeed, "Awaken" is as close to an expression of pure gnosticism, a yearning for unity with a purely transcendent reality, as Yes has ever come. The intertwining of "pagan" and "Christian" themes that is present in Yes's work, especially from *Close to the Edge* onward, is presented here in its most austere and ahistorical form. Early in the work, there is a section of three verses that makes reference to the historical drama of humanity, but more in the sense of the *idea* of history—and, significantly, as "blindness"—rather than through any engagement with sensuous reality. The first of these verses bears this out:

> Workings of man
> Set out to ply historical life;
> Reregaining the flower of the fruit of his tree.
> All awakening.
> All restoring you.

This is the vision of a specifically Jewish gnosticism pared down to its most basic form: all of history can be summarized as the separation from God that befalls humanity because of the incident in the garden. In the second verse in this "workings of man" section, we find a very old gnostic image: humanity "crying out from the fire set aflame." In ancient gnostic lore, going back to the time of Plato and before, the human soul is understood to be a spark that has become separated from the eternal fire. This spark has become trapped in sensuous reality—typical images are of the spark trapped in ice or stone. The transformation of humanity, the setting free of this spark—awakening, restoration—occurs not through the playing out of the historical drama, but in the blink of an eye, as it were, through an act of realization. There is another Jewish tradition—"normative Judaism"—that understands redemption as a work, and that the coming of the messiah must be prepared for *in history.* And, of course, Christianity has similar divisions, usually thematized in terms of salvation by a pure "grace" or, again, a work of redemption that humanity must perform, guided by God's openness to and co-participation in this work (a different sense of "grace"). In marked contrast to works such as "Close to the Edge" or "The Gates of Delirium," "Awaken" seems primarily motivated by this first sense of "grace."[48]

The "gnosticism" question might also be raised in more directly social terms. If the roots of something called "religion" have to do with the fact that, apparently, we human beings *die,* then we might ask whether this fact is something that transcends all social or political or historical categorization. If so, then there is no "politics of mortality," so to speak—or, at least, this is superseded by something more basic about human existence, what Martin Heidegger called "being-toward-death," the idea that "my death" is something that cannot be faced by any other person, at least not in the way that I face it. (I suppose you could say this does yield the minimal political thesis that "death is the great equalizer," a thesis that accompanies a kind of politics of despair that takes solace in the fact that, "at least our enemies will someday day, just as we will." But this doesn't have much to do with Heidegger or, it must be said, any real *politics* that takes as its prime motivation the idea of mutual flourishing of persons in the *polis.*) Some have argued that this is the essence of "religion" (I put the term in scare quotes because I am contesting the definition) and, therefore, to bring in social or political questions is inappropriate in this realm. (This is what Harold Bloom argues with his idea of "religious criticism.")[49] However, we don't simply die, we also live; except in the most narrowly analytical sense (the sense of separating out questions by *category,* without reference to their implication in actual human experience), *how we live* determines to a great degree how we will face death, and it seems quite clear to me that the social (historical, political, cultural) dimensions of this can at no point be factored out from whatever other dimensions there are to the question of mortality. (Incidentally, this is recognized by a number of thinkers who have engaged with—and to some extent are working out of—Heidegger's thought on these issues.)[50]

Considering the main sequence as a whole, one might argue that an oscillation in attitudes toward history, materiality, sensuous reality, and possibilities for active participation in transformation of the world (and therefore consciousness) can be seen, an oscillation between more "gnostic" (*Tales from Topographic Oceans, Going for the One*) and more "engaged" (*The Yes Album, Fragile, Close to the Edge, Relayer*) attitudes. We might consider, as well, the idea that this oscillation works on two levels. First, we might ask to what extent this oscillation represents a shifting point of view in the work of the composers themselves. Relatedly, and considering the three main composers of Yes's music in the main sequence, we might ask if one is more "gnostic," Anderson being the obvious candidate, one more engaged and sensuous, namely Squire, and one somewhere in-between, that person being Howe. However, this is a highly speculative hypothesis; for all that it may be descriptive in a very general sense (Anderson is more "cosmic," Squire more "grounded"), counterexamples abound (for one, the fact that Anderson was the primary composer of "Gates of Delirium"). More significantly, and second, we might ask whether swings in this pendulum are more closely tied to larger social and cultural developments. For example, is it significant that the last swing of the pendulum was more a rejection of the politics of mortality, more toward a pure gnosticism? Or is this a merely contingent fact—just as the fact that "Awaken" is the last epic work of the main sequence may be contingent?

While I would not want to push the reductivistic argument that every piece of Yes music was some sort of direct reaction to changes in the body politic (and the politics of the mortality of the human body), in more general terms I do think there is not only a pole to the oscillation that is more "political," but that there is a politics to the oscillation itself. If one looks at the lyrics for "Awaken" as a whole, the oscillation can be seen in the difference between the "workings of man" verses and all of the other verses, which in fact surround and enclose the "workings" on either side. Here, one might argue, the idea of "religion"-as-gnosis, as having no political dimension, seems to reign supreme. If we look at the purely temporal trajectory of Yes during the main sequence, I suppose that one could say that, "Awaken" provides the gnostic "period" for a long sentence with many clauses.

But there is another way to look at the main sequence, in which we see that the *purely* gnostic expressions are very rare (and even *Tales* is not a purely gnostic expression, nor is *Going for the One*); that, for the most part, these expressions are surrounded by a more engaged poetic expression of the politics of redemption. Human history is, in large part, the history of oppression, suffering, barbarism, the lack of real community, the lack of redemption. Any work that resists and seeks to transcend this history risks offering mere escapism, at best, ideological cover for the "gold stainless nail" and the "cold reigning king" at worst. *This is a risk that cannot be fully avoided*—there are no words, there are no artistic materials, and there are no artistic forms that guarantee this avoidance. Theodor Adorno argued for "determinate negation" as one strategy for *possibly* avoiding the creation of "affirmative" works that let the world as it presently exists off the hook. Jean-Paul Sartre argued for "an ethics and art of the finite." (These themes will be developed further in part 3.) To some extent, these arguments have been transformed into "guerilla" musical strategies that seem to militate against the sort of large-scale, complex works that Yes created in the main sequence. (Important examples of the application of such strategies would be, variously, the work of such punk or quasipunk groups as the Sex Pistols or Gang of Four, and the work by and around Bill Laswell—Material, Praxis, and so on.)

In Adorno's view, to propose an "alternative" structure is to create something akin to a graven image.[51] And yet this did not mean that Adorno rejected large-scale, complex works of music, such as Beethoven's *Missa Solemnis* or Schoenberg's *Moses and Aaron;* indeed, Adorno valued such works precisely because, as Rose Subotnik puts it, they "offer[ed] unusual resistance to neutralization." Subotnik explains further:

> For art to have any chance of resisting neutralization, in Adorno's terms, it must alienate society by making itself difficult for society, as a collective entity, to understand. Stated another way, for the musical subject to preserve the essence of its individuality against social distortion, it must express itself through surface means that are not obviously expressive . . .. This means sacrificing the surface intelligibility of art (the intelligibility of what Adorno calls its "manifest structure") in order to retain the integrity of what Adorno calls the essence or "latent structure." (p. 32)[52]

It seems to me that even works such as "Awaken" embody these principles, and therefore contribute to a work of negation.

Furthermore, for all of those critics of Yes who argued that the group and its music lacked the basic sensuousness and erotic dimension of rock'n'roll, in fact, "Awaken" would have to be a prime offender. For the most part, I would argue, this really has to do with the lack of an overt masculinist program on Yes's part—the sort of logic of the Same (male identity) that many rock commentators seem to need endless confirmation of. In contrast to the two main strategies of sexuality in rock music, either overt masculinism or, what may or may not always be a subversive gesture, gender-bending, Yes seems to offer something at the border of the queer and something like *femininity*. The lack of "rock sensuousness" in Yes's music is in large part the lack of a masculinist sexual dimension, but also an opening to a quite different sense of erotics. This erotics, which exists within the double-bind (and struggles at the double-barricades) of the nonmasculinist and the antimasculinist, is hinted at by, among others, Michel Foucault and Luce Irigaray: they argue for an erotics that is not primarily concerned with self-pleasuring (as an expression of the logic of the Same), but instead with "an erotics of the other."

Another aspect of this lack of sensuousness is the way that formal complexity disrupts ideological smooth functioning. Subotnik explains that Adorno criticized Tchaikovsky's music precisely because it is "conceived as ideology," "ingratiat[ing] itself with society by covering over all inner dichotomies with a smoothly sensuous surface . . ." (p. 32). It seems to me that *this* "resistance to the sensuous" can give rise to another sensuousness, one that is not "smooth" or easily consumed according to the pathways of immediate gratification. "The Gates of Delirium" would perhaps be a better example of such resistance than "Awaken," but the latter is not without this resistant aspect as well.

To conclude this part of the discussion (and to get back into the formal qualities of "Awaken"), I would argue once again that any one work in the main sequence of Yes has to be seen in the overall context of the main sequence as a whole. In other words, the main sequence should be understood as the unfolding of something like a coherent approach to the creation of music. The main character of this approach is well-described by Adorno's charge to "view the world from the standpoint of redemption." If understood in this larger frame, and as a strategic gesture, it may even be the case that, in its austere gnosticism, "Awaken" has a special ability to make us confront the unredeemed nature of the existing world, its essentially fragmented and alienated character.

As I have hinted, "Awaken" begins with an almost unreal clarity, first with Wakeman's rather dazzling piano introduction, then with Anderson's crystalline voice. One thing that stands out like a sore thumb is the fact that, whereas Yes used dissonance on a regular basis in the main sequence, there is exactly *one* moment of dissonance in "Awaken." This moment comes at the end of the second verse, where Anderson sings "Here we can be/We can be here." The dissonant notes, which mainly issue from the twelve-string electric guitar, only sound for a brief instant, to then be swallowed up in the tantric-chanting section of the piece. Do not think for a second that the singularity of this moment is an accident! Indeed, though this moment occurs apart from and some musical distance away from the "workings of man" section, I am inclined to see this dissonant moment as the "ply[ing] out [of] historical life," which passes in the blinking of an eye. We could discuss the meaning of this blinking at greater length, but the political value and potential pitfalls of this idea should be fairly clear by now: on the one hand, there is an element of utopian resistance to the idea that the dissonant moment in the adventure of spirit will seem, in a larger frame, as next to nothing and as inconsequential. On the other hand, this view effectively erases the history of humanity that requires redemption in the first place. This is the risk, however, in any utopian gesture—which doesn't mean that such gestures should be undertaken carelessly. But, then, there is nothing *careless* about the placement of this dissonant moment—on the contrary. This moment disturbs the simple identity-gesture of the "be here."

To say that "Awaken" only has one "dissonant" note is not to say that the rest of the work is conventional in its tonality. The main melodic force of the piece, after the introductions from Wakeman and Anderson, is a very (Eastern) "Indian" line played by Howe on electric twelve-string guitar. Underneath this line is a chunky, pulsing, and sliding line from Squire, which seems to drive Howe's line by running directly into it. (It seems that Squire uses a number of bass guitars in this piece. This initial line is, I think, played on a fretless bass. In concert, Squire used a three-necked monstrosity to cover all these basses—pun intended.) White provides yet another layer of contrast by mainly playing off the beat. At the same time, there is a whole other layer of percussion, including the sleigh bells, that stays on the beat rather insistently, even if the instruments used create a more diffuse sound by their nature. (In the *Yesyears* video retrospective there is a clip of the group recording this percussion track, with everyone contributing.) On top of all of this, Anderson and Squire present the "tantric chant" with extended, almost monotonal notes. As it turns out, there are chants within chants here, one drawn out ("Suns/High/Streams," and so on), the other spoken quickly ("Awaken/Gentle/Mass/Touching"). This second chant gathers urgency, giving way to a series of guitar breaks that are exhilirating, an intense raga.

The "Indian" character of the music changes significantly as we enter the "workings of man" section—indeed, this could be called the "Christian" section of the piece, not only because of the lyrical themes involved, but also because the dominant instrumental voice passes from Howe's guitar to Wakeman's church organ. The music becomes considerably "churchy" at this point as well, the whole section ending with Anderson intoning an extended "Ahhhh. . . ." that, with its rich passion, is in direct contrast to the carefully measured monotonality of what has come before.

This passion is then recapitulated at length, as maximal Yes orchestration gives way to the simplicity of a bell tree playing a simple, almost childish melody. If redemption occurs in the blinking of an eye in the lyrical line, the creation of a human maturity worthy of redemption becomes an extended work in this central instrumental section. White's bell tree remains the ground for much of this section (very much, to my mind, a musical form of Jesus's injunction to come unto him as a child). Two other elements fill out the picture. The first of these is actually a series of elements, basically an entire story that Wakeman unfolds on the church organ. Starting from tentative, innocent, searching notes, played with the organ set on its flute stops, Wakeman develops a rich picture, as musically thick as history itself. This is truly wonderful musicianship on his part, beginning, in a sense, with premises as questionable as those of the human project itself, working out the logic of these premises into an image of the transcendent, the Good. Wakeman has truly captured the mystery of our mortality—not that we die, but that we live, that we even exist. The other element is provided by Howe and Squire, and this is the element of temporality that crosses the mystery of mortality; thus we have not only the momentary nature of our existence, but our existence from moment to moment. The guitar and bass guitar mark this passage of time by creating a musical ticking of the clock. And, as all these elements swirl together—church organ, guitar and bass, bell tree—one feels as if one were inside the workings of an immense temporal mechanism, mortality itself.

At the conclusion of this very magical passage, Howe takes us back into the purely transcendent realm with a surprisingly Frippish (as in Robert) short solo. We begin a kind of post-Christian transformation, as the "Master" invoked by Anderson, the Master of images, soul, light, and time, "hark[ens] thru dark ties/that tunnel us out of sane existence." Finally, Anderson bids "farewell, farewell" to the realm of historical life. It's a big sendoff, with an organ crescendo and a very powerful drum roll, a moving but understated (but also too far down in the mix, to my mind) bass line, and ultimately a more unrestrained and ascending series of guitar parts from the Telecaster (which is quite a contrast to the twelve-string Rickenbacker). All of this christens the ship of the

> Master of Time,
> Setting sail
> Over all of our lands.
> And as we look
> Forever closer,
> Shall we now bid
> Farewell, farewell.

This ship now sails on calm waters, as we return to the initial two verses of "Awaken." Humanity is transformed and even transfigured, "Reaching out to touch our own being, past all mortal as we."

And yet, this transcendence of the mortal human condition is itself transformed by the final verse of "Awaken," sung twice by Anderson alone. Even as a heavenly choir welcomes us into utopia, there is a wistful glance back:

> Like the time I ran away
> And turned around,
> And you were standing close to me.

I find this a much more *personal* statement of the similarly wistful passage at the conclusion of "Close to the Edge":

> Then according to the man who showed his outstretched arm to space,
> He turned around and pointed revealing all the human race.
> I shook my head and smiled a whisper, knowing all about the place.

Likewise, the soulful guitar figure that concludes "Awaken" reminds one that redemption is, finally, not about the transcendent reality of *Being* itself, but instead the ethical relation of sisterhood and brotherhood, of solidarity, of being lost but then found, of me standing next to you, of you standing next to me.

And thus we must now say farewell, farewell, to an extraordinary time in music, a time when Yes worked through the green language toward an immense solidarity with humanity and the cosmos. So much was accomplished in those few years! In saying "farewell," however, let us not bid a final goodbye, but instead work and hope for the greater articulation of this language, this ever-opening flower.

Part 3

In the beginning is the future:
Yes from 1978 into the new millennium

In the last years of the seventies, the time of progressive rock began to draw to a close. A new social dynamic began to open up, one very much defined by urgency. Whereas the early and middle seventies were a time of ideological retreat for capitalism, in the late seventies there was a general retrenchment and new dissemination of reactionary ideas. On a global scale, the two oppressive superpowers—one openly capitalist, the other claiming to be socialist, but in fact capitalist in all significant respects—began to bare their fangs once again. In the West, and especially in the United States, there began a concerted and somewhat coordinated effort to bury the communitarian spirit of the sixties, and to reassert the most narrow forms of self-seeking as fundamental and unchangeable "human nature." The age of youthful experimentation was declared over—it was time to turn things back over to the "grown-ups." Margaret Thatcher and especially Ronald Reagan attempted to bring back, under the cover of a "conservatism" bereft of any drive to conserve anything more traditional than post–World War II "normalcy," the stultifying "culture" of the mainstream 1950s, where anything weird was suspect.

This neoconservatism faced a basic problem, however: the logic of the market is no respecter of values, "conservative" or otherwise. This fundamental "cultural contradiction of capitalism" (as conservative social critic Daniel Bell put it) was still open to radical negotiation by experimental artists. But, against the threat of a very possible global nuclear war, the reassertion of imperialist and colonial "rights" to pillage the Third World, and an unleashing of reactionary forces within the West itself, it seemed that "calls to consciousness" and reminders of utopian possibilities were not enough. The dominant social systems in the world, in competition with one another but driven by the same imperial imperatives (primarily the private accumulation and control of socially produced wealth), were threatening to finally close all spaces of possibility through the enactment of the most violent and brutal counterpossibilities—a "final solution" to the question of human possibility. This "solution," as advanced by the political spokespersons of the "Free World," was put forward in the form of the most banal stupidities. Indeed, this ideological program of "brain damage" required such stupidities.

In the face of this massive reactionary campaign, which operated on every level from the ideological to the military, the call to "awaken" seemed to fall into the trap of what Theodor Adorno and Herbert Marcuse called "affirmative culture." What seemed necessary was, instead, intransigent negation, of the sort that gives no quarter to any kind of "inspirational" possibility. Bertolt Brecht had remarked, "first the bad new things, before the good old things"; with their critique of affirmative culture, Adorno and Marcuse were arguing that there are times when it is an act of irresponsibility to focus on anything other than the bad new things. Marcuse called the alternative the "great refusal." Adorno argued that there are times when it is simply wrong to speak of beauty or to try to create beauty, for this becomes a comfort to the system of oppression and an insult to those who bear the brunt of an overwhelmingly ugly social system.

In his important book, *Lipstick Traces: A Secret History of the Twentieth Century,* Greil Marcus develops some of the arguments of these social critics, as well as the arguments and strategies of French Situationist author and activist Guy Debord, to argue that the appropriate response to the "positivity" of Thatcher's and Reagan's vision of a new "morning" in the West was what the Situationists called *detournement.* While the term really suggests a constellation of concepts and strategies, at the heart of the matter is an approach that combines one-off, "guerilla" negations of "affirmative" ideology and culture with bitter irony. In the realm of music, Marcus's favorite example of this strategy is the Sex Pistols. This is my favorite example as well. The question might be, What is the more effective way to respond to a world where a powerful leader, who has his finger on the button, can spout with impunity false and banal idiocies concocted from a *Reader's Digest*/Hollywood World War II movie perspective—to write a glorious hymn that intones:

> Wish the sun to stand still,
> reaching out to touch our own being.
> Past all mortal as we.
> Here we can be.

—or to declare with snarling, acidic obnoxiousness, "We're so pretty, oh so pretty, we're pretty—pretty vacant"? At the point when the question of mortality is raised with tremendous urgency, it seems inappropriate, at the least, to *dream* of surpassing mortality.

I've argued that the music of Yes does in fact deal with important social questions, urgent questions. I doubt, however, that anyone would attribute to Yes the sort of urgency that seemed to be demanded by the situation of the late seventies and the eighties. But there are two closely related issues that also have to be raised here. First, is it appropriate that, in times that seem intensely "urgent," all cultural production respond in a way that is closely connected to what seems to be the "form" of this larger historical urgency? Perhaps there are times when history demands that we do certain things with whatever abilities we happen to have. But does such a demand issue in a singular logic as to the form that the response must take? Wouldn't such a logic, if given the form of a general principle, simply replicate (even if through the dialectical looking glass) the oppressive system that one is opposing? Second, and relatedly, if there is a need for a cultural response in terms of the urgent logic of the day, does this cancel the need for a response that presents the possibility of some other day? The frame in which artists such as the Sex Pistols, the Clash, the Gang of Four, and other developments of punk music and then hip-hop were responding was such that one had to consider the definite possibility (what I call the ultimate "counterpossibility") that, unless *this* day was dealt with in the most in-your-face fashion, there weren't going to be any other days. For my part, I think it was absolutely right to enter into this consideration and to respond accordingly. The sort of twenty-twenty hindsight that now "knows" that it was a waste of time to oppose the worst violence of the system because, after all, the worst possible outcome (global nuclear war and the destruction of human life through nuclear winter) did not come to pass, is nothing more than the blithe middle-class point of view that rarely rises above the narrow consideration of its career opportunities (a point of view that the Clash responded to quite directly in their song with that title).

What was the place, then, for virtuoso musicians who had established a pattern of musical experimentation, developed through extended forms, and visionary lyrics inspired by an eclectic combination of English Romantic poetry, non-Western wisdom traditions, communitarian and utopian impulses from the sixties, and some sense that the "machine" stands ready to tear all of this to pieces? The late seventies were a period of impasse and confusion for Yes and other progressive rock groups. Essentially, the time of progressive rock came to a close, as did the "main sequence" of Yes.

Perhaps there was more to it than *this* political dynamic. Perhaps the paradigm of progressive rock had been exhausted. I argued earlier that progressive rock is an avant-garde generated out of the elements of rock music. Perhaps these elements were inherently limited and there wasn't much more to be generated out of them. Perhaps there is an even larger question, for it is not only in the case of progressive rock that musical avant-gardes seem exhausted. Everything here is stated under the heading of "perhaps," because it is very difficult to sort out this issue from the larger social issues that intersect with it. I will return to this question in the conclusion.

It is almost impossible to deal with the question of exhaustion in its own right because, toward the end of the seventies and into the eighties, there were two other developments in rock music that complicate the issue. First, record companies began to exercise a great deal more control over their "product." Pure hype was injected into the process of putting out records as never before (the *Frampton Comes Alive* album is a key example, where frenzied audience reaction is dubbed into a live concert performance to make it seem as though this was one bandwagon that no cool person could miss). "Artist and Repertoire" people—the notorious A&R men—began to get involved in the creative control that musicians formerly had over their records. It seemed that a major homogenization drive was underway. The interesting thing is that, in the case of any given artist, group, or album, there was no proof that homogenization would lead to greater popularity. In the case of Yes, the group was already very popular, and even albums such as *Tales from Topographic Oceans* sold in the millions. But, through structural adjustments both conscious and unconscious, capitalism was looking toward the overall benefits of homogenization, of being able to market entertainment product in a more controllable way, based on a more statistically driven conception of "consumer demand." Second, and relatedly, there was an adjustment in the mechanisms of rock music criticism, toward a reentrenchment of what I've been calling "blues orthodoxy." This move may have occurred for quite other reasons than an outright desire to aid the record companies in their drive toward homogenization—though, more and more, as with most "film critics" (that is, movie reviewers), a dependence between industry and "critic" was growing, with almost all power in the hands of the former. Instead, blues orthodoxy was perhaps first of all a response to the increasing complexity of progressive rock and a desire that rock music get back to its roots. However, this orthodoxy has been so co-opted by entertainment industry homogenization that most "music critics" (that is, CD reviewers and promoters) have lost sight of the historical trajectories that brought orthodoxy and homogenization together. One result is that the utopian and experimental sensibility of the progressive rock groups is now cynically dismissed out of hand, with nary a thought.

In this capsule history of the "YesPistols" dynamic of the late seventies, I should mention two further issues. First is the strange issue of what might be called the "double embarrassment" that some musicians and listeners felt in that period. For those folks such as myself, who came from a perspective of thinking that music is important, and that it is important to create good music, but who also felt compelled to respond to the social questions of the day that were being posed with such urgency, there was a bit of a double bind. On the one hand, we felt almost embarrassed by the anthems to the sun, trees, consciousness, and so on that were central to the music of Yes and some other progressive groups. (And we didn't have the language, which would have thematized ecological, gender, and other questions, that might have allowed us to connect this music with more straightforwardly "political" discourses. I hope this book contributes to our having this language.) On the other hand, in terms of the creation of good music, what groups such as the Sex Pistols and the Clash were doing seemed also to be a bit of an embarrassment—after all, compared to progressive rock musicians or to anyone else, for that matter, the punks could hardly play their instruments and didn't seem to care about this. (In *Rotten,* John Lydon says that he isn't a "musician," but instead a "noise structuralist." Well, all right, and I like Lydon, but he's not John Cage, either.) Many musicians were disoriented by the idea that *this stuff* now counted as music. What, then, was the point of trying to be a "good musician" in the more conventional sense of acquiring skill with one's instrument and compositional ability?

In an important section of his book, *What is Literature?,* Jean-Paul Sartre discusses the idea of "writing for one's age." He argues that the pretense of creating art "for the ages" or art that will be "timeless" will only lead to either creating art that is irrelevant to one's own age, or to creating art that participates in the false universalism of the existing order. If a work of art is considered important in some age other than the one it was created in, this will be for reasons that are internal to this other age, reasons that the artist him- or herself can have no knowledge of. In concluding his argument, Sartre calls for "an ethics and an art of the finite."

Still, there is some range even within the finite, and some range for art that resists, on various levels, the order of the existing, finite, time that we find ourselves in. The Sex Pistols gave us something on the order of a bomb, a Molotov cocktail, thrown into the middle of a Western "peace" (the *Pax Britainia/Americana*) that was and is permeated with violence. As the eighties began to open up (starting around 1977–78), this seemed absolutely necessary. No time for screwing around with musicianship! However, the time frame of a pure and absolute negation itself became elongated, and the question of what to do with music came back on the scene. While *Never Mind the Bollocks* retains its power as an especially concentrated example of the art of the finite in a period of great urgency, this cannot be said for many other punk albums of that time (perhaps the Dead Kennedys' *In God We Trust* and a few others). I can remember very well, because I was involved in playing punk music at the time, the impact of two key developments in that kind of music in the early eighties. First, the Clash supposedly sold out by trying to make better records of better music (starting with *London Calling,* incorporating elements of other kinds of music besides punk.) Second, Black Flag supposedly sold out because they attempted to develop the musical material that was there in punk music itself, starting with *My War*—perhaps you could say, using the categories I've tried to develop here, Black Flag began to develop from punk to "experimental punk." (Whether they or anyone else developed—or could have developed; again, there is a question of what's there in the musical material to begin with—"progressive punk" or "avant-punk" is a question that I will leave for another discussion.) I would argue that, in both cases, the musicians were trying to find a way beyond Neil Young's dichotomy of either "burning out" or "fading away." And this meant once again reengaging with formal creativity in music, without, however, losing sight of the fact that the world is radically in need of revolutionary change. Part of my argument in this book has been that Yes's radical affirmation also contains a moment of negation—though, admittedly, never so pure a moment as that created by the Pistols. To create a vision of some other world, *over against* this world, is a way of saying, "not this world." In social-theoretical terms, the dialectic might be described as that between the Sex Pistols' "anarchism" and Yes's radical communitarianism. The former never has any patience, certainly not for any "constructive" task of creating an actual alternative to the world as it is—and there are times when this radical impatience is necessary. On the other hand, in lieu of an alternative, which must be foreshadowed in a culture of the alternative (this claim runs parallel to Lenin's argument that there will be no revolution without revolutionary theory) and artifacts (artworks) thereof, the existing society will simply reassert itself after the debris generated by various incendiary devices has been cleared away (and safely forgotten, or perhaps recuperated as mere fashion, which is what tended to happen with much punk culture).

The second issue that bears mentioning under the heading of "YesPistols" concerns the fact that, however much Yes and the Sex Pistols seem absolute opposites with regard to their approach to music, they had a great deal in common in the fact that both rejected commercial imperatives. Their aim was to not be captured and recuperated by the machinations of profit. As Jon Anderson put it in the *Yesyears* album booklet, "We did what we set out to do, which was to keep going and not feed the pop machine, because it will swallow you." The Sex Pistols gave us something so intensely *immediate* that mere "consumption" of the musical product was not possible. This has its risks, of course, and the Pistols took those risks ingeniously, even if in a way that could in no way be repeated. (As much as some superficial aspects of punk culture have been recuperated, it's still unlikely that we'll ever hear marching bands at the Superbowl game playing "Holiday in the Sun.") From an entirely different musical perspective (or so it seems), Yes also created music that continues to resist consumption. If the Pistols attempted to generate an immediate "connection" to the intensity of a certain period, this was never in the form of a music that could simply be plugged in. In resisting "accessibility," Yes also resisted the niche-driven process of homogenization. Do extremes meet? This question will also have to await another discussion.

Having presented a picture of the character of the times, one that could undoubtedly be developed much further (again, *Lipstick Traces* is to be recommended in this regard), my remaining mission in this final part is to explore the way that Yes negotiated this dangerous minefield. This will be done in four parts. First, though this music predates somewhat the situation just described, we need to spend some time with the "marginalia" of Yes music—some of the solo recordings of the band members, and the *Yessongs* live album and film. Then we will turn to the late seventies proper. Second, then, we will consider the final Yes albums of the seventies, *Tormato* and *Drama*,[1] the first as a misstep, the second as transitional to the Yes of the eighties. Third, we will take up the recordings of Yes from the eighties and moving into the nineties, from *90125* to *Talk*. Fourth, and finally, we will consider the possible futures of Yes.

Solo and live work

In the period of *Tales from Topographic Oceans* and *Relayer,* the members of Yes each pursued projects that they felt were more personal, less something that they wanted to pursue in terms of the group. In some respects this was an opportunity for each band member to get some things out of their system, and to pull back from the heaviness of the group atmosphere for a little while. Especially around *Tales,* and the whole situation with Rick Wakeman, it was probably a good idea to move back a bit and create some breathing room. Again, although this is also anachronistic, I would like to discuss four of the solo albums that came from this period, the four that are perhaps most reflective of "Yes music," as refracted through the individuality of particular members of the group. The four albums that I will discuss, in the following order, are: Rick Wakeman's *Six Wives of Henry VIII,* Steve Howe's *Beginnings,* Jon Anderson's *Olias of Sunhillow,* and Chris Squire's *Fish Out of Water.*[2] Then I will return to Yes music "proper" with a discussion of the *Yessongs* live album and the *Yessongs* film.

The Six Wives of Henry VIII
From the standpoint of pure excitement about what was happening with musical instruments in the early seventies, probably no phenomenon received more attention than that of the "multiple keyboards" artist. In the late sixties, multiple keyboards meant piano and organ (or, in a live setting, Fender Rhodes electric piano and Hammond B-3 organ). With Robert Moog's development of a portable synthesizer (the Mini-Moog, to be followed by other brands), this instrument became a staple of the keyboard artist's studio and live set-up, along with the Mellotron, electric harpsichords, Clavinets, and so forth. Two names stood out as the most adventurous of the new keyboardists, Keith Emerson and Rick Wakeman. Emerson was perhaps better known as the pioneer, as he had already led a keyboard-centered experimental rock group for some years, The Nice (which, as has been noted, influenced Jon Anderson and Chris Squire in forming Yes). He continued in the role of "keyboard power trio" leader with Emerson, Lake, and Palmer, which had already put out three albums by the time that Rick Wakeman joined Yes. However, anyone who was of a certain age, and

interested in this sort of thing, was well aware that a new contender came on the scene in the early seventies.

As much excitement as there was around Yes's new keyboard player and the technology that he was bringing to the group, it is a wonder that this side of things didn't overwhelm the music. Thankfully, music won out, as it did on Wakeman's first solo album. Worries are raised, along with interest, when upon opening the album cover, Rick's keyboard set-up is displayed, with the master himself playing a synthesizer and electric piano simultaneously. (These were the days when the height of keyboard artistry was to play two keyboards that were at different angles or even running in opposite directions, à la some of the well-known live pictures of Keith Emerson.) The record is indeed a tour de force of keyboard work, demonstrating Wakeman's abilities with diverse styles and difficult passages, but it is also a solid piece of music, one that inspires interest quite apart from its element of instrumental virtuosity. Indeed, to its credit, I wouldn't call *Six Wives* a virtuoso showcase. One can argue over how much the six compositions accurately reflect the narrative structure of Wakeman's subjects (the six wives themselves), but taking up this set of structures was a very good way of giving variety to the music and keeping compositional development, rather than mere "blowing," in the forefront.

Six Wives is a pivotal moment in what we might call the "campaign" of progressive rock, its march toward a more general musical credibility. This was the sort of album we got our music teachers in high school, and other "adults" who had some experience with "serious music," to listen to—and we were happy when they pronounced Wakeman's efforts good, and even "valid." The funny thing was that we gave these adults too much credit. They were able to relate to some of these musical structures because they were coming from the keyboard; other instruments common in rock music, especially electric guitars, bass guitars, and drums, they couldn't relate to so well. Therefore, constrained by some rather silly ideas of what it takes to make good music (orchestral instruments, pianos, and operatically trained voices, apparently), they were impressed by *Six Wives,* and yet not impressed by other rock music that was far more adventurous.

Significantly, the playing of Yes-mates Howe, Bruford, and Squire stand out from the very first measures of the album, especially the stabbing bass notes of the latter. "Catherine of Aragon," in fact, begins by sounding very Yes-like, but then it goes off in other directions. Indeed, beyond the initial excitement, this might be a complaint about the album, that it is always going in some new direction without entirely developing what was there. Furthermore, when the new direction seems a bit gimmicky, as with some of the honky-tonk playing or the banjo on track 3 or the gospel-blues-inflected vocals on the first track, one wonders what possible connection this music could have with its ostensive subject matter. On the other hand, Wakeman really put a great deal into this album, especially in terms of the richness of its melodic resources, as well as the harmonies and orchestrations that support the melodies. Indeed, some of these melodies are simply classic. Some of the rhythmic underpinnings are awfully neat, too; in particular, Alan White's drumming on the second track, "Anne of Cleves," really cooks—it's jazzy stuff that also rocks, in a very offbeat rhythm that still manages to go straight ahead. The bass guitarist on this track, Dave Winter, is very good as well, very fluid and romping, and he and White make a return appearance on track 6. Here I find the "gypsy fiddle" part, with the synthesizer replacing the violin, very nicely done—indeed, it could have gone on a bit longer. That part is reminiscent of The Who's "Baba O'Riley," which might not have been an accident, as Wakeman has many times expressed his admiration for that great band.

Beginnings

Perhaps Steve Howe was just as concerned as Wakeman was with not creating a mere virtuoso vehicle. In addition, Howe was clearly interested in writing some good songs—and singing them. *Beginnings* is a mixed bag, with some very strong points and some fairly weak ones. Sometimes I wish that the weak points had just been replaced by what Howe could have easily done, which was to fill in the holes with some monster guitar playing, cutting loose à la the live version of "Yours is No Disgrace." But I have to respect Howe for not doing this, and instead trying to make a coherent album of songs.

First, the weak points. Most obvious, and most remarked upon, of course, is Howe's voice, which doesn't work very well when it takes the lead. In recent interviews Howe has remarked that he realized only in the last few years that he has a minor speech impediment, which affected his singing on his earlier solo albums. I'm not entirely convinced that this is the real problem or that he has overcome his difficulties with lead singing, though I do agree with him that his more recent solo efforts are much better albums on the whole (especially *Turbulence* [1991] and *The Grand Scheme of Things* [1993]). As lousy a thing as this is to say regarding a virtuoso musician who has labored endlessly to develop his craft, Howe's problem with singing may be that he works too hard at it and sometimes ends up sounding forced. Like one of his major influences, Bob Dylan, Howe should just go with the voice he has, and put himself fully into it. (Listening to one of Dylan's greatest performances, "Like a Rolling Stone," you realize that, at one and the same time, this is a guy who doesn't have a very good voice, and yet has one of the greatest voices of all time—and the latter impression wins out, in my humble opinion.)

The other major weak point in Howe's solo efforts, in evidence in *Beginnings* (though even more so in his second solo album, *The Steve Howe Album*), is the overall "grab-bag" feel to the project. Howe simply tried to do too many things with his album, covering too many styles of music. This is a very understandable temptation, for two reasons. First, even an artist such as Steve Howe doesn't know how many solo albums the record companies are going to allow him to make, and so there is the temptation to try to put everything into the most recent one—for it might be the last. Second, Howe is truly a master of many styles, and therefore there is the temptation to display at least one example of each of these styles on any given solo effort. In general, Howe's eclecticism works better for him in a group setting, where his borrowings and extrapolations from Wes Montgomery or Chet Atkins are woven into a larger piece of music. But, even in the solo setting, Howe's eclecticism would be better served by more restraint and some creative grouping, of a counterintuitive sort. In other words, it would be better both for the albums and for his concerts if Howe would group his pieces together by style: the "classical" pieces, the hillbilly flatpicking pieces, the jazz pieces, and so on.

Of course, this criticism wouldn't even be possible except for a remarkable fact: namely that, probably more than any other guitarist in the world, Steve Howe embodies the entire history of the instrument and its practitioners.

In light of these comments, however, I find that there aren't any pieces on *Beginnings* without some redeeming value. They are all good efforts, and, if some of them could be improved on (in some cases by being developed a good deal further, as with "Beginnings"), then let us simply make it a good musical exercise to try to hear them in our heads in their ideal form. Let's turn to the stronger works. "Doors of Sleep" is a very good start for the album, as is "Australia," both having very rich guitar orchestration, chunky bass lines that Howe also plays, and probably the best use of Howe's voice. I would also put the final track, "Break Away From It All," in this category. Notably, the only other musician on any of these pieces is the drummer—in the first two cases Alan White, and in the final case Bill Bruford. This streamlined setting works well for Howe, and he has used it to good effect on his more recent solo albums. "Doors of Sleep" has an eerie side to it that works well, even if Howe has trouble negotiating a few of the lines with his voice. "Australia" has a really neat guitar solo section, especially where Howe interpolates some chords that use tritone intervals, what some consider to be the most dissonant combination. (An example would be the combination of E and A#. Progressive rock listeners probably know the tritone best from King Crimson's "Red," a piece based on these harsh tones. For a useful discussion of the tritone, see Eric Tamm, *Robert Fripp: from King Crimson to Guitar Craft*, p. 78.) In the medieval period (as Tamm explains), this interval was called "the devil in music," and it was banned from compositions by Church authorities. However, Howe's use of the tritone is remarkably playful, devilish only in a mischievous sense. (Howe uses tritones in a similar way in a nice solo at the end of "Shock to the System," from *Union*.) "Pleasure Stole the Night" has a Mediterranean feel to it, and makes nice use of the double bass. There's a short bit at the beginning with bass and some percussive coloring from

Bruford that sounds a little like "The Girl from Ipanema"—and there's nothing wrong with that. Finally, "Break Away From It All" is a strong performance on which to close, and the cadence of the line, "Individuality just won't let him stall" is especially memorable.

In general, the lyrics for *Beginnings* are quite good—nicely understated on the whole, nothing histrionic or over the top. Even though Jon Anderson has been most responsible for Yes's lyrics over the years, *Beginnings* gives us a good look at the sort of contribution that Howe could make—mainly in terms of helping Anderson's cosmic vision stay better grounded, which is a good thing!

Both Howe's and Wakeman's first solo efforts were good, if not quite great. *Six Wives* is perhaps more a part of its time, and therefore doesn't entirely wear well; someone hearing it for the first time today wouldn't be amazed anymore by layers of different keyboards. On the other hand, some of the pieces do transcend their moment; my personal favorites are the first, second, fourth, and sixth tracks. *Beginnings* contributes some good songs that do hold up nicely. If there was some sort of musical scene that tried to preserve good songs and works from progressive rock music—something other than the "tribute band" scene, but instead groups interested in both preserving and developing progressive rock repertory (which wouldn't necessarily mean playing pieces just as they were played on the original recordings)—then many of the songs from *Beginnings* would hold up. In terms of our main subject here, however, perhaps the most significant thing that we see in these efforts are the discrete streams that flow into the larger river that is Yes.

Olias of Sunhillow

Jon Anderson's first solo effort is much more successful in its own terms. Despite the fact that Anderson has told interviewers over the years that he is a "singer, not a musician," *Olias* shows that Anderson is indeed a complete musician—he is a great singer, a great composer, and, if he is not a virtuoso on any other instrument besides voice, he certainly knows very well how to use instruments and how to orchestrate with them. Furthermore, as a complete concept, *Olias of Sunhillow* is a masterwork in its own right, on a level with the Yes albums of the main sequence.

If this is the case, why did Jon Anderson even need Yes? Doesn't *Olias* show that he is capable of putting complete musical works together on his own? Yes and no. Yes, *Olias* showed that Anderson was capable of both envisioning and concretizing an extended musical and lyrical work, at least *once*. His other solo albums are very uneven, to my mind, mixing moments of brilliance and profundity with moments of silliness and superficiality. In general, Anderson needs to work with other people who can give him some grounding and help him separate the wheat from the chaff. (On the other hand, if we have to sift through some of the lesser songs for the really good ones, so be it—I'd rather have the gems, such as "Some Are Born" or "State of Independence," than not have them.) Other people need a Jon Anderson to work with them, as well—somebody who can give vision to virtuosity. But none of this detracts from the fact that *Olias* is an important epic work, something of a rock opera, and I certainly wouldn't be unhappy if Anderson someday creates another work of this calibre.[3]

Anderson plays all of the instruments on *Olias*, a large array that includes various keyboards, guitars, harp (the stringed kind), pipes and little flutes, and all manner of drums and percussion instruments. Starting with *Tales from Topographic Oceans*, Anderson expanded his percussion arsenal from tambourine and the occasional maracas, to include various drums and cymbals, which he played onstage during the *Tales* and *Relayer* tours. One can tell whether or not someone is going to be a good percussionist just by hearing them play the tambourine or some other simple instrument (as simple as it may seem, most people aren't very good at it), and the *Yessongs* film shows that Anderson is indeed a good tambourine player. He turned out to be a good percussionist as well. Of course, *Olias* also features many applications of Anderson's voice, from solo voice to whole choirs. A good deal of credit must be given to the recording engineer, Mike Dunne, for keeping everything sorted out, for the most part with crystal clarity.

Olias is a total work of art, inspired by the album cover paintings of Roger Dean. As a totality, *Olias* consists not only in the music, but also the album cover art by Hipgnosis and the story set out inside the album, which is by Jon Anderson. (On the record sleeve, there is also a short verse which serves as an epigraph; this is by Jenny Anderson.) To really do justice to the entire work would require a discussion as long as what has been provided for each of the main sequence albums of Yes. Unfortunately, this justice cannot be done here, but let us at least visit some of the strongest moments in this uniformly strong work.

Even though *Olias* could be said to be built up out of songs, these building blocks are extremely varied, with hints of all sorts of cultures in them: Irish, Middle Eastern, (Eastern) Indian, Native American, and others. While *Olias* is a work of progressive rock music, there is very little here that one would call "rock." The first, instrumental piece on the album sets the atmosphere, with a hint of sea shanty woven in. This befits the work as a whole and leads nicely into the first "song," "Sound Out the Galleon." Anderson dealt nicely with nautical themes at least once before, in the "As clearer companions" section of *Tales from Topographic Oceans*, Part 4, "Ritual." (This section is anticipated by the line, "till we sail," but the "sailing music" starts a few measures after that.) Here the idea of building a ship and taking it on a long journey is the greater part of the story—along with telling of the circumstances that made the building of the ship necessary. But this ship is meant to travel the sea of stars, from the planet Sunhillow to Earth.

Anderson does some interesting things with language on *Olias*. For example, he has a nice way of using adjectives and adverbs as verbs, as in "Sound Out the Galleon," where he uses the expressions, "to outward" and "to precision." This was before the days when such things became both commonplace and annoying (politicians speaking of "impacting," the television commercial for a chain of photocopy stores that speaks of "the new way to office"). Some philosophers have discussed the priority of the noun over the verb, as indicative of an age of ossified, logocentric metaphysics—and the "reactivation" of the verb as a resistance and alternative to this.[4] All of this fits quite coherently with Anderson's general predilection toward *movement*, a constant theme in the main sequence and beyond. The idea of making alive what seems to be inanimate—or to see that what seems inanimate is indeed alive—is also a constant theme both of *Olias* and of the main sequence. In the former, this theme applies especially to the ship that will fly the people of Sunhillow to Earth, the Moorglade (also known as the Moorglade Mover):

And there they were inside
the Moorglade to move and to chant
all through force to position
As rhythm raced inside the ship came alive
and was struck to the soul of perception

Another interesting thing Anderson does with language is to make up some new words, which are used in chants or invocations. It would be interesting to know whether the melodies or "words" came first. Finally, it is interesting to compare the lyrics for *Olias* with other lyrics from the main sequence. As "cosmic" as some of the latter seem, the *Olias* lyrics are even more cosmic and purely evocative, even while they do manage to tell a substantial part of the story (the other parts of which are set out in the album cover). In any case, if one is interested in getting a sense of the difference between Anderson's approach to ideas and words when he is on his own, as opposed to when the rest of Yes is involved, here is a basis of comparison. One might say that *Olias* is more purely akin to English Romantic poetry than are the Yes albums of the main sequence. For my part I think it is pretty good stuff.

The purely musical part of *Olias* is hard to separate from the lyrics, because Anderson's voice plays such a large role in the album. He often uses his voice as an instrument in the music—quite effectively. The rest of the instrumental parts are relatively simple and straightforward, in terms of structure or their level of difficulty. But Anderson uses textures and rhythms in a masterful way, especially creating a nice *surging* effect in places (for example, "Olias"). The entire work is integrated with obvious care.

Fish Out of Water

Though very different from Jon Anderson's first solo effort, Chris Squire's only solo album to date also very much succeeds in its own terms. Indeed, *Fish Out of Water* may even have stood the test of time better than *Olias*, and certainly Squire's album has lost nothing in the more than twenty years since it was first released. As with Steve Howe's *Beginnings*, *Fish Out of Water* is not an instrumental vehicle, but instead an album of songs and longer musical works that insist on their own musical integrity first of all. There isn't much about the album that doesn't work really well—perhaps the string arrangement on the last piece, "Safe (Canyon Song)," is drawn out just a bit too much; perhaps the stained glass fish on the back cover should have been switched with the fish-like portrait of Squire from the front. But, that's it—otherwise, the album contains great songwriting, great playing, great selection of participating musicians, and great singing.

Starting with the last of these, Squire's voice is simply wonderful, the sort of voice that could easily lead any group. He has range, depth, presence, and warmth. It's almost a sin for one person to have such talent as a singer and as an instrumentalist (but, it couldn't have happened to a better person!). As I said in the portrait of Chris Squire in part 2, in terms of the combination—and this is of course best seen in live playing—Squire is up there with Jimi Hendrix and few others.

Perhaps the first thing that stands out about the group of musicians that Squire chose for his album is what is *not* there, namely, a guitar player. Although Squire adds just a little twelve-string electric guitar in one place, this is basically a guitar-free album, which is a pleasant change of pace. As with *Olias of Sunhillow*, *Fish Out of Water* is rock, but mainly in the sense of where its roots are—where the album goes is somewhere else. The rest of the musicians on this album form a terrific combination. Bill Bruford really has the chance here to weave in and out of Squire's bass lines, and I especially admire the syncopated choppiness of "Lucky Seven." Mel Collins, best known to progressive rock fans for his work with King Crimson, plays various saxophones on the album. Besides the presence of Bruford and Collins, there is yet another small Crimson element in the album, namely, a "thanks" to Pete Sinfield for his suggestions on the lyrics for "Safe." Jimmy Hastings, who plays the flute here, is the brother of Pye Hastings, leader of the miraculous Caravan, a group that occupies some strange territory at the intersection of pop, experimental rock, and progressive rock. Jimmy plays on most of the Caravan albums, and he performs to his usual high standard on *Fish Out of Water*. There are two organists on the album, one being Patrick Moraz, whose playing is tasteful and understated. The other is Barry Rose, who plays the pipe organ. Rose was the choirmaster from the time when Chris Squire was a chorister at St. Andrews Church; it is sweet to see this musical connection reestablished (or fulfilled, as the case may be). The pipe organ lends an especially grand air to the opening measures of the album. The album also features the piano playing of Andrew Pryce Jackman; he does a very nice job with the electric piano in "Lucky Seven," and adds a nice, acoustic backbone to the structure of "Silently Falling" (especially the part accompanying the words, "Hopefully, Eventually"). Finally, there is an orchestra on much of the album.

Squire's own playing is a forceful statement of his uniqueness among practitioners of the bass guitar, and yet, at the same time, there is absolutely nothing show-offy about *Fish Out of Water*. Yes, we are dazzled in certain moments by Squire's digital dexterity, but never without musical reason, never merely for the sake of Squire's showing what he is capable of. Indeed, I would wager that *Fish* was completely unexpected by most fans of Yes and Squire. I know that it wasn't what I expected, and I cannot think of a time when I was more pleased at not getting what I wanted.

The bass guitar does in fact soar—and weave, circle, loop—on *Fish*, right from the opening measures. There are even a number of bass solos on the record, each with its own character. In "Hold Out Your Hand," Squire plays with and against a series of cascading orchestral passages, creating not so much a "solo" as an intregrated part. In "Silently Falling," there is more of a traditional solo, again against the backdrop of the orchestra, where Squire employs some of his trademark "stabbing" notes. In "Lucky Seven" there is a section where Squire and Bruford are weaving into and through each other's syncopated lines, in a way that is both choppy and seamless. In many ways, the bass guitar "leads" the group through the record, but without being obnoxious or overbearing about it. Even to the extent that the bass stands out, it stands out as a means for making music, not as an instrument on display.

The bass part that accompanies the vocals on "Hold Out Your Hand" is a contrapuntal marvel, the very model of Squire's ability to create lines that seem to loop back around on themselves even while propelling the music forward. He also uses repetition and sustain here in a remarkable way—at points it seems as though the music has come to a standstill. (It is not hard to see, incidentally, the affiliation that this song has with "Parallels.") At the expense of sounding like a broken record, I'll say one last time that there simply are no other lines like Squire's, and many of the lines from *Fish* should be included in the great book of "Squire variations" that someday must be composed.

Finally, and at the heart of it all, Squire's songwriting is unpretentious and artful. If a couple of the songs (the final pieces for each side of the record) go on a bit too long, this doesn't detract from the basic soundness of their structures. Thematically, the inescapable conclusion has to be that Squire's lyrics are a more earthy expression of the visionary themes that have motivated Yes and Jon Anderson. (There have been times when this earthiness has been sorely needed.)

Squire's lyrics are more personal, an expression of his feeling for particular persons than for humanity or the cosmos as a whole. And yet, through this particular focus Squire expresses well enough a larger sense of friendship and community: "We're not the only ones reaching for a new kind of wealth."

Having set this extremely high standard, it is not surprising that Chris Squire has gone more than twenty years without producing another solo album—but one hopes that he is about due.[5]

Looking at these four solo albums, it seems both obvious and yet more than a little bit remarkable where the core of Yes is and has been from the beginning. This isn't to downplay the major role that Howe, Wakeman, Bruford, and White played in allowing the core to articulate itself.

Now let us turn, briefly, to some of Yes's live work.

Yessongs (the album)

For most musicians, it is hard to resist live recordings. One wants to know if one's favorite musicians can "pull it off" in a live setting. With the music of Yes, especially from the main sequence, this is no mean feat. In terms of music that is for the most part composed, as opposed to improvised, I doubt that any rock group ever performed more complicated material in a live setting. If the music is already composed, and definitive studio versions exist for the music, however, what is the point of live recordings? In the case of Yes, I can think of two reasons for wanting live recordings (and indeed for wishing for more quality live recordings from the band, as opposed to badly recorded bootlegs).[6]

First, quite apart from the sheer daringness of performing difficult pieces live, there is often a greater urgency and energy to live versions. Tempos tend to be not only a little faster, but also a little more forceful, more infused with energy and enthusiasm.

Second, and relatedly, some of the live versions of Yes music are different from the studio versions in ways that are perhaps small and yet still significant. Sometimes this is a matter of a slight variation, as with the different ending for the live version of "Siberian Khatru." Often it is a matter of nuances in Jon Anderson's vocal performance. With *Yessongs*, there is also the fact that music that was originally performed in the studio with Tony Kaye and Bill Bruford is performed live by Rick Wakeman and Alan White. Perhaps this is only a matter for devoted aficionados of the music, such as myself and some of the other folks who will read this book, but I find that I am grateful for the live versions because, in the ideal versions of each Yes piece that I am constantly revising in my head, a note or a timbre or a nuance or a beat from the live versions gets interpolated into the ideal.

To put it in a less cerebral formulation: if I were preparing an orchestral score of the great works of Yes, I would definitely listen to the live versions for little nuances and variations that might make a big difference. To take what seems an almost insignificant example, it's really neat when, in the midst of the instrumental section that opens "Close to the Edge," Jon Anderson inserts a little vocal sound, something on the order of "bop-ba," that makes for a nice touch. Staying with this example, at the end of "Close to the Edge," when the sounds of the jungle and stream are welling up once again, Steve Howe and Chris Squire provide a very gentle, spacy bit of jamming that is quite nice. Indeed, I wish that part had gone on for another few minutes. (What they're doing, as a spacy jam, reminds me of the Grateful Dead's live performance of "Dark Star," from *Live Dead*.)

Sometimes there is a trade-off between urgency and subtlety. In the live "Siberian Khatru," this is a good trade; the live version just surges along with much energy, as a celebration of life. While on the whole I wish that Alan White wouldn't whack his snare drum quite so much, still there's something to be said for his straightahead approach to this particular song. On the other hand, an example of where a little more subtlety would have been nice is with some of the guitar fills for "Heart of the Sunrise." There is one in particular, just preceding a repetition of the "Sharp-Distance" theme, that sounds like Hendrix going nuts on a line from the "Star Spangled Banner"—which was appropriate there, but not here. I'm sure the audience at that particular Yes concert enjoyed this, but it detracts from the piece in the recorded context. One of the variations from the live "Heart" that is interesting is toward the beginning, when Squire doubles and extends one of the figures in his famous bass line.

On the other hand, some of the great additions to the pieces are made by Howe. The guitar fills in "Roundabout" are simply frightening, the fact that Howe can insert these spontaneous inventions with such seeming ease, any one of which would be a major feat for most guitarists. There is also a part after the first verse where the whole band, but led by Howe and Wakeman (on organ), insert a few extra measures that are not there in the studio version—and they are the sort of thing that keeps me up at night, trying to figure out how they did that. In the instrumental solo section at the end of "Roundabout," Howe absolutely burns; again, "frightening" is the only word I know for it. In the same vein, Howe's solo work in "Yours Is No Disgrace" is simply one of the great extended guitar jams of all time. This solo shows that he can speak the language of rock guitar in a way that is surpassed by no one (even if perhaps equaled by some of the extended live solos of Clapton, Hendrix, or Santana—but this is elite company), even as he also interpolates other material from the larger history of guitar into the solo.

The problem with the sort of guitar solo that just absolutely wrings everything out of the music is that it usually wrings the music out of the solo and becomes mere athleticism. This doesn't happen in Howe's solo in the live "Yours Is No Disgrace"; furthermore, this exhausting foray becomes the basis for two other developments that make the live version a significant addition to studio piece. First, sometimes intervening into the solo, and sometimes propelling it, is some very interesting work from Squire and White. Nothing they do is typical of a standard "guitar jam," but what they create is a rocking jam *par excellence*—if a somewhat warped and weird one. Second, and more significantly, the transition from the end of the solo section to the return of Anderson and the rest of the band captures the spirit of "Yours Is No Disgrace" better than the studio version. Here Anderson's voice seems to rise out of an absolute wreckage, the scorched-earth destruction that the U.S. military did indeed wreak upon the people of Vietnam, and the lyrics assume a special poignancy:

> Death defying, mutilated, armies scatter the earth.
> Crawling out of dirty holes, their morals, their morals disappear.

The entire final vocal section is taken to another plane, and there is a strikingly defiant tone to the last statement of "Yours is no disgrace."

Yessongs also allowed us to have some additional artwork from Roger Dean, including the spores of Earth moving through space, planting seeds of *Olias* in the mind of Jon Anderson.

Yessongs (the film)

Yes made a motion picture during their 1973 tour for *Close to the Edge*, which is now available on video. One thing that comes across abundantly is Steve Howe's encyclopedic knowledge of chords. It is very clear, especially when he plays chords in the middle of improvised parts, that he has devoted a great deal of time to learning and mastering every bit of the guitar neck. Another useful aspect of the film is to see Alan White working his way into music that he had only started playing a little while before the tour started (a matter of a few days, in fact; I don't know how many concerts he had played when the film was made). Though he might be struggling in places, it is a joyful struggling, which he communicates well—indeed, I wish the camera had focused on White more often. All in all, though, from a musician's standpoint, the film is a good one; unlike many films of live concerts, where the director or camara operators show exactly the wrong things, as far as what musicians would like to see is concerned, this one helps musicians and careful listeners get a better sense of how Yes could play some of their music live. This is especially the case with "Close to the Edge," which was almost certainly the most complex piece of rock music played live at that time (and not much has surpassed it since, among the few exceptions being *Topographic Oceans* and perhaps some of King Crimson's music from the *Lark's Tongues/Starless* period). (There are a few moments when someone decided we needed to see a few single-celled organisms undergoing division, but these are mercifully short.)

Other than the purely musical virtues that these live versions have apart from the visual aspect, there is, of course, the fact that we get to see the way that Yes comports itself on stage. I think there is some value to this—again, perhaps especially for musicians. While the group is spirited on stage, especially Howe—who sometimes appears to be possessed—there is a seriousness and quality of concentration to what they are doing that is exemplary. Some critics called the film "dark," and there is certainly that aspect to it. Ironic, isn't it, that the supposedly blissful Yes would make the *film noir* of concert movies? Aside from the serious concentration, however, I was struck by the charm of Jon Anderson, as well as what I would call his "feminine" qualities.

I mentioned the spacy guitar and bass part at the end of the live version of "Close to the Edge," which is heard on the *Yessongs* film as well as the album. In the film, just before Rick Wakeman's solo spot, there is a bit of extemporaneous interplay between Squire and Anderson (bass and vocals), and though this is obviously a piece of fairly marginal Yesiana, I'd still like to hear more of this. When Anderson kisses the microphone, we see someone who is the polar opposite of a strutting, macho rock star.

As with the *Yessongs* album, the version of "Roundabout" on the film simply shreds, especially Howe's guitar fills and solos. I've always liked, as well, some of Anderson's vocal inflections with the live version.

The funny thing is that, just as there are very few books about rock music that actually do deal with music, there are very few concert films of rock groups that allow us insight into the music the way *Yessongs* does. I don't know that everything in this area absolutely needs to come from a musician's perspective, but, on the other hand, this perspective seems to help.

Finally, in this far from exhaustive discussion of Yes marginalia, we might briefly touch on the group's version of Paul Simon's song, "America." This was one of the last pieces that Bill Bruford recorded with the group, and it takes the group back into those aspects of an idealized "America" that most connect with utopian themes. Accordingly, Simon's original song is blown all out of proportion here. Where there is a kind of weariness to Simon's journey to "look for America," Yes is generally much more celebratory—again, revealing that their version is more about some idea of America that may not have much to do with the reality as it was in the late sixties and early seventies. As regards the arrangement, perhaps the most remarkable features are (1) the pedal point bass and hard emphasis on the bell of the cymbal that support the initial vocal line; (2) Howe's several solos, one in a very low, snaky register, another showing his skills with country inflections, and a final one that is in an almost Latin vein; (3) the part where Anderson almost sounds like a rock'n'roll singer, belting out, "Kathy I'm lost I said, even though she was sleeping." This is an enjoyable romp, but perhaps the reservations discussed regarding the Yes–Richie Havens encounter apply here as well. Perhaps, though, we should simply take away the idea that it helps to look at "America" (the place, not the song) from a certain English pastoral perspective, so that the buried history of communitarianism can shine forth.

This is all confusion: *Tormato* and *Drama*

Now let us return to the difficult question of Yes's music after the main sequence. As I've indicated, this was a difficult period for all of the progressive rock groups. King Crimson, always in the forefront, was the first to pack it in. (The record company decided to have the last laugh, as always, issuing the putrid *U.S.A.* live album.) Emerson, Lake, and Palmer spun their wheels for a while in their post–*Brain Salad Surgery* period, issuing a three-record live album and two volumes of *Works*. The first of these featured Keith Emerson's "Piano Concerto No.1," a work that draws on Gershwin and Copeland in a somewhat derivative but all the same quite enjoyable way (those English refractions of "America" again). (It was nice, too, to hear one of the keyboard giants concentrate on a single instrument for a change.) As regards the group, however, this was clearly a period of impasse; the impasse was resolved with a decidedly backward leap, in the form of *Love Beach*. Likewise, Jethro Tull, after exploring their English and Celtic folksong roots in a shorter song format, with *Minstrel in the Gallery*, coughed up *Too Old to Rock 'n' Roll, Too Young to Die*. (In fairness, Ian Anderson went even further with his folk interests following *Too Old*, with *Songs From the Wood*; in any case, as concerns progressive rock, Tull was in the same impasse as the other groups.) After producing two quite good progressive rock albums following the departure of Peter Gabriel (*A Trick of the Tail* and *Wind and Wuthering*), Genesis converted itself into a pop group. Lesser-known groups such as Flash, Gentle Giant, and Focus called it a day.

And, it had been a day, but now there was a new day that progressive rock groups didn't know how to respond to. With Yes, the return of Rick Wakeman for one of their most powerful records, *Going for the One*, must have given the group the idea that, one way or another, they should go on. Thus they came in 1978 to release an album that was markedly below the standard they had previously set.

Tormato

Jon Anderson has said that, after a fairly extended period of large scale works where he played a major role, from "Close to the Edge" to "Awaken," he felt that perhaps he should back off from too heavily "imposing [his] ideology" on the rest of the group (*Yesyears* video). I imagine that many fans of Yes have the same initial reaction as I do to such a statement: "Impose, Jon, *impose*—if only you had imposed!" Perhaps this was the way things should have gone, but I've tried to emphasize that such decisions by individual group members, and the direction taken by the group as a whole, was bound up with its time and the possibilities and necessities of a new cultural and social situation that was emerging. Yes's first response to this new situation was to create another album of progressive rock, but in a weakened, one would have to say watered-down and even somewhat half-hearted, form. There is *some* good music on *Tormato*, but the whole does not hold together as such. Sad to say, the album's goofy title, a conflation of "tornado" and "tomato," and silly cover, is representative of the music that lies within. To the extent that the cover and title were meant as a rebuke to the group's many detractors, this was the wrong sort of response, descending to the level of those who attacked the band with nary a thought—the response itself mimicked this thoughtlessness.

Apparently, the original plan was to call the album "Yes Tor" or simply "Tor" (a "tor" is the peak of a rocky mountain or hill, from the Middle English), and to stress the "quirky English" aspects of the group (*Yesyears* booklet). However, under a variety of pressures, this quirkiness led to a half-cocked approach to the music, on the one hand, and overbearing production, on the other. The work of Eddie Offord, departed since *Relayer*, was especially missed here. If *Tales from Topographic Oceans* represented the full extent of Jon Anderson's single-mindedness—perhaps understood by Rick Wakeman as a syndrome that needed to be kicked—*Tormato* stands at the opposite extreme. Purpose surfaces from time to time, but the project as a whole is rudderless and drifting. Even the first piece on the album is representative of this lack of purpose—it is a two-part work with no title for the whole.

Despite these serious flaws, there are some fine moments on *Tormato*; as with the later *Union*, there is a good album *in there*, waiting to be released (which is what the fourth track on *Tormato* might be begging for). In my view, the highpoints of the album are "Don't Kill the Whale," "Release, Release" (the aforementioned fourth track), and "On the Silent Wings of Freedom." Significantly, the first and last of these feature prominant bass work from Chris Squire.

"Don't Kill the Whale" is often discussed as Yes's first truly "political" statement; I hope that our discussion up until this point has convinced the reader that, in a broader sense, much of Yes's music is quite engaged with political themes. Still, there is a directness to "Don't Kill" that is new and fresh. From the start, the song builds on an appropriately aquatic line from Squire. Unfortunately, the general production for the song is also quite squishy, where it should have been crisp. This especially affects the drums, and it therefore becomes difficult to judge White's performance here. The wordless vocal section is particularly effective, presenting us with whalesong that concludes with, "dig it, dig it." And, of course, they are quite right—it is completely wrong to harm whales (or dolphins or porpoises) or, in my view, to hold them in captivity. But I don't know if "direct politics" is really the best approach for Yes, even if I admire their felt need to engage in making such statements.

"Release, Release" is also a more direct statement, both about music and politics. In some sense, the song is a commentary on Yes's own approach to music—both with regard to the main sequence, at least in the form of a conscious parody, and regarding the group's situation at that time: "The pressure's on, is there lack of concentration?" (punctuation added). The song both addresses and, to some extent, submits to the confusion endemic to the late-seventies impasse:

> Power defy our needs, lift us up, show us now
> Show us how amid the rack of confusion.
> Drive in thoughts of high, satisfy, in a plan
> Set it out for all to understand it.

In fact, the group is not calling on this "craziness of power," but instead calls for release from this craziness:

> Release all, release all, or abandon your hope for your brother.
> Release all, release all, or abandon your hope for your sister.
> Release, release, enough controllers.

These lyrics, in a different musical setting, could almost serve as the kind of "fight the power" anthem that one hears in punk and hip-hop. And yet, if anything, Yes is also responding here to what they seem to take as the power-fascination of some of the antipower militants, which they sum up under the terms "straight jacket" and "campaign everything, anti-right, anti-left." Instead they propose "anticipat[ing] the love of creation." The response continues with a parody of a rock concert, where Steve Howe plays some "hot licks" to tumultuous applause. The whole piece is very interesting, musically and lyrically, but it is also confused, working at cross-purposes. In a way, "Release, Release" by itself sums up what the impasse of progressive rock meant for Yes.

In an album too dominated at times by Wakeman's playing on the "Polymoog" and (something called a) "Birotron," there is a wonderful piece of Hammond work at the end of "Release, Release," inserted, in syncopated fashion, into a nice set of choppy starts and stops from Squire and White.

"Onward" is a pretty song, if a bit mushy. "Circus of Heaven" has a nice part at the end, "Outside great animals as tame as the trees. . . ." But everything before that is hokey, with too much of a keyboard and guitar ditty feel to it. The end devolves into mere sentimentality. The beginning of "Arriving UFO" is a bit wooden, but then the song takes on a fine warmth, infused with hopefulness. The problem is that this kind of "hope" verges on mere escapism. Yes, it isn't hard to see why humanity needs a day when the Earth stands still, because sometimes it seems as though only a god or some intervening alien presence can save us. This is a significant departure, however, from earlier Yes themes, which stress the struggle that humanity must take itself through in order to bring a redeemed world into existence.

Tormato does end on a very strong note, "On the Silent Wings of Freedom." The longest piece on the album, at 7:45, this song comes closest to carrying forward Yes's experimentation with structure and vision. On the whole (despite mushy production with the drums once again) there is a crystal clarity to this song that is very powerful. Few people could have carried off starting such a song with a fairly long bass guitar solo, but Squire does. Indeed, while one might expect "silent wings" to take off with the guitar or perhaps a synthesizer, this is an excellent touch to instead assign this role to the bass. Squire soars here, even when he plays in a lower register; his solo is carefully constructed and testifies once again to his contrapuntal talents. Howe's violin-effect guitar comes in to lift us that extra little bit into the sky, and Anderson's strong, clear voice is well above the clouds. On this clear day, you can see forever. In seeing into the forever, the "balancing of the Sun," "the balance of being one," Anderson presents an otherworldly hymn that all the same means to inspire a certain approach to the here-and-now.

Indeed, the piece takes a severe turn with the second and third verses, which lead from a "forty-second screamdown" to "the darkest night so painful" and a "hunger for love midst the torture of being one." The song turns from the solitary quest for enlightenment to the "common goal of freedom," recognizing the necessarily material dimension of this pursuit. The way to freedom leads through the dark night of the soul, not around or above strife and struggle.

Taking a more objective and less partisan view, however, one might say that what I just provided was more on the order of an ideal interpretation of the song that is buried within the actual song Yes recorded. The latter, I'm afraid, is filled with gratuitously skittish guitar and keyboard parts, a bass guitar that is too effects-laded, and background singing that is often weak and simply there to fill up space. The ideal version of "On the Silent Wings" *might* be in a class with "Roundabout" or "Siberian Khatru," or at least closer to that class, but the actual song is both too trashed up and simply not fully together. This harsh judgment is conditioned by expectations set up by the great music of the main sequence. Something of the main sequence is buried within this impasse, and, clearly, the ideal and the real are fighting it out within the confines of the better pieces from *Tormato*. The group recognized this as an untenable situation. First, in 1979, Yes went even further into the impasse, laying down some basic tracks for an album that would have out-*Tormato*ed *Tormato*, had it been released. Anyone who has heard (bootleg) tapes from these sessions (which were held in Paris) is grateful for the wisdom of the group in not pursuing the project to completion. As with *Tormato*, there are some moments (a couple of which made it into Jon Anderson's solo work), but there is also a fundamental lack of direction.

Drama

The experience with *Tormato* left many followers of Yes, myself included, wondering what this group was going to be about. Many of us didn't feel very hopeful, as it seemed that the time of progressive rock was really at an end, and it was easy to have an "another one bites the dust" mentality about the future of Yes. Needless to say, we were surprised, bewildered, and more than a little shocked and depressed when *Drama* appeared, sans Rick Wakeman and, even more disturbing, sans Jon Anderson. Indeed, the idea of a "Yes" album without Anderson simply seemed unthinkable.

As it turned out, in the midst of the Paris sessions for the abortive post-*Tormato* project, Wakeman and Anderson both reached the conclusion that the group had come to a deep impasse and was not capable, at least as things stood at the time, of producing music worthy of the name Yes. They were right, of course, even if the realization must have been very painful. Being closer to the source of Yes music, Anderson and Wakeman were undoubtedly able to see, better than the group's supporters, that the path forward was cluttered with difficult issues. These issues went beyond Yes, to "the time, the logic, or the reasons we don't understand." Lacking a clear sense of what Yes might do next, Anderson withdrew. This meant that the person who had been the most clear on Yes's direction felt that Yes didn't have anywhere to go at that point. Heavy stuff.

Drama is one of those albums that falls between the cracks, as far as consideration of the different periods of Yes's development goes. With hindsight, however, it isn't very much of a reach to see the album as transitional to the Yes of the eighties. This means that the album represents a transition from the main sequence and progressive rock to a kind of experimental rock that had obvious pop music connections. At first this conclusion may seem elusive. After all, only two musicians, Chris Squire and Alan White, carry over from *Drama* to *90125*. One very strong presence from the main sequence Yes, Steve Howe, is not present in the *90125* group, whereas two other very strong presences with the latter, Jon Anderson and Trevor Rabin, are not a part of *Drama*. But all of this supports my thesis, I would argue, that the transition had as much or more to do with the time and the culture as it did with the members who made up Yes at any particular point. A cultural transition was underway, and it carried Yes along with it. The question as regards *Drama* and Yes's experimental rock work after that is whether there was also a critical edge to Yes's response to the larger transition. Or, was this, for all intents and purposes, the end of the Yes that had made *Fragile* and *Close to the Edge*. I will take up this issue, basically the question whether the Yes of the eighties was essentially a whole other group, when we turn to the albums that feature the work of Trevor Rabin.

The funny thing about *Drama* was that, after we got over the shock of a Yes album without Jon Anderson, we were further shocked by the fact that it was a pretty good album. We weren't sure if we were too happy about that. But the fact is, the influence of Anderson is all over the album, if not his actual vocal and songwriting work. For one thing, the new fellows who came in to replace Anderson and Wakeman, singer Trevor Horn (whose true calling, he later realized, was in recording production) and keyboardist Geoff Downes, were longtime admirers of Yes and Jon Anderson. (As most readers know, Horn and Downes had previously recorded as "The Buggles.") Their aim was to contribute something in that spirit. For another, the whole thrust of *Drama* is aimed at bringing forward some of the elements of Yes's history in the context of making an album in keeping with the spirit of the cultural transition that was underway. This is represented by, as much as anything, the fact that *Drama* returns to cover art by Roger Dean. How much of this thrust was a fully conscious conception I do not know, but, in discussing the album, Chris Squire especially pointed to what was happening in punk and new wave music and the group's desire to engage with that.

Whereas much of *Tormato* seems tentative, disorganized, and even a bit burned out, there is a clear feeling of confidence that comes through with *Drama*, beginning with the initial notes. "Machine Messiah" occupies an interesting bit of territory, an intersection amid protestations against the destruction of English village life by Romantic poets, older, dystopian science fiction scenarios à la *Brave New World*, and more recent cyberpunk scenarios as presented by the genre's acknowledged forerunners, Philip K. Dick and J. G. Ballard. Whereas *Tormato* is full of skittishness, there is a good solid feel to most of *Drama*, and especially "Machine Messiah" which, for many folks, would have to be described as a heavy metal song.

In the main sequence, Yes gathered musical threads from all over the world, interweaving them with a complex classical counterpoint and expressing them through the language and feel of rock music. Ironically, if there was one musical source Yes rarely borrowed from, it was rock music itself. Beginning with *Drama*, Yes went back into that well, attempting to catch up with what had developed while they were away, so to speak.

Steel cables ascend from the ground and descend from the skies, ominously. When the guitar, bass, and drums crash down, this is indeed a very heavy moment for Yes. This *is* hard rock or even heavy metal, but Yes integrates this moment of rock music into their own style, and there is nothing contrived about it. (It should be remembered, too, that there was a kind of hard rock/heavy metal that came before some of the more recent, very screechy and, to my mind, lumbering, boring, and surprisingly bubble-gummish bands. This earlier hard rock was more associated with groups such as Black Sabbath and Deep Purple. The opening chords of "Machine Messiah" especially remind me of the former, particularly their first album.) As these opening power chords fade, Yes does a remarkable job of turning the corner, toward a seemingly different kind of song altogether. I'm not entirely sure how to describe this song; it simply rocks and romps along, with a definite pop aspect. The first vocal lines are delivered with only minimal accompaniment, contributing what might be called a "suspension effect" after the heaviness of the introduction. Although the unfolding subject matter is out of science fiction, Horn does not sing the lines in any kind of cliched techno-dweeb voice—a wise decision. Indeed, Horn's tone of voice communicates well the idea that a society permeated with technological wonders—which here turn out to have dystopian consequences—can still consist in ordinary people with ordinary worries. If anything, the song is about the integration of these people into the technology, rather than vice-versa. Thus, as the three parts of the song progress, the vocals take on an increasingly dominated and alienated tone, but without ever invoking our friends who were "electric" (and who formed tubeway armies)—who were so much in vogue in the late seventies and early eighties.

Especially when compared to Jon Anderson's, Horn's voice had limitations, as he was the first to acknowledge. But he worked well with these limitations. In addition, these limitations provided an opportunity for Chris Squire to increase his vocal contributions, which was much welcome. Yes by this time had had enough experience with different musicians that there was plenty of comparing to do—Peter Banks and Steve Howe; Tony Kaye, Rick Wakeman, Patrick Moraz, and now Geoff Downes; Bill Bruford and Alan White. But the comparisons that were coming into view were perhaps the most difficult: first Anderson and Horn, then Howe and Trevor Rabin. In the case of either comparison, the issues went beyond who was better. Yes without Anderson is almost unthinkable; if his spirit had not been there, in some strong sense, and, even so, if more than one Yes album had been made without him, I think that would have been the end for Yes. We'll turn to the Howe-Rabin question in a moment, but, let us note that, even if the "spirit" issue didn't loom quite as large as in the case of Jon Anderson, still, Howe had become so much a part of Yes that to make a change in the guitarist's position also meant a very significant change in the chemistry of the whole group. Through it all there was Chris Squire (with, as in the case of Anderson, one exception: *ABWH*); he was the crucial carrier of the flame. And that's what matters—not who is a better guitar player, drummer, and so on but whether a certain vision can still carry on and develop.

For a band that might be associated with science fiction by many of its fans and critics, in actuality the connections are somewhat minimal. In some ways, "Machine Messiah" harkens back to "Astral Traveller," in terms of its message of a menacing force. The former is perhaps more ominous, in that it is less ambiguous. (In terms of the perspective presented, "Astral Traveller" might be compared with Genesis's "Watcher of the Skies"—the voice seems to be more one of warning rather than menace.) What is even more frightening, the "machine Messiah" represents the triumph of a force that has welled up from within, rather than dropped down from above. *We want to submit* to the machine messiah; what is especially effective about the song is the way that it works this willful embracing through both alienated and "happy" tones—the latter in the form of "all of us standing in line" and the former in lines such as,

Hold me, machine Messiah,
And show me
The strength of your singular eye.

The intermingling of these emotions is what makes "Machine Messiah" not simply a pop song. This is probably something that the Buggles (Horn and Downes)
brought to this version of Yes, the ability to play off of pop idioms without being
entirely inside these idioms.

As a whole the song has an epic quality about it, and indeed this is the
longest piece the group had recorded since "Awaken." The heaviness of
"Machine Messiah" was completely unexpected, and this is a good example of a
group putting conventional musical strategies to unconventional effect. The hard,
pounding parts of the song went even deeper than the metal of the machine Messiah itself, into the bedrock. When the pounding bass, guitar, and drums are
joined by a chorus, this creates a more Wagnerian metal than most heavy metal
groups have ever approached. (About all that I can compare it to in that genre is
the song "Black Sabbath," from the album and by the group of the same name.)

As the sound of the electrically charged cables that carry power into the
satanic mills finally fades, we take another unexpected turn, toward a miniature
scene, presented under the title, "White Car." We go from a heavily guitar-domi-
nated piece to a piece with no guitar at all, a nice change. And we go from one
of the longer Yes works from recent albums to the shortest piece from any of
their albums. The string and percussion arrangement is charming, especially
Alan White's work with the tympani. (I assume that the strings are keyboard-
generated.) The lyrics are wistful, with an existentialist edge, an image from a
dream—and this in a song that uses the second person to make a statement that
is clearly meant in the first person: "Take all your dreams and you throw them
away." There is continuity with "Machine Messiah," in that both songs deal with
alienation; but "White Car" returns us to a world where people at least know
they are alienated, as evidenced by the whistling synthesizer at the end as much
as by the singing and lyrics.

Can a person be alienated and not know it? Isn't it integral to the concept of
being alienated that a person knows they are alienated? In a well-known essay,
"Postmodernism, or, The Cultural Logic of Late Capitalism," Fredric Jameson
argues that a key aspect of the emerging cultural matrix is "loss of affect." This
results in a kind of postalienation sensibility, wherein one is alienated even from
one's own alienation. The term "postmodernism" has been bandied about so
much, in the arts and philosophy, and I don't know what mileage could be gotten
out of arguing that "Machine Messiah" is a "postmodern" song. Thematically,
however, there's no question but that loss of affect is what "Machine Messiah" is
about. Musically, the song combines different styles, but I wouldn't put this in
the category of "postmodern pastiche" (Jameson identifies this as another aspect

of the postmodern); Yes's approach continues to be synthetic, more in the vein of "world music" than forcing some supposedly unheard of clash of styles. (However, much that is characterized as "postmodern," whether this be in music or painting or architecture, is precisely *forced,* "quirky" in a completely contrived way.) Consider the fact that much postmodern literary criticism has been concerned with English Romantic poetry, however, and one sees that Blake's satanic mills were there from the start—and Yes has been there with Blake for a long time. Loss of affect is to be expected at the point when everything is quantified, something Blake understood many years ago (as did John the Revelator, for that matter, for this is what the "number of the beast" is really all about). Yes is simply carrying forward this "witness against the beast" through the medium of experimental rock music.[7]

Both "Does It Really Happen?" and "Tempus Fugit" deal with the fast pace of modern life, the way that it goes by before you realize that you're supposed to be living it. Indeed, "Into the Lens" could be said to consider this same theme, from the perspective of trying to hang on to memories. Although these songs are all a bit maudlin, and sometimes fall too much into cliches, they remain quite powerful. In my view, "Run Through the Light" shares these weaknesses, without having much in the way of strengths. The vocal performance is too choppy and affected. (Perhaps I'm put off, too, by the idea of someone other than Chris Squire—in this case, Trevor Horn—playing the bass guitar part on a Yes album, especially when Squire is there to play piano on the track.) I simply raise this in order to set the song aside from an album of otherwise strong performances.

Again, from the start, "Does It Really Happen?" is unexpected, at least as a Yes song. Everything in the song seems effortlessly integrated into the whole— the music galavants along without drawing attention to individual parts. What stands out most of all are the vocal performances, not only the harmonies but also the parts sung in unison.

"Into the Lens," even if it is sentimental in places, captures a mood quite nicely. Interestingly, as with "Machine Messiah," the protagonist of the song is again identifying with a mechanical object, in this case a camera. But perhaps all of the pieces after "Machine Messiah" are meant to bring us back to our senses, even if through mechanical mediation (so many years after the Beach Boys, Yes finally does a "car" song!). Even if "time . . . slips away like running water," even if "memories . . . fade so fast," the awareness of loss is vastly superior to the inhuman condition where we "finally unlearn our lessons and alter our stance."

The song as a whole is as good a piece of orchestration as Yes ever did. Beginning with what sounds like a simple enough pedal point in the bass guitar—except for the fact that it's in 12/8 time (and the opening section is in the key of B)—the next instruments that enter in are drums and piano, in a very neat bit of interplay. Alan White's playing here is very crisp, as is Geoff Downes's. (I wish that White and Squire would do more playing of this sort, with just piano;

as with their work on the *E.H. in the U.K.* album, there is a slightly warped and metallic, but also unique and interesting, sort of "jazz" that they are able to play.) Steve Howe pierces through this syncopated cluster with a somewhat angular steel guitar line, more a guitar "part" than a melody, another line in the orchestration. Then we have another "suspension effect," when the first chorus is accompanied mainly by some simple piano chords, with just a little guitar ornamentation. Indeed, there is very good use of space throughout the song. This is perhaps best seen in Alan White's unhurried tom-tom rolls.

The "you and me, by the sea" part would be much too sappy except for the terrific instrumental part that underlies it. (Here's a good example, too, of the difference between poetry and lyrics.) What starts out as vaguely "tropical" sounding becomes very urbane when Squire's four-note bass pattern and Downes's strings come in. The whole section builds up nicely, especially when the guitar takes over the bass line. This is definitely an art of many landscapes, as the "tranquility" of the sea passes into "energy" and then "glass reality." In between the final two verses Squire provides one of those great parts that is not a bass solo, not simply a bass line, but instead a piece of orchestration with the bass guitar, where the bass comes to the forefront. Throughout this piece, the tone of the Rickenbacker is wonderful—clear, punchy, powerful.

Keeping in mind that this is mainly Trevor Horn's song (although the writing credits are shared equally for the entire album, this is a song that Horn would go on to record his own version of with the Buggles), the phrase "to energy" is significant, as Jon Anderson's spirit obviously looms large here.

The lyrics almost seem to alternate sentimental banalities with a kind of cyberpunkish harkening back to the machine messiah. Perhaps there is method in this sadness, as the song also alternates between the freezing of time "into glass reality" and the transference into pure energy. The lyrics are evocative and understated. In a speeded-up time, must I become an unfeeling camera for the sake of memory? Is it one or the other, feeling and forgetting, or unfeeling remembrance?[8]

At the end, the song unfolds in a clean, logical way. Downes contributes a rich organ sequence that heralds the return of Squire's pedal point; finally the piano and drums section from the opening returns to wrap the whole thing up. When Downes and White stop in mid-phrase, this captures nicely the closing of the camera's shutter. Well done!

Drama as a whole is a question and a bundle of questions. "Tempus Fugit," the song that brings the album to a close, even ends with a series of questions:

> If I wait for an answer,
> Will the silence be broken?
> Do we wait for an answer?
> Do we leave it unspoken?

This is a moving way to end the album, especially as it comes at the end of a song that is, if anything, an anthem to the spirit of Yes. These questions seem addressed to that spirit. I don't think it is too far out of line to suggest that, in some sense, these questions are also addressed to Jon Anderson. We will come back to these questions.

Chris Squire describes "Tempus Fugit" as "in the spirit of the times, kind of punky." For my part, I would put anything that is "kind of" punky more into the category of new wave, and here, as with their heavy metal opener, Yes showed that they could also take on this style and integrate it into their larger perspective very well. This song makes a statement on a number of levels, nowhere as much as with its tremendous bass line. This line does double duty, in that it both serves as a lead line and drives the song along. Actually, this line develops out of an initial pedal point section, where Squire uses electronic phasing to good effect. The whole opening, with its fanfare from the rest of the group, is rich with anticipation. Then the signature bass line explodes onto the scene, as if to make a singular pronouncement: this is rocking with counterpoint as only Chris Squire can do it. Despite the element of bombast here, neither Squire nor the rest of the band lose sight of basic musicality.

As "Tempus Fugit" settles down into the groove that will underlie the lyrics, we hear yet another rock style taken up for the first time by Yes, namely Steve Howe's hard, slashing, but definitely *reggae* chords.

"Tempus Fugit" performs what it says; the "leopard that freaks at the sight of a mind beside herself" is perfectly enacted in the frantic pace of the song. The whole cast of the song is reminiscent of "Heart of the Sunrise," except here the running hardly stops, down "all the roads I have travelled," and the language is markedly different. "Punky," perhaps, but with a largeness of mind and more literary turn of phrase:

> If you could see all the roads I have travelled
> Towards some unusable last equilibrium
> Run like an athlete and die like a
> Dead beaten speed freak
> An answer to all of the answers to—yes.

In the song itself this all goes by so quickly that there is no time for a reflective moment; it almost seems that to take a moment to attempt to open up these lyrics runs contrary to the spirit of the song. What is the "last equilibrium" for Yes? Perhaps *Going for the One?* But there is no going back to this previous state of affairs—this bird has flown, and though it is only a few years past, it seems we are in a different era. To raise this issue, and then to end with the series of questions that form the final verse, is an especially poignant finish to an album that was perhaps all the stronger for the absence that is felt as a presence.

Therefore, it seems appropriate to try to recapture that moment, when the future of Yes seemed in doubt as never before. *Drama* is a very good album. On the one hand, after the misstep of *Tormato, Drama* very successfully helped make the transition from progressive rock to a kind of expansive experimental rock with strong pop inclinations. The songwriting throughout is excellent, as is the playing. Trevor Horn had an impossible task set for him, so let it be said that he did a damn good job and that he's got a very nice voice. The whole group was trying to find a way to carry forward the spirit of Yes, and that effort was all the more remarkable for the fact that it included two newcomers. Steve Howe remarked that, in the aftermath of *Tormato* (that is, the Paris sessions), it seemed Yes was losing the "commune feeling." *Drama* went some distance in bringing this feeling back, but perhaps mainly as a kind of defensive gesture, one that was inherently untenable as a long-term strategy. So, on the other hand, and on several levels, there is the sense that, with *Drama,* the group was "standing down." After all, it is one thing to negotiate the distance from *The Yes Album* to *Fragile,* but what is it to go in the other direction, to put one foot back into experimental rock? This means, of course, taking one foot out of progressive rock, and then listeners have to wonder where the whole thing is going from there.

Then things changed completely, the group not to resurface for three more years, and then in Southern California, of all places. What strange beast reared up in that distant place, the original utopia for lads from the sooty factory towns of the English north? Was this the answer to all of the answers?

We exist through this strange disguise: *90125* to *Talk*

Except for the awkward and possibly silly form of the proposition, this section might have been called, "How I finally came to appreciate Trevor Rabin." Like many folks, my first exposure to the idea of a very different Yes was hearing "Owner of a Lonely Heart" on the radio. I had two thoughts: this is a really neat song and, *it's happening again.* I suppose that "happening" is a theme for both *Drama* and *90125* ("Does It Really Happen?" seems to be answered by "It Can Happen"), and indeed for Yes's work as a whole. (There is a moment in the rehearsals for *Tormato,* shown in the *Yesyears* video, where Chris Squire says, "In some ways, it's not really happening, is it?") Everything about "Owner of a Lonely Heart" is so clever, it is easy to overlook what a fine piece of musical construction it is. But then again, like many folks, when I purchased the *90125* album, I wasn't entirely sure that Yes was happening. Like many, I wasn't even sure that this really was Yes.

So, I have some confessions to make. As I mentioned in the Introduction, there was a period in the late seventies and early eighties where it was unclear to me whether Yes was any more a relevant group or approach to music. When punk seemed at its most powerful, and when I was involved in playing that music myself, I even came to doubt whether Yes had ever really been relevant.

When I came out on the other side of that era, and started to consider Yes again—and to look for the language that would help me understand why Yes is indeed important, musically and politically—I focused almost entirely on the main sequence. I still had my doubts about the post-*Drama* Yes, and most of these doubts centered on the presence of Trevor Rabin.

Like many, I started with a series of questions, some completely unfair, others with some degree of validity. The most unfair of these questions was, "Who does this guy think he is replacing Steve Howe?" I didn't take the time to think this through. Steve Howe is, of course, unreplaceable—he's simply a musical treasure of world-historic significance. In addition, to say that some guitarist "isn't as good as Steve Howe" doesn't tell us much. A musician could be half as good as Howe and still be pretty great! More to the point, however, it was never Trevor Rabin's intention to "replace" Steve Howe. Something I didn't know until much later was that it wasn't even Rabin's original intention to "join Yes," but instead to take part in forming a band with Chris Squire and Alan White. Howe had moved on, along with Geoff Downes, to form Asia (on whom I'll simply excuse myself from commenting further). Squire and White wanted to move on as well, and their intention was to start a new band (originally the idea was to form a group with Jimmy Page, but, thanks to the usual gang of legal and managerial cretins, we don't know how that would have come out). Trevor Rabin entered the picture, and the trio proceeded under the working name of "Cinema." Tony Kaye came on board as well, but the real turning point toward making this a new version of Yes was when Jon Anderson got involved.

Still, Anderson got involved in the project late in the game, such that the guiding presence on the group was clearly Rabin. And, at the time (in the early eighties), I doubted that Trevor's vision was really a Yes vision. He certainly offered a number of distractions. Too much about him seemed to reflect a "rock-'n'roll pretty boy" sensibility. In the videos that I saw, he strutted across the stage in a way that seemed to be quite at odds with the whole Yes approach, especially its antimachismo aspects. What's more, it seemed that he was unbothered by his lack of connection with, and even contrast to, the history of Yes's approach to music and (to use one of Jon Anderson's favorite words) ideology. He had chops galore, to be sure, but he also seemed to go in for completely worn-out rock cliches too often. As a guitarist, he seemed unoriginal. As a vocalist, he had a good enough "rock singer" voice, but again there was nothing especially distinctive. Indeed, *on first hearing,* large parts of *90125* reminded me of groups such as Journey or Toto, groups composed of competent musicians, certainly, but who were doing a kind of pop-rock dressed up with just enough progressive rock pretentions to sound very schlocky, and watered down. Such groups seemed intent on "feeding the pop machine," one aspect of which is to not necessarily do the music that you, the musician, think is the best music, but instead to follow the formulaic imperatives of the A&R men. Such music is *fun-*

damentally compromised (and usually isn't even good as straightforward pop music), having nothing of the approach Jon Anderson expressed by saying, "I'll do what I think is the right thing, and hope somebody likes it." Rabin seemed to be going in the other direction.

I think *90125* has some problems, and I still think that Trevor Rabin is problematic as a member of Yes in some ways. But I came around to some extent, and I now think that the "Trevor Yes" has made one excellent album, *Big Generator,* and one very good album, *Talk.*

Why did I come around? For one thing, as I started to once again think intensely about Yes in the later eighties, and to think how much (and here I'm quoting Jon Anderson again) "I wanted Yes to be a force in the world," how important Yes's music can and should be, I started to get a greater appreciation for the difficulty of the question of Yes's ongoingness. It was no easy thing to figure out what Yes could and should have been in the late seventies and early eighties. Someone with a very strong sense of direction, Trevor Rabin, came along at a crucial time, delivering a decisive answer to this question. Though I have some problems with some of the particulars in his answer, I've come to recognize that Rabin did allow yes to reinvent itself. I came to realize that this reinvention was necessary. Most crucially, when the more extended engagement beyond the superficial first listening finally came, I recognized that the elements were indeed there, that *this was indeed Yes.*

The reinvention of Yes occurred in fits and starts, which in the clear light of hindsight makes sense. There is also the simple fact that, without Trevor Rabin, there very likely would not have been a Yes of the eighties and into the nineties—or perhaps there would have been a premature reunion of the seventies group, one that might have been perceived as a mere nostalgia act. (Of course, some people will call it that anyway.)

Asking for originality in rock guitarists in more recent years is just about as shaky a proposition as the reinvention of Yes in the age of punk, new wave, hip-hop, and the reentrenchment of the music *business.* Clearly, Trevor Rabin is a third generation virtuoso guitarist (if Hendrix and Clapton, say, are taken as the first generation, and Steve Howe, Robert Fripp, John McLaughlin, and others are taken as a second generation). There simply isn't as much left for this generation to do. Rabin's roots are fairly easy to see: John McLaughlin refracted through some fairly straightforward rock'n'roll guitarisms. Perhaps McLaughlin meets Joe Walsh—and I intend no put-down of the latter (indeed, I think much of Walsh's playing is very intelligent). Well, that's not such a bad combination, even if it is also not one likely to carry forward the degree of experimentation typical of Steve Howe. Where Howe composed complex guitar parts, as part of larger orchestrations, Rabin divides his "rhythm" and "lead" playing in a more conventional way, often going in for "power chords" in the former and show-offy pyrotechnics in the latter. On the other hand, because of the (acknowledged)

McLaughlin influence, Rabin also brings some (Eastern) Indian and John Coltrane inflections to Yes's music.

As for Rabin's vocal contributions, there is a trade off. As I said, he is a good rock singer; but there are a lot of good rock singers, whereas Jon Anderson brings something very distinctive in that category. On the other hand, Yes with Trevor Rabin is a group with three very strong singers; when they all sing together this produces a "choir" effect that is really powerful. (One of the best examples is the "there in the heart of millions" part of "I'm Running.") To be fair, there are also places where the *contrast* of Anderson's and Rabin's voices is used effectively.

In the larger frame, one might say that Yes was still trying to make the transition—or making it again—from a progressive rock group to an experimental rock group with strong pop inflections. As with the shift from *Tormato* to *Drama,* there was the question of "getting it right." One might say that the *90125* group was doing this for the third time in Yes's history, if one thinks back to *Yes* and *Time and a Word.* As with the "Buggles Yes," the Trevor Rabin Yes was also attempting to "stand down," but without a sense of defeat. In all cases, the first try had some commendable moments, but the second try represented a qualitative advance.

To conclude these "confessions" concerning how I came to appreciate Trevor Rabin, I should mention that what finally made it all come together for me was seeing the group on the tour for the *Talk* album. The thinking I've just discussed had largely been done, but to actually see Jon Anderson and Chris Squire in the flesh had a galvanizing effect. The last time I had seen Yes was for the *Relayer* tour, some nineteen years before. When I saw Yes on the *Talk* tour, I was thirty-eight years old. As the group came on stage, I thought about the fact that I had last seen them half of my lifetime before—really, a *whole* lifetime. As the group began with an instrumental arrangement of "Perpetual Change," I had a very intense feeling: it is happening, it is *still* happening. Thinking back on it, those feelings, and some fairly complicated tears, of joy and melancholy, for the fact that the vision is still happening but also for the fact that the vision is still needed because the world is so far from redemption, well up in me again. The whole group was simply wonderful. They did what Yes is supposed to do—they came out and played great music, with a few nice visual effects, but no posing, no puffery, no strutting, no machismo, no rock'n'roll star trips. And this went for Trevor Rabin as for the rest, and I came to accept his contribution more fully.

My understanding is that the Trevor Rabin period has ended, and that the incarnation of Yes as of this writing (in Spring 1996) consists in Anderson, Squire, Howe, Wakeman, and White. So now Yes is once again happening in another form, a form that happens to recapitulate the group as it was incarnated in the middle seventies. I feel full of hope for this combination. Even though part of this hope is for a Yes that is truer to the spirit of the main sequence, however, I don't want to write off the Trevor Rabin period—as some will be tempted to do, and as I would have been tempted to do at one time. Perhaps the ideal situation would be an ongoing dialectic of two Yeses (awkward word that!); I certainly wouldn't object if we could have albums such as *Big Generator* and *Anderson, Bruford, Wakeman, and Howe,* from some entity, held together by a certain spirit, called Yes. Nor would I object if a *real* attempt were made, with care, to bring these two Yeses into a true *union.* Unfortunately, this is a matter of the time, the reasons, and the logic that we *do* understand, and until the "Shakespeare revolution" is carried out with regard to the music biz lawyers and other keepers of contractural relations, the covenant that should in principle be possible will not become actual. But let us dream, all the same, and work for the day when such dreams can become a reality, when visionary music triumphs over the satanic mills of the culture industry.

The question occurred to me whether I should discuss the albums from *90125* on with the Trevor Rabin albums grouped together, followed by the *Union* project and then the *ABWH* project—or should the discussion proceed chronologically? I opted for the latter course, even though the first option perhaps has a greater musical logic to it. In opting for chronological order, I am staying with my thesis that the reinvention of Yes after the seventies is a matter of a larger historical, social, and cultural logic that envelopes the more narrowly defined musical context. The albums will be discussed, therefore, in the following order: *90125, Big Generator, Anderson, Bruford, Wakeman, and Howe, Union, Talk.*

90125

While there are some similarities, perhaps, between *90125* and Yes's very first album, for the most part the former represents a new synthesis that would have been unthinkable in terms of the group as it had existed before. This goes not only for the music on *90125,* but also for the album cover and even the title. The latter is simply the number assigned to the album by Atlantic Records. Everything else about the album is similarly streamlined, including the bare, not especially colorful cover, dominated by silver, created by artist Garry Mouat, working out of a studio called "Assorted Images." This in itself is characteristic of the "street smart" quality of *90125*—we have gone from urbane London to a Los Angeles where "We'll be waiting for the night to come":

> Fast as lightning
> Go—go get high—he's looking good.
> Once bitten twice shy.
> No woman no cry.
> No woman don't cry.

The quotation of a line from Bob Marley ("No woman no cry") reminds us that the first world and Third World now intersect in the metropolises of the former.

The scene that is set is not especially pretty, or even artfully presented, but there is a certain grittiness to it that captures the period. But how ready was Yes for this grittiness—or, for such an immense change, at any rate? To what extent could Yes become a "street smart" band?

However, lest the wrong impression be created, let us note that the elements of punk and new wave (or even a nascent grunge sensibility) remained precisely *inflections* in the larger synthesis. As in earlier periods, Yes remained eclectic, indeed something of a synthesizing machine. Consider the opening of "Owner of a Lonely Heart," which features a bit of swing era drumming from Alan White, with nice reverb and other production effects from producer Trevor Horn. Right away, we are introduced to Trevor Rabin's chunkier, blockier guitar style—those famous power chords. The backbone of all of this, namely Chris Squire, is streamlined, especially in the main chord progression of the song (A-B-C-C-D-GG), but there is still the essentially propulsive feel of a Squire line. In the chorus, the familiar counterpoint returns. At the same time, there is a new economy of lyrical expression, but basic Yes themes are there: movement, moving oneself, being movement. This economy is welcome. "Owner" is also more than likely the only song in rock music that has the line, "not for pity's sake." In the instrumental section, we hear Jon Anderson scream for the first time in Yes music (actually a series of shrieks that coincide with drum beats), and again there is an interesting synthesis of swing music and more straightahead rock. In his guitar solo Rabin demonstrates his mastery of electronic effects—not for the last time. As with many of Rabin's solos, there is both innovation and cliche, with the latter often tagged on at the end of a line (so why not edit these things out?). Finally, in the last part of the song—"Don't deceive your free will at all"—Anderson hits a note so high and infused with pure joy, on the second repitition of "just receive it," it's inspirational. (This is more readily apparent in the *9012Live* video concert version of "Owner.")

Was "Owner of a Lonely Heart" the "'Roundabout' of the eighties"? In many ways, yes. Not only was the piece a stretched version of a rock song, with interesting admixtures but also a driving feel at the heart of it, but, like "Roundabout," "Owner" served as a rallying point for a new generation of Yes listeners. If everything Yes wasn't in this song, still this song helped everything Yes to keep happening. And, "Owner" is just a good, exciting piece of music.

Other highlights of *90125*. "Hold On" has a solid, rocking feel to it, with excellent vocals. Indeed, the "choir" of Anderson, Rabin, and Squire, presents a solid "united front" here. In the final repetitions of the chorus, Rabin provides some nice harmonics. "It Can Happen" features a trippy bass line that carries most of the song along with it. The singing is again excellent, especially in the "Look up, look down" section. "Changes" is certainly the most Mahavishnu-inflected piece on *90125,* especially in its opening section. Squire uses an eight-string bass guitar here (each of the four standard bass strings is doubled with a string that is an octave higher), to good effect. I especially like the way the song begins with an ascending four-note bass pattern, which then turns back on itself when the guitar comes in. Rabin's lead here is tasteful, precisely that combination of McLaughlin and more straightforward rock guitar at its best. I'm not quite as enthusiastic about his singing here, however, or some of the lyrics, for that matter, both of which tend to give in to cliche. The choruses feature some nice counterpoint, though, and Rabin's voice does work well in the "For some reasoning you're questioning why" verse. Going into the next verse, "One word from you," this is a good example of where the definite contrast between Rabin's and Anderson's voices works well. The line from one of the choruses, "Word to the wise—well you get what's coming" is delivered with a nice edge to it. (In the *9012Live* video, I especially like the way Squire shakes his finger accusingly on this line.) The instrumental track, "Cinema," has a good jazzy feel to it without sounding like "jazz-rock." The singers bring the choir together to optimal effect in "Leave It." There's an interesting shift here, from this united choral front, which opens the song, to one of the more "streetwise" moments on the album, when Rabin sings the "One down, one to go" verse. Here his voice works well. During the chorus ("Aahhh . . . Leave it"), Squire provides a playful, gyrating line, the notes caroming of the ringers in the pinball machine. With *90125* Squire started experimenting more with different bass guitars and electronic effects, and here his line has a peculiar (but intended) thinness to it, but one that is effective. "Our Song" and "Hearts" are pretty songs, though a bit too sentimental for my taste. To end on a stronger note, then, we might mention that "City of Love" is a very hard, crunching, thrashing beast, with a deep, insistent bass line and razor sharp guitar.

I haven't commented on the keyboard work on *90125* in part because it is unclear which parts are played by Trevor Rabin and which by Tony Kaye. I'm guessing that the greater part was played by Rabin. He was originally a pianist (who received an electric guitar as a gift from his parents when he took first place in a classical piano competition), and quite a good one. In addition, Rabin knows all things electronic inside out. Most of the keyboard playing on *90125* is quite understated—though, it should be said, understatement was also one of Kaye's admirable talents—mostly a support rather than a foil for the guitar. This has its good and bad side—I like less keyboards, but I wouldn't have minded a little less guitar as well. In any case, the problem of knowing who is playing what carries over to the next album.

Big Generator

As I've argued, Yes's transitions have often taken two albums to work out, with the second album in the transition representing a qualitative advance over the first. This is certainly the case with the second album of the "Trevor Yes,"

Big Generator, which really integrates all of the elements of an experimental rock album with strong pop inflections. Once one gets into the swing of what Yes is at this point trying to do, I think it is clear that *Big Generator* is an excellent album, from beginning to end.

Although the album cover for *Big Generator* continues the streamlined sensibility of the eighties Yes, the music itself has thickened out somewhat. The street sensibility is replaced, as well, with something that is also new to Yes, a more developed sense of humor. Since its beginnings, Yes had never done a "sex" song; now *Big Generator* comes along and opens with a song about sex, but obviously with tongue in cheek. Indeed, the album begins with a melodramatic string and choral arrangement, reminiscent of sentimental Hollywood pictures from the thirties and forties. When "Rhythm of Love" blasts through the screen, it has the force of an old roadster. The piece is skillfully composed and performed, a very good pop song, but it also has to be understood in the context of "cosmic Yes" up to that point. The group, with Rabin in the lead, is having a playful go at itself. One of the musical elements that stands out is the way that Rabin creates a surface with the guitar that is both sports-car smooth and ripping apart at the edges. Rabin is a skillful user of a kind of snarling dissonance, here and elsewhere. People who think that Yes "went commercial" when Trevor Rabin came onboard should keep in mind the following: given that the group seems to be able to reel off songs in the "Rhythm of Love" mold, why didn't they just make whole albums of this sort of work, and really clean up? To my mind, the answer is that the basic Yes sensibility remains operative, even if sometimes mixed with these pop excursions. In any case, with "White Car" and "Rhythm of Love," Yes finally came around to doing a car song and a sex song (one that was still not a "chick" song), and we see how they did these very much against the grain of the rock canon.

The energy of "Rhythm of Love" continues with "Big Generator." This song has a bass line that hip-hoppers would have to call "phat." Squire is playing a custom instrument that has a longer scale neck and four extra frets at the low end. (This is his solution to having the range of a five-string bass guitar in an instrument with only four strings.) Thus the first note of the piece is a very low A. "Big Generator" is a terrific crossing of science fiction and gangster film genres:

> Big Generator
> Hands upon the wheel
> Big Generator
> In for the kill

At the same time, the song is the funny obverse of "Machine Messiah." Where "Messiah" presents an ominous, dystopian picture, "Big Generator" shows us technology that is not so much friendly as it is *goofy,* inept. As the science fiction gangsters, big talking Chicagoans who tell of the "big gen-a-rad-ah," charge around in their old land yachts, there is a whole other subtext at work, of human possibility: "It can strike a chord inside you, like a generation's need." One of my favorite parts of the song, musically, is the verse toward the end that is presented in an angular, jazzy style, like something by Manhattan Transfer:

Flying out the soft machine, we offer
All surprise to you.
Praise oh praise this anthem generator.

"Soft machine" is, of course, one of William S. Burrough's terms for human being (from his novel, *Naked Lunch*). Again, this is an image of the overblown claims made for the new technology, the legion of robots and cyborgs that will supposedly take us into a bright, chrome-plated future. Given that such images abound nowadays, especially in the vicinity of *Wired* magazine, "Big Generator" was ahead of its time in depicting the 1950s-ish, dweebish, "Mr. Science" character of these innovations.

"Shoot High, Aim Low" continues the interpolation of country music into the synthesis begun by Steve Howe. Indeed, I could imagine hearing this song, along with "Walls," from *Talk,* on country music radio. (I don't know if there ever was such airplay, but I suspect not.) The cast of the piece is bleak, spare, especially with Rabin's clipped guitar sound. There are moments when an almost "Asian" keyboard sound drifts through, and this provides an interesting contrast. The sound is not only "out West," in the desert, but even post-apocalyptic. There is a desperation here, as well as drama: on the one hand, we find a large-scale political scenario in which there are, "Exchanges in the currency of humans/bought and sold/And the leaders seem to lose control"; on the other hand, there is the personal story of two people who are trying to escape this scene: "In the blue sedan we never got much further." In some ways, this song has more pure "atmosphere" than most other Yes works.

I never expected to hear Jon Anderson do anything like a "rap," but this is what we find in parts of "Almost Like Love." It's kind of a "pop rap," but there's a nice bounciness to it, and it is kind of neat to hear Anderson work so many words into such a small space. My favorite line in the song is, "Just like a Shakespeare revolution." Well, let's give it a try! Otherwise, the song is pure pop, very sweet, with some interesting twists. Like many of the other songs here, this one also inserts a concentrated political statement here and there (for example, "in a world of superstition caught in a total nuclear greed") in the midst of a more personal message. Whereas in "Shoot High, Aim Low," both messages were very bleak, here there is a basic sweetness:

So promised in a hundred letters
Should be getting to you any time now.
So promised a surprise for you

For getting so far from now.

It's almost like love.

I suppose that, if I had to say what the weakest song on *Big Generator* is, "Almost Like Love" would probably be it. The song is mostly for fun, but it's a well-crafted fun.

By the same token, one could argue that "Love Will Find a Way" is not much more than a standard pop love song. But it is carefully crafted and, it seems to me, presented with exuberance and heart. The vocals, sung in unison by Anderson and Rabin, are bright and beautiful. In the solo section we get to hear Chris Squire play the harmonica (something he did before only in the live performances of "And You and I"), and Alan White provides some very "big beat" drumming. Mystery line: "I eat at chez nous"—what's that all about?

Finally we come to the two more extended pieces on the album, and what I think are the real masterpieces of *Big Generator.*

First of all, "Final Eyes" is a terrific vocal performance both for its harmony singing and especially for Jon Anderson's powerful solo voice. In addition, the song uses contrasts perfectly, building from an initial, spare, acoustic arrangement, into a larger orchestration. Given that Tony Kaye was always partial to the Hammond B-3, I assume this is his organ work here, and it is very strong. As the acoustic section builds toward the full group arrangement, the final vocalization of the words "final eyes" is magical. In fact, this song is quite simple in structure, but there are many subtle features. For example, in the "I know you think there's nothing" verse, Rabin contributes some two-note guitar fills that add the perfect touch without being obtrusive. The song closes with some very McLaughlin-like acoustic guitar, an interesting ending.

Indeed, this Indian-inflected close of "Final Eyes" segues nicely into "I'm Running," my nomination for the strongest work on the album. As controversial as this may sound, I would also nominate this song as on a par with Yes's best work from any period. Squire is a bit down in the mix in many of the songs from the "Trevor" period—though sometimes he is very much in the fore. "I'm running" opens with an extended bass part from Squire, a line that foreshadows the masterful counterpoint which will unfold in the song. The segue from Rabin's finale for "Final Eyes" to this bass line is a musical journey from India to the islands of the south Pacific. Again the question of "total nuclear greed" rears its hideous head, this time in terms of the nuclear testing that is "tunneling away at the very soul of man." As with some of Yes's greatest works, "I'm Running" unfolds from a very simple, innocent song, into a rather large-scale orchestration. The "island" inflections are something new, and they are used to good effect—both Squire's initial line, and Rabin's acoustic chords that come in slightly off-center. To the extent that there is the pop sound of "happy natives" presented here, this is done self-consciously and in a purely ironic frame.

The drama of the song builds considerably in the first verse, which then gives way to what I find to be Yes's best use of the "suspension effect" in all of their works: when the initial chorus, "And I'm running," comes in, the music really feels as if the bottom has fallen out of it. Apart from the compositional element here, it is especially Alan White who creates this effect with his careful spacing. There is great drama here. Musically, the first part of the song unfolds by repeating the initial verse and chorus, with subtle variations. We then come to the second part, "There in the heart of millions," a verse delivered by Anderson with due intensity. What builds, lyrically, is a human solidarity based on the general threat of nuclear destruction—the words take us from the situation of the islanders, who have "heard the thunder underground," to a projected unity whereby

> All in a sharp step,
> As one together,
> All in all we race
> As one
> This time.

Clearly there is a double entendre at work here: we all race together/all of us together in the human race. This theme will develop even further, in the third part of the song. However, first, there is an interesting instrumental section that is something like a passage through that narrow space where solidarity might come into being (or, as Walter Benjamin put it, "the narrow gate through which the messiah may at any moment come"—which seems in the spirit of "I'm Running": "There in the heart of millions, seen as a godsend to us—there stands our future"). The verse in the inset quotation above gives way to an initial unleashing of the guitar, which then comes to an abrupt halt. We hear the sound of some sort of compartment opening, and in this little box we find a miniature piece of musical interplay that depends especially on the bass and tuned percussion from White (I think he's playing a marimba).

The song returns to its initial simplicity and innocence, building once again through the suspension effect, working finally into a very complex counterpoint involving the Yes chorus at full strength. The musical line of "There in the heart of millions" is crossed with a new line, "Hear this voice now and forever." The harmonies are complex and beautiful, as is Anderson's solo voice in the midst of all this. The song ends rather abruptly, creating a final suspension and a question regarding the possibility of solidarity—"all in all we race."

The pace and complexity of "I'm Running," especially in its final part, is quite taxing. *Big Generator* ends with a more gentle denouement. Jon Anderson's "Holy Lamb," which is very much in the vein of some of his solo compositions, reaffirms Yes's Blakean roots. Even if quite sentimental, the song (and album) closes with a message of utopian hope: "All we need to know is that the future is a friend of yours and mine." The song is somewhat a New Age piece (with the subtitle, "Song for Harmonic Convergence"), somewhat blissed out; on the other hand, "Holy Lamb" also shows that Yes remained committed to vision and had not capitulated to the pop machine.

Anderson, Bruford, Wakeman, and Howe

However, the Yes of the eighties was certainly involved in compromises with this machine. Indeed, this issue was made all the more difficult by the fact that such compromises seemed to come naturally to Trevor Rabin, who probably saw little wrong with them—he came from a different generation and sensibility. Jon Anderson clearly hungered for the opportunity to create works of progressive rock once again, and thus he joined with three other members of the main sequence Yes to form the rather infelicitously named Anderson, Bruford, Wakeman, and Howe. Under this banner the quartet (augmented by three other musicians, most significantly King Crimson and Peter Gabriel bassist Tony Levin) produced a masterful album of visionary, virtuoso rock, *Anderson, Bruford, Wakeman, and Howe*. Perhaps the irony is that this group, with a name that sounds too much like a law firm, could not legally use the name "Yes" precisely because of the growing role of lawyers in the music business. My sense of things is that, rather than choose another name for the group that would, in effect, mean "not-Yes," the group presented itself as four musicians who had indeed played a crucial role in the development of Yes music. This impression is reinforced by Roger Dean's album cover art, one of his more ornate paintings (and a back cover painting that is evocative of Monument Valley, in Utah and Arizona).

My view is that *ABWH* is indeed an album of Yes music, with one important exception. Obviously, Chris Squire is the missing element here. This doesn't automatically mean that the music contained in the album *cannot* be Yes music; if *Drama* could present Yes music—up to a point—without Jon Anderson, then *ABWH* could do likewise without Squire, *if* a certain musical vision had been maintained. Integral to this vision is the complex counterpoint that Squire brings to a piece of music, a line that doesn't just sit at the bottom and play a conventional bass line role, but instead a line that really changes the character of the whole music. I mean no criticism of Tony Levin, who I certainly consider one of the best practitioners of the bass guitar in the past twenty years, but his approach is quite different from Squire's. Having said this, however, I think *ABWH* is a very good album, large parts of which could easily have taken their place in the main sequence.

The album represents a kind of intersection of three main musical elements. First, of course, is the "kind of thing" that Yes was doing in the main sequence—which is already the intersection of many elements, of course. Second, the pieces on *ABWH* take up a number of elements from popular songwriting; for instance, the initial guitar chord sequence in "Birthright" has a distinctively "soul" feel, while "Teakbois" is a rather direct reference to ska and reggae. Third, there is a strong "world music" sensibility on *ABWH* perhaps seen most of all in "Birthright," which uses elements of Australian Aboriginal music (for example, the synthesized sound of the dijeridoo).

There are moments—indeed, whole pieces—where the album becomes a bit too maudlin and sentimental, or too New Agey. I'll concentrate instead on what are the stronger pieces, in my view, and in the following order: "Teakbois," "Themes," "Brother of Mine," "Birthright," and "Order of the Universe."

"Teakbois" ("The Life and Times of Bobby Dread") is appealing mainly for its simplicity, the fact that it tells a more personal sort of story, and its ska-reggae beat. It's one of those things that is quite unexpected and therefore charming when it comes from Yes musicians. I love the play on the standard reggae/Rasta expression, "I and I"—Anderson sings, instead, "you and you and you," which not only repeats the very last words of *Tales from Topographic Oceans,* but also emphasizes the basic "other-orientation" of Yes's approach to music and life.

"Themes" is surely not the most exciting title one might imagine, especially for a piece of music that is quite lively, especially featuring Wakeman's keyboard orchestrations and Bruford's unpredictable spacings. There is a festive sound to both the completely instrumental first part and the second part, "Second Attention," where the vocals come in. This is especially due to the horn sounds from Wakeman's synthesizer, which give us something like a bugle call to present arms, and the joyful clattering from some of Bruford's electronic drums—a bit of a "super-tambourine" sound. In the latter part, Anderson banishes the demons of the music business:

> Be gone you ever piercing
> Power play machine,
> Cutting our musical solidarity . . .

Indeed, Anderson invokes the words of Jesus which the latter used in casting demons out of the possessed: "For I am out of thee with a vengeance" (presented in quotation marks in the song itself). Interestingly, the term "second attention" appears in both "Themes" and "Brother of Mine." I am not sure where this term comes from—though I assume it is an invention of Jon Anderson's—but the associations with messianic themes are fairly clear—second coming, being born again (though I doubt this is meant in any kind of fundamentalist sense). Of course, *ABWH* is itself a kind of second coming or second birth of a certain version of Yes, so perhaps this is the association. Again we see Yes's "other-orientation" in the final verse:

> I don't believe in Devils.
> I don't believe in Demons.
> I only believe in you.

This is also an interesting play on John Lennon's supremely bitter song, "God," from *Plastic Ono Band.* After giving a long list of "I don't believe·"'s a list that includes the Bible, Hitler, Jesus, Zimmerman (Bob Dylan), and the Beatles, Lennon sings, "I only believe in me/Yoko and me/and that's reality." Surely this is one of Lennon's most cynical efforts (thankfully there is another side to him in many of his other songs), and it seems to me that Jon Anderson energy here is directed precisely toward creating an alternative to such cynicism.

"Brother of Mine" begins almost like some sort of droopy, teary-eyed English drinking song, and it pursues this sentimentality at some length. As with "Birthright," most of the references here are to Australian Aboriginal people, the people of the "big dream." After several verses of "never be[ing] afraid to show your heart," there is a subtle change of cadence, as well as the addition of a jaunty, almost rhythm and blues guitar progression. Wakeman also supplies some very nice, understated piano here. The piece becomes a good deal more dramatic with the "Took me by surprise" verse, which carries over into the second part. Indeed, the whole work builds nicely, and subtly, throughout, and the changing cadences are also subtle, understated. Although the song seems male-oriented in the title, in fact it is not: "nothing can come between us, you're a brother of mine"; "nothing can come between us, you're a sister of time." When the song finally builds into the chant that drives the final part, we find a strong statement of a universal "brotherhood" that in fact goes beyond humanism. In the transition from part 2 to part 3, Howe provides a solo that, for all that it has some sting in its tone, is both minimal and friendly. Indeed, there is almost nothing "over the top" in any of the pieces from the album I am discussing here. Finally, in the only grand gesture in the piece, Wakeman uses the full range of the piano keyboard to, in a sense, sum it all up.

Whereas "Brother of Mine" begins in, and mostly stays in, a harmonic universe from a quite different continent than Australia, the song attempts to work its way into some aspects of the Aboriginal world view. Interestingly, "Birthright" works in the opposite direction: its musical material is much more derived from Aboriginal sources, while its perspective is self-consciously external. The work takes as its thematic material the first test of an atomic bomb by the British, which was conducted in the outback of Australia. As the album notes indicate, the British government "failed to contact all of the Aborigine peoples at the time." Once again, then, Yes musicians have taken up the question of the "thunder underground, tunneling away at the very soul of man." As a political statement, "Birthright" is as direct as "Don't Kill the Whale," but I think the Yes musicians did a better job of working with such a statement this time. As I indicated, the synthesized background in this piece evokes Aboriginal music. Bruford adds to this atmosphere with both woodblocks and a deep "thud" from the bass drum. The guitar, however, is in quite a different groove, quite soulful. Anderson's voice has a certain quality to it sometimes that I don't really know how to describe—it's a kind of insistence, but presented in a colorful, really quite beautiful, way. This quality is much in evidence here, especially as he sings the verse that begins, "This road is never lonely." This quality is also heard when Anderson sings, "Like all the empires crumble, will surely change the tide," one of my favorite lines from the song. Of course, to hear Anderson sing, "This place ain't big enough for red and white/This place ain't big enough for stars and stripes" is unexpected—it's direct, and yet the musical context and vocal presentation keep this from sounding like a piece of agit-prop music. When Anderson sings the series of "this place" lines that lead up to "is theirs by their birthright," he paradoxically seems to become both more insistent and to fade from exhaustion. At the end of the song Anderson says something in what I assume is an Aboriginal language; I don't know what he is saying, but it comes across powerfully.

Finally, perhaps taking up the more positive side of themes already presented in "Themes," the group present an anthem of rock music's possibilities. This piece starts at a good clip and only gets faster, until its final chant, "the order of the universe." Indeed, in the first vocal section, "Rock Gives Courage," the lyrics are about as rock'n'roll as anything Yes has ever done. This seems to be a play on the main sequence itself, to use such lyrics to try to articulate the larger themes that were central to that period. Obviously, lines such as the following are quite unexpected:

> Rock gives courage, a way to win the trust.
> Rock gives courage, a way to win or bust.
> Rock gives sisters a way to speak their mind.
> Without this gift of rock and roll
> We'd all be wasting time.

Assuming that this message is not meant to be taken ironically, the idea seems to be that this gift of rock has to burst the bounds of the "power play machine." Can this gift work its way beyond cynicism, beyond the "sick feeling, sick reasoning, sick challenge you, la la la la"? This last little bit, in the way that Anderson sings it on the album, is a wonderfully harsh parody of cynicism. Is there any getting beyond the chatter, to "the order of the universe"?

Is there any getting beyond the music business and the inconsequential garbage, to a rock music that *tries*—"you can't imagine it, how hard it is to grow"—to say something important?

Union

We come down from this lofty challenge to find what might have been two good to very good albums, artificially mushed together in a rather contrived "union." There is some good music there, some real Yes music, but this is so buried under so many layers of production, A&R people, management, and lawyers, that it is very hard to hear—a cynical victory for the power play machine. This album arose out of separate efforts by Anderson, Bruford, Wakeman, and Howe, on the one hand, and the Trevor Rabin Yes, on the other. The trick was to add Anderson's vocals to what the "Trevor Yes" had done, and Squire's voice to the *ABWH* tracks (which again feature Tony Levin on bass). For some reason that I probably wouldn't understand (much less accept) even if I knew it, there is a host of other musicians on these tracks. While I'm sure that they simply did what they were asked to do, and did that well, the result is a very mucked-up album that buries the music. It would have been far better if this "union" had not taken place, and if, instead, there had been two very different albums from these very different incarnations of Yes. At least each might have remained faithful to their own conceptions. The various members of the two Yeses pretty much despised the result (as they said in numerous interviews after the fact), and even felt embarrassed by it. I think every one of the Yes musicians went forward here with the best of intentions, but they really ran into the corporate wall this time.

What is most unfortunate is the fact that we not only missed out on the possibility of a *real* "union," but that, because of this failed, scam union (one is tempted to call it a "company union"), we'll probably never really see the possibilities that might have emerged. For my part, I was especially interested in the idea of an extended interaction between Bill Bruford and Alan White, two of the best percussionists in the world. That the reason we don't know what such an interaction would sound like is because lawyers and management types have other agendas is appalling—and it tells us that things have gotten to the point where *music itself,* in order to be what it is, has to set itself against capitalism, against the idea and institutions of private property.

On a calmer note, there is some pretty decent Yes music buried in *Union,* and I suppose it is a useful listening exercise to ferret this out. "I Would Have Waited Forever" and "Shock to the System" both feature some very good guitar parts from Steve Howe. Both also feature parts where the band drops out momentarily and there is a clear thematic statement from Anderson. In the case of "I Would Have Waited," this part comes when Anderson sings "So in-between the perfect flame of you . . .," while the similar part in "Shock" begins with, "So, in answer to your prayer." Perhaps what is most appealing about these parts is the fact that the overburdened tracks are set aside for a moment, and we get a sense of basic structure. It's interesting how similar these moments are, even beyond both of them beginning with "So." "Masquerade" is a pleasant addition to Steve Howe's collection of solo guitar pieces, this time featuring twelve-string acoustic guitar. With "Lift Me Up" and "Saving My Heart," Trevor Rabin extends his string of potential country classics. The line, "God I hate this town, depending on the day" captures a mood nicely. As I understand it, this song concerns homelessness; as such, it is mostly successful. The first part of "Without Hope You Cannot Start the Day" has a delicate structure that is not too muddled by overproduction; the second part is quite different, and it sounds a bit too much like another song from the album, "Dangerous" (which was written by the same team of Jon Anderson and Jonathan Elias).

In some ways, "Miracle of Life," by Trevor Rabin (and Mark Mancina, one of the many co-writers who somehow made their way into this process) is my favorite piece from the album. The song begins with a nice, complex bit of orchestration featuring acoustic guitar, organ from Tony Kaye I assume, and bass. I especially like Squire's simple line here, reminiscent of what he did in "Owner of a Lonely Heart." The singing is very good, especially Anderson's almost unnaturally high-pitched and fluid ring, and the lyrics bring together themes explored in "Don't Kill the Whale," but with a more redemptive edge: "You'd rather be washed in blood." Throughout there is good orchestration; this is the one place on *Union* where the big production approach works pretty well.

"Silent Talking" has a glamorous and dreamlike feel to it, and it also uses suspension effects at the beginning quite nicely. At the expense of probably irking some readers, I thought the arrangement was not unlike some by Swing Out Sister. The song has a Eurodisco feel. I liked the bass here as much for what it didn't play as for what it did. With its ethereal qualities, there is almost a crossing of the green language with cyberspace when Anderson sings,

> Silent talking
> In the system,
> Bring me to
> This beautiful world.
>
> Silent talking,
> Always dreaming,
> Bring me to this
> Beautiful world.

There is also a basic structure to "The More We Live—Let Go" that is not quite overwhelmed by the production, and this is true of "Angkor Wat" as well. About this time, however, the album begins to sound very stretched out, and though there are some nice parts in the other songs, the musical justification for stringing them all together in this single "union" has pretty much run out of steam. "Evensong," for example, which is piece that Bill Bruford and Tony Levin (playing the Chapman Stick) developed while working with King Crimson, would be interesting in another context of similar and more extended improvisations. Here it just sounds like filler.

Perhaps some day a more perfect union will give this material a more careful treatment.

Talk

After *Union* the future and viability of Yes was once again in question. As I discussed at the outset of this part, the various reinventions of Yes after the time of progressive rock occurred through fits and starts. How is it that Yes could generate such an amazing amount of great music in the years from 1969 to 1977, always growing and developing both in terms of vision and form, while only having a sporadic and fragmentary existence from 1978 on? With the *Union* debacle, it seemed that the reinvention of Yes would remain not only unfinished, but essentially something that would only ever proceed in a hit-or-miss fashion. I've argued that this is mainly for social reasons, including everything from postmodern cybernetic capitalism in its largest outlines to the minute details of the workings of the culture industry, especially its music division. One aspect of this postmodern fragmenation is that, it seems, the outlook of "the group's the thing" can no longer stand up to the corporate music structure. While this outlook was very strong in Yes from its inception up through *Going for the One* (with some bumps in the road, to be sure), the "commune feeling" has been the exception rather than the rule in the post–main sequence period.

In this light, I see the most recent offering from one of the incarnations of Yes as a positive development. To be sure, *Talk* was not made in the sort of group context that prevailed in the days of *Close to the Edge*. Indeed, my understanding is that large parts of the album were made without the musicians playing together at all. The most "group" aspect of the album is that, for once, Trevor Rabin and Jon Anderson worked together on the compositions from the start—in contrast to the other two albums by the "Trevor Yes," where Rabin came with more or less finished songs and Anderson only came in toward the end of the process. The fact of the matter is that Trevor Rabin just isn't that much of a group-oriented musician; as he says in the *Yesyears* video, he tends to put together finished songs and, beyond that, it is "very difficult for [him] to just let things happen." "Letting things happen," in the earlier years of Yes, was itself a kind of democratic discipline, an arena of mutual encouragement and participation. But, if this sort of "letting" is not going to happen in a version of Yes with Trevor Rabin, perhaps there is a next best thing, namely to approach a Yes album in its particularity, as a singular project that will, all the same, try to express something of the Yes vision. This is what has been achieved, at a fairly high level of accomplishment, with *Talk*.

This sense of the singular project is captured well by Peter Max's one-off album cover, displaying the name "Yes" in his minimal but funky pop-art style, and with the album title written in friendly script and sitting unobtrusively in the upper right-hand corner. (This works well, too, in the CD format, where it is hard to display the visually larger and more intricate works of an artist such as Roger Dean. There's an "on the other hand" here that I won't even go into.) *Talk* is the first album to be recorded almost entirely to a computer hard-drive using music production software, and to say that the production is extremely clean is an understatement. The miracle is that the sound is wonderfully clean without being merely slick. This was all master-of-electronic-realities Trevor Rabin's doing. The music was all co-written by Rabin and Anderson, with Squire contributing on two songs, "The Calling" and "Real Love" (and with Roger Hodgson, from Supertramp, contributing on "Walls"). Although I continue to prefer *Big Generator* to *Talk,* among the "Trevor" albums, there are ways in which I can see the latter as more of an achievement. There's an integrity to the whole of *Talk* that perhaps makes it seem more of a real *album,* even more of a real *Yes* album, than the other efforts of the eighties Yes.

Another appealing aspect of *Talk* is that, whereas other Yes albums, or at least works, play around with science fiction themes (from "Astral Traveller" to "Arriving UFO" to "Machine Messiah" to "Big Generator"), there is something about *Talk* that seems as if it *just is* science fiction. This comes through, thematically, in "Real Love," especially in the line, "Far away, in the depths of Hawking's mind" (referring to the physicist, Stephen Hawking, of course, known especially for his work on black holes), but there is something about the whole album that says, "This is Yes for the cybernetic age."

Talk is tremendously varied, but the whole holds together nicely. The first song, "The Calling," begins with that tremendous choir, bigger than ever, of Anderson, Rabin, and Squire, develops with a very sharp attack on the snare drum, an angular and also densely stated bass line, and super-clean, country-inflected guitar. The fifth song on the album, "Walls," takes this country inflection even further, and it also uses the choir to great effect in the chorus. This is definitely one of Rabin's "country classics," perhaps his best. (I wonder what people would make of a compilation of "Yes country"? Of course, whereas the earlier incarnations of Yes used country styles in various pieces that had a larger, synthetic, eclectic character—for example, "Yours Is No Disgrace"—Rabin tends to write straight-out country songs.) "I Am Waiting" is also something out of radioland, but this time Black radio. Its guitar hook and relaxed vocals are a bit too ponderous to my mind, at least as the song simply gets too long. "Real Love" has a swampy, smarmy feel to it—in "the depths of Hawking's mind" we find ourselves led "to the animal, the primalistic grind." "State of Play" is an extraordinarily bright rocker that seems completely plugged into cyberspace. "Where Will You Be," is also electronically ethereal, and yet also engaged with Indian music. Finally, "Endless Dream" is an extended work of progressive rock. Having surveyed these pieces, I'm not sure what holds the album together, but the sense of a musical journey unfolding is pretty strong. One thing that is carefully placed is little bits of thematic material taken from one song and popping up in another.

Let us take just a moment to discuss the strongest and most interesting moments on the album. Finally, for a "Trevor Yes" album, it is clear which keyboard parts are played by Tony Kaye and which are by Rabin. On *Talk,* Kaye only plays the Hammond B-3, and that on only three tracks. The rest of the keyboards are by Rabin. To be honest, when I first got the album and saw that Kaye was listed as playing the Hammond organ, my hope was that there would be a fair amount of his playing on the album *and that* this would be the only keyboard playing on the album. Although Rabin does some interesting things with both piano (especially in "Endless Dream") and electronic keyboards, I still think an album that featured the mighty Hammond as the sole keyboard might have been more interesting. In any case, Kaye's solo on "The Calling" is quite good. "The Calling" also features a juxtaposition of images that is stirring: on the one hand, a kind of global calling to all the corners of the Earth, the

> . . . calling of a miracle
> In the presence of the word.

On the other hand, there is the image of a solitary individual driving through the rain:

> Head into the headlight.
> Don't turn from the rain.
> There's a fire raging
> Somewhere near,
> Like a longtime friend who's
> Seen it darker than ebony.

There's something mysterious and mystical about this juxtaposition, the sense of connection in the midst of unconnectedness.

"The Calling" also features the lines that I have taken the title of this part from, which are about as straightforward an expression of Yes hermeticism as one will find:

> In the beginning is the future,
> And the future is at hand . . .

"I Am Waiting" is the only Yes piece that might be placed in the "soul music" genre. The guitar hook that opens the song is attractive, in that it seems to move while not moving. This is achieved through subtle note-bending on Rabin's part. The other interesting feature of the song is the rather sharp change of direction from the soulful groove to the harsh, almost heavy metal sound of the verse that begins, "It happened in the water." There are parts of this song that are exceedingly schmaltzy, and, although there's something very dreamy about lines such as, "Highways, starways, many ways to be open tonight," I tend to think I'm only drawn into the song because Jon Anderson is singing it. Perhaps if a Luther Vandross version comes out this thesis can be put to the test!

The subterranean, bubbling-under-the-surface, feel of "Real Love" is very effective. As an updating of Yes's longstanding cybernetic primitivism, in the form of a shorter song in any case, this works pretty well.

"State of Play" begins with some intense guitar that sounds as if Rabin is using a slide (though he may have achieved the effect some other way). Although the singing here almost sounds like a TV commercial, there is something very appropriate about it in this context. I don't know if this is *Wired* magazine cyber-optimism or a way of ironically playing off of that, but the added brightness of the vocals is alluring. Significantly, the group sings together in the verses, while the chorus is sung by Anderson alone—just the opposite of the way this is usually done. Anderson offers some very strong singing in the chorus ("Secret needing, from this love I'm feeding"), establishing a pattern of straight-at-you declaiming that is developed to full strength at the end of the song ("Are you looking at it?").

The vocals for "Walls" are at the other end of the spectrum from "State of Play," with a country, beaten-down cast to them. Anderson and Rabin work well here, singing together in a low-key approach. The choir comes on powerfully in the chorus. Again, the guitar work is cleaner than clean.

"Where Will You Be" takes us more into main sequence Yes territory, concerning as it does mortality and the fate of our souls. The song is well-crafted, if not strikingly original. I like the simplicity of it. There is an interesting point where the Indian music gives way to a tango cadence ("No need to fear this love of life"). Neat.

It might be argued that "Endless Dream" is Trevor Rabin's "Close to the Edge," or as close to that edge as Rabin is likely to come. Certainly this is his one piece of full-blown progressive rock with Yes. At its best, "Endless Dream" is a fine piece of work; in places, however, it falls into cliches and bombast. There are some fine moments here, though. Among these, it is simply inspiring in the opening instrumental to hear White and Squire going through the paces of a complex counterpoint once again, with Rabin leading the charge. Rabin is very intelligent in his use of dissonance, but I worry that too much is smoothed out, by and by. And, the snarling guitar is at times too obvious and contrived—as though the snarl simply can't be real. In the opening verses, the vocal and electronic keyboard lines are very reminiscent of Pink Floyd, but perhaps too much so—the line sounds lifted from somewhere. Rabin's voice is electronically modified here, and though I'm not entirely wild about the effect itself, it makes for a nice transition to the third verse ("It's the last time, telling myself everything"), where the keyboard is now a more solid piano (the "acoustic" kind) and Anderson's voice is clear and from the heart. I am assuming that the verses sung by Anderson were also written by him, and the same with Rabin. If so, there is a great contrast, and while the contrast between the soul-searching Anderson verses and the cynical verses by Rabin is clearly intended, the latter are just too silly at times—for example, "How intense I pray depends on how much you pay." Likewise, I can see why Rabin would want to use a "talking guitar" in the middle instrumental break, but this does bring back a few bad memories of "Rocky Mountain Way" (Joe Walsh) and *Frampton Comes Alive*. Still, there is a case to be made for the idea that Rabin is self-consciously playing on these rock cliches. The most beautiful part of the whole piece, to my mind, is when Anderson, Rabin, and Squire intone,

Talk! Talk! Listening . . .
Like the first words ever to reach out.
Talk! Talk!
Like the first sounds, in a silent spring.
Talk! Talk! Listening . . .
Like the first words ever to reach out to you.
Talk! Talk!
Like the first sounds, you start to sing.

The exclamation marks come from the lyrics as published; while there is an insistence to the pronunciation, this verse is overwhelmingly gentle and inviting. The invitation is extended at length in the final, long, verse. In its dialectic of cynicism ("For they talk too loud, and take the hope and peace from your heart") and transcendence, "Endless Dream" works out the possibility that we might belong in this world after all, despite everything. And therefore, despite some of its shortcomings, I look at "Endless Dream" in terms of what it is trying to do, and I can't help but say yes to it.

In the beginning is the future

What will Yes be in the coming years? Or will the coming years be such that a force such as Yes can even exist in this world? Will Yes make a further transition from group to project?

It is simply not possible, of course, to answer these questions in any definitive way. On the one hand, it will be very difficult for Yes to be a true group as long as its members live in different parts of the world. On the other hand, the members of Yes have developed a maturity—exemplified well in the interviews from the *Yesyears* video—that may enable various combinations to come together from time to time to create a "Yes project." While it is unlikely that such an approach will ever give rise to works that are as musically and culturally important as those of the main sequence, one should always be open to possibilities. The very idea of Yes is at odds with the world as it is; at some point, the practicalities of making a constructive project of this necessarily oppositional vision may get worked out. One thing that those who have been listening to the music of Yes—I mean truly listening, with a radical openness—can do to help further a vision that is against the grain is to try to understand it, to articulate and develop the vision in diverse arenas, to make it a force in the world.

A concluding note on form and utopia

There are two basic aspects to the question of musical possibility today. The larger aspect has to do with where the world stands with respect to its possibilities. The other aspect, situated within this larger one, has to do with what appears to be a certain exhaustion of musical form.

Let us take up this second question first. In recent years, we have seen the apparent eclipse of avant-gardes. In Western classical music, post–John Cage experimentation has run its course, whether this is in the form of minimalism, complex apparatuses for the generation of chance procedures, or the micromanagement of tonality, rhythm, and so forth. The present generation of avant-garde composers who come from this tradition (for example, Philip Glass) are distinguished from groups such as the Talking Heads only in the fact that the former went to Julliard or some other conservatory, while the latter are musically adventurous, but also funkier. Jazz seems to have reached a similar limit with the work of Cecil Taylor and Anthony Braxton, whereby its material has been played out, at least as far as anything recognizable as jazz is concerned. And rock music, as every reader knows, has been in a heavy "retro" phase for some time now. This doesn't mean that, in the case of all three of these genres, there isn't more to do with the materials that are already there. In rock music, Lenny Kravitz has shown that there are more good songs to be written in the style of Curtis Mayfield, Jimi Hendrix, and others. Certainly, in jazz and classical music as well, there is room for further exploration in the fields opened up by the various traditions, from Louis Armstrong to John Coltrane and Cecil Taylor, and from Bach to Schoenberg, Ives, Cage, and so on. But this becomes more a matter of pure craft than vision.

Rock music has now become so colonized that there is a stifling *generational* sense of taste that has practically become an *enforced* reality. Originality doesn't matter, except for the generation—if a piece of music is somewhat original as far as what most people in "my" generation have heard on the radio, then it doesn't matter if someone from the previous generation had already done much the same thing, probably in a much better way. There is probably something healthy about each generation's wanting their "own music," but it doesn't seem as though this rebellious impulse is what the present generational divide is mainly about. Instead, the problem seems to be more that music just doesn't seem to matter as much anymore. If music becomes mere entertainment (and this is just as true for the nostalgia-oriented or status-seeking listeners who are inclined more toward classical music or jazz), then what difference does it make if something has already been done, and done better, by an earlier generation of musicians?

This is not a comment about the quality of these generations themselves, of course, but instead an inquiry about what might have happened in the world such that music doesn't seem to have the social and intellectual weight that it might once have had. Yes was interested in creating significant, visionary works of rock music—but why should these works matter, or how can they matter, in a world where music itself doesn't seem so capable of being important? What has happened to music, and what has happened to the world, such that this state of affairs has come about?

Is there an answer to this question purely in terms of music itself? Early in the twentieth century, some composers of Western classical music already seemed to sense the eclipse of the avant-garde that was still to come. The "grid" of tonality, harmony, rhythm, and timbre was increasingly filled out, and it became increasingly clear what it would mean for the rest of the grid to be filled out. In various ways, the major composers of the early twentieth century searched for ways to keep music going—whether this was in terms of expanding the methodology for developing harmony, as in the case of Schoenberg and his followers, or in terms of bringing in resources from outside of classical music proper, as in the cases, variously, of Stravinsky, Shostakovich, Bartok, Sibelius, Ives, and Gershwin. Perhaps a combination of these two approaches is seen in the case of Cage, who extended Schoenberg's system into regions beyond harmony, pushed this system to the point of chance composition, and broke down the distinctions among the concepts of "sound," "silence," "music," and "noise" to the point that, in principle, *anything* could be a piece of music. As profound as Cage's insights have been, philosophically speaking, the point is now upon us where there is little sense of where to go from here.

All of the genres have been emptying out, then, into each other. This has created the generous and expansive meta-genre of "world music"—which, if understood in the broadest terms, would encompass all of those synthetic and eclectic undertakings where there is a meeting of diverse musical materials and cultures. One of my arguments has been that Yes was a forerunner to this genre, a genre that only acquired its present name in more recent years. Much "world music" is rock-based, and this shows something good about rock music, its all-embracing character, its reluctance to pass snobbish and limiting judgments of the "that isn't real music" sort. But the end also seems in sight for the grid of world music—and this "end" doesn't require that every possible combination has already been tried, but rather that these combinations exist more and more simply as predictable slots in the grid. This is what Fredric Jameson calls the "postmodern pastiche."

In the world of the postmodern pastiche, rock music, which has hitherto played the admirable role of being an absolutely wide-open category, simply becomes the repository for the most predictable forms of the "new." This is the "new" and "original" in purely consumerist terms—and, what can that amount to other than, "new for me," or the most "original" fad at present?

The world of the postmodern pastiche is a world of jadedness and exhaustion, not just of musical or other aesthetic forms, but of social forms. To understand musical exhaustion, therefore, we have to move to a larger level of analysis—or, at least, this is my hypothesis—and consider a larger social exhaustion. This world seems to be going in two directions at once: a world where the calculability of every human feeling and interaction creates a general loss of affect, and a world where the material effects of impoverishment and brutality begin to make the world too mean and stupid for redemption. Of what use is significant music, or significant anything, in a world of pure calculation and commodification? Truth, beauty, and other values will have to take a backseat to what sells, and eventually there will be no seat for these values at all. The carrot and the stick have both been adapted to the advanced stage of the power play machine, and any music that seeks to be important will have to contend with this machine. All we can do is *try* to do something significant in a world where significance is itself progressively snuffed out—but an understanding of the conditions in which this trying must take place is essential. I have explored these issues at length in my other books (and I will continue to explore these questions in future works); in brief, however, allow me to set out two possibilities.

The worst case scenario would seem to be that significant music or other art must *await* a radically transformative social revolution, which will break the impasse of postmodern capitalism and attempt once again to find and give meaning to human existence. This is not a possibility, but instead a kind of perverse counterpossibility; unfortunately, this fact does not mean that the counterpossibility cannot come to pass. Quite obviously, any art that seeks to be significant today contends at every moment with this overwhelming counterpossibility.

Even if counterpossibility has already achieved an overwhelming degree of "success" (the pyrrhic, but no less real, victory of the "sick feeling," of the "la la la la"), "trying harder is the only way to go." There is a dialectical relationship between the possibility of bringing a new society into being and creating a radical oppositional culture within the present society—without the latter, I don't believe the former is possible. If we fall into the trap of believing that "only a god can save us now," which is really a way of saying that there is no redemption, that the world is beyond redemption, then we are surely doomed. Perhaps the world *is* beyond redemption, but there is no way forward except for people of good will to fight against this counterpossibility with every iota of our beings.

We have to strive to create and appreciate truly innovative and significant works in the present, and to unfold their possibilities on myriad levels. But our present impasse also issues from a forced disconnection with the more recent periods of vision and innovation; there is a machinery in place that seeks to bury "all that," and the ideological effects of this machinery are immense and subtle. "All that" includes the artistic expressions of sixties radicalism and utopianism; the hip and chic thing to do is to join with the cultural machinery of late capitalism and help ensure that the disconnection sticks. One major aspect of this book, then, has been to go against this hip jadedness and chic cynicism, and to lay the ground for reconnection with that marginal and revolutionary green and communitarian language that, for a brief historical moment, was not so marginal.

Notes

Introduction: the ideologies of form

1. Regarding what has been said here on Robert Fripp and King Crimson, much the same could be said about Ian Anderson's role in Jethro Tull. Fripp does remark, on occasion, that when there is music that can only be played by King Crimson, King Crimson comes into existence in order to play this music. Without getting into the arcane aspects of Fripp's philosophy (about which he is, in any case, quite circumspect), however, it seems clear that, with Yes, there is much more of a sense of "guiding spirit" than with King Crimson.

2. I have not devoted attention, in the main body of the text, to the recent *Symphonic Music of Yes* project. In general, I have found all of the "symphonic music"—of Jethro Tull, Genesis, and so on—projects amusing at best. In the case of the symphonic Yes project, the album does show the great potential of Yes's music in this setting. The best example of this is the transcription for low brass of a Chris Squire bass line from "Close to the Edge." However, the general approach to these projects is to go from progressive rock to "light classical" music; someday I hope we get the chance to hear "Close to the Edge" and other major pieces of Yes music in a "heavy" classical version. My other main problem with these projects is that the approach is to have a rock band at the core of the music, augmented by orchestra. But we already know what this music sounds like played with rock music instruments. I want to hear Yes (or Jethro Tull or Genesis) music creatively arranged for orchestral instruments.

3. Works of purely "conceptual art," such as Yoko Ono's, do raise interesting questions here.

4. Incidentally, many of the European or Europe-based jazz musicians associated with the German label ECM, for example Ralph Towner or Jan Garbarek, build their improvisations as much around transformations of timbre as around the rhythmic and harmonic transformations more typical in jazz.

5. Notice how quaint I am to still refer to "records," despite the fact that the music industry—damn them—has decreed that we shall henceforth listen to compact discs; that is, until they decide on something else, say "compact chips," which you'll simply shove up one or more available orifices.

6. I will leave aside for now the fact that Adorno disliked rock music (and, indeed, any music other than Western classical music). This is a question that would have to be properly taken up after a discussion of the formal structures of Yes's music, the reason for this being that it is not clear that the label "rock music" (and also the label "popular music"), as Adorno understands it, is very helpful here.

7. Another thinker who said some important things on this subject is Ernst Bloch; see especially *The Utopian Function of Art and Literature*.

8. On the question of memory and the "flattening" of meaning, see my *Politics in the impasse*, pp. 13–25.

9. In some respects this book resembles the music of Yes—at times it tends to be sprawling and obscure. Critics who dislike Yes because they aren't cynical will, I hope, dislike this book for the same reason.

Part 1: Before and beyond

1. At the opposite extreme, consider Yes's impromptu performance of the Beatle's "I'm Down," recently released in the *Yesyears* retrospective album. This performance was mainly meant in the spirit of pure fun, but it does demonstrate quite well that Jon Anderson is simply not a "rock'n'roll" singer.

2. For some terrific examples of musical quotations, the reader is referred once again to the magnificent Santana *Lotus* album, where Carlos Santana achieves some of the finest guitar work of any genre and where he skillfully weaves in many borrowings from a range of artists that extends from John Coltrane to the Jackson Five ("Never Can Say Goodbye," a wonderful song).

3. This showiness pops up again about ten years later, in a tune called "Money," which was only released on the *Yesyears* album. Again, it is a demonstration of a genre that Yes would do well to stay away from.

4. Incidentally, given that there are inevitable comparisons between Yes and composers of Western classical music, it will not hurt to mention that there are many examples of lyrics to *Lieder*, "art songs" in the classical tradition (especially German, including Viennese) from Schubert and Beethoven to Mahler, Schoenberg, and so on that also would not stand on their own as poems. (Actually, some of the best examples of *Lieder* were composed by composers, such as Hugo Wolf, who devoted themselves almost entirely to that form.)

5. Perhaps the best known such poem is Wilfrid Owen's "Dulce Et Decorum Est" (1920).

6. Important texts on this question include Edward Said's *Orientalism* and Jacques Derrida's *of Grammatology*. See also my *Matrix and line,* chapter 5.

7. A number of sections of *Tarkus* come to mind, for example, "The preacher said a prayer, save every single hair on his head—he's dead"; "Jerusalem," of course, from *Brain Salad Surgery,* as well as the organ solo from "Karn Evil 9, 3rd Impression."

Part 2: Perpetual change

1. Some useful sources on contemporary Western classical music and contemporary jazz are: H. H. Stuckenschmidt, *Twentieth Century Music,* and Francis Davis, *In the Moment: Jazz in the 1980s.*

2. Although if I were setting out the genealogy of rock music I would begin with rock's Black roots, I accept as valid the direction taken by the makers of the recent "History of Rock and Roll" five-part television series; they began with the folk scene and the moment when Bob Dylan plugged in.

3. If we approach differences in genres in terms of "originality," we often find that there is nothing new under the sun. For instance, what counted as extreme rhythmic innovation in *The Rite of Spring* would be somewhat ordinary in the average Indian raga. The issues involved in musical comparisons are set out in *The Study of Ethnomusicology* by

Bruno Nettl, especially chapters 3, 4, and 5: "The Universal Language," "The Non-Universal Language," and "Apples and Oranges."

4. Perhaps Jacques Derrida's arguments concerning speech and writing would also be relevant here: no speech without (or "before") writing, no spontaneous improvisation "before" composition. See Derrida, *of Grammatology,* pp. 6–73, and Christopher Norris, *Derrida,* pp. 63–141.

5. Please understand, I know that there is a sense in which this is always nothing more than a pretense, and that, if there is anything more silly-looking, indeed ridiculous, than teenagers playing grown-up, it is "adults" playing grown-up.

6. Important discussions of the idea of class entitlement are found in Pierre Bourdieu, *Distinction,* and Benjamin DeMott, *The Imperial Middle.*

7. A useful discussion of this issue is presented by Jonathan Arac, in his editor's Introduction to *Postmodernism and Politics,* pp. xx–xxviii.

8. In addition to Bourdieu, other important sources here include: Lillian Rubin, *Worlds of Pain,* Richard Sennett and Jonathan Cobb, *The Hidden Injuries of Class,* and Michelle Tokarczyk and Elizabeth A. Fay, eds., *Working-Class Women in the Academy.* The central source of inspiration on these questions for me has been the work of my wife, Kathleen League. Among her most insightful works here is the essay, "The New Invisibility of Class (in Discourses of Marginality and Alterity)", as well as the work that she is doing in her dissertation, "Dialectic of Redemption," which attempts to reintegrate the issue of class into Adorno's philosophy.

9. Indeed, I grew up in Miami, Florida, perhaps as culturally distant from the English scene as one could be while still living in the West—and even that is not entirely the case, given that Miami is as much a part of the Caribbean as it is part of North America, and there is also a large immigrant Jewish population there. I'm also reminded of the quip about "two peoples divided by a single language."

10. All of this has been gone into in much greater depth and with far greater insight elsewhere. See especially the recent book on the Beach Boys, *The Nearest Far Away Place,* by Timothy White. Iain Chambers writes to great effect about "why the English are the way they are" in "An island life," from his *Border Dialogues.*

11. See Raymond Williams, *The Country and the City,* esp. pp. 127–41; other important authors and works here would include E. P. Thompson, *Witness Against the Beast: William Blake and the Moral Law,* Jonathan Bate, *Romantic Ecology: Wordsworth and the Environmental Tradition,* and John Mee, *Dangerous Enthusiasm: William Blake and the Culture of Radicalism in the 1790s.*

12. As with many other things English, I must thank Stephen Houlgate for explaining that "Biggles" is a children's storybook character, a World War II fighter pilot who would fly in at the last minute to save the day.

13. The Mormons are perhaps the best example; see D. Michael Quinn, *Early Mormonism and the Magical World View,* and John Brooke, *The Refiner's Fire.*

14. The proof and underside of this argument is the fact that Howe has had difficulties in making a solo album that is musically up to his level of musicianship. With his more recent solo efforts, *Turbulence* and *The Grand Scheme of Things,* he demonstrates a good deal of progress.

15. A useful compendium on these questions is Jay Garfield and Murray Kitely, eds., *Meaning and Truth: The Essential Readings in Modern Semantics.* Also see Donald Davidson, "A Nice Derangement of Epitaphs."

16. See Immanuel Kant, "Idea for a Universal History with a Cosmopolitan Intent"; Derrida, "The Law of Genre," "The Ends of Man," "White Mythology," and *The Other Heading;* Robert Young, *White Mythologies: Writing History and the West;* and my *Humanism and its aftermath,* pp. 127–59.

17. I call this the "shit happens" theory of capitalism: in this pervasively dissemi-nated cynical view, no one is responsible for what happens in the world, whether that be an earthquake or an economic depression or a war. If someone takes responsibility, as in a socialist society (or even in a society that is merely labeled "socialist," or, at any rate, one that is non-Western, for example, the Islamic Republic in Iran), then we can certainly blame them—just don't ever blame "us." For instance, somehow Saddam Hussein is responsible for his actions in Kuwait, but, seemingly, George Bush is on no account responsible, and neither are the rest of the American people responsible, for what the U.S. did in Iraq.

18. It is not clear exactly what the ramifications are, but, given (1) that what goes for logic goes for mathematics, and (2) the close relationship between math and music, it seems there would be ramifications. On the other hand, there is no requirement that music be "logical": it is not clear what it would mean to apply principles of identity and noncon-tradiction to music, and it is unclear how "coherence" and "completeness" apply to music. Clearly there are factors here that are more psychological than logical; there may be questions of complexity and elegance here, but I don't know if there are "principles" to be found. The place to start, other than Plato and Aristotle, is probably Douglas Hofs-tadter, *Gödel, Escher, Bach.*

19. Indeed, Ross Perot, when he first came on the national scene in the period lead-ing up to the 1992 U. S. presidential election, seemed to me to be something Heinlein had invented. About a year before the election, one of Perot's earlier blueprints for remaking the United States was reprinted. On the book jacket was a blurb from Robert Heinlein.

20. This might be fleshed out in terms of Derrida's analysis of Foucault's analysis of Descartes and the question of madness; see my *Humanism and its aftermath,* pp. 51–57.

21. Many of these issues have been fleshed out in what is called the "Gadamer-Habermas debate"; see Thomas McCarthy, *The Critical Theory of Jürgen Habermas,* pp. 187–93; Jerald Wallulis, *The Hermeneutics of Life History,* pp. 31–69; and David Gross, *The Past in Ruins.*

22. Although Kivy does not mention this example, we might think of the fact that it is very difficult for a comedy to win an Academy Award for best film; instead, these awards generally go to more "serious" films. (I put the term in scare quotes because noth-ing that comes out of the Hollywood film industry seems especially serious to me—but lets leave that particular gripe for another day!)

23. This raises interesting questions where rock music is concerned—perhaps its internal conception of craftsmanship is at odds with instrumental virtuosity or taking on profound themes. Perhaps—it's a question worth discussing, at any rate.

24. Kivy has devoted another book to the question of representation: *Sound and Semblance: Reflections on Musical Representation.*

25. What Kivy says about music and meaning might be helpful here; see *Music Alone,* pp. 93–123. The point would be that music alone has no "meaning," at least not in the sense in which that term is ordinarily used. Kivy argues that music is a "quasi-syntac-tical structure without semantics," which is to say that, although music has form (some-thing *like* a "grammar"), and form is one component of a language—which is where we

typically find meanings—there is nothing in form alone that corresponds to words or sentences. And thus there is no way to say, in any kind of straightforward way, what the "meaning" of a musical work is. Therefore, we would do well to drop the talk of "meaning." My experience is that students, especially, are resistant to this point—not for bad reasons, necessarily. But it seems to me that Kivy is right: music is in no strict sense "a language." With languages, in the ordinary sense, we can (even if willy-nilly) translate from one into another. We can write translation manuals. But it would be very hard to get very far in writing, for instance, a "language of music to English language" manual, and any such attempt would definitely do violence to what music is (as opposed to what it is not). Therefore, when I use an expression such as "the language of rock music," this can only be taken in a loose and figurative sense. The main point, to repeat, is that representation in music is a very difficult question.

26. Although most readers probably know this already, I should perhaps explain that "Mellotron" is the name of a particular brand of keyboard instrument made by a company of the same name—hence the upper-case letter. Most early fans of progressive rock first became aware of the Mellotron with *In the Court of the Crimson King,* the first album by you-know-who. The Mellotron is a somewhat unwieldy instrument, best known for producing the sound of a string orchestra. The instrument consists in a series of lengths of recording tape, one for each note on the keyboard. On the tape is a recording of an actual string orchestra playing the note corresponding to the keyboard note. When the key is pressed, the corresponding tape segment is drawn across a playback head, playing the tape. The tape was a finite segment, not a loop, so notes could only be held for a certain amount of time, about eight seconds. Tape sets were available for different instruments as well, most commonly brass sections and choirs. (For instance, in his live "Excerpts from *The Six Wives of Henry VIII,*" on *Yessongs,* Rick Wakeman plays a bit from the Hallelujah Chorus by Handel, and here he is using the Mellotron with choir tapes.) The Mellotron was notoriously temperamental, especially in live or outdoor settings, because the tapes would expand or contract in different climatic conditions, and also stretch from general wear. The Mellotron has been almost entirely supplanted by digital polyphonic synthesizers that are capable of playing "sampled" sounds of strings, brass, choral singers, and so on or of precisely emulating the waveforms of same. Still, the Mellotron played a very important role in the development of progressive rock in the seventies. Besides King Crimson and Yes (who used the instrument in quite different ways, the latter perhaps more conventionally), two other groups that used the Mellotron to very interesting effect were Genesis (for example, "Watcher of the Skies") and, a group that would probably not be familiar to any except the most dedicated progressive rock afficionados, Jonesy (especially their first album, *Keeping Up . . .;* this group was also noteworthy for featuring a solo trumpet player). Perhaps it is significant that Emerson, Lake, and Palmer never really made use of the Mellotron, although I do not know the reason for this. In the main body of the text I will have some other things to say about the relationship between the "music itself" and some of the instruments and technology used to produce it.

27. "Clavinet" is also a brand name; this is a funky-sounding keyboard, perhaps best known from Stevie Wonder's song, "Superstition."

28. In the case of McCartney, however, there was also the tendency to not notice his musical contribution on the bass guitar. This was for all the reasons already stated—that there was nothing else to compare what McCartney was doing with, and the fact that his instrument is the bass guitar—but also because the Beatles were such a huge phenomenon

that it is often easy to forget that they were, after all, *a band,* a group of people playing musical instruments. One result of this is that all of the Beatles have been seriously underrated as musicians. All of these points were brought home to me once again when I saw the "Beatles Anthology" program on television.

29. "Chris Squire Talks About *Talk,*" *Bass Player,* v. 5, n. 7 (Nov. 1994), p. 32.

30. It has recently come to light that the bass line in "Roundabout" owes some of its trebliness to the fact that the Rickenbacker bass is being shadowed by a Gibson "FDH" acoustic f-hole guitar (as discussed in the interview cited in n. 29, as well as in *The Steve Howe Guitar Collection,* p. 29).

31. There are definite limitations to the narrative analysis of music, in which one takes the vocal and instrumental parts of a piece of music to form a whole that tells a story. Even if the piece is intended to be heard this way, the composer's intention does not and cannot fully govern analysis and interpretation. (The difficulty here is intimately connected to the issue of music and meaning, as discussed in n. 25.) Having recognized these limitations, however, it is safe to say that the group works on *Fragile* are strongly narrative in character, and "Heart of the Sunrise" is the most developed of these narratives. Still, I forewarn the reader that, especially whenever an instrumental passage is interpreted as if it were a line or page in a story, the analysis is at best conjectural, and possibly misguided altogether. Again, this is not simply a matter of checking the interpretation against the composer's intentions (what the composer intended to portray, as opposed to what the listener thought she or he heard in the passage), but even more of the very loose fit, at best, between instrumental sounds and silences and narrative verbal discourse.

Another way of putting this is that I am proceeding as if a representational view of music is not very problematic, whereas, in fact, I find such a view highly problematic. For more of the philosophical side of this question, see Peter Kivy, *Music Alone,* pp. 93–123.

32. In case the reader is wondering where the Communist Party of Peru got this nickname, "Sendero Luminoso," it was from a statement by the Peruvian Marxist theorist, Jose Carlos Mariategui. Earlier in the century (before there was a Maoist party in Peru), Mariategui said, "The road to communism is a shining path." Mariategui argued, against more orthodox Marxist notions prevalent at the time, that the question of the indigenous populations of Latin America was pivotal in the movement to overthrow capitalism and imperialism. The Communist Party of Peru has taken up this understanding. I assume that, with his interest in Native American peoples, Mariategui borrowed the metaphor of the "shining path." Another interesting exploration of this theme is found in the *Tales of Alvin Maker* novels by Orson Scott Card.

33. Interestingly, by the time of "Roundabout," King Crimson had largely abandoned this field, perhaps only returning to it with "One More Red Nightmare" from *Red.* "The Great Deceiver," from *Starless and Bible Black,* might also seem to fit the category, though it is a shorter song.

34. On sisterhood, singing, and subjectivity, see my *Matrix and line,* pp. 148–60.

35. See Immanuel Kant, *Fundamental Principles for the Metaphysics of Morals* (often referred to as the *Groundwork*), as well as Robert Paul Wolff's interpretation of Kant's ethical philosophy, *The Autonomy of Reason.*

36. I will simply add, somewhat parenthetically, that, as a social theorist who draws a great deal from various Marxisms, I think there is the possibility of an interpretation of Marxism that is not at odds with this philosophy of process and life. In the case of

Hartshorne and Whitehead, this may seem more than disputable, at least as argued by Randall C. Morris in *Process Philosophy and Political Ideology: The Social and Political Thought of Alfred North Whitehead and Charles Hartshorne;* see esp. pp. 209–19. However, in work on Marx and Hartshorne and Marx and Whitehead, respectively, I think that James Marsh and Ann Pomeroy are demonstrating the viability of a "process Marxism."

37. Two valuable sources on this question are Helmut Peukert, *Science, Action, and Fundamental Theology,* esp. pp. 202–10, and Orson Scott Card's recent novel, *Pastwatch: The Redemption of Christopher Columbus.*

38. This comes from the *Yes Complete* book; I'm not sure if the D# is created by detuning the bass a half step or it is played an octave higher.

39. There is no better exploration of these issues than the novels of Orson Scott Card, which have a specifically Mormon subtext and which cut through a lot of stereotypes about the theology of the Latter-day Saints. At present, I am completing a book on Mormon communitarianism, including its theological-philosophical dimensions, under the title, "Mormon possibilities: Elements of community." I am not LDS (Mormon) myself; however, I find this community a rich source of lessons on the very possibility of community in this hyper-secular, capitalist world.

40. I should mention that my interpretation here is quite at odds with Thomas Mosbø's, even if not at absolutely every point. This disagreement is indicative of our different approaches to Yes more generally; see Mosbø, pp. 139–47. Of course, I encourage readers to compare interpretations and think the issue out for themselves.

41. This question of war and triumphalism is addressed at length in my essay, "A letter on fascism," from *Politics in the impasse,* pp. 197–230.

42. Up to a point I agree with Mosbø on this, but not to the point where he ultimately takes the argument. Yes, all distinctions relating to a just cause *can* disappear in this dialectic; but I don't agree with Mosbø that this is the only thing that can happen in war—and I don't think this is what happens in the war in "Gates of Delirium."

Hovering in the background of any discussion of this sort would have to be the dialectic of Stalin and Hitler, and the dialectic of the Soviet Union and Nazi Germany in the Second World War. This is a dialectic of life and death issues, a dialectic of fundamental directions taken up by parts of humankind. Despite typical caricatures, which have both of these sides collapsing into one another (more or less from the start, though part of the issue is, once again, where to begin), I believe that the issues are vastly more complex. A very important source on these issues, to my mind, is Bob Avakian, *Conquer the World?*

43. Another "hovering issue" is that of "dirty hands." This is taken up in two important plays from the Stalin period, Jean-Paul Sartre's *Dirty Hands,* and Bertolt Brecht's *The Caucasian Chalk Circle.*

44. D. A. Rees, "Platonism and the Platonic Tradition"; from the *Encyclopedia of Philosophy,* edited by Paul Edwards, v. 6; New York: Macmillan and The Free Press, 1967; p. 337.

45. See especially Paul de Man, *The Rhetoric of Romanticism,* as well as Christopher Norris, *Paul de Man.* Perhaps de Man was especially aware and sensitive to the political problems of organicism because of his own involvement with fascist organicism as a young man in occupied Belgium.

46. Useful sources here include: Michael G. Baylor, ed., *The Radical Reformation;* Andrew Weeks, *Boehme: An Intellectual Biography of the Seventeenth-Century Philoso-*

pher and Mystic; and Antoine Faivre, *Access to Western Esotericism.* Also see Bate, *Romantic Ecology.*

47. On the question of "the pursuit of the ideal," see the book with that title by Steven Schwarzschild.

48. Important sources on gnosticism include Hans Jonas, *The Gnostic Religion,* and Ioan Couliano, *Tree of Gnosis.*

49. See Harold Bloom, *The American Religion,* pp. 21–44.

50. For example, see Jacques Derrida, *of Spirit* and *The Gift of Death;* Reiner Schurmann, *Heidegger on Being and Acting: From Principles to Anarchy;* and Jean-Luc Nancy, *The Inoperative Community.*

51. In Adorno's view, to propose an "alternative" structure is to create something akin to a graven image; see his conversation with Ernst Bloch, "Something's Missing," in Bloch, *The Utopian Function of Art and Literature.*

52. The lines elided are, "and that can be apprehended only by a few highly individualized listeners." Does this "can" mean "ought to"? Does Adorno mean "can be apprehended only by a few" as a matter of principle or fact? It seems to me that, with the "time of progressive rock" (roughly the period from 1968 to 1978, as I have defined it), there was the possibility of a "popular" avant-garde—I still think of the fact that *millions* of people, in the early seventies, were interested in works such as *Close to the Edge* and *Lark's Tongues in Aspic.* In other words, this was not a time of cultural or political "business as usual." I worry that formulations such as Adorno's are not sufficiently atuned to the possibility that such a moment may erupt.

Part 3: In the beginning is the future

1. *Drama* was released in 1980, which is technically the last year of the seventies— just as the year 2000 will be the last year of *this* century and millennium; of course, this technicality may have little to do with the social and spiritual "feel" that the year will have.

2. Two albums that I will not be discussing are Alan White's *Ramshackled* and Patrick Moraz's *i.* White's record has some good qualities; it is very unpretentious, and it represents, for the most part, a good "blowing session" on the part of Alan and some of his more R&B-inclined friends. But the record doesn't shed much light on either Yes music as a whole or even White's role in creating this music. (Some might argue that, in fact, *Ramshackled* does shed light on White's role in yes, showing that role to be minimal. I disagree with this interpretation.)

Moraz's *i* is indeed a significant and perhaps brilliant piece of progressive rock music, and it certainly deserves discussion in that context. However, given the brevity of Moraz's time with the group (a time in which he did make, however, important musical contributions), and the fact that *i* comes from a period when he had already left the group, it seems inappropriate to treat this album in the context of Yes's music.

3. I am aware, as many readers are, of an operatic work that Jon Anderson has composed on the life of the painter, Marc Chagall, and I have even heard a tape of this work (or at least a version of it). However, as Anderson has not authorized the release of this work, I feel it is inappropriate to comment on it. I do hope, of course, that this work will someday be heard in the way that Anderson intends it to be heard.

4. This question is taken up in my *Matrix and line,* pp. 127–30.

5. In the interview that Chris Squire gave in *Bass Player* magazine (see part 2, n. 29), Squire says that he has been working on a new solo album. A few years ago, there was a brief appearance by "The Chris Squire Project" at a few clubs in southern California. I have heard a tape of one of these concerts, and the new songs are strong, as are the performances.

6. I should mention that I have a few of these, but I can hardly bear to listen to them because of the excessive audience noise and lack of balance in the recordings.

7. The quoted phrase is a reference to E. P. Thompson's book of the same title.

What exactly counts as "postmodern" music is something deserving of more discussion. This music would have to be distinguished from what ordinarily would be called "avant-garde" music, especially as it comes in the wake of the exhaustion of the avant-garde, and yet there is something intentionally avant about postmodern music. Contenders to the title would include the music of John Zorn, as well as the music of the Talking Heads.

8. I have taken up the discussion of the politics of speed in *Matrix and line,* pp. 185–91, *Humanism and its aftermath,* pp. 165–70, and *Politics in the impasse,* pp. 27–38. Much of my discussion is inspired by Ben Agger's excellent book, *Fast Capitalism.*

Discography

Recordings by Yes as a group

Yes. *Yes*. Atlantic 8243, 1969.
———. *Time and a Word*. Atlantic 8273, 1970.
———. *The Yes Album*. Atlantic 19131, 1971.
———. *Fragile*. Atlantic 19132, 1972.
———. *Close to the Edge*. Atlantic 19133, 1972.
———. *Yessongs*. Atlantic 100, 1973.
———. *Tales from Topographic Oceans*. Atlantic 2–908, 1974
———. *Relayer*. Atlantic 19135, 1974.
———. *Yesterdays*. Atlantic 19134, 1975.
———. *Going for the One*. Atlantic 19106, 1977.
———. *Tormato*. Atlantic 19202, 1978.
———. *Drama*. Atlantic 16019, 1980.
———. *90125*. Atco 90125, 1983.
———. *Big Generator*. Atco 90522, 1987.
———. *Union*. Arista 211 558, 1991.
———. *Talk*. Victory 383-480-033-2, 1994.

Recordings by members of Yes (solo or in other groups)

Jon Anderson. *Olias of Sunhillow*. Atlantic, 1976.
Anderson, Bruford, Wakeman, Howe. *Anderson, Bruford, Wakeman, Howe*. Arista, 1989.
Badger. *One Live Badger*. Atco, 1973.
Peter Banks. *Two Sides of Peter Banks*. Sovereign, 1973.
Bill Bruford. *Feels Good to Me*. Polydor, 1977.
Flash. *Flash*. Sovereign, 1972.
———. *In the Can*. Sovereign, 1972.
———. *Out of Our Hands*. Sovereign, 1973.
Steve Howe. *Beginnings*. Atlantic, 1975.
———. *Turbulence*. Relativity, 1991.
———. *The Grand Scheme of Things*. Relativity, 1993.
Chris Squire. *Fish Out of Water*. Atlantic, 1975.
Rick Wakeman. *The Six Wives of Henry VIII*. A&M, 1973.

Recordings by other artists

The Beach Boys. *Pet Sounds*. Capitol, 1966.
The Beatles. *Rubber Soul*. Capitol, 1965.

————. *Revolver.* Capitol, 1966.

————. *Sergeant Pepper's Lonely Hearts Club Band.* Capitol, 1967.

————. *Magical Mystery Tour.* Capitol, 1967.

————. *The Beatles* ["White Album"]. Capitol, 1968.

————. *Abbey Road.* Capitol, 1969.

Chicago Transit Authority. *Chicago Transit Authority.* Columbia, 1968.

Emerson, Lake, and Palmer. *Tarkus.* Cotillion/Island, 1971.

————. *Brain Salad Surgery.* Manticore, 1973.

————. *Works Volume 1.* Atlantic/Manticore, 1977.

Genesis. *The Lamb Lies Down on Broadway.* ATCO/Charisma, 1974.

The Grateful Dead. *Anthem of the Sun.* Warner Bros., 1968.

Eddie Harris. *E.H. in the U.K.,* Atlantic, 1974.

Henry Cow. *In Praise of Learning.* Virgin, 1975.

Jefferson Airplane. *Volunteers.* RCA, 1969.

————. *Crown of Creation.* RCA, 1968.

Jethro Tull. *Thick as a Brick.* Chrysalis, 1972.

————. *Passion Play.* Chrysalis, 1973.

King Crimson. *In the Court of the Crimson King.* Island, 1969.

————. *In the Wake of Poseidon.* Island, 1970.

————. *Lizard.* Island, 1970.

————. *Lark's Tongues in Aspic.* Island, 1973.

————. *Starless and Bible Black.* Island, 1974.

————. *Red.* Island, 1974.

Magma. *Mekanïk Destruktïw Kommandöh.* A&M, 1973.

The Mahavishnu Orchestra with John McLaughlin. *Inner Mounting Flame.* Columbia, 1971.

————. *Birds of Fire.* Columbia, 1973.

Pink Floyd. *A Saucerful of Secrets.* Columbia, 1968.

————. *Ummagumma.* Harvest, 1969.

The Rolling Stones. *Their Satanic Majesties Request.* London/Decca, 1967.

Santana. *Abraxas.* Columbia, 1970.

Lotus. CBS, 1975.

The Sex Pistols. *Never Mind the Bollocks . . . Here's the Sex Pistols.* Warner Bros./Virgin, 1977.

Bruce Springsteen. *Born In the U.S.A.* Columbia, 1984.

Traffic. *John Barleycorn Must Die.* Island, 1970.

————. *The Low Spark of High-Heeled Boys.* Island, 1971.

The Who. *Tommy.* Decca/Track, 1969.

————. *Quadrophenia.* MCA/Track, 1973.

Bibliography

Sources on Yes

"Change They Must." Editorial from *Yes Magazine,* Fall 1994, p. 34

"Rock Goes to College." (Features Yes prominently, including a photo of Steve Howe.) *Time* magazine, September 23, 1974.

"Tales from a Top Band. Where to Now? Beat Asks the Yes Men." *Beat,* 1974; pp. 36–37.

Cahn, Elliot. "Yes Affirms: There's Life after Wakeman." *Rolling Stone,* August 28, 1975; p. 13.

Clarke, Steve. "New music and old arguments." *New Musical Express,* November 15, 1975; p. 3.

Cohen, Scott. "Chris Squire: The Survivor. How the Yesman Lives and Breathes." *Circus* magazine, c. 1976; pp. 59–61.

Crowe, Cameron. "Yes Soars Back to Earth with "Tales From The [sic] Topographic Ocean." (Sub-heading: "'Tales' is the first signpost on a journey back to basics.") *Circus* magazine, March 1974; pp. 7–10.

Demorest, Steve. "Yes Battles The Skeptics With 'Relayer'." *Circus* magazine, 1975; pp. 67–70.

Farber, Jim. "Going, Going, Gone! Yes Tour Surprises Diehard Fans, Stage Show Finest Ever." *Circus* magazine, c. 1977, p. 35.

Freemantle, Larry, et al. *Yesyears* album booklet. Atlantic Recording Corporation, 1991.

Girard, Jim. "Yes: On the Same Wavelength Again." *Hit Parader,* pp. 36, 38, 65.

Hedges, Dan. *Yes: The Authorised Biography.* London: Sidgwick and Jackson, 1981.

————. "Yes suspends animation on current world tour." *Circus,* 1984; pp. 29–30.

Henderson, Bill. "Yes: In Search of the Absolute". *Street Life,* April 17–30, 1976; pp. 24–30.

Howe, Steve, with Tony Bacon. *The Steve Howe Guitar Collection.* Photographs by Miki Slingsby. San Francisco: GPI Books, 1993.

Jewell, Derek. "Yes and the coming of age" (July 16, 1972), and "Yes at the Summit" (October 30, 1977). In *The Popular Voice: A musical record of the 60s and 70s.* London: Andre Deutsch, 1980; pp. 55–57, 65–66.

Jisi, Chris. "Chris Squire Talks About *Talk." Bass Player* magazine, November 1994; pp. 28–30, 32.

Mackie, Rob. "Don't bother to knock." (On Steve Howe.) *Sounds,* February 22, 1975; pp. 1–2.

Martin, Bill. "Chris Squire: Creating a New Dimension." *Bass Player* magazine, November 1994; pp. 24–26, 34–35.

Mosbø, Thomas. *Yes: But What Does It Mean? Exploring the Music of Yes.* Milton, Wisconsin: Wyndstar (824 Neumann Court, Milton, WI 53563), 1994.

Orme, John. "Yes, we have lift-off. Jon Anderson brings John Orme up to date on Yes after their long silence." *Melody Maker,* July 16, 1977; p. 9.

Prown, Pete. "New Beginnings. Steve Howe Talks Straight about His Gear, His Music and his Revitalized Career Without YES." *Guitar Shop,* Summer 1994; pp. 46–49, 84.

Rule, Greg. "Trevor Rabin Speaks Out on the Making of *Talk.*" *Keyboard* magazine, June 1994; pp. 67–74.

Salewicz, Chris. "The Hippy With the Iron Hand." (Interview with Jon Anderson.) *New Musical Express,* March 22, 1975.

Welch, Chris.

———. "Oui! Paris falls to the Yes invasion! Chris Welch was there." *Melody Maker,* 1974; pp. 47–48.

———. "Wakeman: British groups have gone over the top." *Melody Maker,* April 13, 1974; p. 34.

———. "Yes—art out of electronic orchestration." (Review of *Relayer.*) *Melody Maker,* December 7, 1974; p. 44.

———. "Yes: the edge of delirium." *Melody Maker,* 1975.

———. "Yes: there's no end in sight . . . Jon Anderson talks to Chris Welch." *Melody Maker,* February 22, 1975.

———. "Yes: "When we are perfect we'll stop!" The top band award winners talk to Chris Welch." *Melody Maker,* September 20, 1975; p. 38.

———. "Yes back on course: Jon Anderson talks to Chris Welch." *Melody Maker,* 1977.

———. "Yes it's a classic." (Review of *Going for the One.*) *Melody Maker,* July 9, 1977; p. 22.

———. "Wondrous Stories. As told by Yes' Steve Howe to Chris Welch." *Melody Maker,* October 22, 1977; p. 42.

Yes music books

Yes Complete Deluxe Edition. Secaucus, New Jersey: Warner Bros. Publications, n.d.
Big Generator music book. Secaucus, New Jersey: Warner Bros. Publications, 1988.
Union music book. Secaucus, New Jersey: Warner Bros. Publications, 1991.
Talk music book. Miami, Florida: Warner Bros. Publications, 1994.

Other sources

Adorno, Theodor. *Asthetische Theorie.* 2nd ed. Gretel Adorno and Rolf Tiedemann, eds. Frankfurt am Main: Suhrkamp, 1992.

———. *Introduction to the Sociology of Music.* Trans. E. B. Ashton. New York: Continuum, 1989.

———. *Quasi una fantasia: Essays on Modern Music.* Trans. Rodney Livingstone. London: Verso, 1994.

Agger, Ben. *Fast Capitalism: A Critical Theory of Significance.* Urbana: University of Illinois Press, 1989.

Arac, Jonathan, ed. *Postmodernism and Politics.* Minneapolis: University of Minnesota Press, 1986.

Avakian, Bob. *Conquer the World? The International Proletariat Must and Will.* Chicago: RCP Publications, 1981.

Bate, Jonathan. *Romantic Ecology: Wordsworth and the Environmental Tradition.* London: Routledge, 1991.

Baylor, Michael, ed. *The Radical Reformation.* Cambridge: Cambridge University Press, 1991.

Bloch, Ernst. *The Utopian Function of Art and Literature.* Trans. Jack Zipes and Frank Mecklenburg. Cambridge, Mass.: M. I. T. Press, 1988.

Bloom, Harold. *The American Religion: The Emergence of the Post-Christian Nation.* New York: Simon and Schuster, 1992.

Bourdieu, Pierre. *Distinction: A Social Critique of the Judgment of Taste.* Trans. Richard Nice. Cambridge, Mass.: Harvard University Press, 1984.

Brecht, Bertolt. *The Caucasian Chalk Circle.* Trans. Eric Bentley. New York: Grove Press, 1987.

Brooke, John L. *The Refiner's Fire: The Making of Mormon Cosmology, 1644–1844.* Cambridge: Cambridge University Press, 1994.

Card, Orson Scott. "Alvin Series" *(The Tales of Alvin Maker): Seventh Son, Red Prophet, Prentice Alvin, Alvin Journeyman.* New York: Tor, 1987, 1988, 1989, 1995.

———. "Ender Series": *Ender's Game, Speaker for the Dead, Xenocide.* New York: Tor, 1985, 1986, 1991.

———. *Pastwatch: The Redemption of Christopher Columbus.* New York: Tor, 1996.

Cavell, Stanley. *Conditions Handsome and Unhandsome: The Constitution of Emersonian Perfectionism.* Chicago: University of Chicago Press, 1990.

Chambers, Iain. *Border Dialogues: Journeys in Postmodernity.* London: Routledge, 1990.

Davidson, Donald. "A Nice Derangement of Epitaphs." In Ernest LePore, ed., *Truth and Interpretation: Perspectives on the Philosophy of Donald Davidson.* Oxford: Basil Blackwell, 1986; pp. 433–46.

Davis, Francis. *In the Moment: Jazz in the 1980s.* Oxford: Oxford University Press, 1986.

de Man, Paul. *The Rhetoric of Romanticism.* New York: Columbia University Press, 1984.

DeMott, Benjamin. *The Imperial Middle: Why Americans Can't Think Straight About Class.* New Haven, Connecticut: Yale University Press, 1990.

Derrida, Jacques. *Acts of Literature.* Edited by Derek Attridge. London: Routledge, 1992.

———. "The Ends of Man." In *Margins of Philosophy.*

———. *The Gift of Death.* Trans. David Willis. Chicago: University of Chicago Press, 1995.

———. "The Law of Genre." In *Acts of Literature,* pp. 221–52.

———. *Margins of Philosophy.* Trans. Alan Bass. Chicago: University of Chicago Press, 1982.

———. *of Grammatology.* Trans. Gayatri Chakravorty Spivak. Baltimore: Johns Hopkins University Press, 1974.

———. *of Spirit: Heidegger and the Question.* Trans. Geoffrey Bennington and Rachel Bowlby. Chicago: University of Chicago Press, 1989.

———. *The Other Heading: Reflections on Today's Europe.* Trans. Pascale-Anne Brault and Michael B. Naas. Bloomington: Indiana University Press, 1992.

———. *Specters of Marx: The State of the Debt, the Work of Mourning, and the New International.* Trans. Peggy Kamuf. London: Routledge, 1994.

————. "Ulysses Gramophone: Hear Say Yes in Joyce." In *Acts of Literature*, pp. 253–309.

————. "White Mythology." In *Margins of Philosophy*.

————. *Writing and Difference*. Trans. Alan Bass. Chicago: University of Chicago Press, 1978.

Eagleton, Terry. *Walter Benjamin, or, Towards a Revolutionary Criticism*. London: Verso, 1981.

Faivre, Antoine. *Access to Western Esotericism*. Albany, New York: State University of New York, 1994.

Garfield, Jay L., and Murray Kitely, eds. *Meaning and Truth: The Essential Readings in Modern Semantics*. New York: Paragon House, 1991.

Gross, David. *The Past in Ruins: Tradition and the Critique of Modernity*. Amherst, Massachusetts: University of Massachusetts Press, 1992.

Heinlein, Robert. *Starship Troopers*. New York: Berkley, 1986.

————. *Stranger in a Strange Land*. New York: Berkley, 1961.

Hofstadter, Douglas R. *Godel, Escher, Bach: An Eternal Golden Braid*. New York: Vintage, 1980.

Jameson, Fredric. *Marxism and Form: Twentieth-Century Dialectical Theories of Literature*. Princeton, N.J.: Princeton University Press, 1971.

————. "Postmodernism, or, The Cultural Logic of Late Capitalism." *New Left Review*, n. 146 (July/August 1984).

Jonas, Hans. *The Gnostic Religion*. Boston: Beacon Press, 1958.

Kant, Immanuel. *Critique of Judgment*. Trans. J.H. Bernard. New York: Hafner Press/Macmillan, 1951.

————. "Idea for a Universal History with a Cosmopolitan Intent." In *Perpetual Peace and Other Essays on Politics, History, and Morals*. Trans. Ted Humphrey. Indianapolis: Hackett, 1983.

————. *Fundamental Principles for the Metaphysics of Morals*. Trans. Thomas K. Abbot. New York: Macmillan, 1985.

Kivy, Peter. *Sound and Semblance: Reflections on Musical Representation*. Princeton: Princeton University Press, 1984.

————. *Music Alone: Philosophical Reflections on the Purely Musical Experience*. Ithaca, New York: Cornell University Press, 1991.

League, Kathleen. "The New Invisibility of Class (in Discourses of Alterity and Marginality)." Unpublished essay.

Lydon, John, with Keith and Kent Zimmerman. *Rotten. No Irish, No Blacks, No Dogs*. New York: St. Martin's Press, 1994.

Marcus, Greil. *Lipstick Traces: A Secret History of the 20th Century*. Cambridge, Mass.: Harvard University Press, 1989.

Marcuse, Herbert. *One-Dimensional Man*. Boston: Beacon Press, 1964.

Mariategui, Jose Carlos. *Seven Interpretive Essays on Peruvian Reality*. Trans. Marjory Urquidi. Austin: University of Texas Press, 1971.

Martin, Bill. *Matrix and line: Derrida and the possibilities of postmodern social theory*. Albany, N.Y.: State University of New York Press, 1992.

————. *Humanism and its aftermath: The shared fate of deconstruction and politics*. Atlantic Highlands, N.J.: Humanities Press, 1995.

————. *Politics in the impasse: Explorations in postsecular social theory*. Albany, N.Y.: State University of New York Press, 1996.

McCarthy, Thomas. *The Critical Theory of Jürgen Habermas.* Cambridge, Mass.: M.I.T. Press, 1982.

Mee, Jon. *Dangerous Enthusiasm: William Blake and the Culture of Radicalism in the 1790s.* Oxford: Oxford University Press, 1992.

Morris, Randall C. *Process Philosophy and Political Ideology: The Social and Political Thought of Alfred North Whitehead and Charles Hartshorne.* Albany: State University of New York Press, 1991.

Nancy, Jean-Luc. *The Inoperative Community.* Trans. Peter Connor, Lisa Garbus, Michael Holland, Simona Sawhney. Minneapolis: University of Minnesota Press, 1991.

Nettl, Bruno. *The Study of Ethnomusicology: Twenty-nine Issues and Concepts.* Urbana, Illinois: University of Illinois Press, 1983.

Norris, Christopher. *Derrida.* Cambridge, Mass.: Harvard University Press, 1987.

————. *Paul de Man: Deconstruction and the Critique of Aesthetic Ideology.* London: Routledge, 1988.

Peukert, Helmut. *Science, Action, and Fundamental Theology: Toward a Theology of Communicative Action.* James Bohman, trans. Cambridge: MIT Press, 1984.

Quinn, D. Michael. *Early Mormonism and the Magic World View.* Salt Lake City: Signature Books, 1987.

Rees, D. A. "Platonism and the Platonic Tradition." In *The Encyclopedia of Philosophy.* Paul Edwards, general editor. Vol. 6. New York: Macmillan and The Free Press, 1967, pp. 333–40.

Reynolds, Simon, and Joy Press. *The Sex Revolts: Gender, Rebellion, and Rock'n'Roll.* Cambridge, Mass.: Harvard University Press, 1995.

Rubin, Lillian B. *Worlds of Pain: Life in the Working Class Family.* 2nd ed., revised. New York: Basic Books, 1992.

Ross, Andrew. *The Chicago Gangster Theory of Life: Nature's Debt to Society.* London: Verso, 1994.

Said, Edward W. *Orientalism.* New York: Vintage Books, 1979.

Sartre, Jean-Paul. *Dirty Hands.* Trans. Lionel Abel. In *Three Plays.* New York: Knopf, 1949.

————. "Today's Hope: Conversations with Sartre," by Benny Levy. Lillian Hernandez, George Waterson, Clair Hubert, trans. *Telos* n.44 (Summer 1980), pp. 155–81.

————. *What is Literature? And Other Essays.* Cambridge, Mass.: Harvard University Press, 1988.

Schurmann, Reiner. *Heidegger on Being and Acting: From Principles to Anarchy.* Bloomington, Indiana: Indiana University Press, 1990.

Schwarzschild, Steven. *The Pursuit of the Ideal: Jewish Writings of Steven Schwarzschild.* Edited by Menachem Kellner. Albany, N.Y.: State University of New York Press, 1990.

Sennett, Richard, and Jonathan Cobb. *The Hidden Injuries of Class.* New York: Norton, 1972.

Sontag, Susan. *Against Interpretation.* New York: Farrar, Straus, and Giroux, 1966.

Stevens, Wallace. *The Palm at the End of the Mind. Selected Poems and a Play.* Holly Stevens, ed. New York: Vintage, 1972.

Stuckenschmidt, H. H. *Twentieth Century Music.* Translated by Richard Deveson. New York: McGraw-Hill, 1969.

Subotnik, Rose Rosengard. *Developing Variations: Style and Ideology in Western Music.* Minneapolis: University of Minnesota Press, 1991.

Tamm, Eric. *Robert Fripp: From King Crimson to Guitar Craft.* Boston: Faber and Faber, 1990.

Thompson, Edward P. *Witness Against the Beast: William Blake and the Moral Law.* New York: New Press, 1993.

Tokarczyk, Michelle M., and Elizabeth A. Fay, eds. *Working Class Women in the Academy: Laborers in the Knowledge Factory.* Amherst, Mass.: University of Massachusetts, 1993.

Wallulis, Jerald. *The Hermeneutics of Life History: Personal Achievement and History in Gadamer, Habermas, and Erikson.* Evanston, Illinois: Northwestern University Press, 1990.

Weeks, Andrew. *Boehme: An Intellectual Biography of the Seventeenth-Century Philosopher and Mystic.* Albany, New York: State University of new York Press, 1991.

Willett, Cynthia. *Maternal Ethics and Other Slave Moralities.* London: Routledge, 1995.

Williams, Raymond. *The Country and the City.* New York: Oxford University Press, 1973.

White, Timothy. *The Nearest Faraway Place: Brian Wilson, the Beach Boys, and the Southern California Experience.* New York: Henry Holt, 1994.

Wolff, Robert Paul. *The Autonomy of Reason: A Commentary on Kant's Groundwork of the Metaphysic of Morals.* New York: Harper and Row, 1973.

Young, Robert. *White Mythologies: Writing History and the West.* London: Routledge, 1990.

Zuidervaart, Lambert. *Adorno's Aesthetic Theory: The Redemption of Illusion.* Cambridge, Mass.: M.I.T. Press, 1991.

Permission acknowledgments

RELEASE, RELEASE, by Jon Anderson, Alan White, Chris Squire
© 1978 Topographic Music, Limited (PRS)
All Rights for the World administered by WB Music Corp. (ASCAP)
All Rights Reserved   Used by Permission
WARNER BROS. PUBLICATIONS U.S. INC., Miami, FL. 33014

ROCK GIVES COURAGE (Part 2 from "Order Of The Universe"), by Jon
Anderson, Bill Bruford, Rick Wakeman, Steve Howe, Rhett Lawrence
© 1989 Fizz Music Ltd. (PRS), E.G. Music Ltd. (PRS), Rondor Music (London) Ltd.,
Basedown Music Ltd. (PRS) & Rhett Rhyme Music (ASCAP)
All Rights o/b/o Fizz Music Ltd. administered by WB Music Corp. (ASCAP)
All Rights Reserved   Used by Permission
WARNER BROS. PUBLICATIONS U.S. INC., Miami, FL. 33014

ROUNDABOUT, by Jon Anderson and Steve Howe
© 1971 Topographic Music, Limited (PRS) & Rondor Music (London) Ltd.
All Rights for the World administered by WB Music Corp. (ASCAP)
All Rights Reserved   Used by Permission
WARNER BROS. PUBLICATIONS U.S. INC., Miami, FL. 33014

SECOND ATTENTION, by Jon Anderson, Bill Bruford, Rick Wakeman, Steve Howe
© 1989 Fizz Music Ltd. (PRS), E.G. Music Ltd. (PRS), Rondor Music (London) Ltd.
(PRS), Basedown Music Ltd. (PRS)
All Rights o/b/o Fizz Music Ltd. administered by WB Music Corp. (ASCAP)
All Rights Reserved   Used by Permission
WARNER BROS. PUBLICATIONS U.S. INC., Miami, FL. 33014

SIBERIAN KHATRU, by Jon Anderson, Steve Howe, Rick Wakeman
© 1972 Topographic Music, Limited & Rondor Music (London) Ltd.
All Rights for the World administered by WB Music Corp. (ASCAP)
All Rights Reserved   Used by Permission
WARNER BROS. PUBLICATIONS U.S. INC., Miami, FL. 33014

SILENT TALKING, by Jon Anderson, Steve Howe, Jonathon Elias, Bill Bruford and
Rick Wakeman
© 1991 Affirmative Music (BMI), EMI April Music Inc., Bop Sound, Rondor Music
(London) Ltd., and E.G. Music Inc.
All Rights o/b/o Affirmative Music administered by Warner-Tamerlane Publishing Corp.
All Rights Reserved   Used by Permission
WARNER BROS. PUBLICATIONS U.S. INC., Miami, FL. 33014

SOUND CHASER, by Steve Howe, Jon Anderson, Chris Squire, Alan White and Patrick
Moraz
© 1974 Topographic Music, Limited (PRS)
All Rights for the World administered by WB Music Corp. (ASCAP)
All Rights Reserved   Used by Permission
WARNER BROS. PUBLICATIONS U.S. INC., Miami, FL. 33014

SOUTH SIDE OF THE SKY, by Jon Anderson, Chris Squire
© 1971 Topographic Music, Limited (PRS)
All Rights for the World administered by WB Music Corp. (ASCAP)
All Rights Reserved   Used by Permission
WARNER BROS. PUBLICATIONS U.S. INC., Miami, FL. 33014

SURVIVAL, by Jon Anderson
© 1969 Topographic Music, Limited (PRS)
All Rights for the World administered by WB Music Corp. (ASCAP)
All Rights Reserved   Used by Permission
WARNER BROS. PUBLICATIONS U.S. INC., Miami, FL. 33014

STARSHIP TROOPER(Suite)
includes:
"Disillusion", by Chris Squire/**"Life Seeker"** by Jon Anderson/**"Wurm"** by Steve Howe
© 1971 Topographic Music, Limited (PRS)
All Rights for the World administered by WB Music Corp. (ASCAP)
All Rights Reserved   Used by Permission
WARNER BROS. PUBLICATIONS U.S. INC., Miami, FL. 33014

TEMPUS FUGIT, by Geoff Downes, Trevor Horn, Steve Howe, Chris Squire, Alan White
© 1981 Topographic Music, Limited (PRS) & Island Music Ltd. (PRS)
All Rights o/b/o Topographic Music, Limited administered by WB Music Corp. (ASCAP)
All Rights Reserved   Used by Permission
WARNER BROS. PUBLICATIONS U.S. INC., Miami, FL. 33014

THEN, by Jon Anderson
© 1970 Topographic Music, Limited (PRS)
All Rights for the World administered by WB Music Corp. (ASCAP)
All Rights Reserved   Used by Permission
WARNER BROS. PUBLICATIONS U.S. INC., Miami, FL. 33014

TURN OF THE CENTURY, by Jon Anderson, Steve Howe, Alan White
© 1977 Topographic Music, Limited (PRS)
All Rights for the World administered by WB Music Corp. (ASCAP)
All Rights Reserved   Used by Permission
WARNER BROS. PUBLICATIONS U.S. INC., Miami, FL. 33014

YOURS IS NO DISGRACE, by Jon Anderson, Chris Squire, Steve Howe, Tony Kaye and Bill Bruford
© 1971, 1972 Topographic Music, Limited (PRS)
All Rights for the World administered by WB Music Corp. (ASCAP)
All Rights Reserved   Used by Permission
WARNER BROS. PUBLICATIONS U.S. INC., Miami, FL. 33014

Index